AMERICAN INTERNATIONAL LAW CASES

AMERICAN INTERNATIONAL LAW CASES

Fourth Series

2009

Volume 4

Oceana®
NEW YORK

OXFORD
UNIVERSITY PRESS

Oxford University Press, Inc., publishes works that further Oxford University's objective of excellence in research, scholarship, and education.

Published by Oxford University Press, Inc.
198 Madison Avenue, New York, New York 10016

Cataloging-in-Publication information is available from the Library of Congress.

ISBN 978-0-19-975888-3 (2009, Volume 4)

Note to Readers:

This publication is designed to provide accurate and authoritative information in regard to the subject matter covered. It is based upon sources believed to be accurate and reliable and is intended to be current as of the time it was written. It is sold with the understanding that the publisher is not engaged in rendering legal, accounting, or other professional services. If legal advice or other expert assistance is required, the services of a competent professional person should be sought. Also, to confirm that the information has not been affected or changed by recent developments, traditional legal research techniques should be used, including checking primary sources where appropriate.

(Based on the Declaration of Principles jointly adopted by a Committee of the American Bar Association and a Committee of Publishers and Associations.)

TABLE OF CONTENTS

INTRODUCTORY NOTE

In 2009, American courts dealt with a host of cases incorporating international law, including issues such as the federal government's foreign affairs power and human rights abuses in foreign countries. This year's edition of *AILC* includes cases involving these topics, along with dozens of others critical to understanding the current application of international law in domestic courts.

The force of the foreign affairs doctrine was felt last year when the Ninth Circuit Court of Appeals struck down two California statutes on the grounds that the statutes conflicted with the federal government's foreign affairs power. In the first case, *Von Saher v. Norton Simon Museum of Art at Pasadena*, the statute at issue provided a cause of action to recover artwork looted by the Nazis during World War II. The Ninth Circuit found that California exceeded its authority by allowing all Holocaust victims and their heirs to bring action against any museum or gallery located in the United States. Although the court found that regulating property is generally an activity reserved to the state, the statute's broad scope conflicted with the federal government's power over foreign affairs. In the second case, *Movsesian v. Victoria Versicherung AG*, the Ninth Circuit also struck down a California statute on similar grounds. The California statute at issue in *Movsesian* extended the statute of limitations for claims arising out of life insurance policies issued to Armenian Genocide victims. The statute was held unconstitutional because it conflicted with the executive branch's foreign policy of not providing legislative recognition for the Armenian Genocide. These two California cases demonstrate how a federal court struck down a statute even though the statute did not directly conflict with a treaty, executive agreement, or federal statute.

The Alien Tort Statute and Torture Victim Protection Act also produced a series of cases that dealt with human rights abuses occurring outside of the United States. In *Chavez v. Carranza*, the Sixth Circuit Court of Appeals decided in favor of plaintiffs for crimes committed by a former Salvadoran military officer during the civil war in El Salvador. The court found that a Salvadoran law which granted amnesty to the defendant was not applicable because the plaintiffs were bringing action in the United States. In *Saleh v. Titan Corp.*, the U.S. Court of Appeals for the District of Columbia Circuit discussed whether Alien Tort Statute claims against two private military contractors providing services to the United States at the Abu Ghraib military prison were barred by the federal governmental immunity defense exception. Finally, in *Arar v. Ashcroft*, the U.S. District Court for the Eastern District of New York dismissed an action brought by a Canadian citizen who was arrested by U.S. authorities in New York and deported to Syria, where he was held for a year before being released without charges. The plaintiff brought claims under the Torture Victim Protection Act and the Fifth Amendment against U.S. officials for violations of his rights under international law.

HOW TO USE

Each volume of *American International Law Cases (AILC)* contains a *List of Subjects*, a *List of Abbreviations*, and a *Table of Cases* (by volume). The collection of cases for each year is organized around the *List of Subjects*. Subjects are assigned the same number each year with new subjects added as necessary. This numeration system unifies the collection so that the user can easily locate the topic in any edition of *AILC*. The *Table of Contents* for each volume lists only those subjects covered in the particular edition.

The cases are arranged alphabetically under each subject. Individual Subject Table of Contents for each covered subject provides a complete list of cases dealing with the subject. The Subject Table of Contents includes the page references both for cases printed in the particular volume and for those appearing in other volumes of the edition. Cases are printed under the subject heading with the lowest page number but are included in the Subject Table of Contents under every subject to which they are applicable. For example, the 2009 edition of *AILC* includes three cases that have been classified under the "Service of Process" topic. That topic constitutes subcategory "7. Service of Process" under category "III. PROCEDURE" in the volume's *Table of Contents.* The Subject Table of Contents for "Service of Process" cases appears at Volume 4, page 1291, a page that alphabetically lists the cases falling under that subject. The full text of one of those cases (*STX Panocean (UK) Co., Ltd. v. Glory Wealth Shipping Pte Ltd.*) appears in that section. The text of the other two cases listed there, *Oldfield v. Pueblo De Bahia Lora, S.A.*, and *Transfield ER Cape Ltd. v. Industrial Carriers, Inc.*, appears in Volume 2 in the earlier section of the book devoted to the topic and subtopic under which those cases are cross-referenced: "1.A. Jurisdiction: *In Personam*, over Persons & Corporations", also under "category III. Procedure". You will therefore find the text of those cases at Volume 2, pages 627 and 641.

To assist the user in finding particular cases or in researching particular topics, the 2009 edition includes in the last volume of the edition a "Subject Index of Cases" as well as an expanded Consolidated Table of Cases.

– To research cases by topic, use the *Subject Index of Cases.* The *Subject Index of Cases* lists the titles of *all* cases in the year's entire collection, according to subject, with a reference to the volume and page number where each case is reproduced.

– To locate cases by title, use the *Consolidated Table of Cases.* Cases listed in the alphabetical *Consolidated Table of Cases* are referenced to the volume, page, and topical section where they are reproduced as well as to all the topical sections to which they pertain.

LIST OF SUBJECTS

TABLE OF CASES

Each volume has a Table of Cases covering the materials included in that volume. A Consolidated Table of Cases appears in the last volume.

LIST OF ABBREVIATIONS

Significant abbreviations appearing in *American International Law Cases, 2009* are listed below.

A., A.2d	Atlantic Reporter [1885–1938], *Id.,* 2d Series [1938–date].
App. Div.	Appellate Division Reports [N.Y. 1896–1955].
Bevans	Treaties and Other International Agreements of the United States of America [1776–1949], compiled under the direction of Charles I. Bevans.
B.R.	Bankruptcy Reporter [1979–date].
Cal., Cal. 2d	California Reports [1850–1934], *Id.,* 2d Series [1934–date].
Cal. App.	California Appellate Decisions [1905–1940].
Cal. Rptr.	California Reporter [1959–date].
Cir. (1st, 2d, etc.)	Numbered Circuits of United States Courts of Appeal.
C.M.R.	Court Martial Reports [1951–date].
[state] Ct. App.	Court of Appeals [s] (state)
Ct. Cl.	Court of Claims (U.S.) [1863–1982].
Ct. Int'l Trade or C.I.T.	Court of International Trade [1980–date].
Cust. Ct.	Customs Court (U.S.) [1938–1980].
D. (N.D., S.D., etc.)	District Court (N.D. Northern District, S.D. Southern District, etc.).
D.C.	District of Columbia.
E.A.S.	Executive Agreement Series (replaced in 1945 by T.I.A.S.).
F. App'x or Fed. App'x.	Federal Appendix [2001–date].
F., F.2d, F.3d	Federal Reporter [1910–date].
F.P.C.	Federal Power Commission Reports [1931–date].
F.R.D.	Federal Rules Decisions [1938–date].
F. Supp., F. Supp. 2d	Federal Supplement [1933–date].
Fed. Cir.	Federal Circuit.
Fed. Cl.	Federal Claims Reporter [1992–date].
I.L.M.	International Legal Materials.
L. Ed., L. Ed. 2d	Lawyers' Edition, United States Supreme Court Reports [1754–1956], *Id.,* 2d Series [1956–date].

Misc., Misc. 2d	New York Miscellaneous [1892–1955], *Id.,* 2d Series [1956–date].
M.J.	Military Justice Reporter [1975–date].
N.E., N.E.2d	North Eastern Reporter [1885–1936], *Id.,* 2d Series [1934–date].
N.J.	New Jersey Reports [1948–date].
N.J. Eq.	New Jersey Equity [1830–1948].
N.W., N.W.2d	North Western Reporter [1879–1941], *Id.,* 2d Series [1941–date].
N.Y., N.Y.2d, N.Y.3d	New York Court of Appeals Reports [1846–1956], *Id.*, 2d Series [1956–2003], *Id.*, 3d Series [2004–date].
N.Y.S., N.Y.S.2d	New York Supplement [1888–1937], *Id.,* 2d Series [1937–date].
P., P.2d	Pacific Reporter [1883–1931], *Id.,* 2d Series [1931–date].
S. Ct.	Supreme Court Reporter [1882–date].
S.E., S.E.2d	South Eastern Reporter [1887–1839], *Id.,* 2d Series [1939–date].
So., So. 2d	Southern Reporter [1886–1941], *Id.,* 2d Series [1941–date].
Stat.	United States Statutes at Large.
[state] Super. Ct.	Superior Court
[state] Sup. Ct.	Supreme Court (other)
S.W., S.W.2d	South Western Reporter [1886–1928], *Id.,* 2d Series [1928–date].
T.C.	Tax Court (U.S.) [1942–date].
T.I.A.S.	Treaties and Other International Acts Series [1945–date].
T.S.	Treaty Series [1908–1945].
U.N.T.S.	United Nations Treaty Series [1946–date].
U.S.	United States Supreme Court Reports [1774–date] (Official).
U.S.C.M.A.	United States Court of Military Appeals [1951–date].
U.S.T.	United States Treaties and Other International Agreements [1950–date].
W.L.	Westlaw [1986–date].

III. PROCEDURE

6. Foreign Proceedings

A. Judgment Enforcement and Arbitration*

* Cases are indexed under this subject. The full text of these cases is published in the **volume**-page indicated.

COMISION EJECUTIVA HIDROELECTRICA DEL RIO LEMPA
v.
NEJAPA POWER COMPANY LLC

341 Fed. Appx. 821 (3d Cir. 2009)
Decided August 3, 2009

Joy M. Soloway, Esq. (Argued), C. Mark Baker, Esq., Kevin O'Gorman, Esq., Andrew P. Price, Esq., Fulbright & Jaworski, Houston, TX.

John M. Seaman, Esq., Abrams & Laster, Wilmington, DE, Counsel for Appellant.

Daniel J. Rothstein, Esq., Flemming, Zulack & Williamson, New York, NY, Counsel for Amicus Appellant.

David M. Orta, Esq. (Argued), Arnold & Porter, Washington, DC.

Karl G. Randall, Esq., Donald E. Reid, Esq., Morris, Nichols, Arsht & Tunnell, Wilmington, DE, Counsel for Appellee.

BEFORE: FISHER, CHAGARES and COWEN, Circuit Judges.

COWEN, Circuit Judge

Appellant Nejapa Power Company, L.L.C. ("NPC"), appeals from the order of the United States District Court for the District of Delaware granting the application for discovery assistance filed pursuant to 28 U.S.C. § 1782 by Appellee Comision Ejecutiva Hidroelectrica del Rio Lempa ("CEL"). NPC further challenges the District Court's denial of its subsequent motion for reconsideration. After the appeal was briefed on the merits, NPC filed a "conditional" motion to dismiss the entire appeal as moot. For the following reasons, we will grant this motion, dismiss the appeal as moot, vacate the District Court's judgment, and remand the matter to the District Court with instructions that it likewise dismiss CEL's § 1782 application as moot.

I.

In 1994, El Salvador authorized the country's first private power generation project. CEL awarded the contract for the project to NPC, with the parties entering into a Power Purchase Agreement ("PPA") and the plant commencing operations in 1995. CEL then filed an arbitration proceeding against NPC. This first proceeding resulted in an eventual settlement between the parties, which was confirmed in an arbitration award. Pursuant to this award, CEL terminated the PPA and entered into a Transmission Cost Agreement ("TCA") with NPC.

The TCA provides that disputes between the parties shall be resolved by arbitration "in accordance with the then current United Nations Commission on International Trade Law Arbitration Rules ('UNCITRAL Arbitration Rules')." (A509.) In addition, the "seat of the arbitration shall be Geneva, Switzerland," with the arbitrator or "Arbitral Tribunal" required to apply the substantive law of El Salvador and the procedural law of Switzerland. (A509.)

Following a second arbitration proceeding (which was filed by NPC and ended in its favor), NPC served CEL with a Notice of Arbitration on July 5, 2007. This third arbitration proceeding involves CEL's alleged refusal to perform certain obligations under the TCA. An Arbitral Tribunal was constituted in May 2008, and CEL filed a counterclaim against NPC. The Arbitral Tribunal scheduled the evidentiary hearing to begin on April 27, 2009.

Meanwhile, a dispute arose between the parties regarding the scope and timing of discovery in the arbitration proceeding. In essence, CEL wanted two rounds of document production, while NPC believed that a single round of limited discovery would be sufficient. The Arbitral Tribunal essentially agreed with NPC's discovery position, although it did offer a first round of document requests limited to documents "indispensable" to the parties' initial written submissions. On July 3, 2008, the Arbitral Tribunal issued Procedural Order No. 1 governing the scope of discovery and various procedural aspects of the arbitration proceeding. NPC further agreed to dispense with a limited first round of discovery. The Arbitral Tribunal accordingly issued Procedural Order No. 2 on July 8, 2008. This order, among other things, set forth the deadlines for discovery as well as for the parties' respective first and second written submissions.

On July 3, 2008, CEL filed ex parte applications for discovery "assistance" pursuant to 28 U.S.C. § 1782. One application was filed in the United States District Court for the District of Delaware, and it named NPC as the Respondent.[1] The District Court granted the application on July 18, 2008, expressly authorizing CEL to: (1) "take discovery relating to the issues identified in CEL's application from Respondent . . . including issuing a subpoena to NPC in the form attached as

---

1 The other application was filed in the United States District Court for the Southern District of Texas, and it named El Paso Corporation ("El Paso") as the Respondent. The Texas district court initially granted the application on July 8, 2008. But El Paso sought reconsideration, and the district court ultimately vacated its earlier order and quashed any discovery relating to the foreign arbitration proceeding on November 20, 2008. *See La Comision Ejecutiva Hidroelectrica Del Rio Lempa v. El Paso Corp.*, 617 F. Supp. 2d 481, 2008 WL 5070119, at *6 (S.D. Tex. 2008. CEL's appeal is currently pending before the Fifth Circuit (C.A. No. 08-20771).

Appendix B;" and (2) "take the depositions of the NPC representatives identified in Appendix C and . . . to issue a subpoena for the deposition of these representatives in the form attached as Appendix C." (A4.)

On July 25, 2008, NPC filed both a motion for reconsideration as well as a notice of appeal. The District Court denied the reconsideration motion on October 14, 2008, and NPC responded by filing a motion for a stay pending appeal, a motion to quash the subpoena, and a motion for a protective order on October 21, 2008. It also filed on the same day an amended notice of appeal, referencing both the reconsideration order as well the July 18, 2008 order granting the application. The District Court ultimately granted a stay pending appeal and quashed the subpoena without prejudice in an order entered on November 17, 2008.

NPC repeatedly attempted to obtain various forms of relief from the Arbitral Tribunal with respect to CEL's actions in federal court. The Arbitral Tribunal addressed its requests, as well as various discovery issues, in: (1) Procedural Order No. 3 filed on July 28, 2008; (2) a clarification letter dated August 8, 2008; (3) Procedural Order No. 4 filed on November 27, 2008; and (4) Procedural Order No. 5 also filed on November 27, 2008.[2] The Arbitral Tribunal particularly emphasized that any documents obtained through the § 1782 procedures would have to be submitted pursuant to the already established requirements and timetable, and it expressly reserved its right to accept or reject any submitted evidence.

CEL filed its Submission No. 2 with the Arbitral Tribunal by the applicable deadline of April 1, 2009. This filing included briefing, documents, witness statements, and expert reports. The evidentiary hearing before the Arbitral Tribunal then began as scheduled on April 27, 2009. CEL's counsel argued that documents not included with the parties' previous submissions could not be offered or used by NPC. After three full days, the hearing concluded on April 29, 2009, when the Arbitral Tribunal confirmed that the evidentiary part of the hearing was now closed. Counsel for both parties expressed their satisfaction with the way the hearing had been conducted, and the Arbitral Tribunal indicated that it would work to issue its award by July 2009.

While the foreign arbitration proceeding was moving forward, CEL filed with this Court two separate motions to expedite. We denied the respective motions on December 15, 2008 and March 5, 2009. The Clerk also granted on April 29, 2009 the motion of Daniel J. Rothstein, Esq., for leave to proceed as amicus curiae, for leave to file addendum attached to amicus brief, for leave to file amicus brief out of time, and for leave to file an overlength amicus brief.

---

2 In addition, the Arbitral Tribunal issued Procedural Order No. 6 on February 9, 2009. Among other things, the order dismissed CEL's requests for authorization to pursue the Fifth Circuit appeal and to defend this current appeal. It further reaffirmed the Arbitral Tribunal's previous orders and decisions.

On May 12, 2009, NPC filed a "conditional" motion to dismiss the entire appeal. It specifically asks this Court to "vacate the district court's judgment and dismiss this appeal as moot, and remand this cause to the district court with instructions that it dismiss CEL's application as moot." (Appellant's Conditional Mot. at 12 (citation omitted).) CEL filed its opposition to this motion to dismiss, and amicus sought leave to file his own opposition as well. After NPC filed a reply, CEL moved for leave to file a sur-reply. We heard oral argument on both the motion to dismiss and the merits on May 28, 2009.

II.

The statute at issue in this appeal, 28 U.S.C. § 1782, is entitled "Assistance to foreign and international tribunals and to litigants before such tribunals." It provides as follows:

> (a) The district court of the district in which a person resides or is found may order him to give his testimony or statement or to produce a document or other thing for use in a proceeding in a foreign or international tribunal, including criminal investigations conducted before formal accusation. The order may be made pursuant to a letter rogatory issued, or request made, by a foreign or international tribunal or upon the application of any interested person and may direct that the testimony or statement be given, or the document or other thing be produced, before a person appointed by the court. By virtue of his appointment, the person appointed has power to administer any necessary oath and take the testimony or statement. The order may prescribe the practice and procedure, which may be in whole or part the practice and procedure of the foreign country or the international tribunal, for taking the testimony or statement or producing the document or other thing. To the extent that the order does not prescribe otherwise, the testimony or statement shall be taken, and the document or other thing produced, in accordance with the Federal Rules of Civil Procedure.
>
> A person may not be compelled to give his testimony or statement or to produce a document or other thing in violation of any legally applicable privilege.
>
> (b) This chapter does not preclude a person within the United States from voluntarily giving his testimony or statement, or producing a document or other thing, for use in a proceeding in a foreign or international tribunal before any person and in any manner acceptable to him.

This statutory provision raises a number of difficult issues. In this appeal, the parties (and the amicus) disagree as to whether § 1782 applies to private foreign or international arbitration proceedings, especially in light of the Supreme Court's recent ruling in *Intel Corp. v. Advanced Micro Devices, Inc.*, 542 U.S. 241, 124 S. Ct. 2466, 159 L. Ed. 2d 355 (2004). NPC further contends that, even if the statute authorizes discovery assistance in the arbitration context, the District Court still abused its discretion by granting CEL's ex parte application and then denying NPC's own motion for reconsideration. Nevertheless, we need not (and do not) reach these issues because this entire matter has become moot.

The doctrine of mootness arises out of Article III of the United States Constitution, which limits the federal "judicial power" to the adjudication of "cases" or "controversies." *See, e.g., Am. Bird Conservancy v. Kempthorne*, 559 F.3d 184, 188 (3d Cir. 2009). "If one or more of the issues involved in an action become moot pending appeal or pending the decision of an appellate court, the adjudication of the moot issue or issues should be refused." *N.J. Tpk. Auth. v. Jersey Cent. Power & Light*, 772 F.2d 25, 30 (3d Cir. 1985). In such circumstances, the appellate court generally "will vacate the district court's decision and remand with directions to dismiss the action in order to strip the decision of legal consequences." *Id.* at 34 (citing *United States v. Munsingwear, Inc.*, 340 U.S. 36, 40–41, 71 S. Ct. 104, 95 L. Ed. 36 (1950)); *see also, e.g., Great W. Sugar Co. v. Nelson,* 442 U.S. 92, 92–94, 99 S. Ct. 2149, 60 L. Ed. 2d 735 (1979) (per curiam).

Although the District Court stayed its order granting CEL's § 1782 application pending the outcome of this appeal, the arbitration proceeding itself has moved forward. NPC emphasizes the following three events: (1) the passing of the April 1, 2009 deadline for CEL to file with the Arbitral Tribunal its second written submission and accompanying evidence for the hearing; (2) the completion of the evidentiary hearing conducted by the Arbitral Tribunal between April 27, 2009 and April 29, 2009; and (3) the Arbitral Tribunal's statement at the end of the hearing that the evidentiary phase of the proceeding was now closed.

On the other hand, CEL vigorously denies that its § 1782 application has become moot. Pointing out that a case cannot be considered moot if discovery "could be 'used' in 'a foreign or international proceeding,'" (Appellee's Opp'n at 3 (quoting *Intel*, 542 U.S. 246–47)), CEL argues that it still has the ability to use evidence obtained through its application in the current arbitration proceeding. The dispositive issue accordingly appears to be whether CEL has any real opportunity to introduce or otherwise use evidence obtained pursuant to § 1782 in the *current* arbitration proceeding.[3] CEL turns to two procedural mechanisms: (1) the "reopening" procedure established by Article 29(2) of the UNCITRAL Arbitration Rules; and (2) the

3 This approach appears consistent with the case law discussed by the parties. Compare *In re Ishihara Chem. Co.*, 251 F.3d 120, 125–27 (2d Cir. 2001) (concluding that application seeking discovery assistance in connection with patent invalidity proceeding before Japanese Patent Office ("JPO") was moot because, among other things, there was evidently no method under Japanese law by which applicant on its own could use new evidence in foreign proceeding after JPO conducted evidentiary hearing and because district court neither considered, nor was asked by applicant to consider, filing of new invalidity proceeding), overruled on other grounds by *Intel*, 542 U.S. at 253–54, 259, and *In re Euromepa, S.A.*, 154 F.3d 24, 28–30 (2d Cir. 1998) (affirming district court's dismissal of § 1782 application as moot because, among other things, French Supreme Court refuses to hear and consider new evidence and French Supreme Court otherwise disposed of appeal), with *In re Grupo Qumma, S.A.,* No. M. 8–85, 2005 U.S. Dist. LEXIS 6898, 2005 WL 937486, at *2–*4 (S.D.N.Y. Apr. 22, 2005) (granting § 1782 application filed in connection with Mexican civil court proceeding even though evidence period had allegedly expired because, inter alia, applicant was asking Mexican court for

"revision" procedure available under Swiss procedural law. We, however, must reject both of its theories.

Initially, CEL's various arguments are themselves undercut by some statements it previously made to this Court in support of its unsuccessful motions to expedite. For instance, it asked us to expedite the appeal on the grounds that:

> [F]rom a practical standpoint, absent an expedited appeal, the stay of the order granting the discovery threatens to effectively overturn this decision. Without an Order from this Court expediting the briefing schedule and allowing for a decision on the merits in time to complete production and review of the subpoenaed documents *before the Pending Arbitration on April 27, 2009,* this appeal will become *moot,* and CEL will be irreparably harmed.

(Appellee's Mot. to Expedite Appeal at 6 (emphasis added).) On the other hand, its expedition filings never mentioned any procedures for "reopening" the arbitration hearing or "revising" the arbitration award. At the very least, CEL's prior statements appear to call into question its current theories and provide some additional support for our ultimate finding of mootness. *See Ishihara*, 251 F.3d at 126 (noting that applicant previously represented to Court that it would be unable to use discovery after evidentiary hearing occurred).

In any case, CEL turns to the UNCITRAL Arbitration Rules to contend that, even though the Arbitral Tribunal noted that the evidentiary phase was closed at the end of the hearing, CEL still has an opportunity to introduce new evidence in the proceeding. CEL points to Article 29(2), which expressly states that "'[t]he arbitral tribunal may, if it considers it necessary owing to exceptional circumstances, decide, on its own or upon application of a party, to reopen the hearings at any time before the award is made.'" (Appellee's Opp'n at 6.) We, however, reject this "reopening" theory, primarily because of the past and current circumstances of the foreign arbitration proceeding itself.

CEL's theory does not really take into account the past history of the arbitration proceeding. The Arbitral Tribunal repeatedly and emphatically made clear that any documents obtained through the § 1782 process would have to be submitted pursuant to the Arbitral Tribunal's own directives and deadlines. Accordingly, Procedural Order No. 3 issued on July 28, 2008 stated "that all documents obtained through the Texas and Delaware Discovery process (if maintained) would have to be produced according to the procedural timetable, as provided by the Procedural Order No. 2." (A848.) Procedural Order No. 5 dated November 27, 2008 confirmed that "any documents that might be obtained through the pending Discovery procedures will have to be produced in the arbitration in compliance with the procedural rules set in Procedural Order No. 2." (A1013.) This November 27, 2008 order further reminded the parties that "all documentary evidence relied upon by the parties was

---

ruling allowing additional evidence and there was disagreement over proper translation and meaning of Mexican court's orders).

required to be produced with the parties' first submissions (i.e., Claimant's August 21, 2008 Statement of Claim and Respondent's October 31, 2008 Statement of Defence and Counterclaims)" and that, "[a]s provided by Procedural Order No. 1, Section F. 1, the parties may only produce new documents with their Submission No. 2 insofar as necessary to respond to an argument or allegation of the other party." (A1013–A1014.) Since then, CEL timely filed its second written submission and accompanying documentation with the Arbitral Tribunal, the evidentiary hearing was conducted, and the arbitration record was closed. The Arbitral Tribunal also indicated that it would render its final award promptly, and the parties expect a decision soon. Simply put, the Arbitral Tribunal's own past rulings indicate that the time to submit any evidence in the current arbitration proceeding has passed.

CEL's conduct in the arbitration proceeding further highlights the deficiencies in its "reopening" theory. Initially, it has evidently offered nothing but speculation for its claim that the Arbitral Tribunal *may* reopen the proceeding. In fact, it has not filed any motion for reopening with the Arbitral Tribunal, and there is no indication that it even informed the Arbitral Tribunal of the possibility that such a motion would be filed in the future based on the ultimate outcome of this § 1782 proceeding. *See, e.g., Grupo Qumma*, 2005 U.S. Dist. LEXIS 6898, 2005 WL 937486, at *2 (noting that applicant "is continuing to make efforts in the Mexican proceedings to obtain a ruling that it is not precluded from offering additional evidence"). It similarly never requested an extension of time with respect to either the submission deadlines or the date for the evidentiary hearing itself. On the contrary, it offered no objection to the closure at the end of the evidentiary hearing, and its counsel actually complimented the Arbitral Tribunal for its handling of the proceeding. CEL's attorney even sought to preclude NPC from using any documents at the evidentiary hearing that were not attached to the parties' earlier submissions. Such actions do not appear to be consistent with a party who anticipates filing a motion to reopen in order to present yet more evidence.

CEL alternatively argues that, even after the Arbitral Tribunal makes its award, it could still take advantage of a "revision" procedure available under Swiss law. Relying on a letter provided by an expert on Swiss law, it contends that a party may seek the "revision" of an arbitral award in the Swiss Federal Supreme Court based on newly-discovered evidence. If the party meets the (apparently strict) requirements established by Swiss law, the Swiss court evidently will cancel the arbitral award and remit the case back to the original arbitral tribunal, which then will consider the new facts or evidence. According to CEL, this whole process represents a "continuation" of the arbitration proceeding itself. NPC does not contest the existence of this "revision" procedure. But, with the support of a letter from a Swiss law specialist, it does argue that the procedure constitutes a new proceeding as opposed to a mere "continuation" of the underlying arbitration proceeding. While CEL vigorously defends the "continuation" characterization, we ultimately find that, at least for purposes of § 1782 and the mootness inquiry, the "revision" procedure should be considered a new proceeding.

Simply put, too much has happened in this matter for any judicial "revision" procedure to be considered part of the underlying arbitration proceeding. As already noted, the arbitration proceeding referenced in the application and the underlying District Court orders is nearly over, with the parties simply waiting for a decision from the Arbitral Tribunal. The Supreme Court in Intel emphasized that "a district court is not required to grant a § 1782(a) discovery application simply because it has the authority to do so." *Intel*, 542 U.S. at 264 (citation omitted). It then went on to identify several factors that could be taken into consideration by the district court in its exercise of discretion. *Id.* at 264–65. In this case, the District Court purported to exercise its discretion under § 1782 with respect to an ongoing (and almost finished) *arbitration proceeding*. It obviously did not consider whether the applicable factors supported granting discovery assistance for some future *judicial proceeding* before the Swiss Federal Supreme Court. Because the district courts are vested with the discretion to make the fact-specific determination of whether to grant discovery assistance, it would not be proper for this Court to determine in the first instance whether discovery assistance should be granted with respect to a speculative "revision" procedure. At the very least, CEL should file a new application in the District Court premised on this theory of "revision."

In the end, we must reject both the "reopening" and "revision"[4] theories offered by CEL and find that this entire matter has become moot.[5] In similar circumstances, the Second Circuit vacated the order compelling the production of discovery and remanded the case with instructions for the district court to dismiss the § 1782 application as moot. *See Ishihara*, 251 F.3d at 122–23, 127. We will follow the Second Circuit's example.

III.

For the foregoing reasons, we will grant NPC's "conditional" motion to dismiss, dismiss the appeal as moot, vacate the District Court's judgment, and remand the matter to the District Court with instructions that it dismiss CEL's § 1782 application as moot.

---

4 We further note that, at least according to NPC's Swiss law expert, a party generally has up to ten years to file its "revision" action so long as it is also filed within 90 days from discovering the grounds for revision. Furthermore, the time limit does not even apply if the ground for revision is a criminal act. If we therefore were to accept the logic of CEL's approach, we evidently could not consider the current matter moot until *2019*. Such a result appears absurd and inconsistent with fundamental principles of mootness.

5 We likewise reject the amicus's assertion that NPC's motion to dismiss should be rejected because, "if discovery is permitted, but the arbitrators nonetheless refuse to reopen the arbitration and consider the new evidence, CEL might be able to challenge the arbitral award on the grounds that the arbitrator did not provide CEL with a full opportunity to present its case." (Amicus Opp'n at 1.) Such a highly speculative set of circumstances has no real bearing on the mootness question currently before us.

EL PASO CORPORATION
v.
LA COMISION EJECUTIVA HIDROELECTRICA DEL RIO LEMPA

341 Fed. Appx. 31 (5th Cir. 2009)
Decided August 6, 2009

Before DAVIS, OWEN, and HAYNES, Circuit Judges.

PER CURIAM:*

* Pursuant to 5TH CIR. R. 47.5, the court has determined that this opinion should not be published and is not precedent except under the limited circumstances set forth in 5TH CIR. R. 47.5.4.

La Comision Ejecutiva Hidroelectrica Del Rio Lempa (CEL) appeals the district court's denial of its request for discovery for use in a private international arbitration proceeding pursuant to 28 U.S.C. § 1782. We affirm.

I.

CEL brought this suit to obtain discovery from a party in the United States for use in a private international arbitration in Geneva, Switzerland. The arbitration involves a contractual dispute between CEL, a state-owned utility company in El Salvador, and Nejapa Power Company (NPC), a utility company that contracted to construct a power plant and provide power to CEL for twenty years. Appellee El Paso Corporation is a company related to NPC from whom CEL seeks discovery for use in the arbitration. The arbitration is being conducted pursuant to the parties' agreement under the United Nations Commission on International Trade Law (UNCITRAL) arbitration rules, El Salvadoran substantive law, and Swiss procedural law.

The Swiss arbitral tribunal rejected CEL's request for broad discovery and issued an order limiting document production to those papers that were "relevant and material to the outcome of the case." The arbitral tribunal also established a time line for serving document requests and issuing rulings on any objections. At the same time, CEL filed ex parte § 1782 applications in two federal district courts, one in the District of Delaware and one in the Southern District of Texas, to obtain production of documents and depositions. The Texas application sought depositions from three El Paso employees, as well as Robert Hart, a legal representative for a company acquired by El Paso.

Both district courts granted the ex parte § 1782 applications, and CEL issued document production requests and deposition subpoenas to El Paso and Hart. Up until this point, El Paso, Hart, NPC, and the arbitral tribunal had not been informed of the § 1782 applications. El Paso and Hart filed motions for protection and reconsideration in the Texas district court arguing that CEL made material misrepresentations in its application and failed to apprise the court of Second and Fifth Circuit opinions directly on point. The arbitral tribunal issued an order expressing its views on the § 1782 application, noting that it was not receptive to these discovery efforts.

The Texas district court granted El Paso and Hart's motions for reconsideration, which it treated as a Rule 60(b) motion for relief from a judgment or order; vacated its ex parte order; and quashed the outstanding discovery requests. Relying on the Fifth Circuit's precedent in *Republic of Kazakhstan v. Biedermann International*,[1] the court held that § 1782 did not apply to discovery for use in a private international arbitration. The court also held that, even if it did have the authority under § 1782, "it would not [grant the application], out of respect for the efficient administration of the Swiss arbitration."

CEL appealed the Texas district court's grant of the Rule 60(b) motion and moved for an expedited appeal, arguing that the appeal may be rendered moot if the evidentiary hearing for the arbitration were to take place before the court ruled. This court denied the motion for expedited appeal. Subsequently, the evidentiary hearing in the arbitration concluded, after which the arbitral tribunal closed the evidence. El Paso then filed a motion to dismiss the appeal as moot, which was carried forward with the appeal.

II.

In its motion to dismiss the appeal as moot, El Paso argues that because the evidentiary hearing for the arbitration has concluded and the arbitration panel has closed the evidence, the discovery CEL seeks with its § 1782 application can no longer be used in the arbitration and there is no longer a live case or controversy. This circuit has never addressed the issue of mootness with respect to a request for discovery under § 1782. The Second Circuit has held that, where the proceeding in which the discovery is to be used has already concluded such that the § 1782 discovery can no longer be used in the proceeding, the appeal of a § 1782 application becomes moot.[2]

---

1 168 F.3d 880 (5th Cir. 1999).

2 See In re Application of Ishihara Chem. Co., 251 F.3d 120 (2d Cir. 2001); *Euromepa, S.A. v. R. Esmerian, Inc.* (*In re Application of Euromepa*), 154 F.3d 24 (2d Cir. 1998).

In *In re Application of Ishihara Chemical Co.,* for example, the Second Circuit held that an appeal of the district court's denial of a § 1782 application seeking evidence for use in a Japanese patent invalidity proceeding became moot when the evidentiary hearing in the proceeding concluded while the appeal was pending.[3] But unlike in Ishihara, in which it was clear to the court that the § 1782 movant had no means of using the evidence in the invalidity proceeding after the evidentiary hearing had closed,[4] here, a mechanism exists for CEL to introduce the evidence in the Swiss arbitral tribunal. Under UNCITRAL arbitration rules, an "arbitral tribunal may, if it considers it necessary owing to exceptional circumstances, decide, on its own motion or upon application of a party, to reopen the hearings at any time before the award is made."[5] If CEL discovers new evidence from its § 1782 application, it may ask the arbitral tribunal to reopen the evidentiary hearing to consider the evidence. Though this might be unlikely given the arbitral tribunal's expressed disapproval of CEL's discovery efforts in the United States, the possibility is enough to prevent the appeal from becoming moot. Having concluded that a live case or controversy still exists, we will address the merits of the appeal.

III.

We review the decision to grant a Rule 60(b) motion for abuse of discretion. Such a motion can be granted for a number of reasons, including "mistake, inadvertence, surprise, or excusable neglect" and "any other reason that justifies relief."[6] "The law of this circuit permits a trial judge, in his discretion, to reopen a judgment on the basis of an error of law."[7]

In *Republic of Kazakhstan v. Biedermann International*, we held that a "tribunal" within the meaning of § 1782 did not include a private international arbitral tribunal, and thus § 1782 did not apply to discovery sought for use in such a tribunal.[8] The district court relied on this holding in denying CEL's § 1782 application. CEL argues that *Biedermann* is no longer controlling in light of the Supreme Court's decision in *Intel Corp. v. Advanced Micro Devices, Inc.*[9] We disagree.

In *Intel*, the Supreme Court held that the Commission of European Communities qualified as a "tribunal" within the meaning of § 1782 and that a district court was not categorically barred from ordering discovery for use in a proceeding before the

---

3 *In re: Ishihara*, 251 F.3d at 126.

4 *Id.*

5 UNCITRAL Arb. R. Art. 29(2) (1976), available at http://www.uncitral.org/uncitral/en/uncitral_texts/arbitration/1976Arbitration_rules.html.

6 FED. R. CIV. P. 60(b)(1), (6).

7 *Fed. Deposit Ins. Corp. v. Castle*, 781 F.2d 1101, 1104 (5th Cir. 1986) (quoting *Fackelman v. Bell*, 564 F.2d 734, 736 (5th Cir. 1977)).

8 168 F.3d 880 (5th Cir. 1999).

9 542 U.S. 241, 258, 124 S. Ct. 2466, 159 L. Ed. 2d 355 (2004).

Commission, even though the proceeding was not yet pending or imminent.[10] The question of whether a private international arbitration tribunal also qualifies as a "tribunal" under § 1782 was not before the Court. The only mention of arbitration in the Intel opinion is in a quote in a parenthetical from a law review article by Hans Smit. That quote states that "the term 'tribunal' . . . includes investigating magistrates, administrative and arbitral tribunals, and quasi-judicial agencies, as well as conventional civil, commercial, criminal, and administrative courts."[11] Nothing in the context of the quote suggests that the Court was adopting Smit's definition of "tribunal" in whole.

Moreover, none of the concerns raised in *Biedermann* regarding the application of § 1782 to private international arbitrations were at issue or considered in *Intel*. In *Biedermann*, this court noted that § 1782 authorizes broader discovery than what is authorized for domestic arbitrations by Federal Arbitration Act § 7.[12] If § 1782 were to apply to private international arbitrations, "the differences in available discovery could 'create an entirely new category of disputes concerning the appointment of arbitrators and the characterization of arbitration disputes as domestic, foreign, or international.'"[13] We also noted that empowering parties in international arbitrations to seek ancillary discovery through federal courts could destroy arbitration's principal advantage as "a speedy, economical, and effective means of dispute resolution" if the parties "succumb to fighting over burdensome discovery requests far from the place of arbitration."[14] Neither private arbitration nor these questions were at issue in *Intel*.

Because "[w]e cannot overrule the decision of a prior panel unless such overruling is unequivocally directed by controlling Supreme Court precedent,"[15] we remain bound by our holding in *Biedermann*. Therefore the district court did not abuse its discretion in granting El Paso's Rule 60(b) motion.

* * *

For these reasons, we DENY El Paso's motion to dismiss the appeal as moot and AFFIRM the district court's grant of the Rule 60(b) motion.

---

10 *Id.* at 258–59.

11 *Id.* at 258.

12 *Biedermann*, 168 F.3d at 883.

13 *Id.* (quoting *National Broad. Co. v. Bear Stearns & Co.*, 165 F.3d 184, 188–90 (2d Cir. 1999)).

14 *Id.*

15 *Cain v. Transocean Offshore USA, Inc.*, 518 F.3d 295, 300 (5th Cir. 2008) (quoting *United States v. Zuniga-Salinas*, 945 F.2d 1302, 1306 (5th Cir. 1991)).

MUHAMED SACIRBEY
v.
JOSEPH R. GUCCIONE

589 F.3d 52 (2d Cir. 2009)
Decided December 9, 2009

James J. McGuire (Kesari Ruza, Timothy J. McCarthy, Elizabeth Rotenberg-Schwartz, Sean J. Kirby, of counsel), Sheppard, Mullin, Richter & Hampton LLP, New York, NY, for Petitioner-Appellant Muhamed Sacirbey.

Anjan Sahni, Assistant United States Attorney (Michael J. Garcia, United States Attorney, on the brief, Jonathan S. Kolodner, Assistant United States Attorney, of counsel), Office of the United States Attorney for the Southern District of New York, New York, NY, for Respondents-Appellees Joseph R. Guccione and Dennis Spitzer.

Before: KEARSE, LEVAL, and CABRANES, Circuit Judges.

JOSÉ A. CABRANES, Circuit Judge:

In this appeal we consider whether an arrest warrant issued by a foreign court that no longer has jurisdiction over the accused, nor the power to enforce the warrant, can provide an adequate basis for the extradition of a United States citizen. This is a question of first impression—and the fact that this issue has not been previously decided should not be surprising. It is a rare circumstance where the very document that provides the basis for an extradition request turns out to have been issued by an entity that no longer has lawful authority over the matter. While the factual and procedural history of this case is extraordinary, our resolution of it requires only that we apply the plain meaning of the provisions of the relevant treaty. The treaty authorizes the extradition of an individual who has been "charged" with a crime and requires that an arrest warrant and supporting materials be provided in order to obtain that extradition. Because the arrest warrant at issue in this case was issued by a court that neither has jurisdiction over the matter nor authority to enforce the warrant, the requirement of the treaty that an individual be "charged" with an extraditable offense has not been satisfied. This defect falls within the narrow category of issues that is cognizable on habeas review of an extradition order; we therefore reverse the order of the District Court denying the petition for a writ of habeas corpus.

BACKGROUND

A. Factual Overview[1]

Muhamed Sacirbey, also known as Muhamed Sacirbegovic, was born in 1956 in Sarajevo, Yugoslavia. At that time, the Communist regime led by Josip Broz (Tito) controlled Yugoslavia, and Sacirbey's parents opposed Tito's authoritarian government. For their dissenting political beliefs, Sacirbey's parents were imprisoned for a time. In the 1960s, the Sacirbey family fled Yugoslavia and immigrated to the United States, where they settled in Ohio. On April 27, 1973, at the age of sixteen, Sacirbey became a naturalized citizen of the United States. During the years that followed, Sacirbey attended Tulane University on a football scholarship; he earned a bachelor's degree and a degree in law at Tulane and a Master of Business Administration degree at Columbia University. After his admission to the Bar of the State of New York, Sacirbey worked as a lawyer for a New York law firm. In the 1980s, he left his law firm to work in the financial sector, first as a Vice President at Standard and Poor's, the rating agency, and later as Vice President of an investment bank.

On April 5, 1992, the Republic of Bosnia and Herzegovinia ("Bosnia") declared its independence from Yugoslavia. The United States officially recognized Bosnia's independence two days later, and Bosnia was admitted to membership in the United Nations on May 22, 1992. Shortly thereafter, Bosnian President Alija Izetbegovic, a leader of the Muslim community of Bosnia, appointed Sacirbey to serve as Bosnia's ambassador to the United Nations. Despite international recognition, Bosnian Serbs continued to oppose independence and, with the support of the government of Serbia—a neighboring province in the former Yugoslavia—launched a violent campaign to partition the country along ethnic lines. According to the United States Department of State, "[t]he conflict continued through most of 1995, and many atrocities were committed, including acts of genocide committed by members of the [Bosnian Serb armed forces] in and around Srebrenica from July 12–22, 1995, where approximately 8,000 Bosnian Muslim men and boys were killed." Bureau of European and Eurasian Affairs, U.S. Dep't of State, *Background Note: Bosnia and Herzegovina* (2009), *available at* www.state.gov/r/pa/ei/bgn/2868.htm (last visited December 8, 2009). Sacirbey, appointed Bosnian Foreign Minister upon the assassination of his predecessor in 1995, represented Bosnia at peace talks held in 1995 outside of Dayton, Ohio.[2] Those talks lead to the

---

1 Unless otherwise noted, the following facts are not in dispute.

2 Sacirbey's involvement in the Bosnian peace process has been described in the memoirs of several United States officials. *See* BILL CLINTON, MY LIFE 668 (describing Sacirbey's involvement in the American peace mission to Bosnia and his role as "the eloquent public face of

Dayton Peace Accords, which were formally signed on December 14, 1995 in Paris and which ended the war in Bosnia after more than three years and ensured Bosnia's independence under the supervision of a High Representative selected by the United Nations Security Council. *Id.*

Sacirbey continued to represent Bosnia at the United Nations until 2000. During his eight-year tenure as Bosnia's first United Nations ambassador, Sacirbey opened the Permanent Mission to the United Nations and the General Consulate of Bosnia in New York (the "U.N. Mission"), promoted the creation of the International Criminal Tribunal for the former Yugoslavia (the "ICTY"),[3] and managed the legal team in an action against Yugoslavia for genocide in the International Court of Justice ("ICJ").[4] For much of this period, the finances of the U.N. Mission were in disarray. Sacirbey claims that he received no salary for his services and that he had to open the U.N. Mission using his personal resources, including fees from his speaking engagements, and by soliciting contributions from sympathetic nations. As Sacirbey concedes, funds earmarked for one project were often spent on another, and personal bank accounts were used to house those funds. *See* J.A. 11–12 (Affidavit of Muhamed Sacirbey, Mar. 17, 2005, at ¶¶ 21–27).[5]

Sacirbey resigned from his ambassadorship and returned to private life in the United States in December 2000. After his resignation, Sacirbey claims to have learned that Bosnian Foreign Minister Zlatko Lagumdzija, a perceived political adversary of Sacirbey and allegedly a former official in the Communist Party, had launched an investigation of him. In early 2001, the Foreign Ministry requested that the Cantonal Prosecutors Office in Sarajevo[6] investigate alleged financial irregularities at the U.N. Mission during Sacirbey's tenure. On April 11, 2001, the

---

Bosnia on American television"); RICHARD HOLBROOKE, TO END A WAR 34–35 (stating that Sacirbey was his "first Bosnian friend," and detailing Sacirbey's role in the Dayton peace talks); STROBE TALBOTT, THE GREAT EXPERIMENT: THE STORY OF ANCIENT EMPIRES, MODERN STATES, AND THE QUEST FOR A GLOBAL NATION 306–07 (characterizing Sacirbey as "the pugnacious, thoroughly Americanized foreign minister of Bosnia").

3 Sacirbey also served as Bosnia's representative to the ICTY.

4 Sacirbey served as Bosnia's agent before the ICJ and later as a Vice Chairman of the Preparatory Committee of the International Criminal Court.

5 Sacirbey also claims that he was authorized to reallocate funds in this fashion, and that his efforts before the ICTY and ICJ were approved by President Izetbegovic. *See* J.A. 10 (Affidavit of Muhamed Sacirbey, Mar. 17, 2005, at ¶ 18).

6 Following the Dayton Peace Accords, Bosnia was divided into two sub-divisions: the Federation of Bosnia and Herzegovina and Republika Srpska. The Federation of Bosnia and Herzegovina was, in turn, divided into ten "cantons." *See* Bureau of European and Eurasian Affairs, U.S. Dep't of State, *Background Note: Bosnia and Herzegovina* (2009), *available at* www.state.gov/r/pa/ei/bgn/2868.htm (last visited May 27, 2009). As the District Court observed, "Cantons [are] similar to municipalities or counties in the United States." *Sacirbey v. Guccione,* No. 05 Cv. 2949, 2006 U.S. Dist. LEXIS 64577, at 3 n.3 (S.D.N.Y. Sept. 7, 2006) ("*Sacirbey II*").

Cantonal Prosecutor submitted a Demand for Investigation to the Cantonal Court, alleging that Sacirbey had abused his office in violation of Bosnian law. Specifically, the prosecutor alleged that (1) Sacirbey had embezzled $610,982.46 and (2) there was a $1.8 million shortfall in an investment account over which Sacirbey had signature authority.[7] *See Sacirbey v. Guccione,* No. 05 Cv. 2949, 2006 U.S. Dist. LEXIS 64577, at 4 (S.D.N.Y. Sept. 7, 2006) ("*Sacirbey II*"). In response to the prosecutor's application, the Cantonal Court issued a Decision to Investigate Sacirbey on August 20, 2001, and later, on December 5, 2001, a Decision for Detention and an International Arrest Warrant for Sacirbey. *Id.* at 5–6.

Bosnia sought the extradition of Sacirbey in a formal request to the United States Department of Justice dated January 29, 2002. Bosnia's request was made pursuant to an extradition treaty executed in 1902 by the United States and the Kingdom of Serbia (the "Treaty"),[8] which provides, in part, that

> The Government of the United States and the Government of Servia [sic] mutually agree to deliver up persons who, having been charged with or convicted of any of the crimes and offenses specified in the following article, committed within the jurisdiction of one of the high contracting parties, shall seek an asylum or be found within the territories of the other: Provided, that this shall only be done upon such evidence of criminality as, according to the laws of the place where the fugitive or person so charged shall be found, would justify his or her apprehension and commitment for trial if the crime or offense had been committed there.

Treaty for Mutual Extradition of Fugitives from Justice, U.S.-Serb., art. I, Mar. 7, 1902 (date of ratification by the President), 32 Stat. 1890, 12 Bevans 1238. Under Article II of the Treaty, "[e]mbezzlement by public officers" is among the offenses specified for extradition. *Id.* In order to secure extradition of a "fugitive [who] is merely charged with crime," Article III of the Treaty requires the requesting government to provide "a duly authenticated copy of the warrant of arrest in the country where the crime has been committed, and of the depositions or other evidence upon which such warrant was issued. . . ." Article IV provides that

---

7 The $1.8 million shortfall was determined by a commission that investigated the matter not to be part of the U.N. Mission's deficit because those funds had been donated by the government of Saudi Arabia and therefore did not belong to the Ministry. *Sacirbey II,* 2006 U.S. Dist. LEXIS 64577, at 5 n.6.

8 This treaty applies to Bosnia as a successor state to the former Federal Peoples' Republic of Yugoslavia, which was, in turn, a successor state to the Kingdom of Serbia. *See In re The Extradition of Muhamed Sacirbegovic,* No. 03 Crim. Misc. 01, 2005 U.S. Dist. LEXIS 707, at 30–32 (S.D.N.Y. Jan. 19, 2005) ("*Sacirbey I*") ("[T]he United States . . . consider[s] the Treaty to be in effect between the United States and [Bosnia]."); *see generally 767 Third Ave. Assocs. v. Consulate Gen. of the Socialist Fed. Republic of Yugo.,* 218 F.3d 152, 156 (2d Cir. 2000) (noting that Bosnia is among the successor states of Yugoslavia); *Ivancevic v. Artukovic,* 211 F.2d 565, 573 (9th Cir. 1954) ("[T]he extradition treaty executed by and between the United States and Serbia in 1902 is a present, valid and effective treaty between the United States and the Federal Peoples' Republic of Yugoslavia.").

"in advance of the presentation of formal proofs, complaint on oath . . . shall be made by an agent of the Government of Servia [sic] before a judge or other magistrate authorized to issue warrants of arrest." In addition, the Treaty provides that "[n]either of the high contracting parties shall be bound to deliver up its own citizens or subjects under the stipulations of this Treaty," *id.* at art. V, and that "offense[s] of a political character" may not lead to extradition under the Treaty, *id.* at art. VI.

While the Treaty expressly authorizes the United States to decline to extradite Sacirbey because he is a U.S. citizen, the Department of State is authorized by statute to extradite U.S. citizens who otherwise come within the scope of the relevant extradition treaty. *See* 18 U.S.C. § 3196 ("If the applicable treaty or convention does not obligate the United States to extradite its citizens to a foreign country, the Secretary of State may, nevertheless, order the surrender to that country of a United States citizen whose extradition has been requested by that country if the other requirements of that treaty or convention are met."). The Department of State appears to have chosen to exercise its discretion in this case by requesting Sacireby's extradition. On March 17, 2003, the Department of Justice filed a Complaint for Arrest with a View Towards Extradition of Sacirbey in the United States District Court for the Southern District of New York. Sacirbey was arrested in March 2003 and detained for over a year until he was released on bail in July 2004.[9]

B. Procedural History

The matter was assigned to Magistrate Judge Frank Maas for a determination of whether Sacirbey should be extradited pursuant to Bosnia's request. *See In re The Extradition of Muhamed Sacirbegovic,* No. 03 Crim. Misc. 01, 2005 U.S. Dist. LEXIS 707, at 1 (S.D.N.Y. Jan. 19, 2005) ("*Sacirbey I*"). Judge Maas held a hearing on December 23, 2003, during which the government introduced the following evidence in support of extradition: (1) the Cantonal Court's August 20, 2001 Decision to Investigate; (2) the Cantonal Court's December 5, 2001 Decision for Detention and International Arrest Warrant for Sacirbey; (3) the sworn statements of three witness; and (4) an affidavit from Robert E. Dalton, the Assistant Legal Adviser for Treaty Affairs at the United States Department of State, briefly explaining the history of the Treaty. *See id.* at 10–17; Appellees' Br. 7-8.

Sacirbey opposed extradition on the grounds that (1) there was no valid extradition treaty between the United States and Bosnia, (2) the offense of Abuse of Office or Authority for which extradition was sought failed to meet the Treaty requirements, (3) Bosnia had failed to charge him formally with an extraditable offense; (4) Bosnia had failed to establish probable cause to believe that he committed any

9 By contrast, the Cantonal Court's related Order of Detention authorizes Sacirbey's detention for a "not . . . longer than one month." J.A. 303 ("Decision for Detention," Cantonal Court in Sarajevo, Dec. 5, 2001).

crimes, and (5) his conduct fell within a Treaty exception for crimes of a political character. *Sacirbey I,* 2005 U.S. Dist. LEXIS 707, at 2. In support of his case, Sacirbey offered his own testimony, as well as the testimony of Paul Robert Williams, a former State Department employee and current professor of law, and the declaration of Michael Hartmann, then an adviser to the State Department on matters of criminal prosecution in Afghanistan, as an expert on Bosnian criminal law. Sacirbey testified that the finances of the U.N. mission were haphazard during his tenure and that his political adversaries were using a criminal investigation to retaliate against him. *Id.* at 20–25. Professor Williams corroborated Sacirbey's claims, testifying that "after Sacirbey left office, the party controlling the Bosnian government changed hands, and the new party, 'which was the former communist party, essentially recloaked, had a very specific motive in going after members of the former regime to discredit them for political reasons.'" *Id.* at 19–20.

In an Opinion and Order dated January 19, 2005, Magistrate Judge Maas granted the extradition request. Rejecting Sacirbey's arguments, Magistrate Judge Maas concluded that (1) Bosnia had succeeded to the Treaty, *see id.* at 33–34; (2) the offense of "abuse of authority" was sufficiently equivalent to "embezzlement by public officers" to warrant extradition under the Treaty, *see id.* at 45; (3) a formal criminal charge is not required by the Treaty, *see id.* at 47–48, (4) probable cause had been established by the affidavits submitted in support of the extradition request, *see id.* at 57; and (5) the political-crimes exception did not apply to allegations of embezzlement, *see id.* at 58–61. On January 25, 2005, Judge Maas issued a Certification of Extraditability and Order of Commitment. [A 794]

Three months later, Sacirbey filed a petition for a writ of habeas corpus pursuant to 28 U.S.C § 2241 in the United States District Court for the Southern District of New York (Barbara S. Jones, *Judge).*[10] Observing that the scope of its review was limited to determining whether (1) the magistrate judge had jurisdiction, (2) the charged offense fell within the Treaty and (3) there was a reasonable ground to believe the accused guilty of the charged offense, the District Court denied Sacirbey's petition. *See Sacirbey II,* 2006 U.S. Dist. LEXIS 64577, at 19 (citing *Fernandez v. Phillips,* 268 U.S. 311, 312 (1925)).

In his habeas petition, Sacirbey did not challenge Magistrate Judge Maas's jurisdiction over Bosnia's extradition request, so that ground for habeas relief was effectively conceded. *See id.* at 19 n.10. Instead, he pressed the two other claims cognizable on habeas review, and made several constitutional challenges to the adequacy of the proceedings before Magistrate Judge Maas.

---

10 Sacirbey could not appeal Magistrate Judge Maas's decision because "[a]n order granting or denying [extradition] is not appealable. An extraditee's sole remedy from an adverse decision is to seek a writ of habeas corpus; the Government's sole remedy is to file a new complaint." *Ahmad v. Wigen,* 910 F.2d 1063, 1065 (2d Cir. 1990) (internal citations omitted).

With respect to the second claim cognizable on habeas review, Sacirbey failed to persuade the District Court that he was not "charged" with an extraditable offense.[11] Sacirbey argued, *inter alia,* that legal reforms in Bosnia had deprived the Cantonal Court of jurisdiction over this matter, thereby nullifying the arrest warrant for Sacirbey. At oral argument before the District Court, counsel for Sacirbey emphasized, "The Cantonal Court is done. It does not exist. . . . The old system under which my client was charged has disappeared." J.A. 845 (Tr. of Proceedings 50: 1-4, Oct. 4, 2005). In light of the government's concession that "[t]here is ambiguity" as to whether the Cantonal Court has jurisdiction over the investigation of Sacirbey," J.A. 851 (Tr. of Proceedings 56:15-16, Oct. 4, 2005), the District Court authorized the parties to submit additional briefing on the question of whether a court had jurisdiction over the investigation of Sacirbey.

Pursuant to the District Court's authorization, Sacirbey submitted declarations from his Bosnian lawyer, Zlatan Terzic, and from Michael Hartmann, the same expert who had previously filed a declaration in opposition to the government's application to extradite Sacirbey. The Terzic declaration stated that, based on Terzic's personal inquiries, neither the Cantonal Court nor the Court of Bosnia and Herzegovina (the "National Court") "has been seized of the case against . . . Sacirbey. Therefore, there is no forum available to us to approach for resolution, to petition for appropriate remedies, or to challenge the propriety and legality of this allegedly ongoing investigation." J.A. 871-72 (Nov. 22, 2005 Decl. of Zlatan Terzic ¶ 2). The Hartmann Declaration stated flatly that, "by the admissions of the Bosnian [government] . . . neither the National nor Cantonal Court, nor the Cantonal Prosecutor, have possession of the case. The only state organ not denying possession of the case but rather affirming its possession is the office of the National Prosecutor." J.A. 910 (Nov. 22, 2005 Decl. of Michael Hartmann ¶ 25). Sacirbey argued that, because no court had jurisdiction over his case, he was not charged with a crime, but only the target of an investigation.[12]

---

11 Before Judge Jones, Sacirbey abandoned his argument that Bosnia did not succeed to the Treaty. *See Sacirbey II,* 2006 U.S. Dist. LEXIS 64577, at 21.

12 In a telephonic conference before Magistrate Judge Maas, Professor Cherif Bassiouni, testifying on behalf of Sacirbey, suggested that it was within Bosnia's power to dispel any ambiguity caused by the changes its legal system. He testified as follows:

> As a matter of formal submissions[,] when an extradition is submitted[,] it is submitted by a government and attached to it are judicial documents. When Bosnia filed its request, it had a document presented by its executive branch[,] attached to it were the documents by the judicial branch in accordance with the treaty and in accordance with international practice. What happened is an intervening factor in which as far as we're concerned we do not know its implications which says the person who issued that original warrant no longer ha[s] that authority.
>
> . . .

In response, the government submitted two letters written by Amra Kosovic, Counselor to the Bosnian Embassy in Washington, D.C. Kosovic's first letter, dated October 11, 2005, stated that "[the National Court] will proceed in the matter of [Sacirbey] if the request for extradition would be approved by the appropriate authorities of [the] United States." J.A. 960 (Oct. 11, 2005 Letter of Amra Kosovic). A second letter, dated November 10, 2005, was more equivocal on the question of whether the National Court had jurisdiction over the case. Kosovic's letter stated in relevant part:

> The Cantonal Court . . . exists and hears all cases that are within its jurisdiction. During the period of justice system reforms, the [National Court] was established and the [National] Court *can, on request of the parties in a case, decide to hear this case* of extradition or any other case if the necessary requirements according to the [Bosnian Criminal Procedure Code are met]. As you were informed, [the] Prosecutor's Office of Bosnia . . . has sent notice that [it] took the investigation which was previous[ly] held by [the] Prosecutor's Office of Canton Sarajevo.

J.A. 961 (Nov. 10, 2005 Letter of Amra Kosovic) (emphasis added). Recognizing that these letters "do[ ] not elaborate on the relationship between the Cantonal Court, which originally issued the arrest warrant and demand for investigation against Mr. Sacirbey, and the [National Court], which now appears to be . . . seized of jurisdiction over Mr. Sacirbey's case," the government argued that these letters nevertheless demonstrated that "a Bosnian court . . . would handle Mr. Sacirbey's proceeding upon his extradition." J.A. 958 (Nov. 22, 2005 Letter of Assistant United States Attorney Anjan Sahni).

The District Court agreed with the government. Explaining that the "issue arises because of [Bosnia's] change from a civil law to a common law system[[13]] since the issuance of the original Demand against Sacirbey," the District Court found that "the investigative functions which had been vested in [Bosnia's] civil law

---

> [T]he [United States] Government may be in a better position to save us all the time and effort to have to argue what is the intent of this new Bosnian law by getting some official judicial document from the requesting state [*i.e.,* Bosnia] that confirms the ongoing validity of prior warrants . . . issued by Cantonal prosecutors.

J.A. 405-06 (Tr. of Proceedings 13:12-22, 14:22-15:1, Nov. 3, 2003). The Bosnian government did not make a submission along the lines suggested by Professor Bassiouni.

13 Apparently, this change refers to Bosnia's transition from a system of court-conducted prosecutions to an adversarial system with independent prosecutors and a neutral judge. It cannot be gainsaid that the current administrative and political situation in Bosnia is uncertain. *See* USAID, *Bosnia-Herzegovinia: Overview, available at* www.usaid.gov/locations/europe_eurasia/countries/ba/ (last visited May 27, 2009) ("After extensive negotiations, the European Union (EU) signed a Stabilization and Association agreement with [Bosnia] in 2008, the first step in the process of becoming a candidate for EU membership. However, ethnic tensions and a largely dysfunctional, multi-layered governance structure geared toward safeguarding the rights of the various ethnic groups still hinder development. Reforms, such as establishing strong state-level institutions, privatizing state-owned industry, fighting corruption, and making meaningful progress in the rule of law, require continued effort.").

courts were transferred to independent prosecutors at the cantonal and national levels[, and] a National Court system was established, equivalent to the United States federal court system, and a new National Criminal Code was adopted." *Sacirbey,* 2006 U.S. Dist. LEXIS 64577 at 23 n.12. The District Court concluded that, "by the time the United States Government filed the Complaint, the Investigative Office of the Cantonal Court that had issued the Warrant Order no longer had any power to enforce it." *Id.* These developments were "quite beside the point," in the view of the District Court, because "[a]ll that is required is that Sacirbey be 'charged,' which he had been at the time his extradition was sought, and continues to be." *Id.* at 23.

Relying on authority from the Seventh Circuit and a district court in our Circuit, the District Court observed that "[t]he term 'charge,' in this context, has been interpreted by courts to require something less than a formal charge: for example, the requirement has been deemed satisfied where a subject is 'accused,' or the requesting nation 'intends to prosecute' him." *Id.* at 21 (quoting *In re Assarsson,* 635 F.2d 1237, 1242 (7th Cir. 1980) (*"Assarsson I"); Borodin v. Ashcroft,* 136 F. Supp. 2d 125, 129 (E.D.N.Y. 2001)) (brackets omitted). The District Court held that the evidence showed Bosnia's intent to prosecute Sacirbey for abuse of authority. This determination was based on the record developed in the proceedings before Judge Maas and on the two letters written by Kosovic, the Bosnian Embassy counselor, which demonstrated to the District Court "a *present* intent to prosecute Sacirbey in the National Court [of Bosnia]." *Sacirbey II,* 2006 U.S. Dist. LEXIS 64577, at 23 (emphasis added).

The District Court also determined that the charged offense, "abuse of authority," fell within the Treaty's enumerated offenses—namely, the offense of embezzlement. *See id.* at 24 (citing Art. II of the Treaty). It further held that the requirement of "dual criminality"—*i.e.,* that the alleged conduct constitute a criminal offense in both countries—was "easily satisfied" because "there are numerous federal crimes for which Sacirbey could have been charged in the United States based on the allegations against him." *Id.* at 33. The political offense exception set forth in Article VI of the Treaty did not bar Sacirbey's extradition, according to the District Court, because the exception applied to "political *offenses*—not political figures," *id.* at 34, and the financial misconduct at issue here did not constitute a political offense. Accordingly, the District Court concluded that the charged offense fell within the scope of the Treaty.

Turning to the third claim cognizable on habeas review of an extradition order, the District Court determined that there was a reasonable basis to believe Sacirbey was guilty of the charged offense. The District Court listed the evidence against Sacirbey:

> (i) there were significant shortfalls in the [U.N.] Mission's account, over which Sacirbey had signature authority; (ii) Sacirbey refused to explain certain non-routine expenditures to Ministry representatives, even though [Bosnian] procedures do not allow for confidential expenditures; (iii) President Izetbegovic expressly denied that

> Sacirbey had been authorized to spend [Bosnian] funds on the ICJ and ICTY cases; (iv) Sacirbey represented that he would be able to restore some of the missing funds, but then failed to do so; (v) he may have evaded the efforts of [Bosnian] authorities to question him about the accounting problems; and (vi) he failed to account properly for personal advances that he had taken against the Mission account.

Id. at 38–39. In the District Court's judgment, "[t]his evidence clearly support[ed] [Magistrate] Judge Maas's determination that a finder of fact reasonably could conclude that Sacirbey embezzled funds from the Mission account and used them for his own personal needs." *Id.* at 39 (internal quotation marks omitted).

The District Court also rejected Sacirbey's constitutional challenges to the adequacy of the proceedings before Magistrate Judge Maas. First, Sacirbey argued that the government's refusal to produce evidence relating to the role of United States officials in preparing or pursuing the extradition request violated *Brady v. Maryland,* 373 U.S. 83 (1963). The District Court disagreed, explaining that "[e]ven if *Brady* can be said to apply in the extradition context . . . *Brady* would not extend to Sacirbey's discovery requests . . . because Sacirbey's requests were directed not at *exculpatory* evidence, but rather information regarding the political motivations, if any, behind [Bosnia's] request for his extradition." *Sacirbey II,* 2006 U.S. Dist. LEXIS 64577, at 44 (emphasis in original). Second, Sacirbey challenged Magistrate Judge Maas's refusal to reopen the extradition hearing to allow the submission of a reply declaration in response to an expert declaration submitted by the government. The District Court rejected the challenge because Sacirbey failed to show prejudice. *Id.* at 45–46. Third, Sacirbey urged the District Court to consider the danger and deprivation of due process he would face if extradited to Bosnia. Citing the "well-entrenched rule of non-inquiry" into the legal procedures of a country requesting extradition pursuant to a treaty, the District Court did not entertain this challenge. *Id.* at 47; *see Ahmad v. Wigen,* 910 F.2d 1063, 1066 (2d Cir. 1990) ("A consideration of the procedures that will or may occur in the requesting country is not within the purview of a habeas corpus judge.").

Having made these determinations, the District Court denied Sacribey's habeas corpus petition. This appeal followed.

DISCUSSION

On appeal, Sacirbey reiterates the arguments that he presented to the District Court, including that he was not charged with an extraditable offense under the Treaty. This argument presents a question of first impression for our Court, requiring us to examine a relatively undeveloped area of law.[14]

---

14 Our efforts in this regard are aided by the thorough and well-reasoned opinions of the judges who have previously considered this matter. That our conclusion differs from theirs should not be read to disparage in any way whatsoever the conscientious handling of this case by the District Court.

A. Standard of Review

The basis for Sacirbey's petition for habeas corpus is that, by means of the extradition proceedings against him in the United States District Court for the Southern District of New York, he has been placed "in custody in violation of the Constitution or laws or treaties of the United States." 28 U.S.C. § 2241(c)(3). Our review of the denial of a petition for habeas corpus in extradition proceedings is "narrow" in scope. *Murphy v. United States,* 199 F.3d 599, 601 (2d Cir. 1999). A reviewing court can consider only three issues: "(1) whether the judge below had jurisdiction; (2) whether the offense charged is extraditable under the relevant treaty; and (3) whether the evidence presented by the Government established probable cause to extradite." *Cheung v. United States,* 213 F.3d 82, 88 (2d Cir. 2000); *see also Fernandez,* 268 U.S. at 312.

We are not at liberty to second guess the determination of the magistrate judge to issue an order certifying a request for extradition. Under our precedents, "[h]abeas corpus is not a writ of error, and it is not a means of rehearing what the [extradition] judge or magistrate already has decided." *Ahmad,* 910 F.2d at 1066; *accord Garcia-Guillern v. United States,* 450 F.2d 1189, 1192–93 (5th Cir. 1971) ("A writ of habeas corpus cannot be used to hear for a second time the findings of the court which conducted the initial hearing. As has been said often, habeas corpus cannot take the place of a writ of error.").

It is nevertheless "our duty . . . to ensur[e] that the applicable provisions of the treaty and the governing American statutes are complied with." *Petrushansky v. Marasco,* 325 F.2d 562, 565 (2d Cir. 1963) (Marshall, *J.*); *see also Murphy,* 199 F.3d at 601–02 ("The function of habeas review in this context is to test only the legality of the extradition proceedings." (internal quotation marks omitted)).

With these principles in mind, we review the factual findings of the District Court for clear error and its legal determinations *de novo. See Drake v. Portuondo,* 553 F.3d 230, 239 (2d Cir. 2009) (providing the general standard for review of habeas corpus petitions); *cf. Armstrong v. Guccione,* 470 F.3d 89, 96 (2d Cir. 2006) (reviewing *de novo* a petitioner's legal arguments—raised under 28 U.S.C. § 2241—that his confinement for civil contempt violated the Fifth Amendment and several federal statutes).

B. Sacirbey Was Not Charged with an Extraditable Offense under the Treaty

Sacirbey argues that he has not been "charged" with an extraditable offense pursuant to the terms of the Treaty.[15] On Sacirbey's reading of the record, the evidence shows that an investigative warrant for his arrest was issued in 2001, but the issuing court was subsequently dissolved, with the consequence that "no [c]ourt in

15 Because we conclude that Sacirbey's argument on this point has merit, we do not consider the other grounds for relief raised in his petition.

Bosnia is *currently* seized of the matter." Appellant's Br. 24 (emphasis in original). In Sacirbey's view, the putative interest that Bosnia asserted in correspondence cannot remedy the inadequacy of the warrant that underlies Bosnia's extradition request. The government responds that the Treaty "does not condition extradition on formal charges," and "all that need be shown is that the requesting nation intends to prosecute the extraditee." Appellees' Br. 34-35. Under the government's reading of the record, "Bosnia has repeatedly and unambiguously" indicated its intention to prosecute Sacirbey. *Id.* at 35. As noted above, the District Court agreed with the government's view of the evidence. Relying on non-binding precedents construing similar language in other treaties, the District Court observed that "[t]he term 'charge,' in this context, has been interpreted by courts to require something less than a formal charge: for example, the requirement has been deemed satisfied where a subject is 'accused,' or the requesting nation 'intend[s] to prosecute' him." *Sacirbey II,* 2006 U.S. Dist. LEXIS 64577, at 21 (internal citations omitted).

In one of the cases on which the District Court relied, *Assarsson I,* the petitioner argued that because "a formal document, called a 'charge' in the Swedish criminal code, . . . ha[d] not yet been filed against him, he [could not] be extradited." 635 F.2d at 1239. The Seventh Circuit rejected this argument on the grounds that (1) "[t]he filing of formal charges is not stated anywhere [in the treaty] as a pre-requisite to extradition," *id.* at 1242; and (2) U.S. courts are not empowered to "review compliance with foreign criminal procedure" in the course of ordering extradition pursuant to a valid treaty, *id.* at 1244. The Eighth Circuit reached the same conclusion in a case involving the brother of the petitioner in *Assarsson I. In re Assarsson,* 687 F.2d 1157 (8th Cir. 1982) ("*Assarsson II*"). The Eighth Circuit adopted the Seventh Circuit's holding that, where "[t]he filing of formal charges is not stated anywhere as a prerequisite to extradition. . . ., we may not review the magistrate's determination that [the extraditee] was charged under the terms of the treaty." *Assarsson II,* 687 F.2d at 1160 (quoting *Assarsson I,* 635 F.2d 1242).

The government informs us that the reasoning of *Assarsson I* and *Assarsson II,* has been adopted by the Ninth Circuit as well. Appellees' Br. 35; *see Emami v. U.S. Dist. Court for the N. Dist. of Cal.,* 834 F.2d 1444, 1448–49 (9th Cir. 1987). Like the Seventh and Eighth Circuits, the Ninth Circuit determined that, where an extradition treaty does not condition extradition on the filing of formal charges, it would not read such a requirement into the treaty. That court explained, "We refrain from interpreting the requirements of German criminal procedure [with respect to the filing of a public charge] both out of respect for German sovereignty and because we recognize the chance of erroneous interpretation is much greater when we try to construe the law of a country whose legal system is not based on common law principles." *Id.* at 1449.[16]

16 The government also relies on the conclusory statement of the Fifth Circuit that "[the] contention that [extraditee] has never been properly or legally charged with a crime in accordance with the treaty is . . . not appropriate for consideration [on habeas review]." *Garcia-Guillern,*

Similar "formal-charge" arguments have been rejected by other courts, including district courts in this Circuit. These courts have also addressed the question of how to establish that a crime has been "charged" for the purposes of an extradition treaty, holding that a demonstrated intent to prosecute on the part of the country requesting extradition is sufficient. *See Borodin v. Ashcroft,* 136 F. Supp. 2d 125, 130 (E.D.N.Y. 2001) ("American courts cannot become enmeshed in the technicalities of foreign criminal processes, and . . . the 'charge' requirement is satisfied by a requesting *nation's intent to prosecute as evidenced by the record.*" (emphasis added)); *In re La Salvia,* No. 84 Cr. Misc. 1, 1986 U.S. Dist. LEXIS 29789, at 16–17 (S.D.N.Y. Jan. 31, 1986) ("[T]he reference to 'persons . . . charged' in [the treaty] . . . is a generic term referring to those persons whose extradition is sought *so that they may be brought to trial!"* (emphasis added)); *cf. In re Extradition of Lehming,* 951 F. Supp. 505, 512 (D. Del. 1996) ("[S]ufficient *evidence of an intent to prosecute* exists making extradition proper under these circumstances.") (emphasis added).

The government interprets these precedents to stand for the following proposition: When extradition treaties state that an individual must be "charged" with a crime in order to be extradited, but do not require the filing of an accusatory instrument, a state seeking extradition need show only an intent to prosecute the individual in order to satisfy the requirement that he be "charged" with a crime. This proposition appears reasonable insofar as it gives meaning to treaty language stating that an individual must be "charged" with an offense in order to be extradited, while avoiding unwarranted incursions into the fine details of foreign criminal procedure. *See, e.g., Jhirad v. Ferrandina,* 536 F.2d 478, 484–85 (2d Cir. 1976) ("It is not the business of our courts to assume the responsibility for supervising the integrity of the judicial system of another sovereign nation. Such an assumption would directly conflict with the principle of comity upon which extradition is based."). Applying that teaching to this case, the government urges us to conclude that, because the Treaty requires that an individual be "charged" with a crime but does not require that formal charges be brought, a "clear intent" to prosecute is sufficient to satisfy the terms of the Treaty. Appellees' Br. 44.

---

450 F.2d at 1193 n.1. This statement is at odds with the determinations of the Seventh, Eighth and Ninth Circuits that they have jurisdiction to consider this question on habeas review. *See Emami,* 834 F.2d at 1448 ("Whether a treaty conditions extradition upon the filing of formal charges is a question cognizable on appeal from the denial of a petition for habeas corpus."); *Assarsson II,* 687 F.2d at 1160 ("'The existence of formal charges can be reviewable, then, only if the treaty itself conditions extradition for the offenses listed . . . on the existence of formal charges.'" (quoting *Assarsson I,* 635 F.2d at 1241)). We note that the Fifth Circuit's statement is broader than the government's position, which is that the status of the charges against Sacirbey are not reviewable on a habeas corpus petition *because* the Treaty does not require formal charges as a condition of extradition. *See* Appellees' Br. 38 ("[The Treaty] does not require as a condition of extradition that an extraditee be formally charged. Accordingly, Sacirbey's arguments regarding the status of his charges in Bosnia are beyond the purview of habeas review.").

Sacirbey responds that one additional proposition follows from the cases cited by the District Court and the government—"that there at least be a judicial body in the requesting state seized of the matter, to which the extraditee can petition for relief." Appellant's Reply Br. 8. Sacirbey observes that, in all of these cases, an "instituted judicial proceeding," *id.* was underway in the requesting country. *See Emami,* 834 F.2d at 1447 (Bochum Local Court in Germany); *Assarsson II,* 687 F.2d at 1158 (Malmo District Court in Sweden); *Assarsson* I, 635 F.2d at 1239 (Malmo District Court in Sweden); *Borodin,* 136 F. Supp. 2d at 127 (proceedings before a Swiss Examining Magistrate); *In re Extradition of Lehming,* 951 F. Supp. at 508 (Saarbrucken District Court in Germany); *In re La Salvia,* 1986 U.S. Dist. LEXIS 29789, at 21 (Federal Court of First Instance in Penal and Correctional Matters in Argentina). Based on this observation, Sacirbey argues that the Treaty should be read to require a showing of "[t]he presence of a judicial authority conducting proceedings toward prosecution of the potential extraditee." Appellant's Br. 23. In the absence of such a requirement, Sacirbey fears that "an extraditee may . . . be handed over to political officers of a foreign country for arbitrary and potentially brutal prosecution." *Id.* at 24. He urges us to conclude that, "because no existing [c]ourt has issued a warrant for his arrest or assumed responsibility for his prosecution or protection," he has not been "charged" with a crime under the Treaty. Appellant's Reply Br. 11.

We appreciate the force of Sacirbey's concerns. Indeed, he may be right that extradition treaties *should* contain provisions ensuring that a judicial body in the requesting country stand ready to ensure procedural regularity upon the transfer of custody over the accused. Whether or not the United States should condition extradition—particularly the extradition of its own citizens—on such safeguards is not, however, a question over which this Court has jurisdiction. "[T]he question of the wisdom of extradition remains for the executive branch to decide." *Murphy,* 199 F.3d at 602 (internal quotation marks omitted). Our power, by contrast, is "limited to ensuring that the applicable provisions of the treaty and the governing American statutes are complied with." *Petrushansky,* 325 F.2d at 565.

In keeping with that limited authority, we examine the requirements of the extradition treaty in this case. "In construing a treaty, as in construing a statute, we first look to its terms to determine its meaning." *United States v. Alvarez-Machain,* 504 U.S. 655, 663 (1992); *see also Kahn Lucas Lancaster v. Lark Int'l,* 186 F.3d 210, 215 (2d Cir. 1999) ("Treaties are construed in much the same manner as statutes[,] [and their interpretation] must account for the . . . full text, language as well as punctuation, structure and subject matter." (internal citations and quotation marks omitted)). A basic canon of statutory interpretation, which is equally applicable to interpreting treaties, is to avoid readings that "render statutory language surplusage" or "redundant." *Filler v. Hanvit Bank,* 378 F.3d 213, 220 (2d Cir. 2004); *cf.* Restatement (Second) of Contracts § 203(a) (1981) ("[A]n interpretation which gives a reasonable, lawful, and effective meaning to all the terms is preferred to an interpretation which leaves a part unreasonable, unlawful, or of no effect.").

In addition, we have observed that "the meaning of one term may be determined by reference to the terms it is associated with, and that where specific words follow a general word, the specific words restrict application of the general term to things that are similar to those enumerated." *City of New York v. Beretta U.S.A. Corp.,* 524 F.3d 384, 401 (2d Cir. 2008) (brackets and internal quotation marks omitted); *cf.* Restatement (Second) of Contracts § 203(c) (1981) ("[S]pecific terms and exact terms are given greater weight than general language.").

In the instant case, our review focuses on "whether the offense *charged* is extraditable under the relevant treaty." *Cheung,* 213 F.3d at 88 (emphasis added). Article I of the Treaty sets forth a foundational principle that the states parties "mutually agree to deliver up persons who[ ] hav[e] been *charged* with or convicted of any of the crimes and offenses" (emphasis added), which are supplied in Article II. The remaining articles of the Treaty define the contours of the broad agreement in Article I, including certain limitations on the breadth of the term "charged." Most important to the instant case, Article III of the Treaty imposes a requirement that when "[a] fugitive is merely *charged* with crime, a duly authenticated copy of the warrant of arrest in the country where the crime has been committed, and of the depositions or other evidence upon which such warrant was issued, shall be produced."[17] Treaty art. III (emphases added). In other words, the "warrant of arrest" is a formal legal instrument that is required by the Treaty to show that a person has been charged with an extraditable crime. *See* art. IV (describing the Article III warrant requirement as a "presentation of *formal* proofs" (emphasis added)). Accordingly, we interpret these provisions to mean that the proof required under the Treaty to establish that an individual has been "charged" with a crime is a valid arrest warrant and the evidence submitted in order to obtain that warrant. Any other reading would ignore the express terms of Article III. *Cf. Filler,* 378 F.3d at 220 (stating that courts should avoid readings that "render statutory language surplusage").

Under this construction of the Treaty, Bosnia can satisfy the requirement that Sacirbey be "charged" with a crime only if it can provide, *inter alia,* a valid warrant for his arrest. Bosnia seeks the extradition of Sacirbey pursuant to an "international arrest warrant" issued by the Cantonal Court in Sarajevo. However, as the District Court found, the Cantonal Court currently lacks jurisdiction over the investigation of Sacirbey's alleged crimes and "no longer ha[s] any power to enforce" the arrest warrant. *Sacirbey,* 2006 U.S. Dist. LEXIS 64577, at 23 n.12.[18] Such a warrant—one issued by a court lacking jurisdiction to enforce it—has been described in

---

17 Articles V and VI of the Treaty provide additional limitations on Article I's general extradition agreement for a country's own citizens, *id.* at art. V, and for people accused of political crimes, *id.* at art. VI.

18 The government does not argue that the District Court's findings of fact on the jurisdiction of the Cantonal Court are erroneous, much less clearly erroneous, nor does our review of the record lead us to question the District Court's determination.

another context by the Supreme Court as a "dead letter." *United States v. Verdugo-Urquidez,* 494 U.S. 259, 274 (1990) (rejecting an argument that a warrant issued by a magistrate in the United States would have force in Mexico); *see also In re Terrorist Bombings of U.S. Embassies in E. Afr.,* 552 F.3d 157, 171 n.8 (2d Cir. 2008) (describing the power conferred by a *valid* search warrant). The arrest warrant for Sacirbey was never re-issued—or otherwise ratified—by a Bosnian court with jurisdiction over this case.[19] Accordingly, the existence of this arrest warrant—issued by a court ousted of jurisdiction and no longer able to enforce it—cannot satisfy the Treaty's requirement that Bosnia demonstrate a "charge" by producing a valid arrest warrant.

Consistent with its interpretation of the precedents discussed above, the government maintains that the defect in Bosnia's application can be remedied by official statements indicating Bosnia's intent to prosecute Sacirbey for his alleged crimes. The government points to letters from various Bosnian officials that allegedly show an intention to prosecute Sacirbey, but proof of such an intention is not what the Treaty requires.[20] Even if it did, these letters are equivocal, at best, on the question of whether Bosnian authorities intend to prosecute Sacirbey for his alleged crimes. The letter dated October 2, 2003 from Assistant United States Attorney E. Danya Perry to Magistrate Judge Mass states: "[The Cantonal Prosecutor, Mustafa Bisic, confirmed that there is an ongoing criminal investigation against Sacirbey" and that the Bosnian government sought extradition to further that investigation. J.A 383. The virtually illegible attachment to the October 2 letter also refers to an "investigation against Sacirbey" but does not indicate an intention to prosecute, rather than merely investigate, him. *Id.* at 385.

The letters from Amra Kosovic, Counselor to the Bosnian Embassy in Washington DC, similarly confirm only that Sacirbey is under investigation in Bosnia, not that the Bosnian government seeks to prosecute him. Her letter of October 11, 2005 states ambiguously that "the Court of Bosnia and Herzegovina will proceed in the Matter of Mohamed Sacirbegovic if the request for extradition would be approved." *Id.* at 960. This statement does not hint at *how* the Bosnian court will proceed—that is, whether by immediate prosecution or by permitting the prosecutor to undertake further investigation. Kosovic's letter of November 10, 2005 does nothing to clarify the matter. In that letter, she states that the "Cantonal Court—the one that issued the warrant and demand for investigation of Mr. Muhamed

---

19 In her dissent, Judge Kearse argues that the original warrant for Sacirbey's arrest was transferred to the National Court. However, she provides no evidence or citations to the record that would support this interpretation. Even assuming *arguendo* that Sacirbey's case was transferred, there is no indication that the Bosnia National Court re-issued, ratified, or acknowledged in any fashion the arrest warrant.

20 We take no position on what showing is required when an extradition treaty does not provide any indication of how a requesting state must show that an accused has been "charged" with a crime.

Sacirbegovic—was [not] abolished by the justice system reforms," and she confirms that the "Court exists and hears all cases that are within its jurisdiction." J.A 961. Of course, we know that Sacirbey's case is no longer within that court's jurisdiction pursuant to Bosnia's judicial reforms. *Sacirbey,* 2006 U.S. Dist. LEXIS 64577, at 23 n.12. Perhaps recognizing this fact, the letter notes that "the Court of Bosnia and Herzegovina was established and . . . *can, on request of the parties in a case, decide to hear this case* of extradition." J.A. 961 (emphasis added). Contradicting this conditional statement regarding the Bosnian court's jurisdiction, Kosovic reiterates, verbatim from her earlier letter, that "[t]he Court of Bosnia and Herzegovina *will proceed* in the Matter of Mohamed Sacirbegovic if the request for extradition would be approved." *Id.* (emphasis added). In addition, she observes that the "Prosecutor's office of Bosnia and Herzegovina . . . took the investigation which was previously held by the Prosecutor's Office of the Canton Sarajevo." *Id.* Again, the letter is devoid of any statement that Sacirbey is sought for prosecution in Bosnia.[21]

That nothing more than a criminal investigation of Sacirbey is now pending in Bosnia finds further support in a letter, dated March 3, 2005, from the Cantonal Court in Sarajevo stating that "no indictment against [Sacirbey] . . . has been brought before the Municipal Court Sarajevo or the Cantonal Court in Sarajevo." *Id.* at 749. This letter states that the "criminal investigation against [him] . . . was referred to the Cantonal Prosecutor's Office Sarajevo on 08/06/2003 for appropriate action." *Id.* While formal charges are not required to grant an extradition request, this letter corroborates that an investigation of Sacirbey in the prosecutor's office—rather than a prosecution in court[22]—is pending in Bosnia. Based on our

---

21 In her dissenting opinion, Judge Kearse asserts that "will proceed" reflects an active intent to prosecute by the Bosnian government—a contention for which she provides no supporting authority. Although her interpretation is one feasible reading, the letters are ambiguous. It is that ambiguity which makes us unable to derive from them an active intent to prosecute.

Judge Kearse argues further that we cannot overturn the District Court's "factual finding" as to the meaning of the letters unless that finding is clearly erroneous. We do not base our decision on the meaning of the letters, however, and offer our interpretation of the letters only in response to the argument that an "intent to prosecute" is present. As a matter of law, we hold only that the Treaty requires a valid arrest warrant; there is no valid warrant in the present case; and the terms of the Treaty were, accordingly, not met. Whether an intent to prosecute can be proven by the letters is therefore irrelevant to our holding.

22 Judge Kearse relies on Bosnia's Criminal Procedure Code to support her argument and also to infer the functions and the jurisdictional reach of the National Court. However, she provides no indication, through Bosnian precedent or otherwise, that Bosnian courts would interpret the code provisions in the way that she has chosen to interpret them, and her position is contradicted by the evidence actually in the record: the Cantonal Court was dissolved; no Bosnian authority has provided a clear statement as to whether there is a prosecution now pending in a Bosnian court; and Bosnian authorities have issued only ambiguous letters regarding the status of Sacirbey's case.

review of this evidence, we are dubious that Bosnia seeks to prosecute Sacirbey for a crime.[23]

In any event, whether Bosnia has "intent to prosecute" Sacirbey is not the relevant inquiry. As explained above, the Treaty requires a valid arrest warrant as proof that an individual sought for extradition has been charged with a crime. That requirement is not satisfied by a demonstration of intent to prosecute. The necessary showing has not been made in this case. All of the "formal charges" cases cited by the government indicate the existence of a valid arrest warrant issued by a foreign tribunal. *See Emami,* 834 F.2d at 1447 (arrest warrant issued by a German court); *Assarsson II,* 687 F.2d at 1158 (arrest declaration issued by Swedish court); *Assarsson* I, 635 F.2d at 1239 (arrest declaration issued by Swedish court); *Borodin,* 136 F. Supp. 2d at 127 (arrest warrant issued by Swiss magistrate); *In re Extradition of Lehming,* 951 F. Supp. at 508 (arrest warrant issued by a German court); *In re La Salvia,* 1986 U.S. Dist. LEXIS 29789, at 21 (arrest warrant issued by Argentine court). None of those cases involve a situation where the issuing tribunal subsequently lost jurisdiction over the case owing to a constitutional reorganization, regime change, or any other reason, such that the arrest warrant was no longer valid.

Because the record contains no evidence of a valid warrant authorizing the arrest of Sacirbey, Sacirbey has not been charged with an extraditable offense pursuant to the terms of the Treaty. This defect falls within the narrow category of issues that is cognizable on habeas review of an extradition order, *see Cheung,* 213 F.3d at 88, and we therefore grant Sacirbey's petition for a writ of habeas corpus.

CONCLUSION

For the reasons stated above, we conclude that Sacirbey has not been "charged" with an extraditable offense pursuant to the terms of the extradition treaty between the United States and Bosnia. He is therefore entitled to habeas relief.

We also note, in passing, that, if Bosnia renews its request to extradite Sacirbey, the Department of State is authorized by the extradition treaty and by statute to refrain from extraditing Sacirbey because he is a citizen of the United States. An exercise of that discretion might be warranted if Bosnia renews its extradition request and the Department of State determines that the investigation into Sacirbey's tenure as United Nations Ambassador is motivated by a political vendetta, or that Sacirbey faces mistreatment if he is delivered into Bosnian custody, or for any of the other grounds available to the Department to decline extradition—or, indeed, for no reason at all, as the Treaty does not require any justification for declining to

---

23 As described *ante,* the District Court reached the opposite conclusion, *see Sacirbey,* 2006 U.S. Dist. LEXIS 64577, at 23 ("The letters plainly indicate a present intent to prosecute Sacirbey in the National Court."), but we need not decide whether this ruling was erroneous because it is irrelevant to Sacirbey's extradition.

extradite U.S. citizens. *See* Treaty for Mutual Extradition of Fugitives from Justice, U.S.-Serb., art. V, Mar. 7, 1902 (date of ratification by the President), 32 Stat. 1890, 12 Bevans 1238 ("Neither of the high contracting parties shall be bound to deliver up its own citizens or subjects under the stipulations of this Treaty."). That determination rests, of course, with the Executive Branch of Government, not the Judiciary.

Accordingly, the order of the District Court denying the petition is REVERSED, and Sacirbey's petition for a writ of habeas corpus is hereby GRANTED. The restrictions imposed on Sacirbey's liberty are VACATED and he shall not be extradited to Bosnia pursuant to the formal requests that have been made.

It is so ordered.

KEARSE, Circuit Judge, dissenting:

I respectfully dissent from the majority's decision to overturn the district court's denial of the habeas corpus petition of Muhamed Sacirbey, which sought to forbid his extradition from the United States to the republic of Bosnia and Herzegovina (hereinafter generally "Bosnia"). Extradition was requested by Bosnia in 2002 on the ground that Sacirbey, while serving as its ambassador to the United Nations, abused his official position by misappropriating $610,982.46 in official Bosnian funds to his own private account. There is no dispute that embezzlement by a public official is a criminal offense for which a person who is so "charged" or "convicted" may be extradited pursuant to the treaty between Bosnia, as a successor to the Kingdom of Serbia, and the United States, see Treaty for the Mutual Extradition of Fugitives from Justice, U.S.-Serb., art. I, Oct. 25, 1901, 32 Stat. 1890 ("Treaty") (the parties "mutually agree to deliver up persons who[have] been charged with or convicted of any of the crimes and offenses specified in the following article"); *id.* art. II, para. 6 ("Extradition shall be granted for. . . . Embezzlement by public officers"). Nor do Sacirbey and the majority appear to suggest that it is not within the competence and authority of the Court of Bosnia and Herzegovina (the "National Court" or "Court") to adjudicate such a charge of embezzlement; and the majority recognizes that under the Treaty, "formal charges are not required to grant an extradition request," Majority Opinion *ante* at 25.

The majority, however, concludes that Sacirbey is not "charged" with embezzlement—or any crime—because the majority finds (a) that "the arrest warrant at issue in this case was issued by a court that neither has jurisdiction over the matter nor authority to enforce the warrant," Majority Opinion *ante* at 2, and that a warrant "issued by a court lacking jurisdiction to enforce it" is a nullity, *id.* at 22–23; and (b) that the representation by Bosnia's "Ministry of Justice" that the "Court of Bosnia and Herzegovina will proceed in the Matter of Muhamed Sacirbe[y]" (Letters from Amra Kosovic, Counselor in the Embassy of Bosnia and Herzegovina in Washington, D.C., to the United States Department of State and the United States Department of Justice dated October 11, 2005 ("October 2005 Bosnian Embassy Letter"), and November 10, 2005 ("November 2005 Bosnian Embassy Letter") (collectively the "2005 Bosnian Embassy Letters")), leaves the majority "dubious that Bosnia seeks to prosecute Sacirbey for a crime," *id.* at 25 (emphasis added), because, the majority says, "[t]his statement does not hint at how the Bosnian court will proceed—that is whether by immediate prosecution or by permitting the prosecutor to undertake further investigation," *id.* at 24 (emphasis in original). I disagree with the majority's rationales. I discuss them in reverse order.

(1) The Notion that the Bosnian Court Intends Merely To Permit Investigation

The majority's speculation that the Bosnian National Court may intend merely to permit further investigation of Sacirbey, rather than to entertain his prosecution, is belied by the course of the prior proceedings in Bosnia and by the provisions of the Criminal Procedure Code of Bosnia and Herzegovina ("Bosnia CPC" or "CPC"), adopted in 2003 as part of nationwide judicial reforms. In 2001, Bosnia operated under a civil-law system in which investigations of possible criminal acts were conducted by regional courts in Bosnia's Cantons. In April 2001, the Sarajevo Cantonal prosecutor's office asked the Sarajevo Cantonal Court to investigate allegations that Sacirbey had abused his official position by misappropriating public funds. In August 2001, the Cantonal Court issued a "DECISION TO INVESTIGATE" Sacirbey, based on "a well-founded suspicion" that during his tenure as Bosnia's ambassador to the United Nations, Sacirbey abused his official position by, inter alia, transferring various specified sums of Bosnian United Nations mission money, totaling $610,982.46, to his own private accounts. In December 2001, the Cantonal Court issued a "DECISION FOR DETENTION" and a warrant for the arrest of Sacirbey, "the former Ambassador of [Bosnia] at the Permanent Mission of [Bosnia] with the UN," "because there is a well-founded suspicion that [he] committed the criminal act of abuse of official position or authority." In January 2002, Bosnia submitted to the United States a request for Sacirbey's extradition.

In 2003, Bosnia converted from the civil-law system to a common-law system, and investigative functions that had been vested in the courts were transferred to independent prosecutors. In August 2003, the Sarajevo Cantonal Court transferred the Sacirbey matter to the Sarajevo Cantonal Prosecutor's office for appropriate action. The Bosnian court reforms also included the establishment of the National Court, which serves functions similar to those of the federal courts in the United States. Because Sacirbey was alleged to have abused his position as a representative of the Bosnian nation, the Sacirbey investigation, which had been transferred by the Sarajevo Cantonal Court to the Sarajevo Cantonal Prosecutor, was then transferred from the Cantonal Prosecutor to the office of the National Prosecutor.

The majority's notion that the Bosnian Ministry of Justice's representation that the Bosnian National Court "will proceed" in Sacirbey's case (2005 Bosnian Embassy Letters) means that the Court may merely conduct or "permit[]" "further investigation," Majority Opinion *ante* at 24, is belied by the facts that, pursuant to Bosnia's judicial reforms, the investigation of Sacirbey had already been transferred from court to independent prosecutor, and under the Bosnia CPC, adopted in 2003 as part of the judicial reforms, the Court plays no role in investigations. The provisions of the CPC "set forth the rules of the criminal procedure that are mandatory for the proceedings of 5 the [National] Court" and the conduct of criminal matters by the National Prosecutor. Bosnia CPC art. 1. Under the CPC, "[t]he term 'investigation' refers to all activities," including collection and preservation of information and evidence, "undertaken by the Prosecutor or by authorized officials in accordance with this Code," *id.* art. 20 (j). "[A]uthorized official[s]" are defined as various law enforcement personnel such as members of the "State Border Service," "military police," and "Police bodies of the responsible ministries of" the Bosnian regions, *id.* art. 20(g); those officials are supervised by the Prosecutor, *see id.* art. 218. All of the "INVESTIGATIVE PROCEDURE[S]" set forth in the CPC describe powers and duties of "the Prosecutor" and the officials he or she supervises. *See id.* art. 213-225. There are no CPC provisions placing investigative functions, or the supervision of such functions, in the courts. The investigative procedures section of the CPC begins by stating that public officials are "bound to, " and private citizens "are entitled to, " report the commission of a criminal offense, *id.* art. 213(1), 214(1), and that "[t]he report must be filed with *the Prosecutor*," *id.* art. 215(1) (emphasis added). Further clarifying that investigations are within the sole province of the Prosecutor, not the Court, the CPC provides that

> [i]f the report [of suspected criminal conduct] is filed with the Court, authorized official or some other court or prosecutor in Bosnia and Herzegovina, *they shall accept the report and shall immediately submit the report to the Prosecutor.*

Id. art. 215(3) (emphasis added). There is no provision giving the Court authority to say whether or not an investigation may be pursued.

I thus see no principled reason to infer that the Bosnian Ministry of Justice's statement that the National Court "will proceed" in Sacirbey's case means that the Court may merely "permit[] the prosecutor to undertake further investigation," Majority Opinion *ante* at 24. And surely it disserves the interests of international comity for a court of the United States to forbid extradition on the basis of a mere suspicion that the National Court of the requesting nation intends to proceed in a manner not authorized by that nation's criminal procedure code. In contrast to the dubiety expressed here by the majority, the district court found that "the evidence," including the 2005 Bosnian Embassy Letters, "demonstrates that [Bosnia] intends to prosecute Sacirbey for the offense of abuse of authority." *Sacirbey v. Guccione*, No. 05 CV 2949, 2006 WL 2585561, at 7 (S.D.N.Y. Sept. 7, 2006); *see also id.* ("The letters plainly indicate a present intent to prosecute Sacirbey in the National Court. While the *effectuation* of that intent is conditioned on Sacirbey's extradition, the intent nevertheless presently exists." (emphasis in original)). I cannot view the district court's finding that Bosnia intends to prosecute Sacirbey as clearly erroneous. It is supported not only by the 2005 Bosnian Embassy Letters, but also by (a) the fact that the Sacirbey matter, including the Sarajevo Cantonal Court's finding of a well-founded suspicion that Sacirbey misappropriated $610,982.46 in Bosnian funds, was transferred to the office of the National Prosecutor, and (b) the CPC provision that "*if there is evidence that a criminal offense has been committed*," the National Prosecutor, unless otherwise stated by the CPC, "*is obligated to initiate a prosecution*," Bosnia CPC art. 17 (emphasis added).

(2) The Majority's View that the Arrest Warrant is a Nullity

The majority also reasons that, although the Sarajevo Cantonal Court issued a warrant for Sacirbey's arrest in 2001, the fact that that court no longer has jurisdiction to enforce the warrant makes the warrant a "'dead letter,'" Majority Opinion *ante* at 23, quoting *United States v. Verdugo-Urquidez*, 494 U.S. 259 (1990)—an opinion that observed that a warrant issued by a magistrate in the United States would have no force "outside the United States," *id.* at 274. I do not see the applicability of that observation—as to a warrant's potential extraterritorial effect—to the circumstances here, which involve changes in institutional functions resulting from court reforms within a single country.

Further, the majority apparently assumes that the Bosnian court reforms automatically divested the Sarajevo Cantonal Court of jurisdiction to entertain a prosecution of Sacirbey and assumes that a loss of jurisdiction in the Cantonal Court means that no court has jurisdiction. In my view, neither assumption is correct. Although I agree that the Sarajevo Cantonal Court no longer has jurisdiction, it appears to me, given the provisions of the Bosnia CPC, that the divesture of jurisdiction was not automatic but instead results from the decision of the Bosnian National Court to take the case. I see no reason—and the majority does not explain—why a nation's court reforms cannot entail the transfer of cases from one court to another; and it appears that the Bosnia reforms envision the retention of jurisdiction by the Cantonal Courts in some cases and the transfer to the National Court of other cases of which the National Court wishes to take jurisdiction. The CPC provides that

> [c]ases falling within the competence of the [National] Court *which are pending before other courts or prosecutor's offices and in which the indictment is not legally effective or confirmed*, shall be finalized *by these courts* ***unless*** the [National] Court, *ex officio* ***or*** upon the reasoned proposal of the parties or defense attorney, decide to take such a case.

CPC art. 449(2) (emphases added). I read "shall be finalized by these courts" to mean that even the Sarajevo Cantonal Court could have proceeded to adjudicate Sacirbey's case if the National Court had not decided to take the case. And I read the "unless the Court *ex officio*" clause to mean that the National Court is entitled, simply by virtue of being the National Court, to take jurisdiction of the case. This interpretation is consistent with that of the Bosnian Ministry of Justice, which is Bosnia's "central co-ordinating body for ensuring inter-Entity legislative and justice system harmony and best practice," Law on Ministries and Other Bodies of Administration of Bosnia and Herzegovina, art. 13. The Ministry of Justice is identified in the November 2005 Bosnian Embassy Letter as the source of the information (a) that the National Court can hear Sacirbey's case pursuant to CPC art. 449(2), and (b) that if the United States grants extradition of Sacirbey, the National Court "will proceed." Thus, while I agree with the majority that the Sarajevo Cantonal Court no longer has the power to proceed in the matter of Sacirbey, I reach that conclusion because the Bosnia National Court has decided to take the case. I do not agree with the majority that extradition should be denied on the theory that, rather than having been transferred to the National Court, the original warrant for Sacirbey's arrest has become a "dead letter," Majority Opinion *ante* at 23 (internal quotation marks omitted).

(3) Replies to the Majority's Objections to this Dissent

In response to this dissent, the majority makes several assertions that I find untenable and/or unpersuasive. For example, it asserts that "the Cantonal Court was dissolved," Majority Opinion *ante* at 25 n.22. That contention was advanced in the district court by Sacirbey, but it was explicitly contradicted by the Bosnian government:

> The Ministry of Justice of Bosnia and Herzegovina can not accept the statement that the Cantonal Court—the one that issued the warrant and demand for investigation of Mr. [Sacirbey]—was abolished by the justice system reforms. The mentioned Court exists and hears all cases that are within its jurisdiction.

November 2005 Bosnian Embassy Letter.

In addition, the majority states that "no Bosnian authority has provided a *clear* statement as to whether there is a *prosecution now pending* in a Bosnian court," Majority Opinion *ante* at 25 n.22 (first emphasis in original; second emphasis mine). I cannot see that this provides a basis for requiring the district court to forbid extradition; the majority itself acknowledges that, under the Treaty, "formal charges are not required to grant an extradition request," *id.* at 25.

As to the majority's further suggestion that there is no evidence "that the original warrant for Sacirbey's arrest was transferred to the National Court," Majority Opinion *ante* at 23 n.19, I see nothing in the record to indicate that the arrest warrant was not transferred as part of the transfer of the case. Further, even if the warrant was not transferred, there is nothing in the record to indicate that the warrant is not still extant, given that—contrary to the majority's notion that "the Cantonal Court was dissolved," Majority Opinion *ante* at 25 n.22—the Bosnian Ministry of Justice says that the Cantonal Court was not abolished and still "exists" (November 2005 Bosnian Embassy Letter). I thus do not see the validity of the majority's holding that "there is no valid [arrest] warrant in the present case" "[a]s a matter of law," *id.* at 25 n.21.

Finally, the majority finds that Bosnia's representation that the Bosnia National Court "will proceed" is "ambiguous," Majority Opinion *ante* at 25 n.21, as the majority believes this may mean that that court will merely "permit [] the prosecutor to undertake further investigation," *id.* at 24, and "[i]t is that ambiguity which makes [the majority] unable to derive from the [2005 Bosnian Embassy Letters] an active intent to prosecute," *id.* at 25 n.21. I have three major difficulties with this aspect of the majority opinion. First, as discussed above, I do not see any provision in the Bosnia CPC giving the National Court authority either to "permit[]" or to prohibit "investigation." Second, even linguistically, I cannot view "permit[] the prosecutor to undertake further investigation" as a plausible interpretation of the Bosnia Ministry of Justice's statement that the "Court of Bosnia and Herzegovina will proceed." Third, we are not factfinders; factfinding is the function of the district court. And when the district court has made a finding of fact—here, that "[t]he letters plainly indicate a present intent to prosecute Sacirbey in the National Court," 2006 WL 2585561, at 7—we are not allowed to overturn that finding unless it is "clearly erroneous." Fed. R. Civ. P. 52(a)(6). A feeling that the evidence is "ambiguous," Majority Opinion *ante* at 25 n.21, does not meet the clearly-erroneous test—especially when the majority acknowledges that the judicial interpretation it questions "is one feasible reading," *id.*

In sum, Bosnia has sought the extradition of Sacirbey since January 2002, having issued in December 2001 a warrant for his arrest stating that there was good reason to suspect that, while he was a public official, Sacirbey embezzled Bosnian funds; the matter was thereafter, pursuant to Bosnia's judicial reforms, transferred to Bosnia's National Prosecutor, who has a statutory duty to prosecute where there is evidence that a criminal offense has been committed; and Bosnia's Ministry of Justice has stated that Sacirbey's case will be heard by Bosnia's National Court—a tribunal to which Bosnia's reformed criminal procedure code gives no investigative powers but gives authority *ex officio* to take his case. I thus see no error in the district court's finding that Bosnia intends to prosecute Sacirbey; and I dissent from the majority's decision to reverse on the basis of its speculation, contrary to the Bosnia CPC, that the Bosnian National Court may merely intend to permit further investigation, and of its view, contrary to my reading of CPC art. 449(2), that the warrant for Sacirbey's arrest died with the birth of the Bosnian court reforms.

STEEL CORPORATION OF THE PHILIPPINES
v.
INTERNATIONAL STEEL SERVICES, INC.

Case Nos. 08-1853, 08-2568 (3d Cir. 2009)
Decided November 19, 2009

Leonard Fornella (Argued), Babst, Calland, Clements & Zomnir, Two Gateway Center, 6th Floor, Pittsburgh, PA 15222, Attorney for Appellants.

Paul W. Minnich (Argued), Alex E. Snyder, Sean E. Summers, Barley Snyder, 100 East Market Street, P.O. Box 15012, York, PA 17405, Attorneys for Appellee.

Before: SMITH, FISHER and NYGAARD, Circuit Judges.

NOT PRECEDENTIAL

OPINION OF THE COURT

FISHER, *Circuit Judge.*

International Steel Services, Inc. ("ISSI") appeals from an order of the District Court entering judgment against ISSI in favor of Steel Corporation of the Philippines ("SCP") and an order denying ISSI's motion for relief pursuant to Federal Rule of Civil Procedure 60(b). We will affirm.

I.

We write exclusively for the parties, who are familiar with the factual context and legal history of this case. Therefore, we will set forth only those facts necessary to our analysis.

ISSI, a Delaware corporation headquartered in Pittsburgh, Pennsylvania, and SCP, a Philippine corporation, entered into two separate contracts relevant to this litigation. Under the Acid Regeneration Plant Supply and Installation Agreement ("ARP Contract"), entered into on April 1, 1996, ISSI agreed to construct an acid regeneration plant for SCP. Under the Iron Oxide Sales Agreement ("IOSA Contract"), entered into on April 15, 1997, ISSI agreed to purchase the iron oxide by-product of the plant. Both contracts contained the following arbitration provision:

> "The validity, performance and enforcement of this Contract shall be governed by Philippine Laws. The parties agree that any dispute or claim arising out of this Contract shall be s[e]ttled by arbitration in accordance with the Rules of Conciliation and Arbitration of the International Chamber of Commerce. The proceedings on arbitration shall be conducted in Singapore. The arbitral award shall be final and binding on both parties."

(App. at A-57.) Separate disputes arose under each contract.

On September 18, 2002, ISSI commenced a claim against SCP under the ARP Contract before the Construction Industry Arbitration Commission of the Philippines. The Commission issued an award of $150,000 in ISSI's favor against SCP ("ISSI Award") on August 20, 2003.

On May 5, 2003, SCP instituted a separate claim against ISSI under the IOSA Contract in the International Chamber of Commerce International Court of Arbitration in Singapore. On November 3, 2004, the arbitrator issued a final award of $647,965.50 in SCP's favor against ISSI ("SCP Award"). The SCP Award contained the following provision:

> "The applicable law of the arbitration proceedings is the Singapore International Arbitration Act. The validity, performance and enforcement of . . . the [IOSA Contract is] governed by the laws of the Philippines."

(App. at A-67.) ISSI has not petitioned for judicial review of this award in Singapore.

On August 19, 2004, ISSI filed a petition in the Philippines Regional Trial Court to vacate the SCP Award. Due to an alleged error in service that prevented SCP from receiving an order, on January 4, 2006, the Regional Trial Court declared SCP in default of ISSI's petition to vacate, thereby allowing ISSI to present ex-parte evidence. In response, SCP filed an Urgent Motion for Reconsideration. There is no evidence that the Regional Trial Court ever ruled on this Motion. Instead, a Notice of Pre-Trial indicates that the parties were to attend a pre-trial conference on April 18, 2007. (Addendum Exhibit A.) In an order of that same date, the Regional Trial Court referred the matter to mediation and stayed further proceedings. (Addendum Exhibit B.) The mediation failed.

Meanwhile, on September 13, 2005, ISSI moved to execute the ISSI Award in the Philippines. On July 17, 2007, the Philippine Court of Appeals, in an appeal by SCP, set aside the Award on the basis that ISSI was obligated to pay SCP the greater sum of $647,965.50 under the SCP Award. The Court of Appeals also noted that the Philippine Regional Trial Court, over which the Court has appellate jurisdiction, did not have jurisdiction to set aside the SCP Award. (App. at A-656.)

On January 19, 2006, SCP filed a Petition to Confirm the SCP Award under the Convention on the Recognition and Enforcement of Foreign Arbitral Awards of

June 10, 1958 ("New York Convention"), in the Court of Common Pleas of York County, Pennsylvania. Ultimately, the case was removed to federal court and transferred to the Western District of Pennsylvania. ISSI filed a motion for judgment on the pleadings, which the District Court denied on July 31, 2006.[1] On July 31, 2007, after a discovery phase, the parties filed cross motions for summary judgment.

On February 6, 2008, the District Court denied ISSI's motion for summary judgment, granted SCP's motion for summary judgment, and entered judgment in SCP's favor in the amount of $647,965.50.[2] ISSI filed a motion for relief pursuant to Federal Rule of Civil Procedure 60(b) to reduce the judgment in the amount of $150,000 by offsetting the SCP Award by the amount of the ISSI Award. The District Court denied the motion on April 23, 2008. ISSI filed a timely appeal.

II.

We have jurisdiction over this appeal pursuant to 28 U.S.C. §§ 1291 and 1294. "The District Court's grant of summary judgment and judgment on the pleadings is subject to plenary review." *E.I. DuPont de Nemours & Co. v. United States,* 508 F.3d 126, 131 (3d Cir. 2007). This Court will "construe all facts and inferences in the light most favorable to the non-moving party, and '[j]udgment will not be granted unless the movant clearly establishes there are no material issues of fact, and he is entitled to judgment as a matter of law.'" *Id.* (citations omitted). Likewise, "[w]e review de novo the District Court's interpretation of the [New York] Convention." *Admart AG v. Stephen & Mary Birch Foundation, Inc.,* 457 F.3d 302, 307 (3d Cir. 2006). Finally, "[w]e review grants or denials of relief under Rule 60(b) . . . under an abuse of discretion standard." *Budget Blinds, Inc. v. White,* 536 F.3d 244, 251 (3d Cir. 2008).

III.

ISSI sets forth three arguments on appeal. First and foremost, ISSI contends that the District Court erred in holding that ISSI does not have a valid defense under either Articles V(1)(e) or V(2)(b) of the New York Convention, and thus that the Court erred in enforcing the SCP Award. In the alternative, ISSI argues that the District Court erred in refusing to offset the SCP Award by the smaller ISSI Award pursuant to Federal Rule of Civil Procedure 60(b)(5). We will address each contention in turn.

A.

ISSI argues that under Article V(1)(e) of the New York Convention, the Philippine Regional Trial Court's entry of default against SCP on ISSI's petition to vacate the

1 The District Court also denied reconsideration of the motion on August 28, 2006.

2 The District Court denied ISSI's motion for reconsideration on February 21, 2008.

SCP Award precludes a United States court from enforcing the Award. The applicable language of Article V(1)(e) provides as follows:

> "1. Recognition and enforcement of the award may be refused . . . only if . . .
>
> . . .
>
> (e) The award . . . has been set aside or suspended by a competent authority of the country in which, or under the law of which, that award was made."

Convention on the Recognition and Enforcement of Foreign Arbitral Awards art. V(1), June 10, 1958, T.I.A.S. No. 6997, 21 U.S.T. 2517. To prevail, ISSI must demonstrate that the Philippines is a country with primary jurisdiction by showing that the Philippines is a country "under the law of which"[3] the SCP Award was made.[4] ISSI is unable to do so.

The Sixth Circuit held in *M & C Corp. v. Erwin Behr GmbH & Co., KG* that the Article V(1)(e) language "under the law of which" "'refers exclusively to procedural and not substantive law, and more precisely, to the regimen or scheme of arbitral procedural law *under which the arbitration was conducted.*'" 87 F.3d 844, 848 (6th Cir. 1996) (emphasis added) (quoting *International Standard Electric Corp. v. Bridas Sociedad Anonima Petrolera, Industrial Y Comercial,* 745 F. Supp. 172, 178 (S.D.N.Y. 1990)); *see also Karaha Bodas Co., L.L.C. v. Perusahaan Pertambangan Minyak Dan Gas Bumi Negara,* 364 F.3d 274, 290 (5th Cir. 2004) ("Under the New York Convention, the rulings of the Tribunal interpreting the parties' contract are entitled to deference."). Since the SCP Award indicates that the arbitrator applied Singapore procedural law—"The applicable law of the arbitration proceedings is the Singapore International Arbitration Act" (App. at A-67)—Singapore, not the Philippines, is the country with primary jurisdiction.

In response, ISSI contends that the relevant question is not what procedural law the arbitrator applied, but what procedural law the parties agreed *should* be applied. However, even assuming, *arguendo,* that we look to the parties' choice of procedural law, and not the law applied by the arbitrator, ISSI's argument still fails, as ISSI has not demonstrated that the parties agreed in the IOSA Contract to an application of Philippine procedural law.

Although the Third Circuit has not addressed this issue, the Fifth Circuit held in *Karaha Bodas Co., L.L.C.* that "[u]nder the New York Convention, an agreement specifying the place of the arbitration creates a presumption that the procedural

---

3 The SCP Award was made in Singapore; therefore, the Philippines is not a country "in which" the Award was made.

4 Since the Philippine Regional Trial Court never ruled on SCP's Urgent Motion for Reconsideration of the default judgment, but instead ordered mediation, it is questionable whether the SCP Award has indeed been "set aside or suspended." However, as ISSI is unable to demonstrate that the Philippines is a country with primary jurisdiction, we need not reach this issue.

law of that place applies to the arbitration." 364 F.3d at 291. The Fifth Circuit sensibly explained that any other presumption would be illogical:

> "Authorities on international arbitration describe an agreement providing that one country will be the site of the arbitration but the proceedings w ill be held under the arbitration law of another country by terms such as 'exceptional'; 'almost unknown'; a 'purely academic invention'; 'almost never used in practice'; a possibility 'more theoretical than real'; and a 'once-in-a-blue-moon set of circumstances.' Commentators note that such an agreement would be complex, inconvenient, and inconsistent with the selection of a neutral forum as the arbitral forum."

Id. at 291 (footnotes omitted). We will apply the same presumption here. Accordingly, ISSI bears the burden of showing that Philippine procedural law, not forum procedural law, applies to the arbitration of the SCP Award.

ISSI's primary argument in support of Philippine procedural law is that the parties necessarily agreed to an application of that law by stating in the IOSA Contract that "enforcement" of the Contract would be governed by Philippine law.[5] This is insufficient. Given the difficulty Singapore would likely have in researching, deciphering, and applying another country's procedural law, the use of the term "enforcement," as opposed to the term "procedure," cannot in and of itself create the "once-in-a-blue-moon set of circumstances" w here the forum applies another country's procedural law. *Id.* at 291.

The analogous facts of *Karaha Bodas Co., L.L.C.* support this determination. The litigation in *Karaha Bodas Co., L.L.C.* arose out of an arbitral award made in Switzerland regarding contracts negotiated and allegedly breached in Indonesia. *Id.* at 281. Like the instant case, the parties expressly agreed prior to arbitration that Switzerland would be the site of arbitration and that Indonesian substantive law would apply. *Id.* at 290. Based on these facts, the Fifth Circuit ultimately held that the Swiss tribunal properly applied Swiss procedural law.[6] *Id.* at 293. Similarly, ISSI and SCP expressly agreed to use the substantive law of one country—the

---

5 ISSI attempts to buttress this argument with two additional points, neither of which has merit. First, ISSI argues that the Rules of Conciliation and Arbitration of the International Chamber of Commerce, and in particular Article 15(1), do not limit parties' choice of law. This argument does not help ISSI meet its burden because there is still insufficient evidence that ISSI and SCP actually chose Philippine procedural law over forum procedural law in the IOSA Contract.

Second, ISSI asserts that the deposition testimony of Abeto Uy, the President and Chairman of SCP, and Manuel Pamaran, SCP's expert witness on the application of Philippine law, indicates that SCP clearly understood that Philippine procedural law was to apply. However, contrary to ISSI's assertion, these depositions demonstrate only that Uy and Pamaran neither knew nor understood which procedural law governed the SCP Award.

6 *Karaha Bodas Co., L.L.C.* was arguably a more difficult case. Unlike the instant facts, the parties' contract in *Karaha Bodas Co., L.L.C.* referenced certain Indonesian civil procedure rules. Nevertheless, the Fifth Circuit held that the procedural references "fall far short of an express designation of Indonesian procedural law necessary to rebut the strong presumption

Philippines—while designating another country—Singapore—as the forum, but did not expressly agree to a specific country's procedural law. Therefore, following the Fifth Circuit, we find that ISSI has failed to "rebut the strong presumption that designating the place of the arbitration also designates the law under which the award is made," *id.* at 292, and thus that the Singapore International Court of Arbitration properly applied Singapore procedural law.

In summary, the Philippines is not a country with primary jurisdiction over the SCP Award, and the District Court did not err in holding that ISSI has no defense under Article V(1)(e) of the New York Convention.[7]

B.

Similarly, ISSI contends that under Article V(2)(b) of the New York Convention, enforcing the SCP Award would violate the fundamental principles of res judicata and judicial comity and would run contrary to the public policy against forum shopping in the United States. The relevant provision of Article V(2)(b) provides as follows:

> "2. Recognition and enforcement of an arbitral award may also be refused if the competent authority in the country where recognition and enforcement is sought finds that:
>
> . . .
>
> (b) The recognition or enforcement of the award would be contrary to the public policy of that country."

Convention on the Recognition and Enforcement of Foreign Arbitral Awards art. V(2), June 10, 1958, T.I.A.S. No. 6997, 21 U.S.T. 2517. ISSI argues that because the validity of the SCP Award was already pending in the Philippines, SCP's attempt to enforce the Award in the United States was improper. Accordingly, ISSI asks that we defer to the courts of the Philippines and refrain from enforcing the Award.

ISSI's claim is without merit. To start, we must review Article V public policy defenses narrowly. *Admart AG,* 457 F.3d at 308 ("courts have strictly applied the Article V defenses and generally view them narrowly"). "Enforcement of foreign arbitral awards may be denied [based on the New York Convention's public policy defense] only where enforcement would violate the forum state's most basic notions of morality and justice." *Parsons & Whittemore Overseas Co., Inc. v. Societe Generale De L'Industrie du Papier (RAKTA),* 508 F.2d 969, 974 (2d Cir. 1974).

---

that designating the place of the arbitration also designates the law under which the award is made." 364 F.3d at 292.

7 Although certainly not dispositive, it is worth noting that the Philippine Court of Appeals has also stated, albeit in dicta, that the Philippine Regional Trial Court did not have jurisdiction to set aside the SCP Award. (App. at A-656.)

Here, ISSI's contentions not only do not violate the public policy of the United States, but they contravene the very purpose of the New York Convention. "The principal purpose for acceding to the [New York] Convention was to 'encourage the recognition and enforcement of commercial arbitration agreements in international contracts.'" *Admart AG,* 457 F.3d at 307 (quoting *Scherk v. Alberto-Culver Co.,* 417 U.S. 506, 520 n.15 (1974)). Accordingly, parties may bring suit to enforce awards notwithstanding the existence of ongoing proceedings elsewhere. *See Karaha Bodas Co., L.L.C. v. Perusahaan Pertambangan Minyak Dan Gas Bumi,* 335 F.3d 357, 366–67 (5th Cir. 2003) ("Under the [New York] Convention, a court maintains the discretion to enforce an arbitral award even when nullification proceedings are occurring in the country where the award was rendered. Furthermore, an American court and courts of other countries have enforced awards, or permitted their enforcement, despite prior annulment in courts of primary jurisdiction."). *See also Yusuf Ahmed Alghanim & Sons v. Toys "R" Us, Inc.,* 126 F.3d 15, 22 (2d Cir. 1997) ("The [New York] Convention . . . eradicat[ed] the requirement that a court in the rendering state recognize an award before it could be taken and enforced abroad.").

Applying the foregoing principles to the instant case, SCP was entitled to bring suit to enforce the SCP Award in the United States—where ISSI's assets are located—even though a motion to vacate the SCP Award was pending in the Philippines. Enforcement of the SCP Award does not violate this country's "most basic notions of morality and justice." *Parsons & Whittemore Overseas Co., Inc.,* 508 F.2d at 974. Therefore, the District Court did not err in holding that ISSI does not have an Article V(2)(b) public policy defense against enforcement of the SCP Award in the United States.

C.

Lastly, ISSI challenges the District Court's denial of its motion to offset the SCP Award by the ISSI Award in the amount of $150,000 pursuant to Federal Rule of Civil Procedure 60(b)(5). Because the parties have since resolved this issue,[8] we do not need to address it here.

IV.

For the foregoing reasons, we will affirm the orders of the District Court.

---

8 The parties agreed at oral argument to offset the Awards. Their subsequent stipulation provides, "the Philippine arbitration award in favor of ISSI may be offset against and deducted from the Singapore arbitration award and from the judgment entered in this action in favor of SCP." The agreement calculates the SCP and ISSI Awards, together with interest and costs through October 31, 2009, at $789,427.10 and $281,839.57, respectively. The parties will resolve the continuing calculation of interest after October 31, 2009.

III. PROCEDURE

6. Foreign Proceedings

B. Parallel Proceedings

IN RE BETCORP LIMITED (IN LIQUIDATION)

400 B.R. 266 (Bankr. D. Nev. 2009)
Decided February 9, 2009

Barry F. Irwin, Scott Bennett Kitei, Kirkland & Ellis LLP, Ryan B. Bennett, Chicago, IL, Wade W. Rabenhorst, Campbell & Williams, J. Colby Williams, Las Vegas, NV, for Petitioner.

OPINION ON PETITION FOR RECOGNITION

BRUCE A. MARKELL, Bankruptcy Judge.

I. Introduction

Simon John Cathro, an Australian liquidator, seeks recognition under chapter 15 of the Bankruptcy Code for the ongoing winding up and liquidation, in Australia, of Betcorp Limited, an Australian company. In particular, the petition seeks recognition of the winding up as a "foreign main proceeding." If granted, that recognition would entitle Betcorp to the protections of a variety of Bankruptcy Code provisions, the most important of which for Mr. Cathro's purposes is the automatic stay. *See* 11 U.S.C. § 1520(a)(1) (providing that 11 U.S.C. § 362 applies to a chapter 15 debtor upon recognition).

A United States company, 1st Technology LLC, opposes recognition. It has sued Betcorp for patent infringement, and that lawsuit is currently pending in the United States District Court for the District of Nevada. 1st Technology would prefer (and believes it is entitled) to continue to litigate its claims in a United States court, rather than pursue those claims in Betcorp's Australian liquidation.

Upon consideration of the evidence presented and for the reasons stated below, the court grants Mr. Cathro's petition for recognition of the Australian voluntary winding up as a foreign main proceeding under chapter 15 of the Bankruptcy Code.[1]

---

1 This court has jurisdiction over this proceeding under 28 U.S.C. § 157(b)(1), as this proceeding is a core proceeding, *id.* § 157(b)(2)(P), and this district has entered an order, authorized by 28 U.S.C. § 157(a), referring such matters to this court. NEV. LOC. R. 1001. Given 1st Technology's pending lawsuit against Betcorp, venue in this district is appropriate under 28 U.S.C. § 1410(2).

II. Background

Betcorp was formed and registered as a company under Australian law on February 26, 1998. Declaration of Simon John Cathro ¶ 9 (dkt.# 6) ("Cathro Decl."). When it was active in business, Betcorp was a publicly-traded entity regulated by the Australian Securities and Investments Commission ("ASIC").[2] *Id.* From the time the company was formed until it ceased operations on October 31, 2006, its business activity involved a mélange of gaming activities, conducted through a variety of affiliate and subsidiary entities.[3] Supplemental Declaration of Simon John Cathro ¶ 10 (dkt.#35) ("Cathro Supp."). The company ceased operations after changes in United States law made its business model unworkable. Betcorp's members then voted to liquidate the company through a members' "voluntary winding up" under Australian law, a process which is ongoing. *See* Exhibits to Verified Petition (dkt. # 2, ex. 5 and 6). This process required the appointment of at least one liquidator registered with the ASIC. Throughout most of the winding up process, the appointed liquidators have been in discussions with 1st Technology regarding the patent infringement claims. These events are discussed in more detail below.

A. Betcorp's Gaming Operations and Corporate Governance

When it first began business operations, Betcorp initially created and operated a single subsidiary: Consolidated Sportsbet Australia Pty Limited. Transcript of Testimony of Simon John Cathro, Hearing on Oct. 29, 2008, at p. 54 ("TR").[4] Sportsbet operated solely in Australia, and employed between 20 and 30 people.[5] *Id.* at 54–55. By the end of 2002, Betcorp's management decided to diversify the company's gaming operations. To that end, on January 23, 2003, the company began offering on-line and telephone gaming services through a subsidiary located in Antigua named Tasman Gaming. Cathro Supp. ¶ 12. This business operated under a gaming license issued by the government of Antigua and Barbuda, West Indies. *Id.*

---

2 For a period of approximately eight months in 2006, Betcorp also was listed on the London Stock Exchange's Alternative Investment Market. Cathro Decl. ¶ 10. The company was de-listed in conjunction with its termination of operations and liquidation.

3 "Gaming" is generally regarded as a mild euphemism for gambling, although the OXFORD ENGLISH DICTIONARY indicates that "gaming" was in use to describe wagering and other aleatory activities more than 225 years before "gambling" found its way into the language. *Compare* 6 OXFORD ENGLISH DICTIONARY 342–43 (2d ed.1989) (definition of gambling) *with id.* at 349 (definition of gaming).

4 The testimony of Mr. Cathro and Mr. Ian Walker, one of Betcorp's legal counsel, was taken by video transmission from Australia, after each witness had submitted his direct evidence by written declaration. Although the parties stipulated to the taking of this testimony by video transmission, the court could have found good cause to permit such method of receiving evidence given the cost of bringing the witnesses to the United States for only a half-day of testimony. *See* FED.R.CIV.P. 43(a) (made applicable to this proceeding by FED. R. BANKR.P. 9017).

5 Betcorp sold Sportsbet in October of 2004. TR, pp. 53, 92.

Tasman eventually became the company's primary revenue generator. TR, p. 69. However, Betcorp created and operated other subsidiaries in order to further the company's business strategy of providing a "one-stop shop" for online gamblers. *See* Betcorp's "Annual Report and Accounts 2005" (dkt. # 35, ex. 4–8); *see also* TR, p. 65. As of 2005, Betcorp owned and operated the following subsidiaries:

- BCL (Asia) Pty Limited (incorporated in Australia);
- Tasman Gaming, Inc. (incorporated in Antigua);
- WWI AG Limited (incorporated in Antigua);
- Tasman Investments, Inc. (incorporated in Antigua);
- Swan Holdings (incorporated in Antigua);
- Tartar Sauce Investments, Ltd. (incorporated in Antigua);
- Sinsational Intertainment, Inc. (incorporated in Antigua);
- Oasis Antigua Holdings, Inc. (incorporated in Antigua);
- Applewick Holdings Ltd. (incorporated in Cyprus);
- Betcorp (UK) Limited (incorporated in the United Kingdom); and
- Cyber Processing Corp. Ltd. (incorporated in the Federation of St. Kitts and Nevis).

Cathro Supp. ¶ 11.[6]

Although Betcorp was involved, through these subsidiaries, in business operations in several countries, Australia remained its administrative and executive nerve center. Reflecting the fact that the majority of shareholders resided in or were located in Australia, and that it was an Australian corporation, Australian law governed all corporate activities. Cathro Decl. ¶ 13. The actual statistics overwhelmingly support a center of member ownership in Australia. According to Mr. Cathro, as of September 24, 2007:

- 1,468 of the 1,606 shareholders of Betcorp, or 91.4%, resided in Australia;
- 4,268,617 of the 6,353,426 Betcorp shares (or 67.2%) were held by members who resided in Australia; and
- 138 members (or 8.6%) resided in jurisdictions outside of Australia, of which nine members (or 0.05%) resided in the United States and held but 10,168 (or 0.02%) of the shares of Betcorp.

Id. As an Australian company, all Betcorp shareholder meetings have taken place in Australia. Cathro Supp. ¶ 6.

---

6 Betcorp also operated an information technology and marketing office in Toronto, Canada, which supported its various online gaming operations. Cathro Decl. ¶ 12.

With respect to management, most Betcorp directors have been Australian-born individuals. Of the twenty-five individuals that have served as directors, only five did not reside in Australia. Cathro Supp. ¶ 1. Four of these non-Australian directors resided in the United Kingdom, and one resided in Antigua. *Id.* No Betcorp directors resided in the United States during their tenure. *Id.* These directors participated in both telephonic and in-person meetings. Cathro Supp. ¶ 7. When there were in-person meetings, the majority of them took place in Australia. *Id.*

Corporate audits were performed by the Sydney, Australia offices of two accounting firms: Ernst & Young (prior to 2006), and Grant Thornton (beginning in 2006). Cathro Supp. ¶ 8. Betcorp filed income tax returns with the Australian Tax Office since its incorporation, and paid Australian income tax on its earnings. Cathro Supp. ¶ 9. Finally, Betcorp's registered office has been in Australia from its incorporation to present. Cathro Decl. ¶ 11; TR, pp. 54–55.

B. Changes in United States Gaming Law, Betcorp's Cessation of Operations, and Its Subsequent Winding Up

On October 13, 2006, the United States passed the Unlawful Internet Gambling Enforcement Act, Pub. L. No. 109-347, 120 Stat. 1884 (codified as 31 U.S.C. §§ 5361–67). The Act prevented Betcorp from receiving funds transfers related to gaming activities from United States customers. This was a major blow to Betcorp's business model since at the time of enactment, most of the company's customers resided in the United States. Cathro Decl. ¶¶ 14–16.

Immediately after the passage of the Unlawful Internet Gambling Enforcement Act, the company ceased operations in the United States, and eventually ceased all operations completely.[7] Cathro Decl. ¶ 15. Preparations for the dissolution of the company were made, and in August of 2007, the company engaged the services of two liquidators, Simon John Cathro and Simon Alexander Wallace-Smith, of Deloitte Touche Tohmatsu. Cathro Decl. ¶ 19. An extraordinary general meeting of the company, as provided for under Australian company law, was called for September 28, 2007. Cathro Decl. ¶ 20. At that meeting, held at the company's offices in Australia, the members voted to appoint the liquidators and to begin a voluntary winding up. The vote was 99.9% in favor. *See* Cathro Decl. ¶¶ 2, 20; *see also* Form 505 (dkt.# 2, ex. 6, pp. 4–5). On the day of their appointment, as part of their statutory duty to pay all creditors of the company, the liquidators issued a Notice Inviting Formal Proof of Debt or Claim. *See* Form 534 (dkt.# 6, ex. 2, p. 18). In administering this process, the liquidators became aware of 1st Technology's claims.

7 Soon after the company ceased operations, Tasman was sold to Bodog Entertainment. TR, pp. 62–63.

C. 1st Technology's Claims

1st Technology is owned by Dr. Scott Lewis. Dr. Lewis invented and patented a method and system for interactively transmitting multimedia information over a computer network, in a way that requires less bandwidth than prior art. United States Patent No. 5,564,001 (filed June 24, 1994) (the "'001 patent"). *See* USPTO Patent Full-Text and Image Database, http://patft.uspto.gov/netahtml/PTO/srchnum.htm (search "5564001") (*last visited* Feb. 9, 2009). According to Dr. Lewis, the method is useful to internet gaming companies because it enables a company to transmit data more quickly, using less resources, than would otherwise be the case. Declaration of Dr. Scott Lewis ¶¶ 9–11 (dkt.# 41). Dr. Lewis, through 1st Technology,[8] asserts that Betcorp infringed the '001 patent (either directly or through contributory infringement or inducement), and has sought to vindicate those claims through legal processes undertaken in both the United States and Australia. *Id.* at ¶¶ 22–39.

In early 2006, before Betcorp had ceased operations, 1st Technology sent a letter to Betcorp's offices in Australia, offering to license the '001 patent and other patents for use in Betcorp's operations. Letter from William W. Flachsbart to Betcorp (Feb. 10, 2006) (dkt.# 2, ex. 6, pp. 19–20). This letter also alleged that Betcorp's technology infringed at least one patent owned by 1st Technology. *Id.* Further letters followed on April 20, 2006, and July 21, 2006; neither of which were responded to by Betcorp in a manner satisfactory to 1st Technology.

On February 11, 2008, 1st Technology filed a complaint against Betcorp in the United States District Court for the District of Nevada, alleging infringement of the '001 patent. *1st Tech. v. Betcorp,* No. 2:08-cv-00175. Although 1st Technology did not immediately serve the complaint, its Australian counsel faxed a letter to the liquidators, dated February 13, 2008, which set forth the claims and enclosed a copy of the complaint. Letter from Leon Zwier to Simon Cathro/Simon Wallace-Smith (dkt.# 2, ex. 6, pp. 7–25). The letter requested additional information from Betcorp regarding some transactions in which Betcorp had been a participant. *Id.* Presumably, this information was sought to assist 1st Technology in the United States lawsuit, as well as in the Australian legal processes that would soon follow.

On April 16, 2008, 1st Technology submitted a proof of debt to the Australian liquidators. Letter from Leon Zwier to Ian Walker (April 16, 2008) (dkt.# 2, ex. 7, pp. 2–4). The liquidators responded to this proof of debt with a request for further evidence, pursuant to Regulation 5.6.53(1) of Australia's *Corporations*

---

8 Betcorp has not questioned that 1st Technology has standing to pursue claims of infringement of a patent originally issued to Dr. Lewis.

Regulations 2001.[9] Letter from Simon Wallace-Smith to Leon Zwier (April 30, 2008) (dkt.# 2, ex. 7, pp. 6–8).

1st Technology and the liquidators engaged in further communications, but the liquidators believed that the information received was insufficient to permit the liquidators to make a final decision on the proof of debt.[10] With the matter unresolved, 1st Technology then went forward with its United States lawsuit by formally serving it upon the liquidators on August 15, 2008. Return of Service (dkt.# 2, ex. 7, pp. 25–27). Although Betcorp has appeared in the infringement lawsuit, it has not answered the complaint. The liquidators instead prefer to resolve 1st Technology's claims through the Australian winding up process.[11] This reasoning lead to Mr. Cathro's filing the petition for recognition on October 2, 2008 (dkt.# 1).

III. Recognition of Betcorp's Winding Up

Recognition of any proceeding as a foreign main proceeding requires several findings, and Mr. Cathro's request to recognize Betcorp's voluntary winding up in Australia is no different. As a preliminary matter, however, the court must determine whether Betcorp's winding up is a "foreign proceeding" within the meaning of 11 U.S.C. § 101(23). If 1st Technology is correct that the winding up fails to qualify under section 101(23), the matter ends there, and no recognition will be given. If, however, the winding up is a foreign proceeding, the court must look to section 1517(a) to see if Mr. Cathro has met his burden of proving that the winding up proceeding is entitled to recognition either as a "foreign main" proceeding or as a "foreign nonmain" proceeding. Each of these issues is discussed below.

A. Is Betcorp's Winding Up a "Foreign Proceeding" as Defined by 11 U.S.C. § 101(23)?

1st Technology argues that Betcorp's winding up is not a "foreign proceeding" within the meaning of chapter 15. It asserts, correctly, that (i) there is no lawsuit or legal proceeding pending in an Australian court (or anywhere else except the United States) involving any of Betcorp's creditors; (ii) Betcorp is not a bankrupt or in administration under Australian bankruptcy laws, or any other bankruptcy laws; and (iii) there is no lawsuit or other legal process by which a judge or other judicial officer directly supervises the liquidators' actions in the winding up. Based upon these facts, 1st Technology contends that Betcorp's actions are nothing more

9 This request was made pursuant to authority granted to the liquidators under Australian regulatory law. *See* Corporations Regulations 2001, *available at* http://www.comlaw.gov.au/ (click "Compilations—Current" under "Select Legislative Instruments (SLIs) and Statutory Rules (SRs)"; search for "F2008C00509") (*last visited* Feb. 9, 2009).

10 The liquidators, as of the submission of this matter, still have not made a decision on the proof of debt. At the hearing on the petition for recognition, Betcorp indicated that the liquidators would grant additional extensions after the court's decision to allow 1st Technology to submit additional evidence regarding their proof of debt.

11 The parties have stipulated to stay the patent infringement action pending this court's decision on Betcorp's recognition petition.

than a unilateral cessation of business followed by a private and unregulated settling of accounts.

1st Technology's interpretation of Australia's statutory scheme of liquidation is misguided. Both the text and existing interpretations of Australia's corporations statute indicate that an Australian voluntary winding up has all of the necessary elements of a "foreign proceeding" as that term is used in section 101(23). Although no United States court has examined section 101(23) in great detail, the court does not write without guidance. Chapter 15, which uses the term to define its scope, "incorporate[s] the Model Law on Cross-Border Insolvency" drafted by UNCITRAL, the United Nations Commission on International Trade Law. 11 U.S.C. § 1501(a). The statutory intent to meld American law into international law is explicit in the text of section 1501(a), and also is expressed in section 1508, which states that "[i]n interpreting this chapter, the court shall consider its international origin, and the need to promote an application of this chapter that is consistent with the application of similar statutes adopted by foreign jurisdictions." 11 U.S.C. § 1508; *see also* HOUSE REPORT ON THE BANKRUPTCY ABUSE PREVENTION AND CONSUMER PROTECTION ACT OF 2005, H.R.REP. NO. 109-31, pt. I, at 105 (2005), *reprinted in* 2005 U.S.C.C.A.N. 88, 169 ("[Chapter 15] incorporates the Model Law on Cross-Border Insolvency to encourage cooperation between the United States and foreign countries with respect to transnational insolvency cases . . . . [These provisions are] intended to provide greater legal certainty for trade and investment as well as to provide for the fair and efficient administration of cross-border insolvencies, which protects the interests of creditors and other interested parties, including the debtor.") [hereinafter "HOUSE REPORT"]; 8 COLLIER ON BANKRUPTCY ¶ 1501.01 (Alan N. Resnick & Henry J. Sommer eds., 15th ed. rev.2008) (explaining the basis for chapter 15).

Against this background, the scope of the Model Law's definition of "proceeding" is quite relevant. The Model Law's *Guide to Enactment,* published by UNCITRAL, states:

> To fall within the scope of the Model Law, a foreign insolvency proceeding needs to possess certain attributes. These include the following: basis in insolvency-related law of the originating State; involvement of creditors collectively; control or supervision of the assets and affairs of the debtor by a court or another official body; and reorganization or liquidation of the debtor as the purpose of the proceeding . . . .

UNITED NATIONS COMMISSION ON INTERNATIONAL TRADE LAW (UNCITRAL), UNCITRAL MODEL LAW ON CROSS-BORDER INSOLVENCY WITH GUIDE TO ENACTMENT ¶ 23, at 10, U.N. Gen. Assembly, UNCITRAL 30th Sess., U.N. Doc. A/CN.9/442 (1997), *available at* http://www.uncitral.org/uncitral/en/commission/sessions/30th.html [hereinafter *"Guide to Enactment"*].[12]

---

12 As Congress noted, the *Guide to Enactment* is very useful in construing chapter 15. "Interpretation of this chapter [15] on a uniform basis will be aided by reference to the Guide and the Reports cited therein, which explain the reasons for the terms used and often cite their origins as well." HOUSE REPORT. *supra,* at 109.

These attributes, as stated in the *Guide to Enactment,* follow from the text of Article 2(a) of the Model Law, which is codified almost word-for-word in this country in section 101(23).[13]

Section 101(23) states:

> The term "foreign proceeding" means a collective judicial or administrative proceeding in a foreign country, including an interim proceeding, under a law relating to insolvency or adjustment of debt in which proceeding the assets and affairs of the debtor are subject to control or supervision by a foreign court, for the purpose of reorganization or liquidation.

11 U.S.C. § 101(23).

This definition can be broken down in seven criteria or elements, each of which must be satisfied before Betcorp's winding up can be called a "foreign proceeding." These elements are:

(i) a proceeding;

(ii) that is either judicial or administrative;

(iii) that is collective in nature;

(iv) that is in a foreign country;

(v) that is authorized or conducted under a law related to insolvency or the adjustment of debts;

(vi) in which the debtor's assets and affairs are subject to the control or supervision of a foreign court; and

(vii) which proceeding is for the purpose of reorganization or liquidation.

Each of these is analyzed below.

1. A "Proceeding"

The first step in this analysis is to determine whether a "voluntary winding up" under Australian law is even a "proceeding." 1st Technology argues that it is not, since there is no petition or application to any court. To an American ear, this argument has some initial appeal. In cases under title 11, the term "proceeding" has a fairly circumscribed meaning—it is used to refer to in-court events, such as hearings, as well as being used to refer to self-contained lawsuits brought within a particular bankruptcy case, such as adversary proceedings. *See* BLACK'S LAW

---

13 Article 2(a) of the Model Law and section 101(23) have only minor differences. Section 101(23) adds the two words "The term" at the beginning of the definition, uses the term "foreign country" instead of the Model Law's "foreign State", substitutes the phrase "under a law" instead of using the word "pursuant", and adds the phrase "or adjustment of debt" after "insolvency." For purposes of this case, these are insignificant differences.

DICTIONARY 1241 (8th ed.2004) (definition of proceeding); *see also* FED. R. BANKR. P. 7001.

In the context of chapter 15, however, the word "proceeding" requires a broader definition in order to achieve the statutory directive of interpretation consistent with the understandings and the usages of international law and the UNCITRAL Model Law. Although not directly applicable under the circumstances, the *European Union Regulation on Insolvency Proceedings* is helpful with regard to the accepted meaning of the word "proceeding" in international insolvency law.[14] Paragraph 10 of the introductory recitals of the EU Regulation states:

> Insolvency proceedings do not necessarily involve the intervention of a judicial authority; the expression "court" in this Regulation should be given a broad meaning and include a person or body empowered by national law to open insolvency proceedings. In order for this Regulation to apply, *proceedings (comprising acts and formalities set down in law)* should not only have to comply with the provisions of this Regulation, but they should also be officially recognized and legally effective in the Member State in which the insolvency proceedings are opened . . . .

COUNCIL REGULATION 1346/2000, 2000 O.J. (L 160), at 2, *available at* http://eurlex.europa.eu/LexUriServ/LexUriServ.do?uri=OJ:L:2000:160:0001:0018:EN:PDF (emphasis supplied) [hereinafter "EU Regulation"].[15]

This excerpt identifies the essence of a "proceeding": acts and formalities set down in law so that courts, merchants and creditors can know them in advance, and apply them evenly in practice. In the context of corporate insolvencies, the hallmark of

---

14 The EU Regulation applies in cross-border cases among all members of the European Union except Denmark. After its promulgation in 2000, it came into effect in 2002. That the controlling instrument is a regulation rather than a law arises because the European Union was unable to agree, for nonbankruptcy reasons, on an earlier draft law, known as the European Union Convention on Insolvency Proceedings (the "EU Convention"). For a brief overview of the history and the current text of the EU Regulation, see Ian F. Fletcher, *The European Union Regulation on Insolvency Proceedings, reprinted in* INSOL INTERNATIONAL, CROSS-BORDER INSOLVENCY: A GUIDE TO RECOGNITION AND ENFORCEMENT, 15–45 (2003).

Even though the EU Convention was never adopted, the *Guide to Enactment's* references to the EU Convention's text are still relevant and valid, inasmuch as the *Guide to Enactment* was drafted during a time when it was possible to think that the EU Convention would be adopted, and the final text of the EU Regulation is based upon and closely parallels the earlier text of the EU Convention. These close connections are discussed in *In re Ran,* 390 B.R. 257, 264 n. 3 (Bankr.S.D.Tex.2008) (quoting the opinion of Mr. Advocate General Ruiz-Jarabo Colomer in Case C-1/04, *Proceedings brought by Staubitz-Schreiber,* [2006] E.C.R. I-701, 2005 WL 2138235 (ECJ Grand Chamber)).

15 The breadth of this definition is significant in light of the more restrictive scope of the EU Regulation. The EU Regulation only applies to collective proceedings which "entail the partial or total divestment of a debtor and an appointment of a liquidator." EU Regulation, at 4 (art. 1(1)). Section 101(23) and Article 2(a) of the Model Law, however, have a broader scope, extending to reorganization proceedings such as the United States' chapter 11 when a debtor in possession is in control.

a "proceeding" is a statutory framework that constrains a company's actions and that regulates the final distribution of a company's assets. In this case, that framework is provided by the Australian *Corporations Act (Cth) 2001.*[16] Under Australian law, this Act governs voluntary winding up, as well as a multitude of other procedures used to end a corporation's existence. Chapter 5 of the *Corporations Act,* entitled "External Administration," governs the termination of businesses through the appointment of an administrator or liquidator, and is applicable to Betcorp.

1st Technology argues that a voluntary winding up is not a proceeding because commencement of that type of process does not require an application or petition to any court. Mr. Cathro responds that this bare fact obscures the nature of a voluntary winding up. He argues that to understand the voluntary winding up process, the court must consider all of the *Corporations Act's* external administration provisions, along with the duties those provisions impose on a liquidator (who is necessarily appointed as part of a voluntary winding up). *See CA § 495(1), CA § 499(1).*

Chapter 5 of the Australian *Corporations Act* is obviously intended to be read as an integrated whole. It purports to contain all of the provisions necessary to wind up any company and has been interpreted to be the exclusive procedure under which any such winding up may occur. *See* MICHAEL GRONOW, McPHERSON'S LAW OF COMPANY LIQUIDATION ¶ 1.40, at 1–52 (5th ed.2006); Rosalind Mason, *Local Proceedings in a Multi-State Liquidation: Issues of Jurisdiction,* 30 MELB.U.L.REV. 145, 160–61 & nn. 112–13 (2006) (citing ANDREW KEAY, McPHERSON: THE LAW OF COMPANY LIQUIDATION 2–3 (4th ed.1999)).[17] To augment this exclusivity, the provisions allow, but do not require, court

---

16 The court permitted Mr. Cathro to introduce the entire Australian *Corporations Act (Cth) 2001* into evidence, but that was not necessary. Rule 44.1 would have permitted the court to have looked to the version generally available on the Internet. *See* FED. R.CIV.P. 44.1 (made applicable to this proceeding by FED. R. BANKR.P. 9017) ("In determining foreign law, the court may consider any relevant material or source, including testimony, whether or not submitted by a party or admissible under the Federal Rules of Evidence.").

The *Corporations Act* is divided into 10 chapters, consisting in total of over 2,000 pages. It is comprehensive, dealing with matters affecting all stages of the corporate life-cycle, from the formation and registration of corporate entities through termination of operations, liquidation and dissolution. Corporations Act (Cth) 2001, *available at* http://www.comlaw.gov.au/ (click "Compilations—Current" under "Acts"; search for "C2009C00042") (*last visited* Feb. 9, 2009) (The abbreviation "Cth" stands for "Commonwealth of Australia," the full name of that country, and is the official designator for laws enacted by Australia's federal government.)

In this opinion, sections of the *Corporations Act* will be cited as "CA." Although the *Corporations Act* was amended after submission of this matter, the amendments do not affect the analysis of whether Betcorp's winding up is entitled to recognition under chapter 15.

17 It also requires notice to the ASIC, the Australian regulatory agency responsible for and which oversees Australian corporations. *CA § 5B; see* ROBERT P. AUSTIN & IAN M. RAMSAY, FORD'S PRINCIPLES OF CORPORATIONS LAW ¶ 3.140 (13th ed.2007) (describing the functions of the ASIC).

involvement, and provide, in appropriate cases, for the conversion from voluntary winding up to court-supervised external administration, and vice versa. *See CA § 459P* (setting out who may apply to a court for a company to be wound up in insolvency); *CA § 461* (setting out grounds other than insolvency upon which a court may wind up a company); *CA § 496* (explaining the duties of liquidators when a company turns out to be insolvent); *CA § 467B* (allowing the court to take control of a voluntary winding up); *CA § 482* (permitting the court to terminate or stay a court ordered winding up and return company control to the corporate principals).

So although a voluntary winding up may never be placed squarely in front of a judge, once the provisions of Part 5 are invoked, the nature of the process changes, and changes in ways that are beyond the debtor's control. The terms of these changes are laid out in the statute, providing the necessary "act and formalities" for conversion and supervision.

As an example, if a company initiates a voluntary winding up, and is found during the course of that winding up to be insolvent, the liquidator must convert to another type of administration or call a creditors' meeting. *CA § 496.* Either action will likely lead to court involvement. Similarly, if a corporation chooses liquidation under a type of court-supervised external administration known as a voluntary administration (not this case), and all creditors are paid 100 cents on the dollar, then that proceeding must be terminated and the company wound up under other Chapter 5 provisions. *See CA § 445FA; CA § 446A.* A court may also order the end of such a voluntary administration if it thinks a company is solvent. *CA § 447A.* Numerous other provisions of Chapter 5 also require conversion among the various types of external administration or otherwise govern the effects of conversion.[18]

Australian case law also indicates that viewing the voluntary winding up process as a "proceeding" is appropriate. As stated in *Lofthouse v. Austl. Sec. Invs. Comm'n,* (2004) 82 A.L.D. 481, ¶¶ 50–52, 2004 WL 674816 (Austl.):

> Subject to its being solvent and a Court's not having ordered that it be wound up in insolvency, a company may resolve by special resolution that it be wound up [*CA §§ 490, 491*]. If such a resolution is made, a liquidator must be appointed by the company in a general meeting [*CA § 495(1)*] and all the powers of the directors cease [*CA § 495(2)*]. If it should transpire that the company is insolvent, the liquidator may choose to apply to the Court under [*CA § 459P*] for the company to be wound up in

18 For example, the provisions of Chapter 5.2, regarding the appointment of a receiver, explain how the receiver's powers are affected when a company is being wound up. *CA § 420C.* The provisions of Chapter 5.3A, in section 436B, explains that a liquidator may appoint an administrator, which is something a liquidator might choose to do after determining the liquidator has a statutory duty to convert a winding up into some other time of external administration. Sections 459 and 462 also provide mechanisms for a liquidator to convert a proceeding from one type of external administration to another.

> insolvency, appoint an administrator of the company under [*CA § 436B*] or convene a meeting of the company's creditors [*CA § 496(1)*] . . . . Subject to the provisions of the Act as to preferential payments, the property of the company must be applied in satisfaction of its liabilities equally and, subject to the company's constitution, be distributed amongst its members according to their rights and interests in the company [*CA § 501*].

The fact that commencing this type of external administration terminates the authority of the company's directors, combined with the fact that the winding up cannot be stopped by the equity interest holders once they have passed the special resolution, lends further support to a finding that this Australian legal process is a proceeding.

1st Technology's sole argument on this issue—that the absence of an application or a petition to an Australian court proves the winding up is not a proceeding—is not persuasive given the explanation found in *Lofthouse* and this court's reading of the Australian *Corporations Act. See also* EU Regulation, Recital ¶ 10 ("Insolvency proceedings do not necessarily involve the intervention of a judicial authority; the expression 'court' in this Regulation should be given a broad meaning and include a person or body empowered by national law to open insolvency proceedings."). The court thus finds that an Australian voluntary winding up is a "proceeding" under section 101(23) and, by extension, chapter 15.

2. Judicial or Administrative in Character

Section 101(23) requires that the proceeding be judicial or administrative in character. An Australian voluntary winding is, generally, a proceeding with an administrative character, although under certain circumstances the proceeding may temporarily become more appropriately characterized as judicial.

The Australian *Corporations Act* provides that a company commences a voluntary winding up by passing a "special resolution." *CA § 491.* Once passed, the liquidating company must appoint a liquidator that is registered with the ASIC. *CA § 495(1); see* Part 9.2 of the *Corporations Act.* The initial actions of the liquidator, such as sending a notice of liquidation and requesting proofs of debt, have an administrative character. *See CA §§ 490–581.* The submission of proofs of debt and the ultimate payments to creditors are made pursuant to the administrative framework created by the *Corporations Act. Id.* If no party objects, and every creditor is paid in full, it is possible that the entire voluntary winding up may progress from commencement to final disbursal of funds and company de-registration as a purely administrative proceeding.[19]

---

19 The payment in full is critical; "creditors have no involvement [in a voluntary winding up] because they will be repaid in full." MICHAEL MURRAY, KEAY'S INSOLVENCY: PERSONAL AND CORPORATE LAW AND PRACTICE ¶ 11.10, at 273 (6th ed.2008).

In order to protect creditors' rights, however, a voluntary winding up may change from a proceeding with an administrative character to one with a judicial character. As discussed in Part III.A.6, *infra,* the actions of the liquidator are subject to review by the courts of Australia upon application by parties in interest. If such review is sought, the proceeding will take on a judicial character while a judge reviews the request. More importantly, however, if it appears to the liquidators that there may not be sufficient funds to pay all creditors in full, the proceeding will generally have to be converted into a form of external administration requiring more judicial involvement. *Lofthouse,* 82 A.L.D. at ¶ 50.

In any event, section 101(23) requires only that a proceeding have either an administrative *or* a judicial character. Therefore, because the court finds that the voluntary winding up necessarily has an administrative character, this element of section 101(23) is satisfied.

3. A Collective Proceeding

Section 101(23) also requires the proceeding be "collective." A collective proceeding is one that considers the rights and obligations of all creditors. This is in contrast, for example, to a receivership remedy instigated at the request, and for the benefit, of a single secured creditor.

A voluntary winding up fits this "collective" criterion. As a leading Australian treatise states: "Liquidation is, like bankruptcy, a procedure of an inherently collective nature . . . . The procedure is compulsory, in order to ensure that there is an orderly, cooperative system. The result is that any attempt by a creditor to undermine the collective nature of liquidation is outlawed." GRONOW, *supra,* ¶ 1.20, at 1–51. Australian courts have also consistently held that private remedies, such as a receivership or a private deed of arrangement, cannot accomplish the goals of a statutory winding up. *Id.* at ¶ 1.40, at 1–51 (citing cases); Re Island Air Pty Ltd, (1983) 7 ACLR 844 (Austl.) (scheme of arrangement); Re Tillers Pty Ltd, [1970] 3 NSWR 202 (Austl.) (similar); Re Swallow Footwear Ltd, (1956) 222 LT 229 (Austl.) (court-appointed receiver); *see also CA § 501.*[20]

The voluntary winding up provisions, combined with the case law from Australian courts, provide substantial evidence that this type of external administration is properly understood as collective. Thus, this criterion of section 101(23) is satisfied by Betcorp's proceeding.

---

20 The liquidator has a duty to account for the rights of all creditors in the course of distributing a company's property. *CA § 501.* Provisions of the *Corporations Act* facilitate and enhance this collective process by permitting a high degree of creditor involvement. For example, if a creditor so chooses, the liquidator must hold meetings to determine the need for the formation of creditor Committees of Inspection. *CA §§ 548–52.* If the liquidator refuses to form these committees, that decision is immediately appealable to a court, which in turn may order their formation. *Id.*

4. Located in a Foreign Country

The voluntary winding up must be located in a foreign country. The special resolution commencing Betcorp's voluntary winding up was made at a meeting that was held at the company's registered office, which is located in Melbourne, Australia. The voluntary winding up is operating under the provisions of Australian law. The liquidators—whom are currently the only persons authorized to act for the company—are appointed pursuant to Australian law, and both are citizens and residents of Australia. Based on this evidence, the court finds that Betcorp's winding up is located in a foreign country, thereby satisfying this section 101(23) criterion.

5. Authorized or Conducted under a Law Related to Insolvency or the Adjustment of Debts

For Betcorp's winding up to qualify as a foreign proceeding, the winding up must be authorized or conducted under a law related to insolvency or the adjustment of debts. Importantly, this element does not require the company to be either insolvent or to be contemplating using the provisions of Australian law to adjust any debts.[21] Two facts favor a finding that Betcorp's winding up satisfies this fifth criterion: (1) the unified structure of the external administration provisions of the *Corporations Act;* and (2) the Australian Parliament's own interpretation that Australia's company laws qualify under the Model Law.

As explained above, the *Corporations Act* regulates the whole of the corporate life-cycle of an Australian corporation. In this regard, several sub-parts of Chapter 5 contain provisions that deal with corporate insolvency and allow for the adjustment of debts. *See* Parts 5.3, 5.4A, and 5.4B of Chapter 5 of the *Corporations Act.* These facts, combined with the statutory ability to shift among various forms of dissolution given changing circumstances, demonstrate that winding up is achieved under a law relating to insolvency or the adjustment of debts.

Additionally, the court finds persuasive the Australian legislature's interpretation of its *Corporations Act,* published in connection with Australia's adoption of the Model Law. In Australia, proposed legislation is often accompanied by "explanatory memoranda" that serve as an aid to understanding the purpose and structure of the legislation. Pursuant to statutory authority, Australian courts may use these explanatory memoranda to interpret legislation that has been enacted. *See* Austl. Acts Interpretation Act 1901 (2009) § 15AB(2)(e) (providing that a court may use

---

21 *See* UNCITRAL, Working Group on Insolvency Law, *Draft Legislative Provisions on Judicial Cooperation and Access and Recognition in Cases of Cross-border Insolvency,* p. 9, at n. 2, U.N. Doc. A/CN.9/WG.V/WP.44 (Mar. 8, 1996) (explaining that the phrase "or other law relating to insolvency" is intended to "allude to the fact that liquidations . . . might be conducted under other than, strictly speaking, insolvency laws" and giving the example of company laws), *available at* http://www.uncitral.org/pdf/ english/travaux/insolvency/acn9-wg5-wp44-e.pdf.

an explanatory memorandum to interpret legislation), *available at* http://www.comlaw.gov.au/ (click "Compilations—Current" under "Acts"; search for "C2009C00046"; click the PDF) (*last visited* Feb. 9, 2009). Given that this court may look to any relevant material or source to interpret foreign law, *see* FED. R.CIV.P. 44.1, the court will thus consider these memoranda as relevant sources and interpretative guides to Australian law.

The Senate of the Parliament of the Commonwealth of Australia has issued an "Explanatory Memorandum" which interprets Australia's version of the UNCITRAL Model Law, enacted as part of Australia's Cross-Border Insolvency Bill 2008. CROSS-BORDER INSOLVENCY BILL 2008, EXPLANATORY MEMORANDUM, *available at* http://www.comlaw.gov.au/ (click "1996 + by title" under "Bills"; search for "C2008B00008"; select "Cross-Border Insolvency Bill 2008"; click "EM/Supp Material"; click the PDF) (*last visited* Feb. 9, 2009) [hereinafter "Explanatory Memorandum"]. That memorandum states:

> Many articles of the Model Law require an insertion for 'laws of the enacting State relating to insolvency' (or similar). It is intended that the Model Law will apply to collective judicial or administrative proceedings pursuant to a law relating to bankruptcy or corporate insolvency. As such, the relevant Australian laws are the Bankruptcy Act and Chapter 5 (other than Parts 5.2 and 5.4A) of the Corporations Act, and also section 601CL of the Corporations Act [Part 2, clause 8].

Explanatory Memorandum ¶ .13, at 7–8.

A voluntary winding up is governed by Part 5.5 of Chapter 5 of the *Corporations Act.* It is telling that this is *not* one of the sub-parts excluded in the *Explanatory Memorandum.* Accordingly, based upon the Australian legislature's interpretation of the UNCITRAL Model Law and Australian domestic law, a company engaged in a voluntary winding up is being administered under a law relating to insolvency. This evidence supports the court's determination that Betcorp's winding up satisfies the "law relating to insolvency" criterion of section 101(23). Therefore, the court finds that this element of section 101(23) is satisfied.[22]

6. Foreign Court's Control or Supervision of the Debtor's Assets and Affairs

Section 101(23) requires that the voluntary winding is conducted such that the assets and affairs of the debtor are subject to control or supervision by a foreign court. In chapter 15, the term "foreign court" has a defined meaning. Section 1502

22 The United States' expansion of the types of laws that can be considered-the addition in section 101(23) of laws related to "adjustment of debt" to laws related to "insolvency," see note 13—bolsters this conclusion but is not necessary to it. For proceedings for which this addition might be relevant, *see* Jennifer D. Morton, Note, *Recognition of Cross-Border Insolvency Proceedings: An Evaluation of Solvent Schemes of Arrangement and Part VII Transfers Under U.S. Chapter 15,* 29 FORD. INT'L L.J. 1312 (2006).

of the Bankruptcy Code defines "foreign court" as "a judicial or other authority competent to control or supervise a foreign proceeding."[23]

In Betcorp's case, the liquidators, Mr. Cathro and Mr. Wallace-Smith, have direct control of the debtor's assets. The ASIC, in turn, directly regulates all liquidators. As stated in section 5B of the *Corporations Act,* "Subject to the ASIC Act, ASIC has the general administration of this Act." The ASIC supervises liquidators in the performance of their duties, and requires that liquidators request permission of the ASIC before undertaking certain actions. *See, e.g.,* ASIC POLICY STATEMENT 81, DESTRUCTION OF BOOKS (May 3, 2000) (requiring liquidators conducting a voluntary winding up to submit a written request to the ASIC before destroying any books and records). Also, pursuant to Part 9.2 of the *Corporations Act,* the ASIC may remove or revoke the authority of any person to be a liquidator. Therefore, a reasonable interpretation of the relationship between the ASIC and any liquidator is that the ASIC itself is "an authority competent to control and supervise a foreign proceeding" within the meaning of sections 101(23) and 1502. *See In re Tradex Swiss AG,* 384 B.R. 34, 42 (Bankr. D.Mass.2008) (Swiss Federal Banking Commission held to be a foreign court under chapter 15 because it controls and supervises liquidation of entities, such as debtor, that are in brokerage trade).

Alternatively, the voluntary winding up proceedings are also subject to supervision by a more traditional judicial authority: the Australian courts.[24] Section 511 of

---

23 There is a slight problem with the use and interpretation of "foreign court" in section 101(23). The chapter 15 definition of "foreign court" is not directly applicable to chapter 1 of the Bankruptcy Code in which section 101(23) is found. *Compare* 11 U.S.C. § 103(k) (stating, with exceptions not relevant here, that chapter 15 applies only in cases under that chapter) *with id.* § 1502 (stating that the listed definitions are "[f]or the purposes of this chapter [15]"). The question thus arises as to whether the definition of "foreign court" found in section 1502(3) can be used to interpret that same phrase in section 101(23).

While recognizing that the suggested reading—that an administrative agency is a court—is somewhat contrary to plain meaning, this court will use the definition found in section 1502(3) to construe section 101(23). This deviation from accepted methods of statutory interpretation is justified by the international context of this case, and by Congress' directives, contained in section 1501 and 1508, to construe chapter 15 so that it is consistent with international understandings.

Initially, the Model Law was drafted with the definition of "foreign proceeding" and the definition of "foreign court" in the same Article. *Compare* Model Law, Arts. 2(a) (definition of "foreign proceeding") *with id.* Art. 2(e) (definition of "foreign court"). The separation of the two definitions in chapter 15 does not appear to have been done with the intent of limiting the scope of section 101(23). *See* HOUSE REPORT, *supra,* 110 (discussing definitions, including "foreign court," as if adapted without change from Model Law). To the contrary, section 1501(a)'s instruction is to interpret chapter 15 in line with the Model Law so as to promote, among other things, "greater legal certainty." 11 U.S.C. § 1501(a)(3). That certainly would be undermined if United States courts refused to recognize, as a foreign proceeding, foreign liquidations and reorganizations simply because they were being administered by an administrative agency rather than a judicial officer.

24 As explained in section 58AA of the *Corporations Act,* "Court," as used in the Act, may, under the circumstances, refer to either the Federal Court of Australia or the Supreme Court of a State or Territory.

the *Corporations Act* allows both liquidators and creditors to request a court to determine "any question arising in the winding up of a company." Even in the absence of a creditor's appeal, the Australian courts have a broad mandate to review actions of liquidators. Under section 536, if it appears to a court that the actions of a liquidator are in derogation of the *Corporations Act,* the court "may take such action as it thinks fit." *See also Cresvale Far East (in liq) v. Cresvale Sec. Ltd,* (2001) 39 A.C.S.R. 622, ¶ 63, 2001 WL 1353240 (Austl.) (reversed in part on unrelated grounds) ("In a voluntary winding up, the appointment of the liquidator is consensual but a liquidator's duties and powers are prescribed by the Corporations Act, and there are elements of supervision by the Court.").

Further, under section 1321 of the *Corporations Act,* any person "aggrieved by any act, omission or decision of . . . a liquidator" may appeal to an Australian court. The court may then "confirm, reverse or modify the act or decision or remedy the omission, as the case may be, and make such orders and give such directions as it thinks fit."[25] *Id.* If cause is shown, the court may remove the liquidator from his or her position. *CA § 503; cf. Tradex Swiss,* 384 B.R. at 42 (alternatively holding the Swiss Federal Banking Commission to be a foreign court under chapter 15 because its decisions are subject to review by Swiss courts).

Based on this evidence, the court finds that Betcorp's winding up proceeding is being conducted such that the assets and affairs of Betcorp are subject to control or supervision by a foreign court, within the meaning of section 101(23).

7. Reorganization or Liquidation Purpose

The final requirement of section 101(23) is that the purpose of the foreign proceeding be for reorganization or liquidation. A voluntary winding up is a statutory process under the law of Australia through which a company is liquidated. *See CA § 501.* The directors' minutes and memo to equity interest holders explain that the purpose of the winding up is to liquidate Betcorp. *See* Director's Minutes (dkt.#2, ex. 5, pp. 2–29). The special resolution commencing Betcorp's winding up indicates the same. *See* Resolution (dkt.# 2, ex. 6, p. 2). The declaration filed by Mr. Cathro also states that the purpose of the winding up is to liquidate the company. Cathro Decl. ¶¶ 25, 44. Therefore, the court finds this final element of section 101(23) is satisfied.

Having determined that each of the seven criteria required by section 101(23) are satisfied, the court finds that Betcorp's voluntary winding up is a "foreign proceeding." With this substantial preliminary question settled, the court now turns to the requirements for recognition that are stated in section 1517.

---

25 Also, if a creditor does not believe a liquidator is dealing appropriately with its proof of claim, it "may apply to the Court for a decision in respect of it." *Corporations Regulations 5.6.53(2).*

B. Does Betcorp's Winding Up Proceeding Meet the Requirements for Recognition Under Section 1517?

Section 1517 requires recognition of a foreign proceeding if:

(1) such foreign proceeding for which recognition is sought is a foreign main proceeding or foreign nonmain proceeding within the meaning of section 1502;

(2) the foreign representative applying for recognition is a person or body; and

(3) the petition meets the requirements of section 1515.

Assessing whether these three requirements are satisfied necessitates reference to other chapter 15 provisions and the Code's definition section. These elements are addressed in turn.

1. Is the Foreign Proceeding for Which Recognition Is Sought a Foreign Main Proceeding or Foreign Nonmain Proceeding?

Section 1517's first requirement is that the foreign proceeding for which recognition is sought is either a foreign main or a foreign nonmain proceeding. In this case, Mr. Cathro specifically seeks Betcorp's winding up to be recognized as a foreign main proceeding.

Under section 1502(4), a foreign main proceeding is a "foreign proceeding pending in the country where the debtor has the center of its main interests." As Betcorp's winding up qualifies as a "foreign proceeding," the question then becomes where Betcorp's "center of main interests" or "COMI" as it is often referred to, is located.

COMI is not defined in the Bankruptcy Code or in the Model Law. To aid courts in simple or uncontested cases, section 1516(c) states that, "[i]n the absence of evidence to the contrary, the debtor's registered office . . . is presumed to be the center of the debtor's main interests."[26] If this presumption applied, it is undisputed that at all times the debtor's registered office was in Australia.

1st Technology, however, has in good faith introduced evidence raising a legitimate question as to whether Betcorp's COMI is in Australia. Because of this, this court cannot rely solely upon section 1516(c)'s presumption in determining whether Betcorp's COMI is in Australia. It must consider all evidence, while keeping in mind that it is Mr. Cathro's burden to persuade the court, by a preponderance of the evidence, that Betcorp's COMI is in Australia. *In re Bear Stearns High-Grade Structured Credit Strategies Master Fund, Ltd.,* 389 B.R. 325, 335–36

26 "The presumption that the place of the registered office is also the center of the debtor's main interest is included for speed and convenience of proof where there is no serious controversy." HOUSE REPORT, *supra* at 113; *see In re Basis Yield Alpha Fund (Master),* 381 B.R. 37, 52–53 (Bankr.S.D.N.Y. 2008).

(S.D.N.Y.2008) (quoting HOUSE REPORT, *supra,* at 112–13); *Tradex Swiss,* 384 B.R. at 43; *see* FED.R.EVID. 301 (explaining that a party's rebuttal of a presumption does not shift the burden of proof; rather, the risk of nonpersuasion remains upon the party on whom it was originally cast-in this case, the joint liquidators of Betcorp); *see also In re Tri-Continental Exchange Ltd.,* 349 B.R. 627, 635 (Bankr.E.D.Cal.2006) (discussing the 11 U.S.C. § 1516(c) presumption).

The next section, Part III.B.1.i, analyzes cases discussing and applying the COMI concept. Part III.B.1.ii then addresses a particular COMI issue raised by 1st Technology: should COMI be determined as of the time of the filing of the petition for recognition, or should the court look back and determine COMI in light of a debtor's operational history? Following that, Part III.B.1.iii will address Mr. Cathro's contention that Betcorp's COMI is located in Australia.

i. Factors Relevant to the COMI Determination

The term "center of main interests" is taken from the UNCITRAL Model Law. *Tri-Continental,* 349 B.R. at 633. The *Guide to Enactment* to that law indicates the phrase's origin to be in the EU Convention.[27] As stated in paragraph 31 of the *Guide to Enactment:*

> A foreign proceeding is deemed to be the "main" proceeding if it has been commenced in the State where "the debtor has the centre of its main interests". This corresponds to the formulation in the European Union Convention on Insolvency Proceedings (art. 3 of that Convention), thus building on the emerging harmonization as regards the notion of a "main" proceeding.[28]

Guide to Enactment, ¶ 31, at 12.

In the preliminary paragraphs of the EU Regulation, in turn, elaborate upon COMI as "the place where the debtor conducts the administration of his interests on a regular basis and is therefore ascertainable by third parties." EU Regulation ¶ 13. As explained in a report generally thought to be expressive of the intent of the EU Convention, and upon which the EU Regulation is based:

> The rationale of this rule is not difficult to explain. Insolvency is a foreseeable risk. It is therefore important that international jurisdiction ... be based on a place known to the debtor's potential creditors. This enables the legal risks which would have to be assumed in the case of insolvency to be calculated.

27 The connections between the failed EU Convention and the current EU Regulation are examined in note 14, *supra.*

28 This borrowing is confirmed by paragraph 72 of the *Guide to Enactment:*

> The expression "centre of main interests" in subparagraph (b) to define a foreign main proceeding is used also in the European Union Convention on Insolvency Proceedings.

Guide to Enactment, ¶ 72.

MIGUEL VIRGOS & ETIENNE SCHMIT, REPORT ON THE CONVENTION ON INSOLVENCY PROCEEDINGS ¶ 75, at 51 (1996), *available at* http://aei.pitt.edu/952/01/insolvency_report_schmidt_1988.pdf.[29]

Although examining these origins helps, it leaves much open; after all, the term "center of main interests" is not specifically defined, either in chapter 15 or the Model Law. Such uncertainty was not intended. One of the United States' representatives to the UNCITRAL meetings that produced the Model Law, Professor Jay Westbrook, has explained that the adoption of the term in chapter 15 was not intended to create a new concept of location, but to build upon existing concepts:

> Chapter 15 was drafted to follow the Model Law as closely as possible, with the idea of encouraging other countries to do the same. One example is use of the phrase "center of main interests," which could have been replaced by "principal place of business" as a phrase more familiar to American judges and lawyers. The drafters of Chapter 15 believed, however, that such a crucial jurisdictional test should be uniform around the world and hoped that its adoption by the United States would encourage other countries to use it as well.

Jay Lawrence Westbrook, *Chapter 15 at Last,* 79 AM. BANKR.L.J. 713, 719–20 (2005) (citations omitted). This gloss on "center of main interests"—that it is virtually identical to the more commonly used (at least in the United States) concept of "principal place of business"—has been analyzed recently by several domestic courts. *See also* Jay Lawrence Westbrook, *Locating the Eye of the Financial Storm,* 32 BROOK. J. INT'L L. 1019, 1020 (2007) ("COMI is similar to standards like 'principal place of business,' 'chief executive offices,' or 'real seat' that one finds in many statutes in the United States and elsewhere.") [hereinafter "Westbrook, *Financial Storm*"].

---

29 This report was originally designed to be the authorized guide to the EU Convention. While the EU Convention was never adopted, however, it still retains interpretative vitality so long as its origins are properly understood. When discussing the provenance of this report, Professor Ian Fletcher has noted that:

> The exact status of the *Virgos-Schmit* Report is somewhat uncertain since it has never been officially placed in the public domain, although the text has been published in various languages, using the version prepared and revised by the linguistic experts of the EC Council during 1995–1996 in anticipation of formal publication in the *Official Journal.*

Ian F. Fletcher, *The European Union Regulation on Insolvency Proceedings, reprinted in* INSOL INTERNATIONAL, CROSS-BORDER INSOLVENCY: A GUIDE TO RECOGNITION AND ENFORCEMENT 19 (2003). Professor Fletcher goes on to note that:

> To provide for some measure of atonement for the abrogation of the proposed explanatory report, many of the numbered Recitals [of the EU Regulation] attempt to provide a much-compressed summary of the information that the Report contained concerning many of the key provisions or expressions now embodied in the Regulation.

Id.

Although the Internet citation refers to "Schmidt," the report itself indicates that the author's name does not contain a "d."

In *Bear Stearns,* the only appellate case thus far to address chapter 15's COMI concept, official liquidators for two hedge funds registered as Cayman Islands limited liability companies sought chapter 15 recognition for liquidation proceedings opened in the Cayman Islands. In determining whether the funds' COMI was in the Cayman Islands, or elsewhere, the court began with *Tri-Continental Exchange's* observation that COMI could be "equate[d]" with "the United States' concept of 'principal place of business.'" *Id.* at 336 (quoting *Tri-Continental,* 349 B.R. at 629); *see also In re Basis Yield Alpha Fund (Master),* 381 B.R. 37, 47 (Bankr. S.D.N.Y.2008).

The *Bear Stearns* court then recited the bankruptcy court's listing of potential factors that could be relevant to a COMI determination. 389 B.R. at 336. These included:

> the location of the debtor's headquarters; the location of those who actually manage the debtor (which, conceivably could be the headquarters of a holding company); the location of the debtor's primary assets; the location of the majority of the debtor's creditors or of a majority of the creditors who would be affected by the case; and/or the jurisdiction whose law would apply to most disputes.

Id. (quoting *In re Bear Stearns High-Grade Structured Credit Strategies Master Fund, Ltd.,* 374 B.R. 122, 128 (Bankr. S.D.N.Y.2007)) (in turn quoting *In re SPhinX, Ltd.,* 351 B.R. 103, 117 (Bankr. S.D.N.Y.2007)). This formulation has been adopted or used by most courts that have subsequently addressed the components of COMI. *See* Tradex Swiss, 384 B.R. at 42–43; *In re Ernst & Young, Inc.,* 383 B.R. 773, 779 (Bankr.D.Colo.2008); *Basis Yield,* 381 B.R. at 47; *In re Loy,* 380 B.R. 154, 162 (Bankr.E.D.Va.2007).

Ultimately, *Bear Stearns* affirmed the bankruptcy court's finding that the debtor's COMI was not in the Cayman Islands, and thus the Cayman Islands proceeding was not entitled to recognition as a foreign main proceeding.[30] 389 B.R. at 337–38. Aside from being registered in the Cayman Islands, the bankruptcy court had found that the Funds had no other "adhesive connection" with that country. 374 B.R. at 129–30. Further, no managers or employees were located in the Caymans, the Funds were administered from offices located in the United States, and neither the books and records of the Funds, nor the Funds' assets, were held in the Caymans. *Id.* In sum, the court denied recognition because the Funds existed in the Caymans as merely shells or "letterbox" companies. *Id.* at 130 n. 8.

Tradex Swiss used the same analysis in a somewhat different setting. There, a foreign exchange trading company had activities in Switzerland and the United States. Swiss banking authorities had commenced an investigation into the debtor's activities; the testimony was that the Swiss regulator had oversight responsibility for all

30 Indeed, the bankruptcy court had gone further and found that the debtor did not even have an "establishment" in the Cayman Islands, and denied recognition as a foreign nonmain proceeding as well. The district court affirmed this finding and conclusion. 389 B.R. at 338–39.

currency traders such as Tradex (because it acted as a securities broker as defined in Swiss law). 384 B.R. at 37–38. The regulator had the power to act as a bankruptcy court for the restructuring or liquidation of securities brokers such as Tradex. *Id.*

Tradex was registered as a Swiss company, but had offices in the United States and in Switzerland. Tradex's trades were accomplished at its United States office, and the officer with signing authority over bank accounts was located there. *Id.* at 39. Its physical files were in Boston, and its email correspondence with customers originated there. *Id.* Its money was in United States' banks, and a plurality of its creditors (in number) and a majority in amount were in the United States. *Id.* The United States office had 18 employees, and the Swiss office had only 4, one of which was a girlfriend of a principal, and another was a cleaning person. *Id.*

The foreign representatives wanted a halt to United States proceedings, including an involuntary chapter 7 case filed against the debtor. To achieve this goal, they filed a chapter 15 case, seeking to establish that the debtor's COMI was in Switzerland, thus making the Swiss proceeding a foreign main proceeding.

The court did not grant recognition as a foreign main proceeding. Adopting the principal place of business framework, the court analyzed the debtor's business activities as of the chapter 15 filing. *Id.* at 42–43. The court found that the presence of a business location, and a principal, of the debtor in Switzerland was not enough to establish COMI there; rather, the fact that the debtor's cash, assets, main trading platform, and records were in the United States made the United States the debtor's COMI.[31] *Id.* at 43.

These domestic decisions do not stand alone. Cases from other countries also support a focus on the principal place of business.[32] An instructive case from the European Court of Justice is *Bondi v. Bank of America,* N.A. (*In re Eurofood IFSC Ltd.*), Case 341/04, 2006 E.C.R. I-3813, 2006 ECJ Celex Lexis 777, 2006 WL 1142304 (E.C.J. May 2, 2006). The case concerned an entity named Eurofood, which was a subsidiary of an Italian entity named Parmalat SpA. Eurofood's registered office was in Ireland, and it did business throughout that country. *Id.* at ¶ 17. In January of 2004, Eurofood was sought to be involuntarily wound up, pursuant to the provisions of Irish law. *Id.* at ¶¶ 19–20. That proceeding was immediately opened, and ultimately the Irish court found Ireland to be Eurofood's COMI. *Id.* ¶ 20.

---

31 The Swiss proceedings were recognized, however, as a foreign nonmain proceeding because the facts indicated that Tradex had an establishment in Switzerland, just not a principal place of business. *Id.* at 43–44.

32 Looking at these foreign cases is appropriate. Section 1508 states in interpreting phrases such as "center of main interests," "the court shall consider" how those phrases have been construed in other jurisdictions which have adopted similar statutes. This means looking not only at domestic cases, but also at cases decided by the courts of other countries. As stated in the legislative history, "[n]ot only are these sources persuasive, but they advance the crucial goal of uniformity of interpretation." HOUSE REPORT, *supra,* at 110.

Eurofood's parent Parmalat was, at the time of the commencement of the Eurofood Irish proceeding, itself the subject of an "extraordinary administration" proceeding in Italy. In conjunction with Parmalat's proceeding, an Italian proceeding was opened against Eurofood, and in late February 2004 that court found Eurofood insolvent and declared Italy to be Eurofood's COMI. Finally, in March, the Irish courts determined that the Irish proceeding had primacy under the EU Regulation, found Eurofood's COMI to be in Ireland, and refused to recognize the decisions made in Eurofood's Italian proceeding. *Id.*

The European Court of Justice found that Parmalat, by virtue of its position as corporate parent, had ultimate control over Eurofood, but that Eurofood's main interests were objectively in Ireland, and were ascertainable to be in Ireland by third parties. *Id.* at ¶ 37. Given this conduct, the European court found that the relationship of parent and subsidiary was insufficient to rebut the presumption that the registered office of Eurofood, Ireland, was Eurofood's center of main interests. *Id.*

Other cases confirm the strength of an ascertainable principal place of business even when it is not located in the country in which the debtor is registered or incorporated. In *Re* BRAC Budget Rent-a-Car Int'l Inc., [2003] EWHC 128(Ch), 2003 WL 117146 (Eng.), for example, a company incorporated in Delaware and with its registered address in the United States, petitioned for an administration order under United Kingdom law. The company had never traded in the United States and, for the most part, conducted its business in the United Kingdom. In addition, most of its employees worked in England and had contracts of employment governed by English law. Given this background, the court found the debtor's COMI to be in the United Kingdom, thus giving it the power to take jurisdiction over the proceeding. A similar holding was issued in Collins & Aikman Corp. Group, [2005] EWHC (Ch) 1754, ¶ 38, 2005 WL 4829623 (Eng.), in which the court found that the debtor's centralization of human resources systems, cash systems, sales functions and engineering design function in England lead to a finding that England was the debtor's COMI. *See also* Scott A. Bomhof & Adam M. Slavens, *Shifting Gears in Cross-Border Insolvencies: From Comity to COMI,* 24 Bank. & Fin. L. Rev. 31, 46–53 (2008).

In sum, a commonality of cases analyzing debtors' COMI demonstrates that courts do not apply any rigid formula or consistently find one factor dispositive; instead, courts analyze a variety of factors to discern, objectively, where a particular debtor has its principal place of business. This inquiry examines the debtor's administration, management, and operations along with whether reasonable and ordinary third parties can discern or perceive where the debtor is conducting these various functions.[33]

---

33 Professor Westbrook, in *Financial Storm,* proposes that the determination of COMI be influenced not only by the predictability that the principal place of business standard provides, but also by the likelihood of selection of an acceptable substantive law. Westbrook, *Financial*

ii. Timing of the COMI Determination

Even if the objective facts at the time of Betcorp's filing establish its COMI in Australia, 1st Technology has a further argument. It contends that the COMI determination should be made with reference to a company's operational history, and not merely by assessing where COMI lies on the petition date. If this perspective is adopted, so 1st Technology argues, it demonstrates that Australia is not Betcorp's COMI.

This argument is flawed. To accept it would frustrate the goals of using COMI to "harmonize" insolvency proceeding recognition transnationally, and it would make the determination of COMI imprecise and often incorrect.

A good example of the various policy choices is found in *In re Ran,* 390 B.R. 257 (Bankr.S.D.Tex.2008). In *Ran,* an Israeli bankruptcy trustee sought recognition of the Israeli bankruptcy under chapter 15 as a foreign main proceeding. The bankruptcy involved an individual, one Yuval Ran, an Israeli citizen who had a prolonged history of business activities in Israel, but who had relocated to the United States and continuously resided in Texas for approximately a decade prior to the chapter 15 filing. *Id.* at 260–61.

Ran is a prime example of why the court cannot make the COMI determination with an eye toward a debtor's operational history. Timing was a decisive issue in *Ran* because, in his past, Mr. Ran had substantial interests in Israel, but on the date of the petition for recognition, he had effectively no interests in that country. *Ran,* 390 B.R. at 260. In an argument closely tracking that of 1st Technology in this case, Mr. Ran essentially argued that the court must consider his entire operational history in making its COMI determination. *Id.* at 300.

Prior to 1997, Mr. Ran was the CEO of a publicly-traded Israeli company and had been associated with nearly 100 Israeli companies. *Id.* at 260, 285. Some of the companies Mr. Ran was associated with began experiencing large losses, prompting Mr. Ran and his family to leave Israel and come to America.

Storm, supra, at 1020. Professor Westbrook's proposal is driven by the understandable desire to avoid the application of law chosen by the debtor which would lead to predictably abusive results for the debtor's creditors. *Id.* at 1030–35. The use of such debtor havens raises the difficulty that "both formally and in action, [the results produced by the haven law] is too likely to fall outside that range of acceptable outcomes. It may also lack essential procedural characteristics, such as sufficient transparency and an acceptable judicial system." *Id.* at 1032. The ultimate result would be a unwelcome drift back to territorialism and the unprincipled preference for local law. *Id.*

Whatever the merits of this proposal—and they are considerable—this court does not have to decide whether a COMI determination needs to consider the quality of the applicable substantive law. In this case, Betcorp's country of registry, its principal place of business, and the likelihood that an acceptable substantive law will govern its liquidation, all point to Australia as Betcorp's COMI.

Id. at 260.[34] Since 1998, Mr. Ran had not conducted business in Israel. *Id.* Mr. Ran took up work in America, applied to be a United States citizen, and at the COMI hearing, he stated that he intended to remain in America for the rest of his life. *Id.* Nonetheless, the Israeli bankruptcy trustee argued fervently that a longitudinal assessment of Mr. Ran's business activities proved his COMI was in Israel. *Id.* The trustee pointed out that in 1999, an Israeli court—the District Court of Tel-Aviv-Jaffa—had appointed him as trustee to administer Mr. Ran's assets. *Id.*

Ran rejected the trustee's arguments. *Id.* at 300. It based that rejection on a common sense argument: If courts assess COMI with an eye to a debtor's operational history, there is an increased likelihood of conflicting COMI determinations, as courts may tend to attach greater importance to activities in their own countries, or may simply weigh the evidence differently. Giving consideration to a debtor's operational history increases the possibility of competing main proceedings, thus defeating the purpose of using the COMI construct. Requiring courts to give weight to the debtor's interests over the course of its operational history may destroy the uniformity and harmonization that is the goal of employing the COMI inquiry.

Moreover, it is important that the debtor's COMI be ascertainable by third parties. *Ran's* analysis correctly proceeds on the assumption that COMI is affected not only by what a debtor does, but by what a debtor is perceived as doing. *See id.* at 274–75. If the debtor's main interests are in a particular country and third parties observe this situation, it should be irrelevant that the debtor's interests were previously centered in a different country. The presumption is that creditors will look to the law of the jurisdiction in which they perceive the debtor to be operating to resolve any difficulties they have with that debtor, regardless of whether such resolution is informal, administrative or judicial.[35]

In fact, an inquiry into the debtor's past interests could lead to a denial of recognition in a country where a debtor's interests are truly centered, merely because of past activities. This frustrates two of the purposes of the COMI inquiry—it decreases the effectiveness of the insolvency proceeding for which recognition is sought, and it may lead to a sub-optimal distribution of the debtor's assets, inasmuch as non-recognition where recognition is due may forestall needed inter-nation cooperation. *See* Westbrook, *Financial Storm, supra.*

As a result, *Ran* held that the appropriate time to determine COMI was when the chapter 15 case commenced. This is consistent with English cases interpreting the EU Regulation, which seem to select a time linked to the commencement or service of the relevant insolvency proceeding. *Shierson v. Vlieland-Boddy,* [2005] EWCA

---

34 There were also personal reasons. His car and his brother's office were firebombed, and he and his family had received several death and kidnaping threats. 390 B.R. at 260–61 n. 1.

35 As *Ran* also recognizes, due regard must be given for the debtor's choice to conduct his business where he or she sees fit. *Id.* at 272–75 (citing *Shierson v. Vlieland-Boddy,* [2005] EWCA (Civ) 974, 2005 WL 1860177 (Eng.)).

(Civ) 974, ¶¶ 39, 55, 2005 WL 1860177(Eng); Re Collins & Aikman Corp. Group, [2005] EWHC (Ch) 1754, ¶ 39, 2005 WL 4829623 (Eng).

iii. Betcorp's COMI

This brings the analysis to the determination of Betcorp's center of main interests. Viewing Betcorp as of the time of the petition for recognition, almost all of the factors considered by courts lead to a determination that Betcorp's COMI is Australia. *See Bear Stearns,* 389 B.R. at 336 (listing potentially relevant factors such as: the locale of debtor's headquarters; its management; its assets; its creditors and the jurisdiction whose law would apply to most disputes). The location of Betcorp's registered office and the place from where the winding up is being administered is Australia.[36] The location of those that manage Betcorp—the liquidators (since commencing the winding up divests the directors of their authority)—is Australia. Betcorp has no employees, save and except for those selected by the liquidators. Betcorp's primary asset; in fact, its only asset, is the cash in its Australian bank account. The voluntary winding up is being conducted pursuant to the Australian *Corporations Act,* and therefore this is the law that would apply to most disputes.

The only factor that does not support a finding that Betcorp's COMI is Australia is the location of its creditors. Betcorp currently has two creditors. One is located in the United Kingdom, and will apparently be paid when the liquidators have settled all outstanding creditor disputes. The other creditor is 1st Technology, which is located in the United States. 1st Technology argues that notwithstanding all of the factors indicating Betcorp's COMI is in Australia, the court should determine COMI is in the United States, based upon 1st Technology's allegations of patent infringement.[37]

Based on a consideration of all of the relevant factors and the evidence presented, the court finds that Betcorp's COMI is Australia. This is the place from which Betcorp conducts the administration of its interests, and this fact has proved ascertainable not only by third parties, but by 1st Technology itself (e.g., the letters from 1st Technology regarding alleged patent infringement, and submitting its proof of debt to the Australian liquidators). This finding is in line with recent English decisions under the EU Regulation finding that the identity of the country in which an individual debtor's debts were incurred was not a relevant consideration in

---

36 Although the presumption of section 1516 does not apply in this case, that does not mean that the location of Betcorp's registered office is irrelevant. *See Bear Stearns,* 389 B.R. at 336; *Tri-Continental,* 349 B.R. at 629–30.

37 1st Technology also argues that the court should consider that many of Betcorp's former customers were from the United States. The court declines this invitation, considering that Betcorp had no customers as of the date of the petition for recognition, and this date cabins the court's inquiry.

establishing where COMI might be. *Shierson,* [2005] EWCA (Civ) 974; *Official Receiver v. Eichler,* [2007] B.P.I.R. (Ch D.) 1636, 2007 WL 4947537 (Eng.).

Consideration of the consequences of 1st Technology's argument also support Australian COMI. If 1st Technology is correct, then Betcorp's COMI is in the United States, and only a United States court could open a main proceeding for its assets and creditors. This court would then be faced with administering the estate of an Australian company, with its assets and management some eighteen time zones away, all for the sake of one lawsuit. This is especially wasteful when Australia, the other candidate for Betcorp's COMI, has a liquidation process in place that is both rational and fair, and which provides for full payment to creditors such as1st Technology, or if Betcorp proves insolvent, for a fair aliquot share of any remaining assets.[38]

Further, even if the court accepted 1st Technology's invitation to determine COMI with respect to the company's operational history—an invitation this court rejects—the outcome would not change. When the company was first formed, its sole subsidiary operated only in Australia. As the company grew, it began to operate subsidiaries in other countries, given rise to "interests" in each place it did business. But as discussed in Part II of this opinion, at all times Betcorp's administrative and executive nerve center was Australia. It is where its decisions were made and where most of its management and shareholdings were concentrated. 1st Technology's evidence with respect to Betcorp's customers, while relevant, is not as probative as the other objective and external indica of where Betcorp's executive decisions were made. Against this, Mr. Cathro has introduced extensive evidence showing Betcorp's COMI was and is Australia. Therefore, the court's decision on Betcorp's COMI would not be changed by taking into account the operational history of the company. Based on the evidence presented, Mr. Cathro has carried his burden of showing Betcorp's center of main interests to be in Australia. Accordingly, the court finds the first element of section 1517 is satisfied and that Betcorp's winding up is a "foreign main" proceeding.[39]

---

38 1st Technology's focus has been on having a United States court decide its United States patent claims. But chapter 15 recognition will not preclude that from occurring; rather, it simply means that the company's liquidators will have the ability to make the initial determination as to where the claim will be liquidated. It could be that the liquidators may permit the United States lawsuit to proceed, or the parties could agree to some other form of resolution. If 1st Technology disagrees with the liquidators' determination, this court is convinced that it will have appropriate recourse to Australian courts to have that decision reviewed.

39 Because the court has determined that Betcorp's winding up is a foreign main proceeding, it need not discuss whether the proceeding would qualify as a nonmain proceeding, since the definitions of main and nonmain make those terms mutually exclusive. *See* 11 U.S.C. §§ 1502(4) and (5). This also renders moot 1st Technology's request for denial of recognition on the basis that Betcorp does not have an "establishment" in Australia because of its liquidation. *See* 11 U.S.C. § 1501(2) (definition of establishment).

2. Is the Foreign Representative Applying for Recognition a Person or Body?

The second requirement under section 1517 is that the foreign representative applying for recognition is a person or body. Section 101(24) defines the term "foreign representative" as "a person or body, including a person or body appointed on an interim basis, authorized in a foreign proceeding to administer the reorganization or the liquidation of the debtor's assets or affairs or to act as a representative of such foreign proceeding." This requirement is satisfied in this case.

The court has already found that the voluntary winding up qualifies as a foreign proceeding under section 101(23). In that voluntary winding up, the liquidators are officially authorized by statute to liquidate the debtor's assets. *See CA § 506; see also id. § 501.* The Betcorp member vote authorizing the winding up specifically gave the liquidators control over the debtor's assets and allowed them to liquidate those assets. Cathro Decl. ¶¶ 19–22. Mr. Cathro and Mr. Wallace-Smith are the only representatives of the debtor currently authorized to act on its behalf and have been actively carrying out the duties required of them as liquidators. *See* Cathro Decl. ¶ 23. Mr. Cathro, an individual and the liquidator named in the petition for recognition, is therefore both a person[40] and a "foreign representative" applying for recognition. The court thus finds this second requirement of section 1517 is satisfied.

3. Does the Petition Meet the Requirements of Section 1515?

The final item necessary for recognition is that all four requirements of section 1515 are met. 11 U.S.C. § 1517(a), (b)(1) – (3). Section 1515's first requirement is found in subsection (a) and simply that the foreign representative has filed a petition for recognition. 11 U.S.C. § 1515(a). Mr. Cathro has complied with this requirement. *See* Petition for Recognition (dkt.# 1).

The existence of an establishment in the country in which the proceeding is pending is only relevant to the determination of whether a foreign proceeding is a "foreign nonmain proceeding." Only that definition uses the definition of "establishment." *Compare* 11 U.S.C. § 1517(b)(1) (providing for recognition as foreign main proceeding if proceeding is pending in country where debtor has center of main interests) *with id.* § 1517(b)(2) (providing for recognition as a foreign nonmain proceeding if proceeding is pending in country where the debtor has an establishment). Since foreign main and foreign nonmain proceedings are mutually exclusive, and since the court has found that Betcorp's winding up qualifies as a foreign main proceeding, there is no legal need to make any findings on whether or where Betcorp has an "establishment."

40 The Bankruptcy Code states that "[t]he term person includes individual, partnership, and corporation . . . ." 11 U.S.C. § 101(41). As Mr. Cathro is an individual—that is, a living human being—the court need not construe what is meant by "body," a term undefined in either chapter 1 or chapter 15 of the Bankruptcy Code.

The second requirement of section 1515 is found in subsection (b). It requires that the petitioner establish that a foreign proceeding exists and that the petitioner has been appointed as the foreign representative. The first two paragraphs of section 1515(b) provide for the sufficient evidence; they specify that the petitioner may satisfy this requirement by providing a "certified copy of the decision commencing such foreign proceeding and appointing the foreign representative" and "a certificate from the foreign court affirming the existence of the foreign proceeding and the appointment of the foreign representative." 11 U.S.C. § 1515(b)(1) & (2). In cases such as Betcorp's, however, in which there is no formal court proceeding, the statute may be satisfied with "any other evidence acceptable to the court of the existence of such foreign proceeding and of the appointment of the foreign representative." 11 U.S.C. § 1515(b)(3).

Mr. Cathro has satisfied the second requirement. In conjunction with the filing of its petition for recognition, Mr. Cathro filed a document from the ASIC showing that liquidators had been appointed pursuant to provisions of the *Corporations Act. See* Form 505 (dkt.#2, ex. 6, pp. 4–5). Given that section 1502(3)'s definition of "foreign court" refers to "a judicial *or other authority* competent to control or supervise a foreign proceeding," documents from the ASIC, for reasons stated earlier, suffice for this requirement.[41] In combination with the other evidence presented, this documentary evidence submitted by Mr. Cathro satisfies this section 1517(a)(3).

The third requirement under section 1515 is that the petition for recognition is accompanied by a statement identifying all foreign proceedings with respect to the debtor that are known to the foreign representative. 11 U.S.C. § 1515(c). Mr. Cathro's declaration explains that the Australian proceeding is the only foreign proceeding the debtor is involved with, and therefore the court finds this requirement is satisfied. *See* Verified Petition Under Chapter 15 For Recognition of a Foreign Main Proceeding ¶¶ 28–31 (dkt.# 2); *see also* Cathro Decl. ¶ 44.

The fourth and final requirement is simply that certain documents be translated into English. 11 U.S.C. § 1515(d). As the native language of all documents produced is English, this requirement is also satisfied.

Accordingly, all requirements of section 1515 are satisfied.

IV. Conclusion

As all of the requirements under section 1517(a) have been met, the petition for recognition is granted. In accordance with section 1517(b), Betcorp's winding up is hereby recognized as a foreign main proceeding. This opinion shall constitute

---

41 (emphasis supplied). There is no issue of the applicability of section 1502(3)'s definition in this context, as section 1515 is found in chapter 3, the stated scope of the definitions in section 1502.

the court's findings of fact and conclusions of law, in accordance with FED. R. BANKR.P. 7052 (incorporating FED.R.CIV.P. 52), made applicable to this proceeding under FED. R. BANKR. P. 1018. The court will enter a separate order under FED. R. BANKR. P. 9021.

IT IS SO ORDERED.

III. PROCEDURE

6. Foreign Proceedings

C. Discovery*

* Cases are indexed under this subject. The full text of these cases is published on the pages indicated.

III. PROCEDURE

6. Foreign Proceedings

D. Fifth Amendment and *Habeas Corpus* in Foreign Jurisdictions*

* The case indexed under this subject is published on the page indicated.

III. PROCEDURE

7. Service of Process*

* Cases are indexed under this subject. The full text of these cases is published in the **volume**-page indicated.

STX PANOCEAN (UK) CO., LTD.
v.
GLORY WEALTH SHIPPING PTE LTD.

560 F.3d 127 (2d Cir. 2009)
Decided March 19, 2009

Christopher Carlsen, Clyde and Co. U.S. LLP, New York, NY, for Plaintiff-Appellant.

James H. Power, (Lisa D. Schaupp on the brief), Holland & Knight, LLP, New York, NY, for Defendants-Appellees.

Before: WALKER, CALABRESI, and WESLEY, Circuit Judges.

PER CURIAM:

Plaintiff-Appellant STX Panocean (UK) Co., Ltd. ("STX") appeals from and seeks a stay, pursuant to Federal Rule of Appellate Procedure 8(a), of the December 10, 2008 order of the United States District Court for the Southern District of New York (Daniels, J.) vacating the *ex parte* Process of Maritime Attachment and Garnishment obtained by STX in the amount of $900,000 against Glory Wealth Shipping Pte Ltd. ("Glory Wealth") and Glory Wealth Shipping Service Ltd. ("Glory Service") (collectively, the "Defendants"). We find that registration with the New York Department of State, pursuant to New York Business Corporation Law § 1304, to conduct business in New York, and designation of an agent within the district upon whom process may be served constitutes being "found" within the district for purposes of Rule B of the Supplemental Rules for Admiralty or Maritime Claims and Asset Forfeiture Actions. We therefore affirm the district court's vacatur of the maritime attachment and dismiss the motion for a stay as moot.

BACKGROUND

In November 2008, STX filed a complaint against Defendants, alleging that Glory Wealth agreed to charter one of its vessels, but then failed to produce the required hire payment for a fifteen-day period, and that Glory Service served as guarantor of Glory Wealth's performance. The district court issued an *ex parte* order pursuant to Rule B of the Supplemental Rules for Admiralty or Maritime Claims and

Asset Forfeiture Actions granting an attachment against Glory Wealth in the amount of $900,000. *See STX Panocean (UK) Co., Ltd. v. Glory Wealth Shipping Pte Ltd.,* No. 08-CV-9762 (GBD) (S.D.N.Y. Nov. 13, 2008) (*Ex Parte Order*).

The Defendants responded with a letter motion to vacate the attachment. The Defendants argued that they were not subject to a Rule B attachment because they had registered with the New York Department of State and therefore could be "found" in New York for Rule B purposes.

On December 10, 2008, the district court conducted a hearing to assess whether Glory Wealth in fact met Rule B's requirements. At the conclusion of the hearing, the district court vacated the attachment, finding that "[i]n the absence of a clear statement by the Second Circuit to the contrary," the court agreed with the sizable majority of Southern District judges who concluded "that the requirements [for a finding that the defendant is] found in this district are not a set of greater requirements than [those required to exercise] personal jurisdiction over the defendant[s] in this case." *Id.* (Hr'g Tr.) 27. The district court also noted that if STX won an arbitration award, it could return to the Southern District to satisfy that judgment against the Defendants. *Id.* at 28. STX reiterated its request for a stay of the vacatur pending the outcome of the appeal before this Court of *Centauri Shipping Ltd. v. W. Bulk Carriers KS,* 528 F. Supp. 2d 186 (S.D.N.Y.2007), *appeal docketed,* No. 07-4193-cv (2d Cir. Sept. 18, 2007). The district court denied the application. *Id.* at 29–30. The district court explained that "the balance of hardships doesn't weigh towards a stay" where the attachment affected a significant amount of funds that were intended to flow to other parties. *STX Panocean,* No. 08-CV-9762 (Hr'g Tr.) 29–30. The district court added that "there's no reason to believe that, if appropriate, future funds can't be attached in further support of an arbitration award," particularly where it was unclear whether STX had even filed for arbitration. *Id.* at 30. On December 16, 2008, STX filed a timely notice of appeal.

On December 18, 2008, STX filed a motion for a stay of execution of the order vacating the attachment. The applications judge granted a temporary stay pending this Court's hearing of that motion.

Because this is an issue of frequent occurrence in this circuit, *see, e.g., Marimed Shipping, Inc. v. Persian Gulf Shipping Co.,* 567 F. Supp. 2d 524 (S.D.N.Y.2008); *Pioneer Navigation Ltd. v. STX Pan Ocean (U.K.) Co.,* 08 Civ. 10490(JGK), 2008 WL 5334550 (S.D.N.Y. Dec. 18, 2008); *Minmetals Shipping & Forwarding Co. v. HBC Hamburg Bulk Carriers GmbH & Co.,* No. 08 Civ. 3533(RWS), 2008 U.S. Dist. LEXIS 48639, 2008 WL 2518709 (S.D.N.Y. June 24, 2008); *Carolina Shipping, Ltd. v. Renaissance Ins. Group,* No. 08 Civ 4711 (BSJ), 2008 U.S. Dist. Lexis 104432 (S.D.N.Y. Jun. 10, 2008), *appeal docketed,* No. 08-3142-cv (2d Cir. Jun. 24, 2008); *Centauri,* 528 F. Supp. 2d at 186, and disposition of the motion requires analysis of the merits of the underlying appeal, we consolidated the motion and underlying appeal to resolve the merits of plaintiff's claim for an attachment. The parties were instructed to brief the substance of the appeal as well as the motion.

DISCUSSION

This Court, in its discretion, may issue a stay pending appeal under Rule 8(a) of the Supplemental Rules for Admiralty or Maritime Claims and Asset Forfeiture Actions. A factor to be considered in granting a stay is whether the movant has demonstrated "a strong showing that he is likely to succeed on the merits." *McCue v. City of New York (In re World Trade Ctr. Disaster Site Litig.),* 503 F.3d 167, 170 (2d Cir.2007). In our view, STX cannot demonstrate any likelihood of success on the merits.

Rule B provides, in relevant part: "If a defendant is not found within the district . . . a verified complaint may contain a prayer for process to attach the defendant's tangible or intangible personal property—up to the amount sued for—in the hands of garnishees named in the process." Fed. R. Civ. P. Supp. R. B(1)(a). STX argues that Defendants' registration pursuant to § 1304 alone is insufficient to avoid attachment in the Southern District of New York. However, for the following reasons, we find that registration under the statute is sufficient—defendants who have registered with the Department of State pursuant to § 1304 may be "found" within the district for purposes of Rule B analysis.[1]

Maritime attachments arose because it is often more difficult to obtain jurisdiction over parties to a maritime dispute than parties to a traditional civil action. Maritime parties are itinerant, their assets transitory. *See In re Louisville Underwriters,* 134 U.S. 488, 493, 10 S. Ct. 587, 33 L.Ed 991 (1890). Thus, the traditional policy underlying maritime attachment has been to permit the attachment of assets wherever they can be found, thereby obviating the need for a plaintiff to "scour the globe" to find a proper forum for suit, or property of the defendant sufficient to satisfy a judgment. *Aqua Stoli Shipping Ltd. v. Gardner Smith Pty Ltd.,* 460 F.3d 434, 443 (2d Cir.2006).

As such, an attachment under Admiralty Rule B serves two purposes. The attachment establishes jurisdiction over a portion of a defendant's property and thereby creates a fund from which a judgment may be satisfied. *See Seawind Compania, S.A. v. Crescent Line, Inc.,* 320 F.2d 580, 581–82 (2d Cir.1963). However, this Court has stated that "[t]he two purposes may not be separated . . . for security cannot be obtained except as an adjunct to obtaining jurisdiction." *Id.* at 582. Thus, Rule B gives potential defendants the choice between subjecting themselves to the jurisdiction of the courts of the district in question, or making themselves vulnerable to the possibility that their property in the district will be attached. *See Daehan Shipping Co., Ltd. v. Farenco Shipping Co., Ltd.,* No. 08 Civ. 10052, 2008 WL 5068952, at 1 (S.D.N.Y. Nov. 24, 2008).

---

1 We note that there has been some disagreement among district court judges as to the meaning of the term "district." However, this issue is not before us as the parties both agree that the district in question in this case is the Southern District of New York.

Although Rule B does not expressly define "found within the district," this Court has interpreted it to require "a two-pronged inquiry: first, whether [Defendants] can be found within the district in terms of jurisdiction, and second, if so, whether [they] can be found for service of process." (the "*Seawind* Test"). *Seawind,* 320 F.2d at 582 (internal citations and quotation marks omitted); *see also Integrated Container Serv. Inc. v. Starlines Container Shipping Ltd.,* 476 F. Supp. 119, 122 (S.D.N.Y.1979) (stating that "[a] maritime attachment is precluded under [Rule B] only if the defendants have engaged in sufficient activity in the district or the cause of action has sufficient contacts with the district to permit the court to exercise in personam jurisdiction over the defendants," and the defendant "can be found within the geographical confines of the district for service of process."). While the purpose of the prongs cannot be separated, they are distinct: the presence of an agent authorized to accept process is, alone, insufficient to establish that a defendant is "found" within that district. *See Seawind,* 320 F.2d at 583. Similarly, sufficient contacts to establish in personam jurisdiction in the *International Shoe* sense, absent a showing of actual presence that would allow a plaintiff to locate the defendant in the district for service of process, will not support a conclusion that a defendant is found within that district. *Id.* at 583–84; *see also Integrated Container,* 476 F. Supp. at 122.

Federal law defines the requirements necessary for satisfaction of Rule B; however, federal courts look to the relevant state law to determine if those requirements are met. Therefore, we look to New York law to determine whether the Defendants can be found within the Southern District. *See, e.g., Seawind,* 320 F.2d at 583 (looking to state law governing service of process and personal jurisdiction to analyze whether the defendant was found within the Southern District).

It is undisputed that Defendants in this case satisfy the second prong of the *Seawind* Test, as both parties agree that Defendants have designated an in-state agent to receive service of process in the district at issue. *See STX Panocean,* No. 08 CV 9762, (Hr'g Tr.) 7. Therefore, we need only address the first prong of the test: whether Defendants are subject to personal jurisdiction in the district.

It is well-settled under New York law that registration under § 1304 subjects foreign companies to personal jurisdiction in New York. *See, e.g., Augsbury Corp. v. Petrokey Corp.,* 97 A.D.2d 173, 470 N.Y.S.2d 787 (3d Dep't 1983); *Robfogel Mill-Andrews Corp. v. Cupples Co., Mfrs.,* 67 Misc.2d 623, 624, 323 N.Y.S.2d 381 (1971). Federal courts have applied this doctrine as well. *See, e.g., Iyalla v. TRT Holdings, Inc.,* No. 04 Civ. 8114(NRB), 2005 WL 1765707, at 3 (S.D.N.Y. July 25, 2005); *Cannon v. Newmar Corp.,* 210 F. Supp. 2d 461, 463 n. 2 (S.D.N.Y.2002); *see also Rockefeller Univ. v. Ligand Pharms.,* 581 F. Supp. 2d 461, 467 (S.D.N.Y. 2008) (holding that authorization to do business in New York and designation of a registered agent for service of process "amount to consent to personal jurisdiction in New York.").

Only one Southern District of New York case, *Erne Shipping Inc. v. HBC Hamburg Bulk Carriers, GmbH & Co. KG,* 409 F. Supp. 2d 427 (S.D.N.Y.2006), *overruled in part by Aqua Stoli,* 460 F.3d at 446, has found a foreign corporation's "mere filing for authorization to do business" in New York to be insufficient under Rule B, which the district court interpreted as requiring more "systematic and continuous" contacts. In contrast, every subsequent Southern District court to have considered the issue has held that registration with the Department of State pursuant to New York Business Corporation Law § 1304, constitutes being "found" within the district for purposes of Rule B. *See Marimed Shipping,* 567 F. Supp. 2d at 528 (citing cases). *Erne* has been widely discussed, criticized, and rejected by the judges in the Southern District. *See, e.g., id.; Centauri Shipping,* 528 F. Supp. 2d at 191–92.

Under this majority view, amenability to suit, rather than a party's economic and physical activities in the district at issue, is the touchstone of the first prong of the *Seawind* Test. *See Integrated Container,* 476 F. Supp. at 123; *Centauri Shipping,* 528 F. Supp. 2d at 191. Recently, in *Aqua Stoli,* this Court declined to specifically discuss the "found" factor of the Rule B test, stating that district courts have not "experienced any confusion in its application," and citing *Integrated Container,* 476 F. Supp. at 123, in support of this contention. 460 F.3d at 445 n. 4. In *Integrated Container,* Judge Pierre N. Leval, then sitting on the district court, held that the jurisdictional presence factor is satisfied either where the defendant's "activity in the district" or its "contacts within the district . . . permit the court to exercise *in personam* jurisdiction over the defendant." *Id.* at 122. Applying this standard, the court in *Integrated Container* found that the defendant's registration as a foreign corporation with the New York Department of State, as well as its contractual consent to suit in New York, were sufficient to establish the defendant's presence within the district for purposes of Rule B. *Id.*

Moreover, the district courts' reasoning that registration with the State satisfies the jurisdictional prong of the test for being "found" is persuasive in light of the underlying purpose of maritime attachment. In the context of peripatetic defendants with transient assets, maritime attachment is aimed at obviating a plaintiff's need to determine where the defendant is amenable to suit. *See In re Louisville Underwriters,* 134 U.S. at 493, 10 S. Ct. 587. However, no "scour[ing of] the globe"—and, therefore, no attachment—is necessary where the defendant has already voluntarily subjected itself to the district's jurisdiction by reason of its registration with the State. *See Amoco Overseas Oil,* 605 F.2d at 655.

"Maritime attachment is centuries old." *Winter Storm Shipping, Ltd. v. TPI,* 310 F.3d 263, 267 (2d Cir.2003); *accord Aurora Maritime Co. v. Abdullah Mohamed Fahem & Co.,* 85 F.3d 44, 47 (2d Cir.1996) ("[M]aritime attachment is a feature of admiralty jurisprudence that antedates both the congressional grant of admiralty jurisdiction to the federal district courts and the promulgation of the first Supreme Court Admiralty Rules in 1844."); *see also Atkins v. Fibre Disintegrating Co.,* 85 U.S. (18 Wall.) 272, 303, 21 L.Ed. 841 (1873). It has long existed because of the highly international nature of maritime commerce and the transitory nature of maritime assets within a given jurisdiction. *See Aqua Stoli,* 460 F.3d at 443; *Aurora*

Maritime Co., 85 F.3d at 48; *Amoco Overseas Oil Co. v. Compangie Nationale Algerienne de Navigation,* 605 F.2d 648, 655 (2d Cir. 1979). But as the world changed, so too did the exact nature and necessity of maritime attachment. In 1966, when Supplemental Rule B was created, the Advisory Committee drew heavily upon Admiralty Rule 2. *See* Supp. R. B, Advisory Committee's Notes. By 1966, however, it was clear that the precise need for maritime attachment and nature of maritime commerce had changed a great deal over the previous several hundred years and was likely to continue to change. For that reason, neither Supplemental Rule B nor the Advisory Committee attempted to define what it means to be "found within the district." *See id.* Rather, the Advisory Committee stated that "[t]he subject seems one best left for the time being to development on a case-by-case basis." *Id.* This, we believe, invited courts to define what it means to be "found" in a common law fashion. But common law development in time can yield firm rules. And that is precisely what we hold today.

In the modern era, although maritime commerce is still international and maritime assets are still transitory, companies that have both appointed an agent for service of process and registered in New York, consenting to jurisdiction, do not pose the same needs for maritime attachment. Indeed, in today's era of electronic banking, many of the assets that are attached in New York are not ships, but rather electronic wire transfers routed through banks. And in today's era, "[t]he frustrated creditor" is not "much like Evangeline, the poor Arcadian girl separated from her lover, . . . tragically left to roam the shores awaiting the debtor's next arrival." *Schiffahartsgesellschaft Leonhardt & Co. v. A. Bottacchi S.A. De Navegacion,* 732 F.2d 1543, 1548 (11th Cir.1984) (referencing HENRY WADSWORTH LONGFELLOW, EVANGELINE, A TALE OF ACADIE (1843)). Rather, when that debtor is registered to do business in New York, there are generally any number of means to prosecute a civil claim and, upon receiving judgment, collect on that claim.

Thus, we hold that a defendant's registration under New York Business Corporation Law § 1304 is sufficient to satisfy both prongs of the *Seawind* Test and, therefore, a company registered with the Department of State is "found" for purposes of Rule B of the Supplemental Rules for Admiralty or Maritime Claims and Asset Forfeiture Actions.

Applying this rule to the case at hand, we find that STX is present in the district both jurisdictionally, by virtue of its registration with the Department of State, and in terms of its ability to accept service of process, by virtue of its appointment of a designated agent for service of process within the district. Both of these are accomplished through its registration with the Department of State pursuant to § 1304.[2]

---

2 STX itself conceded that Defendants' registration with the State subjects them to personal jurisdiction. When asked "Is there any way they can argue they can't be sued and a judgment enforced against them in this jurisdiction," by Judge Daniels, counsel for STX answered, "I don't believe so . . ." Previously, counsel for STX had stated that "[Defendants are] subject to personal jurisdiction by virtue of their registration."

Because STX is not entitled to maintain its attachment by virtue of the Defendants' being "found" within the district, it cannot demonstrate a likelihood of success on the merits for purposes of its motion, and, necessarily, it also loses the underlying appeal. We thus affirm the district court's vacatur of the maritime attachment and dismiss the motion as moot.

CONCLUSION

For the foregoing reasons, the district court's order of December 10, 2008 vacating the *ex parte* Process of Maritime Attachment and Garnishment is hereby AFFIRMED. The motion for a stay of that order pursuant to Federal Rule of Appellate Procedure 8(a) is DISMISSED AS MOOT.

III. PROCEDURE

8. Exceptions & Limitations

A. Foreign Sovereign Immunities Act

i. In General*

* Cases are indexed under this subject. The full text of these cases is published in the **volume**-page indicated.

EMIL ALPERIN
v.
VATICAN BANK

360 Fed. Appx. 847 (9th Cir. 2009)
Decided December 29, 2009

Before: B. FLETCHER, THOMAS and N.R. SMITH, Circuit Judges.

MEMORANDUM*

* This disposition is not appropriate for publication and is not precedent except as provided by 9th Cir. R. 36-3.

Survivors and descendants of victims of the Holocaust, and associated organizations (collectively referred to herein as "Alperin"), appeal the dismissal of their purported class action lawsuit against the Vatican Bank, also known by its official title Istituto per le Opere di Religione (the "IOR"). On a previous appeal, we held that the political question doctrine barred broad allegations of violation of international law but did not bar certain property claims. *Alperin v. Vatican Bank*, 410 F.3d 532 (9th Cir. 2005). We are now asked whether the IOR is a foreign sovereign protected by the Foreign Sovereign Immunity Act (the "FSIA"), and if so, whether Alperin's claims fall within the international takings exception or commercial takings exception to the FSIA's jurisdictional bar. We have jurisdiction under 28 U.S.C. § 1291, and we affirm.

"The existence of sovereign immunity and subject matter jurisdiction under the [FSIA] are questions of law that [this Court] review[s] de novo." *Af-Cap, Inc. v. Chevron Overseas (Congo) Ltd.*, 475 F.3d 1080, 1085c86 (9th Cir. 2007) (internal quotation marks and citation omitted) (alteration in original). A District Court's interpretation of foreign law is also reviewed *de novo. Brady v. Brown*, 51 F.3d 810, 816 (9th Cir. 1995). On a motion to dismiss, the court "assume[s] that [it has] truthful factual allegations before [it]." *Saudi Arabia v. Nelson,* 507 U.S. 349, 351, 113 S. Ct. 1471, 123 L. Ed. 2d 47 (1993). "To survive a motion to dismiss, a complaint must contain sufficient factual matter, accepted as true, to 'state a claim to relief that is plausible on its face.'" *Ashcroft v. Iqbal,* ____U.S.____, 129 S. Ct. 1937, 1949, 173 L. Ed. 2d 868 (2009) (quoting *Bell Atl. Corp. v. Twombly,* 550 U.S. 544, 570, 127 S. Ct. 1955, 167 L. Ed. 2d 929 (2007)).

I.

The district court did not err in holding that the IOR is an organ of a foreign state entitled to FSIA immunity. In assessing whether an entity is an organ of a foreign state, *see* 28 U.S.C. § 1603(b)(2), we "[t]ak[e] a holistic view" of the defendant, *Cal. Dep't of Water Res. v. Powerex Corp.,* 533 F.3d 1087, 1102 (9th Cir. 2008). In doing so, we examine

> "[1] the circumstances surrounding the entity's creation, [2] the purpose of its activities, [3] its independence from the government, [4] the level of government financial support, [5] its employment policies, and [6] its obligations and privileges under state law. An entity may be an organ of a foreign state even if it has some autonomy from the foreign government."

Powerex, 533 F.3d at 1098 (quoting *EIE Guam Corp. v. Long Term Credit Bank of Japan, Ltd.*, 322 F.3d 635, 640 (9th Cir. 2003)) (internal quotation marks omitted).

A showing of organ status may be based exclusively on foreign law. *See, e.g. Gates v. Victor Fine Foods,* 54 F.3d 1457, 1460–64 (9th Cir. 1995) (using Alberta statutes and regulation to determine defendant's organ status). *But see EOTT Energy Operating Ltd. P'ship v. Winterthur Swiss Ins. Co.,* 257 F.3d 992, 999 (9th Cir. 2001) (remanding for "factual inquiry" where record "incomplete[]" and contained "ambiguities"). The defendant bears the burden of establishing a prima facie case of immunity. *Phaneuf v. Republic of Indonesia,* 106 F.3d 302, 306 (9th Cir. 1997).

Through its affidavit showing its status, structure, and role under Vatican law, the IOR made a prima facie case that it is an agency or instrumentality of the Vatican, and thus entitled to FSIA immunity. The affidavit shows that the modern IOR was created by the Pope as a public and independent juridic entity that is responsible for managing assets placed in its care for the purpose of supporting religious or charitable works. The highest administrative level of the IOR is composed of high-ranking government officials all appointed by the Vatican. The IOR has exclusive control over several obligations created and assigned by Vatican law. *See Kelly v. Syria Shell Petroleum Dev. B.V.,* 213 F.3d 841, 848 (9th Cir. 2000) (emphasizing monopoly over task); Corporacion *Mexicana de Servicios Maritimos, S.A. de C.V. v. M/T Respect*, 89 F.3d 650, 655 (9th Cir. 1996) (same). And the IOR is immune from suit in Italy as a foreign sovereign. Alperin did not challenge the affidavit or provide a counter-affidavit. Therefore, we conclude that the district court correctly held that the IOR established a prima facie case that it was an organ of a foreign state entitled to FSIA immunity.

Contrary to Alperin's argument, the historical origins and activities of the IOR are not relevant to this inquiry. *Dole Food Co. v. Patrickson*, 538 U.S. 468, 480, 123 S. Ct. 1655, 155 L. Ed. 2d 643 (2003) ("[I]nstrumentality status is determined at the time of the filing of the complaint."). Accordingly, this court has not considered evidence pertaining to the IOR's organ status prior to 1999, when the first Complaint was filed. The IOR need not be the Vatican Central Bank for it to have a public purpose. *See Powerex*, 533 F.3d at 1098. Its involvement in commercial affairs does not automatically render the IOR non-governmental. *EIE Guam*, 322 F.3d at 641. Nor is it necessary that the Vatican maintain day-to-day control over the IOR's activities. *Gates*, 54 F.3d at 1461. Notwithstanding the IOR's commercial activities and arms-length supervision by the Vatican, the record, viewed holistically, supports the district court's conclusion that the IOR is an agency or instrumentality of the Vatican.

II.

The district court did not err in holding that the international takings exception does not apply to remove FSIA immunity. Where the defendant sovereign succeeds in "establish[ing] a prima facie case of immunity, the burden of production shifts to the plaintiff to offer evidence that an exception applies." *Phaneuf*, 106 F.3d at 307.

FSIA's international taking exception provides that:

> A foreign state shall not be immune from the jurisdiction of the courts of the United States . . . in any case . . . (3) in which rights in property taken in violation of international law are in issue and [1] that property or any property exchanged for such property is present in the United States in connection with a commercial activity carried on in the United States by the foreign state; or [2] that property or any property exchanged for such property is owned or operated by an agency or instrumentality of the foreign state and that agency or instrumentality is engaged in a commercial activity in the United States.

28 U.S.C. § 1605(a).

Of critical importance to any analysis under this exception is that plaintiffs not only must plead a right to property taken in violation of international law—and we do not reach the question of whether they have in this case—but that they must plead a jurisdictional nexus to the United States. Under either prong of § 1605(a)(3), this involves pleading the current status of the property at issue (or any property exchanged for such property)—that it either is present in the United States or is owned or operated by an agency or instrumentality of the foreign state.

While we recognize that it could be difficult to prove that a fungible article such as the gold alleged to have been taken in this case is currently present in the United States, Alperin did not even make such an allegation in the pleadings. Therefore, assuming without deciding that plaintiffs may meet their burden under the first prong through pleadings about the commercial activities of an agency or instrumentality of a foreign state rather than the foreign state itself, Alperin failed to do so in this case. *Cf. Garb v. Republic of Poland*, 440 F.3d 579 (2d Cir. 2006) (holding that only the first clause of the takings exception applies where the jurisdictional nexus is based on allegations regarding the commercial activity of the Ministry of the Treasury, since the Ministry is the state itself, not an agency or instrumentality). *But see* 28 U.S.C. § 1603(a) ("A 'foreign state' . . . includes . . . an agency or instrumentality of a foreign state . . . .").

Nor, under the second prong of § 1605(a)(3), did Alperin sufficiently plead that the IOR has current ownership of the expropriated property or property exchanged for expropriated property. At most, Alperin asserted that "defendants" (in this multi-defendant case) "retained" some portion of the Ustasha Treasury, after other portions were laundered in the 1940s. They never allege that the expropriated property "retained" by the defendants includes property that properly belongs to the named plaintiffs. This is insufficient where the FSIA requires present ownership of the expropriated property (or any property exchanged for such property).

III.

The district court also did not err in determining that the commercial activity exception does not remove FSIA immunity in this case. A second exception to FSIA is for cases "in which the action is based upon a commercial activity carried on in the United States by the foreign state" or based "upon an act outside the territory of the United States in connection with a commercial activity of the foreign state elsewhere and that act causes a direct effect in the United States." 28 U.S.C. § 1605(a)(2).

Nor does Alperin's complaint meet either prong of the commercial activities exception. Plaintiffs allege that a different defendant used funds laundered by the IOR to establish publishing houses and other commercial activities in Chicago, and they argue that the IOR was enabled to store gold in the United States and trade it on U.S. markets because its gold collection was enhanced by the Ustasha Treasury. These alleged commercial activities in the United States are too tangentially related to their legal claims to be considered "the basis for [the] suit." *Nelson*, 507 U.S. at 358; *see also Alder v. Fed'l Republic of Nigeria*, 219 F.3d 869, 874–75 (9th Cir. 2000) (analyzing claim based on money-laundering under direct effects prong only). Nor are the effects that Alperin alleges—the cumulative impact of Ustasha gold on the IOR's holdings and on its commercial activities in the United States over a decade later; and the results of another party allegedly investing laundered funds in Chicago—sufficiently direct to fall within this exception. *See Corzo v. Banco Cent. de Reserva del Peru*, 243 F.3d 519, 525 (9th Cir. 2001) (holding that "secondary or incidental results" do not count under direct effects prong).

IV.

The district court correctly dismissed the complaint. Given our reasoning, we need not—and do not—reach any other issue raised by the parties. All motions for judicial notice filed by both parties are DENIED.

AFFIRMED.

JAMES L. BUTLER, JR.
v.
SUKHOI COMPANY

579 F.3d 1307 (11th Cir. 2009)
Decided August 19, 2009

For Sukhoi Company, United Aircraft Manufacturing Corp., Irkut Corporation, Sukhoi Civil Aircraft, Russian Federation, Appellants: Socarras, Michael Peter, McDermott Will & Emery LLP, WASHINGTON, DC.

For Appellant: Rodriguez, Raquel A., McDermott Will & Emery LLP, Miami, FL.

For Butler, James L. Jr., Appellee: Stewart, Kelley B., Krupnick, Campbell, Malone, et al, P.A., FT LAUDERDALE, FL.

For Bari L. Butler, Appellee: Edward Royce Curtis, Tripp Scott, P.A., FT LAUDERDALE, FL.

Before DUBINA, Chief Judge, BIRCH and WILSON, Circuit Judges.

BIRCH, Circuit Judge:

Sukhoi Company ("Sukhoi"), United Aircraft Manufacturing Corporation ("UAC"), Irkut Corporation ("Irkut"), Sukhoi Civil Aircraft ("SCA"), and The Russian Federation ("Russia") (collectively, "appellants") appeal the order of the district court denying their motion to dismiss the complaint filed by appellees James Butler and his wife, Bari Butler (hereinafter "the Butlers"), in which the Butlers sought to enforce a default judgment entered in their favor in a previous cause of action against appellants' alleged predecessor-in-interest, Sukhoi Design Bureau ("SDB"). Because the district court lacked subject matter jurisdiction over the Butlers' claims, we REVERSE and REMAND to the district court with instructions to dismiss the case.

I. Background

The Butlers filed suit (hereinafter "*Butler I*") in 2003 in the United States District Court for the Southern District of Florida against SDB and Advanced Sukhoi

Technologies[1] seeking damages for injuries James Butler sustained when a Sukhoi SU-29 aircraft he was piloting crashed in Broward County, Florida as a result of defects in the aircraft. The district court denied SDB's motion to dismiss for lack of personal jurisdiction and SDB answered the complaint. SDB admitted that it was a subject of the Russian Federation and asserted various affirmative defenses, including lack of personal jurisdiction and failure to state a claim, but did not invoke immunity under the Foreign Sovereign Immunities Act ("FSIA"), 28 U.S.C. § 1602, *et seq*. After SDB failed to respond to discovery or to comply with the district court's order compelling discovery, the Butlers filed a motion for default judgment, which the district court granted. Following a jury trial on damages, the district court entered an amended final judgment, in accordance with the jury's verdict, ordering SDB to pay damages to the Butlers in the amount of $3,592,500 plus post-judgment interest.

On 2 August 2007, the Butlers filed the instant action (hereinafter "*Butler II*") against SDB, naming as additional defendants Sukhoi, UAC, Irkut, SCA, and Russia.[2] In their complaint, the Butlers alleged that appellants were a foreign state and/or instrumentalities or agencies of a foreign state not entitled to immunity under the FSIA and sought a declaration that appellants - none of whom were parties in *Butler I* - were jointly and severally liable for the *Butler I* judgment as successors in interest to and/or alter-egos of SDB.[3] Appellants filed a motion to dismiss, asserting immunity from liability and execution under the FSIA. They argued that the complaint's allegations were insufficient as a matter of law to establish the court's subject matter jurisdiction under the FSIA.[4]

---

1 In its motion to dismiss the *Butler I* complaint, SDB stated that it was a company separate and independent from "Advanced Sukhoi Technologies," which, according to SDB, was operating under the name "Advanced Technologies for Aircraft Manufacturing" at the time of the lawsuit.

2 Though named as a defendant, SDB has not appeared in *Butler II*.

3 Specifically, the complaint alleged that: (1) Sukhoi is a Russian corporation wholly owned by Russia, an agency and instrumentality of Russia, and Russia's alter-ego; (2) SDB is a Russian corporation owned 50% + 1 share by Sukhoi Company and is the alter-ego of Russia and Sukhoi Company; (3) Irkut is a Russian corporation owned in part by Sukhoi; (4) SCA is a Russian company owned 86.84% by Sukhoi; (5) UAC is a Russian corporation that was organized and incorporated by a decree of Russian president Vladimir Putin "to maintain the scientific-industrial potential of Russia's aircraft manufacturing complex, and to ensure the country's security and defense capabilities," and is controlled by Russia; (6) all other corporate defendants merged into UAC as the successor in interest to Sukhoi Company, SDB, Irkut, and SCA; and (7) UAC and Russia are alter-egos of one another. R1-1 at 2-4 (internal quotation marks omitted).

4 Appellants contended additionally that the complaint was due to be dismissed because: (1) the *Butler I* judgment was entered by default and in accordance with a jury verdict and thus unenforceable under 28 U.S.C. §§ 1608(e) and 1330(a), respectively; (2) the complaint actually alleged a basis for absolute immunity under 28 U.S.C. § 1611(b)(2) by stating that appellants' bank accounts were used to facilitate international civil and military aircraft transactions; (3) the court lacked personal jurisdiction due to improper service of process under the

The Butlers responded that SDB waived immunity from suit by failing to invoke the protections of the FSIA in *Butler I.* They argued additionally that they were merely seeking to execute a judgment entered against SDB and that Rule 69 of the Federal Rules of Civil Procedure allows for enforcement of such judgments in federal courts. They contended that they were entitled to limited jurisdictional discovery as to the alter-ego basis for subject matter jurisdiction and to discovery in aid of execution as to the location of the judgment debtors' assets. The Butlers did not, however, identify any specific undiscovered facts that were necessary to make an immunity determination.

The district court denied appellants' motion on 29 July 2008, finding that it would be "premature" to dismiss the complaint because the Butlers were entitled to discovery on the "jurisdictional issues" raised by appellants. R1-41. This appeal followed.

II. Discussion

We have jurisdiction under 28 U.S.C. § 1291 only over appeals from "final decisions" of the district courts. *W.R. Huff Asset Mgmt Co. v. Kohlberg, Kravis, Roberts & Co.*, 566 F.3d 979, 984 (11th Cir. 2009) (quotation marks and citation omitted). "[A] district court order is considered final and appealable only if it ends the litigation on the merits and leaves nothing for the court to do but execute the judgment." *Id.* Because the district court's order denying appellants' motion to dismiss did not end the litigation on the merits, we must, as an initial matter, determine whether we have jurisdiction over this appeal.

It is well-settled that a court of appeals has jurisdiction over interlocutory orders denying claims of immunity under the FSIA. *See O'Bryan v. Holy See*, 556 F.3d 361, 372 (6th Cir. 2009) (noting that because sovereign immunity is immunity from trial, not merely a defense to liability, the denial of a claim of sovereign immunity is immediately appealable as a final decision under 28 U.S.C. § 1291); *S & Davis Int'l, Inc. v. Republic of Yemen*, 218 F.3d 1292, 1295, 1297 (11th Cir. 2000). Inasmuch as the order on appeal required appellants to answer the complaint and called for discovery, it denied them immunity from suit under the FSIA. *See McMahon v. Presidential Airways, Inc.*, 502 F.3d 1331, 1339 (11th Cir. 2007) (noting that "immunity from suit entails a right to be free from the burdens of litigation"); *Kelly v. Syria Shell Petroleum Dev. B.V.*, 213 F.3d 841, 849 (5th Cir. 2000) ("FSIA immunity is immunity not only from liability, but also from the

---

FSIA and, even if the FSIA were inapplicable, the court lacked personal jurisdiction under Florida's long arm statute; (4) venue was improper under the FSIA because the complaint's sole claim was that appellants were alter-egos of one another and thus any acts or omissions upon which the claim was based could only have occurred, if at all, in Russia; and (5) the complaint failed to state a claim under Rule 12(b)(6). Finally, appellants asserted that summary judgment was appropriate because the complaint asserted only a conclusory alter-ego claim and thus failed to raise genuine issues of material fact for discovery or trial.

costs, in time and expense, and other disruptions attendant to litigation."). Accordingly, we have jurisdiction over appellants' assertion of immunity under the FSIA, notwithstanding the lack of a final judgment in this case. We now turn to the merits.

Appellants argue that the district court erred in denying their motion to dismiss and abused its discretion in ordering jurisdictional discovery because the Butlers' complaint failed to allege a basis for subject matter jurisdiction. The Butlers, on the other hand, contend that the district court correctly denied the motion because they were entitled to limited jurisdictional discovery in order to further define appellants' alter-ego relationship with SDB. We conclude that, even accepting as true the Butlers' allegations that appellants are alter-egos of one another and of SDB, they are insufficient as a matter of law to demonstrate the existence of subject matter jurisdiction.

The FSIA provides "the sole basis for obtaining jurisdiction over a foreign state in [United States] courts." *Argentine Republic v. Amerada Hess Shipping Corp.*, 488 U.S. 428, 434, 109 S. Ct. 683, 688, 102 L. Ed. 2d 818 (1989); *see also Vermeulen v. Renault, U.S.A., Inc.*, 985 F.2d 1534, 1543 (11th Cir. 1993) (noting that FSIA is "[t]he only possible source of federal jurisdiction in suits against corporations owned by foreign states"). Under the FSIA, foreign states and their agencies and/or instrumentalities[5] are immune from suit in the United States *unless* an FSIA statutory exception applies.[6] See 28 U.S.C. §§ 1603, 1604, 1605; *Aquamar, S.A. v.*

---

5 A "foreign state" under the FSIA includes an "agency or instrumentality of a foreign state," defined as "a separate legal person, corporate or otherwise, . . . a majority of whose shares or other ownership interest is owned by a foreign state or political subdivision thereof." 28 U.S.C. § 1603(a), (b); *see S & Davis Int'l*, 218 F.3d at 1300. Accordingly, any such agency or instrumentality of a foreign state also enjoys immunity from suit and execution under the FSIA. *See Alejandre v. Telefonica Larga Distancia de Puerto Rico, Inc.*, 183 F.3d 1277, 1283 (11th Cir. 1999). Appellants conceded for purposes of their motion to dismiss and on appeal that they are instrumentalities of Russia.

6 The FSIA does not immunize foreign states from suit cases in which: (1) "the foreign state has waived its immunity either explicitly or by implication"; (2) "the action is based upon a commercial activity carried on in the United States by the foreign state"; (3) "rights in property taken in violation of international law are in issue and that property or any property exchanged for such property is present in the United States in connection with a commercial activity carried on in the United States by the foreign state;" (4) "rights in property in the United States acquired by succession or gift or rights in immovable property situated in the United States are in issue"; (5) "money damages are sought against a foreign state for personal injury or death, or damage to or loss of property, occurring in the United States and caused by the tortious act or omission of that foreign state"; (6) "the action is brought, either to enforce an agreement made by the foreign state with or for the benefit of a private party to submit to arbitration all or any differences which have arisen or which may arise between the parties with respect to a defined legal relationship . . . concerning a subject matter capable of settlement by arbitration under the laws of the United States, or to confirm an award made pursuant to such an agreement to arbitrate"; (7) "a suit in admiralty is brought to enforce a maritime lien against a vessel or cargo of the foreign state, which maritime lien is based upon a commercial activity of the foreign state"; (8) an action is brought to foreclose a preferred mortgage. 28 U.S.C. § 1605; see also 28 U.S.C. § 1605A (addressing terrorist exception to jurisdictional immunity); § 1607

Del Monte Fresh Produce N.A., Inc., 179 F.3d 1279, 1290 (11th Cir. 1999). If none of the exceptions applies, then the district court lacks subject matter jurisdiction over the plaintiff's claims. *Mwani v. BinLaden*, 417 F.3d 1, 15, 368 U.S. App. D.C. 1 (D.C. Cir. 2005) (citing 28 U.S.C. § 1604). Conversely, "[i]f an exception does apply, the district court has jurisdiction." *Id.* (citing 28 U.S.C. § 1330(a)[7]). Thus, in order to establish subject matter jurisdiction under the FSIA, the plaintiff must overcome the presumption that the foreign state is immune from suit by producing evidence that "the conduct which forms the basis of [the] complaint falls within one of the statutorily defined exceptions." *S & Davis Int'l,* 218 F.3d at 1300; *see also In re Terrorist Attacks* on September 11, 2001, 538 F.3d 71, 80 (2d Cir. 2008) (plaintiff has burden of producing evidence showing that, under exceptions to the FSIA, immunity should not be granted). Whether the plaintiff has satisfied his burden of production in this regard is determined by looking at "the allegations in the complaint [and] the undisputed facts, if any, placed before the court by the parties." *In re Terrorist Attacks,* 538 F.3d at 80 (quotation marks, alterations, and citation omitted). Once the plaintiff demonstrates that one of the statutory exceptions to FSIA immunity applies, the burden then shifts to the defendant to prove, by a preponderance of the evidence, that the plaintiff's claims do not fall within that exception. *See S & Davis Int'l,* 218 F.3d at 1300; *Aquamar*, 179 F.3d at 1290; *Arango v. Guzman Travel Advisors Corp.,* 621 F.2d 1371, 1378 (5th Cir. Unit B 1980).

Because the Butlers sought to invoke the jurisdiction of the United States courts to enter a new judgment in a separate cause of action against appellants, they bore the burden of presenting a prima facie case that jurisdiction existed.[8] *See S & Davis Int'l*, 218 F.3d at 1300. Where, as here, the party asserting immunity under the FSIA does not contest the alleged jurisdictional facts, but rather, challenges their legal adequacy, we review de novo the complaint's jurisdictional allegations to determine whether they were sufficient to eliminate the appellants' presumptive immunity. *See Mwani*, 417 F.3d at 15–16 (where foreign sovereign did not expressly concede plaintiffs' factual allegations but argued that the allegations, even if substantiated, were insufficient to trigger FSIA exception, sovereign's argument was a challenge to the legal sufficiency of the allegations subject to

---

(addressing counterclaims against foreign states that bring actions in the United States courts); §§ 1610–11 (setting forth exceptions to immunity from attachment or execution).

7 Section 1330(a) provides: "The district courts shall have original jurisdiction without regard to amount in controversy of any nonjury civil action against a foreign state as defined in section 1603(a) of this title as to any claim for relief in personam with respect to which the foreign state is not entitled to immunity either under sections 1605–1607 of this title or under any applicable international agreement." 28 U.S.C. § 1330(a).

8 Although a defendant challenging subject matter jurisdiction under the FSIA has the initial urden of presenting a prima facie case that it is a foreign state, *see In re Terrorist Attacks,* 58 F.3d at 80, the appellants' status as "foreign states" under the FSIA was uncontested in this case.

de novo review); *see also Chudasama v. Mazda Motor Corp.*, 123 F.3d 1353, 1367 (11th Cir. 1997) (noting that a facial challenge to the legal sufficiency of a claim or defense, unlike a denial of the complaint's factual allegations, "always presents a purely legal question").

The complaint in this case pleads the FSIA as the district court's basis for subject matter jurisdiction, but fails to specifically invoke any of the FSIA's statutory exceptions. The only "conduct" alleged in the complaint is that appellants and SDB are alter-egos. We agree with appellants that this conduct is insufficient to divest appellants of their sovereign immunity because, even if substantiated through discovery, it does not bring the claim within one of one the statutorily-enumerated exceptions either to pre-judgment or post-judgment immunity under the FSIA. *See Mwani,* 417 F.3d at 17. Moreover, although the complaint makes the bald assertion that jurisdiction exists under § 1605 because the action "involves a foreign state and instrumentalities or agencies of a foreign state not entitled to immunity under 28 U.S.C. §§ 1603, et seq. of the [FSIA] and under FRCP 69(a) to enforce its own judgments," this is a legal conclusion that we need not accept as true. R1–1 at 4; *see O'Bryan*, 556 F.3d at 376 (where defendant asserts a facial attack on the subject-matter jurisdiction alleged in the complaint, "conclusory allegations or legal conclusions masquerading as factual conclusions will not suffice to prevent a motion to dismiss" (quotation marks and citation omitted)); *S & Davis Int'l,* 218 F.3d at 1298. Inasmuch as the complaint was insufficient as a matter of law to establish a prima facie case that the district court had jurisdiction, the district court abused its discretion in allowing the case to proceed and granting discovery on the jurisdictional issue. *See United Techs. Corp. v. Mazer*, 556 F.3d 1260, 1280–81 (11th Cir. 2009) (reviewing district court's decision to allow jurisdictional discovery for an abuse of discretion); *see, e.g., In re Terrorist Attacks*, 538 F.3d at 96 (finding no error in district court's denial of jurisdictional discovery against foreign state where plaintiffs failed to establish a prima facie case that the district court had jurisdiction over defendants); *Mwani*, 417 F.3d at 17 (finding no error in district court's denial of jurisdictional discovery where, even assuming defendant/sovereign engaged in conduct alleged in the complaint, commercial activity exception to FSIA would not apply as a matter of law).

Further, we note that the principles of comity underlying the FSIA require the district court, when deciding whether or not to allow jurisdictional discovery from a foreign sovereign, to balance the need for "discovery to substantiate exceptions to statutory foreign sovereign immunity" against the need to "protect[] a sovereign's or sovereign agency's legitimate claim to immunity from discovery." *First City, Texas-Houston, N.A. v. Rafidain Bank,* 150 F.3d 172, 176 (2d Cir. 1998) (quotation marks and citation omitted). Such an analysis serves to ensure that jurisdictional discovery is "ordered circumspectly and only to verify allegations of specific facts crucial to an immunity determination." *Id.* (quotation marks and citation omitted); *In re Papandreou*, 139 F.3d 247, 253, 329 U.S. App. D.C. 210 (D.C. Cir. 1998)

("[A] district court authorizing discovery to determine whether immunity bars jurisdiction must proceed with circumspection, lest the evaluation of the immunity itself encroach unduly on the benefits the immunity was to ensure."); *Federal Ins. Co. v. Richard I. Rubin & Co., Inc.,* 12 F.3d 1270, 1284 n.11 (3d Cir. 1993) ("[D]iscovery and fact-finding should be limited to the essentials necessary to determining the preliminary question of jurisdiction." (quotation marks and citation omitted)).

As previously noted, the complaint in this case fails to allege an FSIA statutory exception to sovereign immunity that could be subjected to verification through discovery. The Butlers simply assert that they are entitled to further discovery regarding appellants' and SDB's alter-ego status. Given that appellants conceded for purposes of their motion to dismiss that they were alter-egos of SDB, we are unable to see what specific facts additional discovery might reveal that would be crucial to the court's immunity determination. *See Goodman Holdings v. Rafidain Bank*, 26 F.3d 1143, 1147, 307 U.S. App. D.C. 79 (D.C. Cir. 1994) (affirming district court's dismissal for lack of jurisdiction in FSIA case where additional discovery was unlikely to produce facts affecting court's jurisdictional analysis); *see also America West Airlines, Inc. v. GPA Group, Ltd.,* 877 F.2d 793, 801 (9th Cir. 1989) (where discovery sought was unlikely to substantiate plaintiff's assertion of jurisdiction, district court did not abuse its discretion in deciding the jurisdictional issue without allowing additional time for discovery); *Wells Fargo & Co. v. Wells Fargo Express Co.,* 556 F.2d 406, 430 n.24 (9th Cir. 1977) (noting that a district court's refusal to allow discovery to determine whether subject matter jurisdiction exists "is not an abuse of discretion when it is clear that further discovery would not demonstrate facts sufficient to constitute a basis for jurisdiction"). Because the complaint's alter-ego allegations, if proven through additional discovery, would not demonstrate a basis for jurisdiction in any event, we have little difficulty concluding that the need to protect appellants' claim to immunity from discovery greatly outweighed any competing need for further discovery. *See First City*, 150 F.3d at 176; *Kaylor v. Fields*, 661 F.2d 1177, 1184 (8th Cir. 1981) (noting that the purpose of discovery is not "to enable a plaintiff to make a case when his complaint has failed to state a claim"). In sum, requiring Russia and its instrumentalities to engage in the burdens and costs of responding to discovery, especially when the jurisdictional question in this case may be resolved simply by reference to the undisputed allegations in the complaint, would "frustrate the significance and benefit of entitlement to immunity from suit" under the FSIA. *Belhas v. Ya'alon*, 515 F.3d 1279, 1290, 380 U.S. App. D.C. 56 (D.C. Cir. 2008) (quotation marks and citation omitted).

III. Conclusion

Appellants appeal the order of the district court denying their motion to dismiss and ordering them to answer the Butlers' complaint. Because the complaint failed to allege any facts that, if verified, would demonstrate the applicability of a statutorily-enumerated exception to foreign sovereign immunity under the FSIA, it was plainly insufficient to establish subject matter jurisdiction. Accordingly, we REVERSE the order of the district court and REMAND to the district court with instructions to dismiss the case.

REVERSED and REMANDED.

JOHN V. DOE
v.
HOLY SEE

557 F.3d 1066 (9th Cir. 2009)
Decided March 3, 2009

Jeffrey S. Lena, Law Office of Jeffrey S. Lena, Berkeley, California for the defendant-appellant-cross-appellee.

Marci A. Hamilton, Washington Crossing, Pennsylvania, for the plaintiff-appellee-cross-appellant.

Before: Ferdinand F. Fernandez and Marsha S. Berzon, Circuit Judges, and Otis D. Wright, II*, District Judge. Dissent by Judge Berzon; Concurrence by Judge Fernandez.

PER CURIAM:

We consider whether, on the allegations made in the Plaintiff's complaint in this case, the Holy See is entitled to immunity from suit under the Foreign Sovereign Immunities Act ("FSIA"), 28 U.S.C. §§ 1330, 1602–1611.

John V. Doe brought suit in the United States District Court for the District of Oregon against the Holy See, the Archdiocese of Portland, Oregon ("Archdiocese"), the Catholic Bishop of Chicago ("Chicago Bishop"), and the Order of the Friar Servants ("Order"), alleging that when he was fifteen or sixteen years old he was sexually abused by Father Ronan, a priest in the Archdiocese and a member of the Order. Doe alleged various causes of action against the Holy See: (1) for vicarious liability based on the actions of the Holy See's instrumentalities, the Archdiocese, the Chicago Bishop, and the Order; (2) for respondeat superior liability based on the actions of the Holy See's employee, Ronan; and (3) for direct liability for the Holy See's own negligent retention and supervision of Ronan and its negligent failure to warn Doe of Ronan's dangerous proclivities. The Holy See contended in the district court that all of Doe's causes of action against it must be dismissed

* The Honorable Otis D. Wright, II, United States District Judge for the Central District of California, sitting by designation.

because, as a foreign sovereign, it is immune from suit in U.S. courts. The district court disagreed, holding that it has jurisdiction over all but one of Doe's claims under the FSIA's tortious act exception to sovereign immunity. The Holy See appeals.

For the reasons explained below, we affirm the district court in part and reverse in part as to the Holy See's appeal. As to the Holy See's vicarious liability for the acts of the Archdiocese, the Chicago Bishop, and the Order, we conclude that Doe has not alleged facts sufficient to overcome the presumption of separate juridical status for governmental instrumentalities, so the negligent acts of those entities cannot be attributed to the Holy See for jurisdictional purposes. Doe's vicarious liability claims therefore cannot go forward as pleaded. As to the Holy See's respondeat superior liability for Ronan's acts, we conclude that, because Doe has sufficiently alleged that Ronan was an employee of the Holy See acting within the "scope of his employment" under Oregon law, Ronan's acts can be attributed to the Holy See for jurisdictional purposes. Further, we agree with the district court that Ronan's acts come within the FSIA's tortious act exception, so the Holy See is not immune from suit for the respondeat superior cause of action. Although the district court held that Doe's negligence claims against the Holy See could proceed under the FSIA's tortious act exception, we conclude that they cannot, because the FSIA preserves immunity for discretionary acts. However, we do not have jurisdiction to consider the cross-appeal as to the commercial activity exception at this time. The decision of the district court on the appeal by the Holy See is therefore affirmed in part, reversed in part, and remanded for further proceedings not inconsistent with this opinion. We dismiss the cross-appeal.

I. Procedural Background

A. Complaint

In his amended complaint, filed April 1, 2004, Doe describes as follows Father Andrew Ronan's alleged sexual abuse of young boys: In 1955 or 1956, while employed as a parish priest in the Archdiocese of Armagh, Ireland, Father Ronan molested a minor and admitted to doing so. Ronan was later removed from Our Lady of Benburb and placed in the employ of the Chicago Bishop, at St. Philip's High School. At St. Philip's, Ronan molested at least three male students. Confronted with allegations of abuse, Ronan admitted to molesting the boys. The Chicago Bishop, "acting in accordance with the policies, practices, and procedures" of the Holy See, did not discipline or remove Ronan from his post.[1]

In approximately 1965, when Doe was 15 or 16 years old, the Holy See and the Order of the Friar Servants, of which Ronan was a member, "placed" Ronan in a parish priest position at St. Albert's Church in Portland, Oregon. Doe met Ronan

1 These are, of course, only allegations, but we are required to take them as true for the purposes of this appeal. *See infra*, Part III.A.

at St. Albert's and came to know Ronan "as his priest, counselor and spiritual adviser." Doe was a devout Roman Catholic, and for him "Ronan was a person of great influence and persuasion as a holy man and authority figure." Using his position of trust and authority, Ronan "engaged in harmful sexual contact upon" Doe on repeated occasions. The sexual contact occurred "in several places including the monastery and surrounding areas."

Based on these facts, Doe alleged causes of action against the Holy See, its "instrumentalities or agents" ("Does 1–10"), the Archdiocese, the Chicago Bishop, and the Order, all of whom it alleged were employers of Ronan. According to the amended complaint:

> Defendant Holy See is the ecclesiastical, governmental, and administrative capital of the Roman Catholic Church. Defendant Holy See is the composite of the authority, jurisdiction, and sovereignty vested in the Pope and his delegated advisors to direct the world-wide Roman Catholic Church. Defendant Holy See has unqualified power over the Catholic Church including each and every individual and section of the [C]hurch. Defendant Holy See directs, supervises, supports, promotes[,] and engages in providing religious and pastoral guidance, education[,] and counseling services to Roman Catholics world-wide in exchange for all or a portion of the revenues derived from its members for these services. The Holy See engages in these activities through its agents, cardinals, bishops[,] and clergy, including religious order priests, brothers[,] and sisters, who engage in pastoral work under the authority of its bishop[s]. The Holy See is supported through the contributions of the faithful[,] which are received through donations from the dioceses around the world, including those in the United States. Defendant Holy See promotes and safeguards the morals and standards of conduct of the clergy of the [C]atholic [C]hurch. Defendant Holy See does this by and through its agents and instrumentalities, including the Congregation for the Clergy and the Congregation for Religious both delegated by the Pope and acting on his behalf. It creates, divides[,] and re-aligns dioceses, archdioceses[,] and ecclesiastical provinces. It also gives final approval to the creation, division[,] or suppression of provinces of religious orders. . . . It creates, appoints, assigns and re-assigns bishops [and] superiors of religious orders, and through the bishops and superiors of religious orders [it] has the power to directly assign and remove individual clergy. All bishops, clergy, and priests, including religious order priests, vow to show respect and obedience to the Pope and their bishop. Defendant Holy See also examines and is responsible for the work and discipline and all those things which concern bishops, superiors of religious orders, priests[,] and deacons of the religious clergy. In furtherance of this duty, Defendant Holy See requires bishops to file a report, on a regular basis, outlining the status of, and any problems with, clergy. Defendant Holy See promulgates and enforces the laws and regulations regarding the education, training[,] and standards of conduct and discipline for its members and those who serve in the governmental, administrative, judicial, educational[,] and pastoral workings of the Catholic [C]hurch world-wide. Defendant Holy See is also directly responsible for removing superiors of religious orders, bishops, archbishops[,] and cardinals from service and/or making them ineligible for positions of leadership in the various divisions and offices of the Catholic [C]hurch.

The Archdiocese, according to the amendment complaint, is a corporation incorporated under the laws of the state of Oregon and is therefore a citizen of that state. It "provided pastoral services to [Doe] and his immediate family through its parishes." The Chicago Bishop is incorporated under the laws of the state of Illinois and is a citizen of that state. Finally, the Order is "a citizen of the state of Illinois," but it operates worldwide. It is under the "ultimate authority of" the Holy See.

Doe alleged that the Archdiocese and the Order were vicariously liable for Ronan's abuse of Doe, and that the Chicago Bishop and the Order were negligent in failing to warn the Archdiocese and Doe of Ronan's propensities. Doe also alleged that the Holy See was vicariously liable for Ronan's abuse of Doe and for the negligent actions of the Archdiocese, the Order, and the Chicago Bishop, and that the Holy See was itself negligent in its retention and supervision of Ronan and in failing to warn of his propensities.

B. District Court Decision

The Holy See moved to dismiss the complaint in its entirety for lack of subject-matter jurisdiction, arguing that as a foreign sovereign, it is presumptively immune from suit under the FSIA, and that neither the "tortious act" exception to sovereign immunity, 28 U.S.C. § 1605(a)(5), nor the "commercial activity" exception to sovereign immunity, 28 U.S.C. § 1605(a)(2), applies. The district court held that the commercial activity exception does not apply to permit the exercise of jurisdiction over Doe's claims; the court did not view the Holy See's activities as commercial because "the true essence of the complaint . . . clearly sound[s] in tort." *Doe v. Holy See*, 434 F. Supp. 2d 925, 942 (D. Or. 2006). In contrast, the district court held that the tortious act exception does apply, permitting it to exercise jurisdiction over all Doe's claims except for the fraud claim. *Id.* at 957. The district court therefore granted the Holy See's motion to dismiss as to the fraud claim, but it denied the motion as to all of Doe's other claims.

The Holy See appeals the district court's decision that the tortious act exception applies. Doe cross-appeals the district court's dismissal of his fraud claim, contending that the commercial activity exception permits federal court jurisdiction over that cause of action.

II. Statutory Framework

For much of our nation's history, from at least 1812 until 1952, "the United States generally granted foreign sovereigns complete immunity from suit in the courts of this country." *Verlinden B.V. v. Cent. Bank of Nigeria*, 461 U.S. 480, 486, 103 S. Ct. 1962, 76 L. Ed. 2d 81 (1983) (citing *The Schooner Exchange v. M'Faddon*, 11 U.S. 116, 7 *Cranch* 116, 3 L. Ed. 287 (1812)). In 1952, however, the State Department adopted a more "restrictive" theory of foreign sovereign immunity, under which sovereign "immunity is confined to suits involving the foreign sovereign's public acts." *Id.* at 487. Applying this restrictive approach, questions of foreign sovereign immunity arising in U.S. courts were decided on a case-by-case basis, often with the assistance of letters from the State Department containing "suggestions of immunity." *Id.*

In 1976, to "clarify the governing standards" and to insulate the issue of sovereign immunity from the impact of "case-by-case diplomatic pressures," Congress enacted the FSIA, 28 U.S.C. §§ 1330, 1602–1611. *Verlinden*, 461 U.S. at 488. The FSIA contains "a comprehensive set of legal standards governing claims of immunity in every civil action against a foreign state or its political subdivisions, agencies, or instrumentalities." *Id.* at 488. It is this set of legal standards with which we deal today.

Under the FSIA, a foreign state is "immune from the jurisdiction of the courts of the United States and of the States" unless one of the statute's enumerated exceptions applies. 28 U.S.C. § 1604. A foreign state "includes a political subdivision of a foreign state or an agency or instrumentality of a foreign state." *Id.* § 1603(a). An "agency or instrumentality of a foreign state" is defined in turn as any entity:

> (1) which is a separate legal person, corporate or otherwise, and
>
> (2) which is an organ of a foreign state or political subdivision thereof, . . . and
>
> (3) which is neither a citizen of a State of the United States . . . nor created under the laws of any third country.

Id. § 1603(b).

Section 1605[2] contains "[g]eneral exceptions to the jurisdictional immunity of a foreign state," providing in relevant part that:

> (a) A foreign state shall not be immune from the jurisdiction of courts of the United States or of the States in any case –
>
> . . .
>
> (2) in which the action is based upon a commercial activity carried on in the United States by the foreign state; or upon an act performed in the United States in connection with a commercial activity of the foreign state elsewhere; or upon an act outside the territory of the United States in connection with a commercial activity of the foreign state elsewhere and that act causes a direct effect in the United States;
>
> . . .
>
> (5) not otherwise encompassed in paragraph (2) above, in which money damages are sought against a foreign state for personal injury or death, or damage to or loss of property, occurring in the United States and caused by the tortious act of that foreign state or of any official or employee of that foreign state while acting within the scope of his office or employment; except this paragraph shall not apply to –
>
> (A) any claim based upon the exercise or performance or the failure to exercise or perform a discretionary function regardless of whether the discretion be abused, or

2 All statutory citations are to Title 28 of the United States Code unless otherwise indicated.

> (B) any claim arising out of malicious prosecution, abuse of process, libel, slander, misrepresentation, deceit, or interference with contract rights . . .

The statute further defines the elements of the commercial activity exception: A "'commercial activity' means either a regular course of commercial conduct or a particular commercial transaction or act. The commercial character of an activity shall be determined by reference to the nature of the course of conduct or particular transaction or act, rather than by reference to its purpose." *Id.* § 1603(d). A "'commercial activity carried on in the United States by a foreign state' means commercial activity carried on by such state and having substantial contact with the United States." *Id.* § 1603(e).

The statute does not set out any substantive rules of liability, but instead provides that, "[a]s to any claim for relief with respect to which a foreign state is not entitled to immunity under" the statute, "the foreign state shall be liable in the same manner and to the same extent as a private individual under like circumstances." *Id.* § 1606.

III. Analysis

A. Standard for Motions to Dismiss Based on Foreign Sovereign Immunity

The Holy See has brought a facial attack on the subject matter jurisdiction of the district court under Rule 12(b)(1). We therefore "assume [plaintiff's] [factual] allegations to be true and draw all reasonable inferences in his favor." *Wolfe v. Strankman*, 392 F.3d 358, 362 (9th Cir. 2004); *see also McNatt v. Apfel*, 201 F.3d 1084, 1087 (9th Cir. 2000) (holding that we "favorably view[ ] the facts alleged to support jurisdiction"). We do not, however, accept the "truth of *legal* conclusions merely because they are cast in the form of factual allegations." *Warren v. Fox Family Worldwide, Inc.*, 328 F.3d 1136, 1139 (9th Cir. 2003) (emphasis added; internal quotations omitted) (quoting *W. Mining Council v. Watt,* 643 F.2d 618, 624 (9th Cir. 1981)).

The Holy See suggests that when evaluating facial motions to dismiss based on foreign sovereign immunity, we must require a greater-than-usual level of detail in the pleadings, and may not construe factual allegations in favor of the plaintiff. Neither contention is correct. The cases on which the Holy See relies involve *fact-based* challenges to subject-matter jurisdiction. *See, e.g., Robinson v. Gov't of Malaysia*, 269 F.3d 133, 137–38, 146 (2d Cir. 2001) (relying on testimony and affidavits from the parties in concluding that the "generic allegations" in the complaint were insufficient to establish subject matter jurisdiction under the FSIA). In such cases, "no presumptive truthfulness attaches to plaintiff's allegations, and the existence of disputed material facts will not preclude the trial court from evaluating for itself the merits of jurisdictional claims." *Roberts v. Corrothers,* 812 F.2d 1173, 1177 (9th Cir. 1987).

Here, in contrast, the Holy See is contending that on the face of the complaint, we lack subject matter jurisdiction; it has introduced no evidence contesting any of the allegations. With regard to such a challenge, a motion to dismiss for lack of jurisdiction under the FSIA is no different from any other motion to dismiss on the pleadings for lack of jurisdiction, and we apply the same standards in evaluating its merit. *See, e.g., Safe Air for Everyone v. Meyer,* 373 F.3d 1035, 1039 (9th Cir. 2004). As the D.C. Circuit explained in *Rong v. Liaoning Province Gov't,* 371 U.S. App. D.C. 507, 452 F.3d 883, 888 (D.C. Cir. 2006), in the foreign sovereign immunity context, "[i]f the defendant challenges only the legal sufficiency of the plaintiff's jurisdictional allegations, then the district court should take the plaintiff's factual allegations as true and determine whether they bring the case within any of the exceptions to immunity invoked by the plaintiff."

Moreover, we have never held that anything other than our usual notice pleading standard applies to complaints that allege an exception to foreign sovereign immunity. Under notice pleading rules, we require only "a short and plain statement" of the grounds for jurisdiction and the claim for relief. Fed. R. Civ. P. 8(a)(1), (2); *see also Bell Atlantic Corp. v. Twombly,* 550 U.S. 544, 127 S. Ct. 1955, 1964–65, 167 L. Ed. 2d 929 (2007). We do not impose a heightened pleading standard in the absence of "an explicit requirement in a statute or federal rule," *Skaff v. Meridien North America Beverly Hills, LLC,* 506 F.3d 832, 841 (9th Cir. 2007); there is no such explicit requirement here applicable. In evaluating assertions of subject-matter jurisdiction based on an exception to foreign sovereign immunity, then, we apply the same notice pleading requirements we would apply to any other assertion of subject-matter jurisdiction and look only for a "short and plain statement" of the basis for jurisdiction.

B. Appellate Jurisdiction

1. Jurisdiction Over Appeal

A district court's denial of immunity to a foreign sovereign is an appealable order under the collateral order doctrine. *See Schoenberg v. Exportadora de Sal, S.A.,* 930 F.2d 777, 779 (9th Cir. 1991); *see also In re Republic of the Phil.,* 309 F.3d 1143, 1148 (9th Cir. 2002) (explaining that refusal to dismiss on grounds of sovereign immunity is within the collateral order doctrine because it "may result in the parties having to litigate claims over which the court lacks jurisdiction").

2. Jurisdiction over Cross-Appeal

Doe cross-appeals and argues that his claims come within the FSIA's commercial activity exception to sovereign immunity, § 1605(a)(2). The Holy See contends that we do not have jurisdiction over Doe's cross-appeal because it is not "inextricably intertwined" with the collaterally appealable issue of whether the Holy See is immune from suit. *See Burlington N. & Santa Fe Ry. Co. v. Vaughn,* 509 F.3d 1085, 1093–94 (9th Cir. 2007) (in a case involving a collaterally appealable order, denying a tribe sovereign immunity, but holding that the court could not reach other issues raised on appeal because they were not "inextricably intertwined" with the collaterally appealable issue). According to the Holy See, we do not have jurisdiction to consider Doe's argument that his claims come within the commercial activity exception. We agree.

As a general rule, the collateral order doctrine permits appellate jurisdiction only over those decisions of a district court that "conclusively determine the disputed question, resolve an important issue completely separate from the merits of the action, and [are] effectively unreviewable on appeal from a final judgment." *See In re Copley Press, Inc.*, 518 F.3d 1022, 1025 (9th Cir. 2008) (quoting *Coopers & Lybrand v. Livesay,* 437 U.S. 463, 468, 98 S. Ct. 2454, 57 L. Ed. 2d 351 (1978)). A decision denying immunity to a foreign sovereign meets those requirements. *See Gupta v. Thai Airways Int'l, Ltd.*, 487 F.3d 759, 763–64 & n.6 (9th Cir. 2007). Additionally, permitting a trial to go forward against a foreign sovereign when there is a claim of sovereign immunity "imperil[s] a substantial public interest." *See Will v. Hallock,* 546 U.S. 345, 353, 126 S. Ct. 952, 163 L. Ed. 2d 836 (2006) (explaining why decisions denying absolute, qualified, and Eleventh Amendment immunity come within the collaterally appealable order doctrine).

The collaterally appealable order doctrine does not automatically permit review of district court rulings contained in the same district court opinion as the appealable determination, if they do not themselves meet these requirements. *See Abney v. United States*, 431 U.S. 651, 663, 97 S. Ct. 2034, 52 L. Ed. 2d 651 (1977) (after concluding that the collateral order doctrine applies to a decision denying a motion to dismiss on double jeopardy grounds, holding that "other claims presented to, and rejected by, the district court in passing on the . . . motion to dismiss . . . are appealable if, and only if, they too fall within [the] collateral-order exception to the final-judgment rule"); *Burlington N.,* 509 F.3d at 1089, 1093–94 (refusing to exercise pendent appellate jurisdiction over an exhaustion issue decided in the same district court order as the collaterally appealable question); *United States v. Yellow Freight Sys., Inc.,* 637 F.2d 1248, 1251 (9th Cir. 1980) ("Inquiry into the immediate appealability of a particular pretrial order must focus upon each claim asserted."); *but cf. Joseph v. Office of Consulate Gen. of Nig.*, 830 F.2d 1018, 1021 (9th Cir. 1987) (assuming jurisdiction over cross-appeal in FSIA case, without explanation).

Here, the tort causes of action are not inextricably intertwined with Doe's other claims. Thus, that concept is not sufficient to allow Doe to appeal the district court's grant of immunity as far as that exception is concerned.[3]

3 We are aware of the fact that § 1605(a)(5), identifying the tortious act exception, is applicable to cases "not otherwise encompassed in paragraph (2) [the commercial activity exception] above." This language does not mean that, in interpreting the tortious act exception in (a)(5), we must always first consider whether the commercial activity exception in (a)(2) applies. Courts have not proceeded in that fashion. *See, e.g., Argentine Republic v. Amerada Hess Shipping Corp.,* 488 U.S. 428, 439–43, 109 S. Ct. 683, 102 L. Ed. 2d 818 (1989); *Blaxland v. Commonwealth Dir. of Public Prosecutions,* 323 F.3d 1198, 1203–04 (9th Cir. 2003); *Risk v. Halvorsen*, 936 F.2d 393, 395–96 (9th Cir. 1991). Indeed, in *Joseph*, 830 F.2d at 1025, we explicitly stated that because we could decide the question presented under subsection (a)(5),

Nor do we agree that we ought to simply take up the commercial activity issue on the basis that it is no more than an alternate ground to uphold the district court. In fact, the need for review of immunity denials—avoiding the undermining of the purpose of the grant of immunity[4]—has no weight where immunity has been granted. Were there any doubt about that, the sensitive nature of the issues dealing with sovereigns would convince us that it would generally be prudentially unsound to expand review into the area of immunity grants when an appeal is taken from a denial of immunity.

This case points up one of the perils of undertaking unnecessary review of grants of immunity. On this appeal we are presented with comparatively straightforward questions about the relationship between the Holy See and local priests under the tort exception. But the cross-appeal seeks to expand our inquiry into the arcane question of whether church functions are commercial activity because churches receive financial support from their parishioners, or otherwise. That is an issue that actually has nothing to do with the issues on interlocutory appeal.

To say it another way, it is well established that, although an interlocutory appeal can be taken whenever immunity (absolute or qualified) is denied to a person or entity claiming entitlement thereto, an expansion to other issues is not usually allowed. *See Swint v. Chambers County Comm'n*., 514 U.S. 35, 43–51, 115 S. Ct. 1203, 131 L. Ed. 2d 60 (1995); *Cunningham v. Gates*, 229 F.3d 1271, 1284–86 (9th Cir. 2000). We are asked to, in effect, change that rule so that whenever immunity is denied on one set of issues but granted on another set, a cross-appeal can be taken regarding the granted set. Surely that would be the ineluctable effect of Doe's request. One would not even need to show, by the way, a true interlocking of issues beyond the fact that both deal with immunity. One would only need to argue that the alternative set will support the denial of immunity on a wholly different basis. That approach would be followed even if the district court had expressly ruled to the contrary on the alternative set of issues.[5] In other words, here we would be

---

there was no need to consider subsection (a)(2) at all. Other courts have reached the same result. *See, e.g., Robinson v. Gov't of Malay.*, 269 F.3d 133, 145–47 (2d Cir. 2001); *Cabiri v. Gov't of Republic of Ghana*, 165 F.3d 193, 199–201 (2d Cir. 1999); *Frolova v. Union of Soviet Socialist Republics,* 761 F.2d 370, 379 (7th Cir. 1985); *Asociacion de Reclamantes v. United Mexican States*, 237 U.S. App. D.C. 81, 735 F.2d 1517, 1524–25 (D.C. Cir. 1984); *Persinger v. Islamic Republic of Iran*, 234 U.S. App. D.C. 349, 729 F.2d 835, 838–39 (D.C. Cir. 1984).

4 *See Gupta*, 487 F.3d at 763–64.

5 We are aware of the theory that allows alternate grounds to be used to support a district court decision, even where no cross-appeal has been filed. *See El Paso Natural Gas Co. v. Neztsosie*, 526 U.S. 473, 479–80, 119 S. Ct. 1430, 143 L. Ed. 2d 635 (1999); *Rivero v. City & County of San Francisco*, 316 F.3d 857, 861–62 (9th Cir. 2002). We have said that taking jurisdiction in that instance is prudential and discretionary. *See Lee v. Burlington N. Santa Fe Ry. Co.,* 245 F.3d 1102, 1107 (9th Cir. 2001); *Bryant v. Tech. Research Co.,* 654 F.2d 1337, 1341–42 (9th Cir. 1981). For reasons explained in the text, we would decline to exercise that jurisdiction. The theory makes a good deal of jurisprudential sense when both the grant and the denial of relief were actually appealable issues; it makes much less sense where, as here,

asked to take up the appeal from that grant and reverse the district court's determination; we would have to reach out and engage in a lengthy disquisition on the commercial activity exception to FSIA, which we neither must nor should do.

Thus, we will not consider issues regarding the district court's grant of immunity under the commercial exception to the FSIA.

C. Determining Which Acts May Be Attributed to the Holy See for Jurisdictional Purposes

Before turning to the question of which, if any, of the FSIA's exceptions to immunity apply, we must determine which of the acts alleged in the complaint may legitimately be attributed to the Holy See for purposes of establishing jurisdiction. Doe's complaint alleges tortious acts by the Archdiocese, the Order, and the Bishop, all alleged to be corporations created by the Holy See. The Holy See argues that we may not consider these alleged acts by the Archdiocese, the Order, and the Bishop when determining whether jurisdiction exists over the Holy See, because Doe has not alleged facts that would overcome the presumption of separate juridical status such that the acts of the latter could be attributed to the former.[6] For the reasons explained below, given the allegations that Doe has pleaded, we agree with the Holy See. In addition, however, the complaint alleges a number of actions performed by the Holy See itself, such as "creat[ing]" dioceses and archdioceses, "giv[ing] final approval to the creation, division or suppression of provinces of religious orders," "employ[ing]" Ronan, and "plac[ing]" Ronan in the Archdiocese in Portland, Oregon. We conclude below that these acts do establish jurisdiction over the Holy See for the claims to which the acts are relevant.

1. Determining Whether an Agency Relationship Exists Between the Holy See and Its Domestic Corporations for Purposes of Establishing Jurisdiction over the Holy See

a. The Bancec *Standard*

In arguing that the actions of the corporations are not attributable to Holy See for purposes of determining jurisdiction, the Holy See relies on *First Nat. City Bank v.*

---

a grant of immunity is not interlocutorily appealable at all and would involve, as we have said, a vast expansion of the issues in and complexity of the appeal.

6 We note that the question we address here is distinct from the question whether the Archdiocese, the Chicago Bishop, and the Order are themselves immune from suit under the FSIA. An "agency or instrumentality" of a foreign state, as defined by the FSIA, is immune from suit because it is itself a "foreign state" within the meaning of the Act. § 1603(a), (b). On the allegation of the complaint, however, the Archdiocese, the Chicago Bishop, and the Order are not "agencies or instrumentalities" of a foreign state within the meaning of the FSIA, because they are all citizens of the United States. *See* § 1603(b) (an agency or instrumentality of a foreign state means, among other things, an entity "which is neither a citizen of a State of the United States . . . nor created under the laws of any third country"). They are therefore not immune from suit.

Banco Para el Comercio Exterior de Cuba ("Bancec"), 462 U.S. 611, 103 S. Ct. 2591, 77 L. Ed. 2d 46 (1983). In *Bancec*, the Supreme Court considered whether an instrumentality created by a foreign state could be held liable for the actions of the foreign state itself, a question the reverse of ours. Bancec was "the Cuban Government's exclusive agent in foreign trade," and the "government supplied all of [Bancec]'s capital and owned all of its stock." *Id.* at 614. Soon after Bancec sought to collect on a letter of credit that had been issued in its favor by Citibank, the Cuban government seized and nationalized all of Citibank's assets in Cuba. *Id.* So, when Bancec filed an action in U.S. federal court to recover on the letter of credit, Citibank counterclaimed, seeking a setoff for the value of its expropriated Cuban branches. *Id.* at 614–15. In the meantime, Bancec was dissolved, and Bancec filed a stipulation "stating that . . . its claim had been transferred to the Ministry of Foreign Trade" of Cuba. *Id.* at 615–16.

Jurisdiction in *Bancec* existed under FSIA's counterclaim provision, 28 U.S.C. § 1607(c).[7] *Id.* at 620–21. Because jurisdiction was not at issue, the question for the Supreme Court was one of liability: whether Bancec could be held liable for the act of expropriation committed by the Cuban government. *Id.* at 617.

The Supreme Court began by noting that, although Bancec was an "agency or instrumentality" of Cuba within the meaning of FSIA § 1603(b), this status was relevant only to jurisdiction; it did not control the question of Bancec's liability for Cuba's actions. The FSIA "was not intended to affect the substantive law determining the liability of a foreign state or instrumentality." *Id.* at 620. Instead, liability was to be assessed according to corporate law principles "common to both international law and federal common law." *Id.* at 623. Surveying international and federal law on the status of corporations, the Supreme Court recognized a presumption of "separate juridical [status]" for the instrumentalities of foreign states. *Id.* at 624, 624–28.

That presumption can be overcome, the Court explained, in two instances: when "a corporate entity is so extensively controlled by its owner that a relationship of principal and agent is created," or when recognizing the separate status of a corporation "would work fraud or injustice." *Id.* at 629. The Court then held the latter standard dispositive of Bancec's case: The Cuban government could not have sued in its own name in a U.S. court "without waiving its sovereign immunity and answering for [its] seizure of Citibank's assets." *Id.* at 633. Instead, Cuba had transferred its assets to separate entities, and Bancec then sought to avoid liability for the seizure. "[T]he Cuban government . . . [and] not any third parties that may have relied on Bancec's separate juridical identity" would be the real beneficiary

---

7 "In any action brought by a foreign state [or its agency or instrumentality] . . . in a court of the United States or of a State, the foreign state shall not be accorded immunity with respect to any counterclaim . . . to the extent that the counterclaim does not seek relief exceeding in amount or differing in kind from that sought by the foreign state." 28 U.S.C. § 1607(c).

if Bancec was not held liable for the Cuban government's actions. *Id.* at 631–32. Given this circumstance, the Court concluded that to "adhere blindly to the corporate form" would work such an "injustice" that the presumption of separate juridical status had been overcome. *Id.* at 632. Holding Bancec liable for the Cuban government's actions, the Court held that Citibank was entitled to offset the value of its seized assets from the amount it owed to Bancec. *Id.* at 634.

The Supreme Court in *Bancec* did not have the opportunity to consider whether the actions of a *corporation* may be attributed to the *sovereign*—the reverse of the *Bancec* scenario—for purposes of determining whether jurisdiction over that sovereign exists. This Circuit has not previously addressed that question either.[8] At least two other circuits, however, faced with such a scenario, have applied Bancec's substantive corporate law principles in determining whether jurisdiction exists under the FSIA.

In *Transamerica Leasing v. La Republica de Venezuela*, 339 U.S. App. D.C. 385, 200 F.3d 843 (D.C. Cir. 2000), a plaintiff sued Venezuela, alleging that Venezuela was liable for the commercial acts of a government instrumentality, CAVN. *Id.* at 846. To determine whether Venezuela was amenable to suit under the commercial activity exception, the court turned to the *Bancec* test and asked whether (1) Venezuela and CAVN had a principal-agent relationship, or (2) recognizing CAVN as a separate entity would work an injustice. *Id.* at 848. Although it acknowledged that "*Bancec* recognized these as exceptions to the rule that a foreign sovereign is not *liable* for the acts of an instrumentality of the state," the D.C. Circuit held that "they serve also as exceptions to the rule that a foreign sovereign is not *amenable to suit* based on the acts of such an instrumentality." *Id.* (emphasis added). *See also Foremost-McKesson, Inc. v. Islamic Republic of Iran,* 284 U.S. App. D.C. 333, 905 F.2d 438, 446 (D.C. Cir. 1990) ("The presumption of juridical separateness of entities also applies to jurisdictional issues."). The Fifth Circuit adopted the same principle in *Arriba Ltd. v. Petroleos Mexicanos*, 962 F.2d 528, 533–36 (5th Cir. 1992), refusing to attribute the actions of a private labor union to the Mexican state-owned oil company for purposes of determining FSIA jurisdiction.

We join the D.C. Circuit and the Fifth Circuit in extending *Bancec's* analysis to the question whether the actions of a corporation may render a foreign sovereign amenable to suit. A foreign state can only "act[ ] through its agents," be they corporations or individual people. *Phaneuf v. Republic of Indonesia*, 106 F.3d 302, 307–08 (9th Cir. 1997) ("Because a foreign state acts through its agents, an agent's deed . . . constitutes activity 'of the foreign state.'"); *see also Gilson v. Republic of Ireland*, 221 U.S. App. D.C. 73, 682 F.2d 1022, 1026 n.16 (D.C. Cir. 1982) (noting

8 We have, however, applied the *Bancec* presumption of separate juridical status at the merits phase of FSIA litigation. *See Flatow v. Islamic Republic of Iran*, 308 F.3d 1065 (9th Cir. 2002) (applying *Bancec* in a case in which an individual who had obtained a judgment against Iran attempted to enforce it against the Bank Saderat Iran).

that "the activities of an agent may be attributed to the principal for jurisdictional purposes"). Therefore, in applying the jurisdictional provisions of the FSIA, courts will routinely have to decide whether a particular individual or corporation is an agent of a foreign state.

Bancec provides a workable standard for deciding this question. Applying *Bancec's* presumption in favor of separate juridical status for foreign state instrumentalities at the jurisdiction phase, not just at the liability phase, is consistent with the FSIA's broad policy goals. In *Bancec*, the Court discussed at length the comity considerations at play when entertaining suits against foreign government instrumentalities in U.S. courts. 462 U.S. at 626; *see also Republic of Austria v. Altmann*, 541 U.S. 677, 688, 124 S. Ct. 2240, 159 L. Ed. 2d 1 (2004). As at the merits phase, failing to recognize the presumption of separate juridical status at the jurisdictional phase could "result in substantial uncertainty over whether an instrumentality's assets would be diverted to satisfy a claim against the sovereign," and might frustrate "the efforts of sovereign nations to structure their governmental activities in a manner deemed necessary to promote economic development and efficient administration." *Bancec*, 462 U.S. at 626. Applying *Bancec's* presumption—as well as the standard for overcoming that presumption—at the outset of a suit as well as at the merits phase makes good sense.

With these considerations in mind, we conclude that it is appropriate to use the *Bancec* standard to determine whether Doe's allegations are sufficient to permit jurisdiction over the Holy See based on acts committed by its affiliated domestic corporations.

b. Applying the Bancec standard to Doe's complaint

Applying the rule of *Bancec* to the allegations in Doe's complaint, we conclude that Doe has not alleged sufficient facts to overcome the "presumption of separate juridical status," for reasons similar to those dispositive in the converse situation in *Flatow v. Islamic Republic of Iran,* 308 F.3d 1065 (9th Cir. 2002). In *Flatow*, we applied *Bancec* to the relationship between the Iranian government and the Bank Saderat Iran ("BSI"). BSI was created by the Iranian government and fully owned by it. *Id.* at 1072–73. Its actions were regulated by Iran's General Assembly of Banks and High Council of Banks, which reviewed BSI's annual statements and "perform[ed] broad policymaking functions." *Id.* at 1073. *Flatow* held these facts insufficient to overcome the presumption of separate juridical status, because the government's "involvement [did not] rise to a [sufficiently] high[ ] level," and in particular, did not involve "day-to-day" control. *Id.* (citing *McKesson Corp v. Islamic Republic of Iran*, 311 U.S. App. D.C. 197, 52 F.3d 346, 351–52 (D.C. Cir. 1995) (holding the presumption of separateness overcome where Iran controlled routine business decisions, such as declaring and paying dividends and honoring contracts).

Doe's complaint does not allege day-to-day, routine involvement of the Holy See in the affairs of the Archdiocese, the Order, and the Bishop. Instead, it alleges that the Holy See "creates, divides[,] and re-aligns dioceses, archdioceses and ecclesiastical provinces" and "gives final approval to the creation, division or suppression of provinces of religious orders." Doe also alleges that the Holy See "promulgates and enforces the laws and regulations regarding the education, training[,] and standards of conduct and discipline for its members and those who serve in the governmental, administrative, judicial, educational[,] and pastoral workings of the Catholic [C]hurch world-wide." These factual allegations—that the Holy See participated in creating the corporations and continues to promulgate laws and regulations that apply to them—are quite similar to the facts in *Flatow*, and are, as in *Flatow*, insufficient to overcome the presumption of separate juridical status.

Doe does directly allege in his complaint that the corporations are "agents" of the Holy See. In this context, however, the term "agent" is not self-explanatory. "Agent" can have more than one legal meaning: the standard for determining that a natural person is the agent of another differs from the standard for attribution of the actions of a corporation to another entity. *See, e.g., Rough & Ready Lumber Co. v. Blue Sky Forest Products,* 105 Ore. App. 227, 231, 804 P.2d 498 (1991) (an agency relationship between two natural persons "results from the manifestation of consent by one person to another that the other shall act on his behalf and subject to his control, and consent by the other so to act.") (quoting Restatement (Second) of Agency § 1 (1958)). The *Bancec* standard is in fact most similar to the "alter ego" or "piercing the corporate veil" standards applied in many state courts to determine whether the actions of a corporation are attributable to its owners. *See, e.g., Amfac Foods, Inc. v. Int'l Sys. & Controls Corp.,* 294 Ore. 94, 107–08, 654 P.2d 1092 (1982) (holding that to demonstrate alter ego status, plaintiff must show control of the subsidiary and that "the plaintiff's inability to collect from the corporation resulted from some form of improper conduct" on part of parent corporation). Even reading the complaint generously to Doe, as we must, we cannot infer from the use of the word "agent" that Doe is alleging the type of day-to-day control that *Bancec* and *Flatow* require to overcome the presumption of separate juridical status.

The district court apparently found jurisdiction proper by relying on the second, equitable prong of *Bancec*, noting that "foreign states cannot avoid their obligations to third parties by engaging in abuses of the corporate form." *Doe*, 434 F. Supp. 2d at 936. But Doe has not alleged that the Holy See has inappropriately used the separate status of the corporations to its own benefit, as in *Bancec*, or that the Holy See created the corporations for the purpose of evading liability for its own wrongs. Rather, in ruling for Doe on this point, the district court seemed to be influenced by the complaint's allegations of wrongful acts perpetrated directly by the Holy See. *See Doe*, 434 F. Supp. 2d at 937. The existence of such *direct* wrongful acts cannot determine whether the distinct wrongful acts of the affiliated *corporations* should also be attributed to the Holy See.

Doe's vicarious liability claim for the actions of the Archdiocese, Chicago Bishop, and Order is based entirely on an allegation that the actions of the domestic corporations are attributable to the Holy See. Doe has therefore not alleged sufficient facts to demonstrate that any exception to sovereign immunity applies to that cause of action. We therefore conclude that the district court lacked jurisdiction over the Holy See for the tortious acts allegedly committed by the Archdiocese, the Chicago Bishop, and the Order.

2. Actions Performed by the Holy See Itself

As to Doe's other causes of action, the Holy See contends that Doe has failed to allege any facts in support of his claims based on the actions of the Holy See itself, rather than of its domestic corporations. We do not agree. Doe has made several allegations regarding actions taken by the Holy See itself—namely, its negligent retention and supervision of Ronan and its failure to warn Doe of Ronan's dangerousness. Doe has also alleged respondeat superior liability against the Holy See for Ronan's actions as an alleged employee of the Holy See. We turn now to those allegations, considering whether they are sufficient to support jurisdiction over the Holy See.

We will now examine whether the district court could exercise jurisdiction over the Holy See for these causes of action under the FSIA's tortious act exception.

D. Tortious Act Exception

The district court held that all of Doe's claims, except the one for fraud, come within the exception to immunity for a "tortious act or omission of [a] foreign state or of any official or employee of that foreign state while acting within the scope of his or her employment." § 1605(a)(2); *Doe*, 434 F. Supp. 2d at 950. We agree in part.

Doe's respondeat superior claim based on Ronan's actions comes within the tortious act exception. Doe has clearly alleged that Ronan was an employee of the Holy See, acting within the scope of his employment, when he molested Doe. We conclude, however, that Doe's claims against the Holy See for negligent retention and supervision and failure to warn cannot be brought under the tort exception because they are barred by the FSIA's exclusion for discretionary functions, § 1605(a)(5)(A).

1. Respondeat superior for Father Ronan's tortious acts

a. The meaning of "employee"

In his complaint, Doe alleges that the Holy See "employed priests, including one Father Andrew Ronan" and that Ronan was under the "direct supervision and control" of the Holy See. The Holy See was further "responsible for the work and discipline [of] . . . priests." According to the complaint, the Holy See on at least one occasion was responsible for controlling where Ronan performed his functions: the Holy See "placed Ronan in [the] Archdiocese at St. Albert's Church in Portland, Oregon."

The Holy See maintains that Doe has not alleged sufficient facts to demonstrate that Ronan was an "employee" of the Holy See for purposes of the tortious act exception, because the word "employee" is a legal conclusion we are not required to accept as true. We are highly skeptical of the notion that, under notice pleading, use of the word "employee" in a complaint is insufficient to establish an allegation of an employment relationship. True, in addition to being a word used in everyday speech, "employee" does have a common law legal definition. *See, e.g., Schaff v. Ray's Land & Sea Food Co.,* 334 Ore. 94, 45 P.3d 936, 939 (Or. 2002) (defining "employee" for purposes of Oregon law). But then, of course, so do the words "person," "corporation," "citizen," and "molest," also used in this complaint—and, undoubtedly, in many other complaints filed each year in federal courts—without further definition. Were we to require that every such word used in a complaint be broken down into its constituent factual predicates, we would undermine the purpose of notice pleading—that is, "to focus litigation on the merits of a claim" rather than on procedural requirements. *Galbraith v. County of Santa Clara,* 307 F.3d 1119, 1125 (9th Cir. 2002). Thus, while we do not accept Doe's legal conclusions as true, we also do not engage in "a hypertechnical reading of the complaint inconsistent with the generous notice pleading standard." *Mendoza v. Zirkle Fruit Co.,* 301 F.3d 1163, 1168 (9th Cir. 2002). Although there is undoubtedly a line beyond which the legal definition of a commonly used term is so complex or contentious that failure to allege each element of the definition would prevent a defendant from understanding the factual basis for the claim, use of the word "employee" falls well short of that line.

b. The meaning of "within the scope of employment"

More complicated under Oregon law is the question of whether Ronan's actions were "within the scope of employment" as the FSIA requires. In *Joseph*, we indicated that the "'scope of employment' provision of the tortious activity exception essentially requires a finding that the doctrine of respondeat superior applies to the tortious acts of individuals." 830 F.2d at 1025. "This determination is governed by state law." *Id.; see also Randolph*, 97 F.3d at 327.

As it happens, the Oregon Supreme Court has directly addressed whether a church can be liable under respondeat superior for the actions of a priest who sexually assaults a parishioner. In *Fearing v. Bucher*, 328 Ore. 367, 977 P.2d 1163 (Or. 1999), the plaintiff alleged that he had been sexually molested by a Catholic priest who "used his position as youth pastor, spiritual guide, confessor, and priest to plaintiff and his family to gain their trust and confidence" and "[b]y virtue of that relationship . . . gained the opportunity to be alone with plaintiff" and sexually assault him. *Id.* at 1166. *Fearing* began its analysis from the proposition that, in a respondeat superior action, an employer can be liable for intentional as well as unintentional torts of an employee if committed "within the scope of employment." *Id.* Generally, under Oregon law, "three requirements must be met to demonstrate that an employee was acting within the course and scope of employment":

> (1) the act must have occurred substantially within the time and space limits authorized by the employment;

> (2) the employee must have been motivated, at least partially, by a purpose to serve the employer; and
>
> (3) the act must have been of a kind which the employee was hired to perform.

Id. at 1166.

Applying these three factors, *Fearing* stated that the priest's "alleged sexual assaults on plaintiff clearly were outside the scope of his employment" under the traditional test, but held that the "inquiry does not end there." *Id.* at 1166. Instead, the court went on to ask whether "acts that *were* within [the priest's] scope of employment resulted in the acts which led to injury to [the] plaintiff." *Id.* (emphasis added; internal quotation marks and citation omitted). The court concluded that because a jury could infer from the facts alleged that "performance of . . . pastoral duties with respect to plaintiff and his family were a necessary precursor to the sexual abuse and that the assaults thus were a direct outgrowth of and were engendered by conduct that was within the scope of . . . employment," *id.* at 1168, the complaint satisfied "all three . . . requirements for establishing that employee conduct was within the scope of employment." *Id.* at 1167.

The Oregon Supreme Court has since clarified that Fearing created a "scope of employment" test specifically applicable to intentional torts. *Minnis v. Oregon Mut. Ins. Co.,* 334 Ore. 191, 48 P.3d 137 (Or. 2002), observed that, in *Fearing*, there was no question that the first requirement of "the within the scope of employment" test was met, because the abuse occurred "within the time and space limits" of the priest's employment. 48 P.3d at 144–45. But because *Fearing* involved an intentional tort, it was inappropriate to focus on whether the tort itself was committed in furtherance of the employer's objectives or was an act of the kind the employee was hired to perform:

> Rather, for the purpose of determining whether a complaint meets the second and third . . . requirements . . . , the focus properly is directed at whether the complaint contains sufficient allegations of employee's conduct that was within the scope of his employment, that is, conduct that the employee was hired to perform, that arguably resulted in the acts that caused plaintiff's injury.

Id. at 144–45 (internal quotation marks, alterations, and citations omitted). *Minnis* thus makes clear that, rather than holding that sexual abuse is not within the scope of employment, *Fearing* created an alternative test with respect to the second and third factors of the "within the scope of employment" standard, applicable when a plaintiff has alleged an intentional tort: An intentional tort is within the scope of employment, and can support respondeat superior liability for the employer, if conduct that was within the scope of employment was "a necessary precursor to the" intentional tort and the intentional tort was "a direct outgrowth of . . . conduct that was within the scope of . . . employment." *Fearing*, 977 P.2d at 1163.

Doe's allegations meet this standard. Doe has asserted that he "came to know Ronan as his priest, counselor and spiritual adviser," and that Ronan used his "position of authority" to "engage in harmful sexual contact upon" Doe in "several places including the monastery and surrounding areas in Portland, Oregon." His allegations are thus very similar to those in *Fearing*. 977 P.2d at 1166.

Under Oregon law, then, Doe has clearly alleged sufficient facts to show that his claim is based on an injury caused by an "employee" of the foreign state while acting "within the scope of his . . . employment," as required to come within the FSIA's tortious act exception. § 1605(a)(5). The Holy See is therefore not immune from Doe's respondeat superior claim.[9]

2. Negligent retention, supervision, and failure to warn

According to Doe's complaint, the Holy See "negligently retained Ronan and failed to warn those coming into contact with him," even though it knew or should have known that Ronan had a history of sexually abusing children. The Holy See also "failed to provide reasonable supervision of Ronan." Whether or not this alleged negligence otherwise comes within the language of the FSIA's tortious act exception—a question we do not decide—these causes of action may not go forward under that section because they are barred by the exclusion for "discretionary functions." The district court thus erred in exercising jurisdiction over these claims.

The discretionary function exclusion shields foreign sovereigns from tort claims "based upon the exercise or performance or the failure to exercise or perform a discretionary function regardless of whether the discretion be abused." § 1605(a)(5)(A). The language of the discretionary function exclusion closely parallels the language of a similar exclusion in the Federal Tort Claims Act ("FTCA"), so we look to case law on the FTCA when interpreting the FSIA's discretionary function exclusion. *See* 28 U.S.C. § 2680(a); *Joseph*, 830 F.2d at 1026. Extrapolating from FTCA case law, the Holy See is protected by the discretionary function exclusion if the challenged action meets two criteria: (1) it is "discretionary in nature" or "involve[s] an element of judgment or choice" and (2) "the judgment is of the kind that the discretionary function exception was designed to shield." *United States v. Gaubert*, 499 U.S. 315, 322, 111 S. Ct. 1267, 113 L. Ed. 2d 335 (1991) (internal quotation marks and citation omitted); *see also Soldano v. United States*, 453 F.3d 1140, 1145 (9th Cir. 2006) (clarifying that judgments "of the kind that the discretionary function exception was designed to shield" are "governmental actions and decisions based on considerations of public policy.") (internal quotation marks and citations omitted).

---

9 We are aware of the fact that the Sixth Circuit has reached a different result, but the law of Kentucky, which it was construing, differs from the law of Oregon. *See O'Bryan v. Holy See*, Nos. 07-5078, 07-5163, 556 F.3d 361, 382–83, 2009 U.S. App. LEXIS 2412 at *46, 2009 WL 305342, at *14 (6th Cir. Feb. 10, 2009).

As to the first *Gaubert* criterion, Doe refers vaguely in his complaint to the Holy See's "policies, practices, and procedures" of not firing priests for, and not warning others about, their abusive acts. He also refers in his brief to a "policy promulgated by the Holy See to cover up incidents of child abuse," which he argues removed "an[y] element of judgment or choice" from the Holy See's actions "to the extent that Appellants were acting pursuant to" it. Yet nowhere does Doe allege the existence of a policy that is "*specific* and *mandatory*" on the Holy See. *Kennewick Irrigation Dist. v. United States*, 880 F.2d 1018, 1026 (9th Cir. 1989) (emphasis in original). He does not state the terms of this alleged policy, or describe any documents, promulgations, or orders embodying it. Nor does the complaint in any other way allege that the Holy See's decisions to retain Doe and not warn about his proclivities involved no element of judgment, choice, or discretion. While the burden of proving the *Gaubert* factors ultimately falls on the sovereign entity asserting the discretionary function exception, "a plaintiff must advance a claim that is facially outside the discretionary function exception in order to survive a motion to dismiss." *Prescott v. United States*, 973 F.2d 696, 702 & n.4 (9th Cir. 1992) (citing *Carlyle v. U.S. Dep't of the Army*, 674 F.2d 554, 556 (6th Cir. 1982) ("Only after a plaintiff has successfully invoked jurisdiction by a pleading that facially alleges matters not excepted by [the FTCA] does the burden fall on the government to prove the applicability of a specific provision of [the FTCA].")). Doe has not pled any actions that fall facially outside the discretionary function exception.

As to the second *Gaubert* criterion, the decision of whether and how to retain and supervise an employee, as well as whether to warn about his dangerous proclivities, are the type of discretionary judgments that the exclusion was designed to protect. We have held the hiring, supervision, and training of employees to be discretionary acts. *See Nurse v. United States*, 226 F.3d 996, 1001 (9th Cir. 2000) (holding that plaintiff's claims of "negligent and reckless employment, supervision and training of" employees "fall squarely within the discretionary function exception"); *see also Burkhart v. Washington Metro. Area Transit Auth.*, 324 U.S. App. D.C. 241, 112 F.3d 1207, 1217 (D.C. Cir. 1997) (holding that "decisions concerning the hiring, training, and super[vision]" of employees are discretionary). Moreover, failure to warn about an individual's dangerousness is discretionary.[10]

---

10 Even were it not the case that the "failure to warn" claim is barred by the discretionary function exclusion, it would be barred by the "misrepresentation" exclusion. Like the discretionary function exclusion, the misrepresentation exclusion in the FSIA, § 1605(a)(5)(B), has been interpreted in light of the misrepresentation exclusion in the FTCA, § 2680(h). *See de Sanchez v. Banco Central de Nicaragua*, 770 F.2d 1385, 1398 (5th Cir. 1985). The misrepresentation exclusion covers both acts of affirmative misrepresentation and failure to warn. *See City and County of San Francisco v. United States,* 615 F.2d 498, 505 (9th Cir. 1980) (holding that "a negligent failure to inform, without more, is misrepresentation within the meaning of" the misrepresentation exclusion). In particular, we have held that government officials' failure to warn about an individual's dangerousness, which ultimately led to sexual abuse of a minor,

See Sigman v. United States, 217 F.3d 785, 797 (9th Cir. 2000) (failure to warn individuals on Air Force Base about potentially dangerous serviceman was a discretionary function, because it "brought into play sensitive and competing policy considerations of protecting safety while preserving resources and preventing unwarranted alarm"); *Weissich v. United States*, 4 F.3d 810, 814–15 (9th Cir. 1993) (failure of probation officers to warn a prosecutor that probationer was a threat to him was a discretionary decision).

The Holy See's failure to present any evidence that its actions were actually based on policy considerations is not relevant to whether the discretionary function exception applies. A foreign state's decision "need not *actually* be grounded in policy considerations so long as it is, by its nature[,] *susceptible* to a policy analysis." *See Kelly v. United States,* 241 F.3d 755, 764 n.5 (9th Cir. 2001) (second emphasis added). A policy analysis is one that implements "political, social, and economic judgments.*" Berkovitz v. United States,* 486 U.S. 531, 539, 108 S. Ct. 1954, 100 L. Ed. 2d 531 (1988) (internal quotation marks and citations omitted). In the case of Father Ronan's alleged abuse, the Holy See might have decided to retain him and not to warn his parishioners because it felt that to do otherwise would have harmed the Church's reputation locally, or because it felt that pastoral stability was sufficiently important for the parishioners' well-being, or because low ordination rates or staffing shortages made it necessary to keep Ronan on. That such social, economic, or political policy considerations could have influenced the decision renders it the kind of judgment that the discretionary function exception was designed to shield.

In sum, the tortious act exception does not provide jurisdiction over Doe's negligent hiring, supervision, and failure to warn claims because they are barred by the discretionary function exclusion.[11] We therefore cannot affirm the district court's judgment on this ground.

IV. Conclusion

In conclusion, we observe once again that the Holy See has brought a facial attack on the allegations of subject-matter jurisdiction in the complaint. It remains to be seen whether Doe can prove his allegations. While the Holy See was certainly entitled to bring a facial attack on the complaint, such an approach is not without risk, for it "call[s] upon [us] to decide far-reaching . . . questions" of some importance

---

comes within the misrepresentation exclusion. *See Lawrence v. United States*, 340 F.3d 952, 958 (9th Cir. 2003).

11 Because we conclude that the tortious act exception does not apply to the above claims, we have no occasion to consider whether the *entire* tort must occur in the United States, as the Sixth and D.C. Circuits have held. *See O'Bryan v. Holy See,* Nos. 07-5078, 07-5163, 556 F.3d 361, 382, 2009 U.S. App. LEXIS 2412 at *42, 2009 WL 305342, at *13 (6th Cir. Feb. 10, 2009); *Asociacion de Reclamantes v. United Mexican States*, 237 U.S. App. D.C. 81, 735 F.2d 1517, 1524–25 (D.C. Cir. 1984). *But see Olsen v. Gov't of Mexico*, 729 F.2d 641, 646 (9th Cir. 1984).

"on a nonexistent factual record, even where . . . discovery" might "reveal the plaintiff's claims to be factually baseless." *Kwai Fun Wong v. United States*, 373 F.3d 952, 957 (9th Cir. 2004). After careful consideration, we have reached the conclusion that most of Doe's causes of action are not covered by the tort exception and overturn the district court's denial of immunity as to those. However, because it would be improper to consider the commercial activity exception, we express no opinion regarding that exception.

For the foregoing reasons, in appeal No. 06-35563 the decision of the district court is AFFIRMED in part, REVERSED in part, and REMANDED. The cross-appeal (No. 06-35587) is DISMISSED. Each party shall bear their own costs.

DISSENT

BERZON, Circuit Judge, dissenting in part:

I agree with the majority that Doe's negligence claims against the Holy See, as currently pleaded, cannot proceed under the tortious act exception to the Foreign Sovereign Immunities Act ("FSIA"). Unlike the majority, however, I would affirm the district court's holding that the FSIA does not give the Holy See immunity from Doe's claims of negligent retention, supervision, and failure to warn. As explained below, we have jurisdiction to affirm the district court on any grounds that were raised below and supported by the record, and our case law compels the conclusion that Doe's negligence claims come within the FSIA's commercial activity exception.

I. Jurisdiction

We have before us an appeal (by the Holy See) and a cross-appeal (by Doe), both seeking reversal of different aspects of the district court's decision. The Holy See's appeal, which is authorized under the collateral order doctrine, challenges the district court's ruling that the FSIA does not provide it with immunity from Doe's negligence claims. The district court held that although the commercial activity exception does not apply to defeat the Holy See's assertion of immunity, the tortious act exception does apply, permitting all Doe's claims except for the fraud claim to go forward. *See Doe v. Holy See*, 434 F. Supp. 2d 925, 957 (D. Or. 2006). The Holy See asks us to reverse the district court's immunity ruling, arguing that the tortious act exception is not applicable to Doe's negligence claims.

Doe argues, in response, that we should affirm the district court's ruling that the FSIA does not give the Holy See immunity from his negligence claims—either because the district court correctly held that the tortious act exception applies, or, in the alternative, because the commercial activity exception applies. In addition, Doe filed a cross-appeal, urging us to reverse the district court's dismissal of his fraud claim, because the commercial activity exception preserves federal subject matter jurisdiction over that claim. His argument concerning his cross-appeal and his response to the Holy See's appeal of the district court's ruling as to his negligence claims are presented to us in a single brief, but they are clearly separable.

I agree with the majority and the Holy See that we lack jurisdiction over Doe's *actual* cross-appeal—that is, over the question whether the Holy See is immune from Doe's fraud cause of action. We do, however, have jurisdiction over Doe's arguments in favor of *upholding* the district court's order, including his argument that the non-fraud causes of action, which the district court allowed to go forward, are within the commercial activity exception.

Specifically, I agree that the district court's grant of immunity with regard to the fraud cause of action is not independently appealable under the collateral order doctrine at this stage in the proceedings. As the majority notes, where a district court has *granted* sovereign immunity on a particular claim, as opposed to where it has *denied* immunity and let the claim go forward, the concerns for foreign sovereigns that animate the collateral order doctrine do not apply. *See* Maj. Op. at 2559 (quoting *Will v. Hallock*, 546 U.S. 345, 353, 126 S. Ct. 952, 163 L. Ed. 2d 836 (2006)). Further, the district court's grant of immunity and denial of jurisdiction over Doe's fraud cause of action will be reviewable at the end of the entire action, so there is no need to allow review of that decision at this time, before there has been a final judgment on the case as a whole. *See In re Copley Press, Inc.,* 518 F.3d 1022, 1025–26 (9th Cir. 2008).

Nor may we exercise pendent jurisdiction over Doe's fraud cause of action in the course of deciding the Holy See's appeal. To establish jurisdiction over an entity covered by the FSIA, each *individual* claim contained in the complaint must come within an exception to foreign sovereign immunity. *See Joseph v. Office of the Consulate Gen. of Nigeria,* 830 F.2d 1018, 1023–25 (9th Cir. 1987) (analyzing separately whether each of plaintiff's claims came within an exception to foreign sovereign immunity). Therefore, a holding that Doe's respondeat superior or negligence claims come within one of the FSIA's exceptions does not necessarily decide the question whether the fraud claim does so as well. So the fraud cause of action cannot be viewed as "inextricably intertwined" with Doe's other claims, which would permit us to exercise pendent jurisdiction over it. *Burlington N. & Santa Fe Ry. Co. v. Vaughn,* 509 F.3d 1085, 1093–94 (9th Cir. 2007).

Our consideration of the fraud claim is also not "'necessary to ensure meaningful review of'" the other questions that are properly before us. *Meredith v. Oregon*, 321 F.3d 807, 812 (9th Cir. 2003) (quoting *Swint v. Chambers County Comm'n*, 514 U.S. 35, 51, 115 S. Ct. 1203, 131 L. Ed. 2d 60 (1995)). We have held that decision of an issue is "necessary to ensure meaningful review of" another question only if the assertedly pendent issue provided the basis for the district court's jurisdiction to reach the otherwise appealable question. *Id.* (internal quotation marks omitted) (holding that review of *Younger* abstention decision was necessary to ensure meaningful review of the district court's grant of a preliminary injunction, because in the absence of its *Younger* holding, the district court would not have had jurisdiction to issue the injunction). The denial of the fraud claim in this case, in contrast, was not an essential precursor to the district court's determination that it had jurisdiction over Doe's other causes of action. For these reasons, I agree with the majority that the district court's dismissal of Doe's fraud claim is not properly before us.

At the same time, I entirely disagree with the majority's insistence that we lack jurisdiction to decide in full the question that the Holy See *has* appealed to us: whether the district court erred in denying immunity and exercising jurisdiction over all Doe's non-fraud causes of action. Doe argues in response that the district court's ruling should stand, because either the tortious act exception or the commercial activity exception applies and precludes immunity from suit.

As we have stated over and over again, we may affirm the district court on any ground raised below and supported by the record. *See, e.g., Atel Fin. Corp. v. Quaker Coal Co.,* 321 F.3d 924, 926 (9th Cir. 2003) (*per curiam*) ("We may affirm a district court's judgment on any ground supported by the record, whether or not the decision of the district court relied on the same grounds or reasoning we adopt."); *accord Cigna Prop. & Cas. Ins. Co. v. Polaris Pictures Corp.,* 159 F.3d 412, 418–19 (9th Cir. 1998); *Jackson v. S. Cal. Gas Co.,* 881 F.2d 638, 643 (9th Cir. 1989).

No cross-appeal is required—or appropriate—where we are being asked only to affirm the district court's judgment in full, albeit on a ground rejected by the district court. We have long held that an appellee is required to file a cross-appeal if he seeks "to support modification of the judgment." *Engleson v. Burlington N. R.R. Co.,* 972 F.2d 1038, 1041 (9th Cir. 1992) (internal quotation marks and citation omitted). In contrast, "arguments that support the judgment as entered can be made without a cross-appeal . . . even where the argument being raised has been explicitly rejected by the district court." *Id.* (internal quotation marks and citation omitted); *accord Gilliam v. Nev. Power Co.*, 488 F.3d 1189, 1192 n.3 (9th Cir. 2007) (citing *Engleson*, and holding that an appellee did not need to cross-appeal to argue for a different standard of review than that used by the district court as an alternative ground for affirming the district court's judgment). In other words, "[s]o long as the appellee does not seek to 'enlarge' the rights it obtained under the district court judgment, or to 'lessen' the rights the appellant obtained under that judgment, appellee need not cross-appeal in order to present arguments supporting the judgment." *Rivero v. City & County of San Francisco*, 316 F.3d 857, 862 (9th Cir. 2002); *see also Lee v. Burlington N. Santa Fe Ry. Co.,* 245 F.3d 1102, 1107 (9th Cir. 2001) ("A prevailing party need not cross-petition to defend a judgment on any ground properly raised below, so long as that party seeks to preserve, and not to change, the judgment.").

So, if we conclude that the tortious act exception is insufficient to support jurisdiction over any of Doe's non-fraud claims, we may look to the commercial activity exception as an alternative ground on which to affirm the district court. Contrary to the majority's assertion, by doing so we would not be exercising jurisdiction over Doe's cross-appeal, in which Doe raises a commercial activity exception argument that would permit the exercise of jurisdiction over his fraud claim. Rather, we would be determining whether the record supports *affirmance* of the district court's order as to Doe's non-fraud claims, which is the subject of the Holy See's appeal. Put another way, Doe's cross-appeal asks us to "'enlarge' the rights [he] obtained under the district court judgment," *Rivero*, 316 F.3d at 862, so the majority is quite right that we may not consider his arguments regarding the fraud claim. But Doe needed no cross-appeal to respond to the Holy See's appeal; Doe could—and did—respond by asking us simply to preserve the result that the district court reached, either by following the district court's reasoning or by a different rationale. Our case law clearly permits us to do so.

The majority concludes otherwise, maintaining that deciding the commercial activity issues involves review of a *grant* of immunity. *See* Maj. Op. at 2560–61, 2562 & n.5. But that is simply not so. The district court did decide that the commercial activity exception does not apply, but—except for the fraud cause of action—it did not grant immunity on that basis, as it concluded that there was another basis for denying immunity. So the majority is just wrong when it states, repeatedly, that our reaching the commercial activity exception would entail reviewing a *grant* of immunity.

Moreover, I see no prudential reasons whatever for refusing to exercise our jurisdiction. The application of the commercial activity exception was fully litigated below, the district court decided the question, and the issue has been fully briefed and argued here. *See McClure v. Life Ins. Co. of N. Am.,* 84 F.3d 1129, 1133 (9th Cir. 1996) (holding that we can decline on appeal to affirm a summary judgment on grounds not relied on by the district court if the record is inadequate or the grounds not purely legal); *Badea v. Cox,* 931 F.2d 573, 575 n.2 (9th Cir. 1991) (declining to affirm the district court on an alternative basis "as a prudential matter," because the issue had not been briefed by the government, and raised a question of first impression in this Circuit) (internal quotation marks omitted).

The majority disagrees, maintaining that we should not exercise our prudential jurisdiction to support the district court's denial of immunity, because "a grant of immunity is not interlocutorily appealable at all." Maj. Op. at 2562 n.5. This reasoning, once more, mischaracterizes the state of play. The district court did not grant the Holy See immunity except with regard to the fraud cause of action; as to the rest of Doe's complaint, the district court denied immunity. The exercise of available jurisdiction is thus necessary to decide whether the district court's denial of immunity should stand. I would conclude that we have jurisdiction to decide the applicability of both the tortious act and commercial activity exceptions to the causes of action that are the subject of the Holy See's appeal—that is, all the causes of action alleged against the Holy See in Doe's complaint except for the fraud cause of action.

II. The Commercial Activity Exception

Given my view of the jurisdictional posture of the case, I would reach the merits of the commercial activity question and hold that, although the district court erred in applying the tortious act exception to preserve federal jurisdiction over Doe's non-fraud negligence claims, the district court's result should be affirmed on the alternative rationale that the commercial activity exception applies.[1]

---

1 The discretionary function exclusion, 28 U.S.C. § 1605(a)(5)(A), and the misrepresentation exclusion, *id.* § 1605(a)(5)(B), only provide foreign states and their instrumentalities a safe harbor from the FSIA's tortious act exception, not from the commercial activity exception. *See Export Group v. Reef Indus., Inc.,* 54 F.3d 1466, 1477 (9th Cir. 1995).

As the majority explains, Doe's complaint sufficiently alleged an employment relationship between Ronan and the Holy See under Oregon law. Maj. Op. at 2572–75 (citing *Fearing v. Bucher*, 328 Ore. 367, 977 P.2d 1163 (Or. 1999)). For the reasons explained in greater detail below, I would hold that that relationship constitutes "commercial activity" for purposes of the FSIA.

Ronan was employed not as a member of the Vatican's diplomatic, civil service, or military personnel, the employment of whom we have held to be a quintessentially sovereign activity under the FSIA, but in a non-sovereign—here, religious—capacity. *See Holden v. Canadian Consulate*, 92 F.3d 918, 921 (9th Cir. 1996). Further, Doe's negligence claims are "based upon" the employment relationship between Ronan and the Holy See, as the FSIA requires. 28 U.S.C. § 1605(a)(2). Doe's negligent retention, supervision, and failure to warn causes of action against the Holy See therefore fall within FSIA's commercial activity exception, and the district court has jurisdiction to decide them.

A. The definition of "commercial activity" under the FSIA

The FSIA is often described as having codified the "restrictive" theory of sovereign immunity. *See, e.g.*, H.R. Rep. No. 94-1487, at 7 (1976); *Verlinden B.V. v. Cent. Bank of Nigeria,* 461 U.S. 480, 487, 103 S. Ct. 1962, 76 L. Ed. 2d 81 (1983). Under the restrictive theory, "a state is immune from the jurisdiction of foreign courts as to its sovereign or public acts (*jure imperii*), but not as to those that are private or commercial in character (*jure gestionis*)." *Saudi Arabia v. Nelson*, 507 U.S. 349, 359–60, 113 S. Ct. 1471, 123 L. Ed. 2d 47 (1993). The Supreme Court has explained that a foreign state engages in "commercial" activities when it "do[es] not exercise powers peculiar to sovereigns," but rather "exercise[s] only those powers that can be exercised by private citizens." *Republic of Argentina v. Weltover*, 504 U.S. 607, 614, 112 S. Ct. 2160, 119 L. Ed. 2d 394 (1992) (alteration in original) (internal quotation marks omitted). Clarifying the statute's requirement that courts look not at the "purpose" of a foreign state's actions but rather at the "nature" of its actions, 28 U.S.C. § 1603(e), *Weltover* explained that "the question is not whether the foreign government is acting with a profit motive or instead with the aim of fulfilling uniquely sovereign objectives," but whether the government's actions "are the *type* of actions by which a private party engages in" commerce. 504 U.S. at 614. The reason *why* the sovereign engages in that activity—its purpose or motive—is immaterial.

What is more, no profit need be made, or need even be possible, for the activity to qualify as "commercial." In *Weltover*, Argentina's issuance of bonds to refinance its debt was held to be "commercial activity," even though the consideration Argentina received for them was "in no way commensurate with [their] value." *Id.* at 616 (alteration in original). That fact, the Court held, "ma[de] no difference," because "[e]ngaging in a commercial act does not require the receipt of fair value, or even compliance with the common-law requirements of consideration." *Id.* Applying this understanding, courts have found that non-profit organizations can engage in commercial activity. *See, e.g., Malewicz v. City of Amsterdam,* 362 F. Supp. 2d 298, 314 (D. D.C. 2005) (holding that the loan of artwork by a Dutch non-profit museum to non-profit museums in the United States constitutes commercial activity, because exchanging artwork is an activity in which private individuals *can* engage, sometimes for profit).

In sum, a foreign state engages in commercial activity when it engages in acts that any private citizen has the power to undertake, regardless of the state's motive or the possibility of making a profit therefrom. Applying the *Weltover* definition of "commercial activity," this Circuit has repeatedly held that an employment relationship between a foreign sovereign and its employee constitutes commercial activity, so long as the employee is not a civil service, diplomatic, or military employee. In *Holden v. Canadian Consulate,* 92 F.3d 918 (9th Cir. 1996), for example, a former "Commercial Officer" in the "Trade and Investment Section" of the Canadian Consulate in San Francisco brought an action alleging that the Canadian government illegally discriminated against her on the basis of sex and age. *Id.* at 919–20. Examining the FSIA's legislative history, we noted that the House Report listed "the employment of diplomatic, civil service, or military personnel . . . by the Foreign state in the United States" as examples of acts that are "public or governmental and not commercial in nature." *Id.* at 921 (quoting H.R. Rep. No. 94-1487, at 16). In contrast, the "employment or engagement of [such other employees as] laborers, clerical staff or public relations or marketing agents would be . . . included within the definition of commercial activity." *Id.* (quoting H.R. Rep. No. 94-1487, at 16). Based on this legislative history, we held that employment "of diplomatic, civil service or military personnel is governmental and the employment of other personnel is commercial." *Id.*

We applied the *Holden* standard to the hiring of a domestic servant for a diplomat's residence in *Park v. Shin,* 313 F.3d 1138 (9th Cir. 2002). Park brought an action against the Deputy Consul General of the Korean Consulate in San Francisco, alleging that during her tenure as a domestic servant in the Deputy Consul General's home, the Deputy Consul General withheld her pay, denied her medical care, and confiscated her passport. *Id.* at 1140–41. We held that the commercial activity exception applied because "[t]he act of hiring a domestic servant is not an inherently public act that only a government could perform." *Id.* at 1145. Because the plaintiff's claims were based on an employment relationship with the defendant, the defendant was not entitled to sovereign immunity. *Id.*

B. The employment relationship between Ronan and the Holy See

Under this understanding of the phrase "commercial activity," Doe's negligence claims without doubt come within the commercial activity exception.

Doe's amended complaint explains that the Holy See has both "ecclesiastical" and "governmental" functions. In its governmental role, the Holy See undertakes certain functions that are undoubtedly sovereign. It maintains a volunteer military to defend the territory of Vatican City, over which it has complete control; it may enact laws with domestic effect and enter into international treaties and compacts with other nations; and it sends and receives diplomatic representatives to and from other states.[2] Under the analysis we set forth in *Holden*, had Ronan been employed to perform any of these "diplomatic, civil service, or military" functions, his employment by the Vatican would have fallen outside the FSIA's commercial activity exception. 92 F.3d at 921.

But, on the allegations in the complaint, Ronan was not a civil service, diplomatic, or military employee—the types of employees that only sovereign states can employ. Nor is there any evidence that Ronan was "privy to any governmental policy deliberations" or that he engaged in "legislative work" on behalf of the Holy See. *Id.* at 922. Rather, the Holy See hired Ronan to perform ecclesiastical and parochial services—to provide "religious and pastoral guidance, education and counseling services" to the Church's faithful. Providing religious, educational, and counseling services is not a peculiarly governmental function; it is something that non-governmental employers can do.

To reach this conclusion, I do not rely at all on the consideration that "churches receive financial support from their parishioners." Maj. Op. at 2561. The fact that Ronan's provision of pastoral services coincides with and depends upon his parishioners giving donations is neither necessary nor sufficient to show that the Holy See's employment of Ronan is a commercial activity under *Weltover's* nature-not-purpose test. *Weltover*, 504 U.S. at 614. Instead, the critical factor in the commercial activity analysis in this case is that the Holy See's employment activities alleged in Doe's complaint are not distinctly *sovereign* in nature—that they are the sort of functions that private parties, not just sovereign governments, can perform. *See Holden*, 92 F.3d at 921. So approached, the application of the FSIA commercial activity exception to Doe's complaint is not an "arcane question," *see* Maj. Op. at 2561, but a straightforward matter of applying our own binding case law.

I recognize that the Holy See's dual role as not only a sovereign government but also the head of a worldwide church gives this case a peculiar complexion. But that sense of oddity comes about because the Holy See is a sovereign of a very unusual kind. Both in physical size and number of inhabitants, the land it governs is tiny. Its role as a traditional, sovereign government entity is correspondingly small, when compared to its role in running an extremely large international religious organization.

The fact that the Holy See is unique among sovereigns in this respect does not, however, necessitate deviating from the rules we normally follow in construing and applying the FSIA. The operation of a huge international religious institution

---

2 *See* U.S. Dep't of State, Background Note: Holy See, July 2008, http://www.state.gov/r/pa/ei/bgn/3819.htm. Although these facts are not mentioned in the complaint, I take judicial notice of them pursuant to Fed. R. Evid. 201(b).

is a large task, and one of great importance to many people. But it is not an activity that may be undertaken only by *sovereign* states, which is the focus of the FSIA's commercial activity exception.

Indeed, in most cases it is nongovernmental entities, not governments, that operate international religious institutions, the Mormon Church and the Greek Orthodox Church being two prominent examples. The FSIA's purpose is not to insulate religious institutions from suit; it juxtaposes commercial activities not to *religious* activities, but to *governmental* activities. The Holy See differs from other foreign states in the *nature* of the non-sovereign activities it carries out and, in all likelihood, in the ratio of its non-sovereign activities to its sovereign activities. But it is like other sovereigns in the respect essential here: It engages in a range of non-sovereign activities in the United States, and the FSIA's commercial activity exception lifts the shield of immunity from such non-sovereign activities.

The district court nonetheless expressed discomfort with characterizing the Holy See's employment of Ronan as "commercial" activity for FSIA purposes, observing that the Holy See's employment of clergy is "widely viewed as the antithesis of commerciality." *Doe*, 434 F. Supp. 2d at 941. Commerciality and religiosity are, indeed, often viewed as antithetical categories. But, as I have explained, the FSIA's "commercial activity" phrase, as it has been interpreted in the case law, is a term of art, not reliant on common usage, which reflects the special concerns of a sovereign immunity statute. The district court's discomfort notwithstanding, under well-established FSIA principles and our own binding case law the employment relationship that existed between Ronan and the Holy See does constitute "commercial activity of a foreign state."

C. Doe's negligence claims are "based upon" commercial activity

Under the FSIA's commercial activity exception, it is not enough for the plaintiff to show that the defendant engaged in something that qualifies as a commercial activity under the *Weltover* test. The plaintiff must also show that his cause of action is related to that commercial activity in one of three ways, depending upon the geographical location where the activity occurred. 28 U.S.C. § 1605(a)(2). In Clause 1 of § 1605(a)(2), the FSIA requires that if the foreign state's commercial activity is carried on inside the United States, the plaintiff's cause of action must be "based upon" that activity itself. Alternatively, if the commercial activity is not carried on inside the United States, the plaintiff's cause of action must be "[based] upon" an act performed inside the United States in connection with the commercial activity elsewhere, *id.* [Clause 2], or else "[based] upon" an act performed outside the United States in connection with commercial activity elsewhere that causes a "direct effect" in the United States. *Id.* [Clause 3]. Doe asserts that his claims may go forward under either Clause 1 or Clause 3 of the commercial activity exception.

Saudi Arabia v. Nelson, 507 U.S. 349, 113 S. Ct. 1471, 123 L. Ed. 2d 47 (1993), provides the leading interpretation of the FSIA's "based upon" requirement.

Nelson explained that "[i]n denoting conduct that forms the 'basis,' or 'foundation,' for a claim, the phrase is read most naturally to mean those elements of a claim that, if proven, would entitle a plaintiff to relief under his theory of the case." *Id.* at 357 (internal citations omitted). As the district court here correctly noted, "[t]he commercial activity must do more than *lead to* the injuries plaintiff suffered"; it must be "involved in proving" one of the elements of plaintiff's cause of action. *Doe*, 434 F. Supp. 2d at 943 (quoting *Sun v. Taiwan,* 201 F.3d 1105, 1110 (9th Cir. 2000)) (internal quotations omitted).

Applying this standard, I would hold that Doe's negligence claims were "based upon" the Holy See's employment of Ronan within the meaning of the statute. The existence of that employment relationship is a necessary element of at least the negligent retention and supervision claims. *See Chesterman v. Barmon*, 82 Ore. App. 1, 4, 727 P.2d 130 (1986) (in assessing whether plaintiff had sufficiently alleged a negligent retention claim, requiring that the individual who caused the harm be an "employee" of defendant). *See also* Restatement (Second) of Torts § 317 ("A master is under a duty to exercise reasonable care so to control his servant.")[3]; *accord DiPietro v. Lighthouse Ministries,* 159 Ohio App. 3d 766, 772, 2005 Ohio 639, 825 N.E.2d 630 (2005) (holding that "[i]n order to prevail on a claim of negligent retention, plaintiff must establish . . . the existence of an employment relationship") (internal quotation marks and citation omitted).

Because Ronan's activities pursuant to the employment relationship occurred inside the United States, it may be that Clause 1 of the FSIA's commercial activity provision is satisfied: Arguably, the Holy See's alleged negligent acts were "based on" an employment relationship that, at least in part, was "carried on in the United States," as well as in Rome. 28 U.S.C. § 1605(a)(2) [Clause 1]. Whether or not Clause 1 applies, however, I think it quite clear that jurisdiction arises under § 1605(a)(2)'s Clause 3, regarding acts performed outside U.S. territory in connection with a foreign state's commercial activity that have a "direct effect" inside the United States. *Id.* [Clause 3].

Doe alleges that the Holy See participated in the decision to retain and reassign Ronan rather than terminating his employment, an act that we can infer was taken outside the United States in connection with Ronan's employment, and that had a direct effect in the United States—Ronan's ability to carry out his molestation of Doe. Taking his allegations as true, Doe has satisfied Clause 3 as to his negligent supervision and retention claims.

Determining whether Doe's "failure to warn" claim is based upon the alleged employment relationship requires looking to Oregon's "failure to warn" case law,

---

3 I rely on the Restatement (Second) of Torts as evidence of Oregon law because it is frequently relied on by the Oregon Supreme Court in negligence cases. *See, e.g., Wallach v. Allstate Ins. Co.*, 344 Ore. 314, 320, 180 P.3d 19 (2008); *Bailey v. Lewis Farm, Inc.*, 343 Ore. 276, 285, 171 P.3d 336 (2007).

of which there is relatively little. In general, under Oregon law, a defendant is not liable for a negligent omission that leads to a plaintiff being harmed by a third party unless the defendant has a "special relationship" either to the third party or to the plaintiff. *See* Restatement (Second) of Torts § 302 cmt. a. Such a special relationship may exist if, for example, the defendant "has brought into contact or association with the other a person whom the actor knows or should know to be peculiarly likely to commit intentional misconduct." Restatement (Second) of Torts § 302B cmt. e(D); *cf. Brown v. Washington County,* 163 Ore. App. 362, 987 P.2d 1254 (1999) (holding that defendant could be held liable for failure to warn about the dangerousness of an inmate within its custody).

According to Doe's complaint, it was the Holy See's continued employment of Ronan in a position of authority that led to Doe's contact with Ronan, and thus to the Holy See's duty to warn Doe and the other parishioners about Ronan's abusive past and potential future dangerousness. So Doe's negligent failure to warn claim is also "based upon" a commercial activity, in that it is the result of non-sovereign actions undertaken elsewhere - the decision not to warn about an employee's dangerousness - with a "direct effect" in the United States. § 1605(a)(2) [Clause 3]. I would therefore hold that the district court has jurisdiction to decide it.

D. The "essence" of Doe's claims

Although the district court determined, as I would, that Doe's allegations satisfied the requirements of the commercial activity exception, it ultimately held the commercial activity exception inapplicable. *See Doe*, 434 F. Supp. 2d at 941–42. It did so because, following what it considered to be "the overarching principle in *Nelson*," it concluded that it could not "fairly characterize[ ] [the activities described in the complaint] as commercial." *Id.* at 947. Rather, it explained that "at the heart of plaintiff's complaint is the injury inflicted by a sexually abusive priest at plaintiff's church, a claim clearly sounding in tort." *Id.* at 942. On the district court's reading of *Nelson*, if the "essence" of a plaintiff's complaint sounds in tort, *id.*, the plaintiff's claims can proceed only under the FSIA's tortious act exception, or not at all.

The Sixth Circuit recently came to a similar conclusion in *O'Bryan v. Holy See*, Nos. 07-5078, 07-5163, 556 F.3d 361, 2009 U.S. App. LEXIS 2412, 2009 WL 305342 (6th Cir. Feb. 10, 2009). *O'Bryan* held that, because the "true essence" or "gravamen" of the wrongful activities alleged in the plaintiff's complaint sounded like torts, the court could exercise jurisdiction over the Holy See only through the FSIA's tortious act exception. *O'Bryan*, 2009 U.S. App. LEXIS 2412, 2009 WL 305342, at *11–12, 16–17. It therefore held the commercial activity exception inapplicable to the Holy See's employment activities.

I disagree that the arguably tortious "essence" of Doe's claims renders the commercial activity exception unavailable to him. Nothing in the FSIA suggests that the commercial activity exception and the tortious act exception are mutually exclusive and cannot possibly apply to the same conduct. Nor does *Nelson*, or any other controlling case, authorize reading such a requirement into the statute.

In *Nelson*, the plaintiff entered into an employment contract in the United States with a Saudi Arabian hospital operated by the government of Saudi Arabia. 507 U.S. at 351–52. He then moved to Saudi Arabia, where he worked as an engineer for the hospital. *Id.* at 352. After he reported several safety violations to his superiors, he was arrested by the Saudi national police, imprisoned, and tortured. *Id.* at 352–53. He sued in U.S. federal court, alleging several intentional tort causes of action based on his imprisonment and torture, as well as a claim regarding the hospital's negligent failure to warn him, during the contract negotiations in the United States, that he would be subject to imprisonment and torture if he reported safety violations. *Id.* at 353–54. He argued that there was jurisdiction over his claims under the first clause of the commercial activity exception.

The Supreme Court concluded that there was no jurisdiction over any of his causes of action. His intentional tort claims could not proceed under the commercial activity exception because "a foreign state's exercise of the power of its police" is an act "which is peculiarly sovereign in nature," and therefore not "commercial" within the meaning of the FSIA. *Id.* at 361. As to the "failure to warn" claim, the Court concluded that the plaintiff could not meet the statute's requirement that his claim be "based upon the commercial activity" of Saudi Arabia merely by phrasing his claim in terms of the contract negotiations in the United States during which the failure to warn allegedly occurred. "[A] plaintiff could recast virtually any claim of intentional tort committed by sovereign act as a claim of failure to warn. . . . To give jurisdictional significance to this feint of language would effectively thwart the Act's manifest purpose." *Id.* at 363.

In analyzing the failure to warn claim, then, *Nelson* simply applied the general principle that the court does not accept a plaintiff's mischaracterization of the legal significance of the facts he has alleged, but will look "beyond the complaint's characterization to the conduct on which the claim is based." *Blaxland v. Commonwealth Dir. of Pub. Prosecutions*, 323 F.3d 1198, 1203 (9th Cir. 2003) (quoting *Mt. Homes, Inc. v. United States*, 912 F.2d 352, 356 (9th Cir. 1990)).[4]

Here, unlike in *Nelson*, Doe's negligent retention, supervision, and failure to warn claims are not simply a "feint of language" to obtain jurisdiction through the commercial activity exception. *Nelson*, 507 U.S. at 363. Doe has alleged that the Holy See continued to employee Ronan, and placed him in the Archdiocese where he molested Doe, even after the Holy See was aware that Ronan had molested young boys on at least two prior occasions while in its employ. He has alleged further that the Holy See did not inform Doe or his parents of what it knew about Ronan's

4 For example, if a plaintiff has alleged conduct that clearly amounts to false arrest, but has called his claim one for "false imprisonment," the court will not simply accept that latter characterization. *Blaxland*, 323 F.3d at 1204–06.

dangerousness, despite its position of trust with respect to Doe and its employment relationship with Ronan. Doe's negligence claims are not a mischaracterization of the factual allegations he has made, but are in fact among the central wrongs he alleges.[5]

In summary, I see no reason why claims arising from actions with an arguably tortious "essence" cannot proceed under the commercial activity exception. As noted above, the phrase "commercial activity" in the FSIA is a term of art. Neither the statute, nor any controlling case, requires the conclusion that the commercial activity exception is necessarily inapplicable whenever the label "tort" would be, in common usage, a better description of the harms a plaintiff alleges.

E. The Holy See's First Amendment argument

The Holy See contends that reading the FSIA to allow federal jurisdiction over Doe's claims via the commercial activity exception would violate the First Amendment, because adjudicating the case will require the judicial interpretation of such religious doctrine as the vow of obedience that members of the clergy offer to the Pope. This contention cannot get off the ground because, as a foreign sovereign, the Holy See has no rights under the First Amendment.[6]

Neither we nor the Supreme Court have previously addressed whether foreign sovereigns enjoy the benefit of any rights under the Constitution of the United States. *Cf. Weltover,* 504 U.S. at 619 (leaving open the question whether foreign states enjoy rights under the due process clause). The D.C. Circuit, however, has

---

5 Nor does our decision in *Randolph v. Budget Rent-A-Car*, 97 F.3d 319 (9th Cir. 1996), require any different result. *Randolph* concerned a Saudi student trainee studying in the United States on a scholarship from Saudia airlines, an instrumentality of the Saudi government. *Id.* at 327. While living in this country, the student "negligently crashed his rented automobile into John Randolph's motorcycle." *Id.* at 323. We held that Randolph's respondeat superior claims against Saudia could not come within the tortious act exception to the FSIA because the student was not an "employee" of Saudia. *Id.* at 325–29. Addressing the commercial activity exception, we concluded that the lack of an employment relationship meant that the allegations simply had no nexus to any commercial activity of Saudia: "[N]ot only must the activity be commercial in nature, but the commercial activity must cause the harm alleged. . . . The specific acts of which plaintiff complains did not arise out of Saudia's commercial activity in the United States." *Id.* at 324.

We also observed that "plaintiffs' personal injury lawsuit sounds in tort and centers on the non-commercial negligence of a purported employee." *Id.* This observation, however, must be considered in the context of the conclusion that there was no employment relationship between Saudia and the student. In the absence of such a connection, there was only the tort of negligent driving by a student unconnected to Saudia, and no "commercial activity." In this case, in contrast, Doe has clearly alleged an employment relationship between the Holy See and Ronan and a nexus between the employment relationship and the harm he suffered. That relationship supplies the commercial activity missing in *Randolph*.

6 The Archdiocese, the Catholic Bishop, and the Order, which are not foreign sovereigns and are residents of the United States, are, of course, entitled to First Amendment protections.

concluded that foreign sovereigns are not entitled to rights under the due process clause of the Fifth Amendment, and much of its reasoning on that question is relevant here. *See Price v. Socialist People's Libyan Arab Jamahiriya*, 352 U.S. App. D.C. 284, 294 F.3d 82, 96 (D.C. Cir. 2002).

The D.C. Circuit explained that foreign sovereign nations are not members of the political community for whose benefit the *Bill of Rights* was adopted. They "are entirely alien to our constitutional system," *id.*, and so the protections to which they are entitled have traditionally been governed not by domestic constitutional law, but by international law. *Id.* at 97; *see also Principality of Monaco v. Mississippi*, 292 U.S. 313, 330, 54 S. Ct. 745, 78 L. Ed. 1282 (1934) (foreign sovereigns are "outside the structure of the Union."). Unlike private individuals, "sovereign states interact with each other through diplomacy and even coercion in ways not affected by constitutional protections." *Nat'l Council of Resistance of Iran v. Dep't of State,* 346 U.S. App. D.C. 131, 251 F.3d 192, 202 (D.C. Cir. 2001). They also have recourse to international dispute-resolution mechanisms to which private individuals have no access. Indeed, the FSIA is in part a recognition that grievances against foreign states are sometimes better resolved in these other arenas, not in U.S. courts. In this context, there seems no basis for extending constitutional protections to foreign states in their capacity as such. *Accord O'Bryan v. Holy See*, 471 F. Supp. 2d 784, 794 (W.D. Ky. 2007) (the "Holy See cannot simultaneously seek the protections of the FSIA and the United States Constitution.").

In addition, as the D.C. Circuit observed in *Price*, "serious practical problems might arise were we to hold that foreign states may cloak themselves in the protections of the" Constitution. *Price*, 294 F.3d at 99. It would be thoroughly anomalous to permit the executive branch to be constrained in its conduct of foreign relations by assertions by foreign sovereigns of entitlement to the protections of the First Amendment. I would therefore reject the Holy See's contention that foreign sovereigns have First Amendment rights under the U.S. Constitution, holding that the district court's exercise of jurisdiction over Doe's claims presents no First Amendment concerns.

III. Conclusion

For the foregoing reasons, I would affirm the district court's judgment, holding that the FSIA's commercial activity exception permits it to exercise jurisdiction over Doe's non-fraud negligence claims.

CONCUR

FERNANDEZ, Circuit Judge, concurring: I agree that we cannot consider the commercial exception to the Foreign Sovereign Immunities Act, 28 USC § 1605(a)(2). But, Judge Berzon does not and has, therefore, gone on to opine that all (or virtually all) activities by churches are actually commercial activity. While I recognize that her opinion cannot be precedential and that a response from me cannot be either, I am loath to leave her disquisition standing alone. Thus, I cannot (or at least will not) refrain from offering my own view on the rather oxymoronic proposition that church functions are commercial.

As I see it, Doe's claim that church functions are simply commercial transactions because parishioners do give donations to the church bespeaks the veriest cynicism about religion and a church's position within religion.[1] Could a church spread the word of God without some funds? Would that it could, but the need for support does not mean that the holy activity is commercial. Is the Mass the marketing of a form of edifying entertainment? Is hearing confessions and giving religious advice—an age-old function of churches—really no more than a commercial activity similar to psychological counseling? Is the sacrament of Holy Eucharist the marketing of bread and wine or is the sacrament of Extreme Unction the marketing of oil? I think not. Normal legal usage and common sense recoil from those possibilities. *See United States v. Lamont*, 330 F.3d 1249, 1254–55 (9th Cir. 2003).

Nor does the statute or the case law suggest that the Holy See's religious activities must be commercial. The FSIA tells us that "[a] 'commercial activity' means either a regular course of commercial conduct or a particular commercial transaction or act." 28 U.S.C. § 1603(d). That does not help much, but it also does not say that every possibly private activity is commercial. It says only that commercial behavior is commercial activity. As the Supreme Court has, somewhat more helpfully, stated:

> [W]e conclude that when a foreign government acts, not as a regulator of a market, but in the manner of private player within it, the foreign sovereign's actions are "commercial" within the meaning of the FSIA. Moreover, because the Act provides that the commercial character of an act is to be determined by reference to its "nature" rather than its "purpose" . . . , the question is not whether the foreign government is acting with a profit motive or instead with the aim of fulfilling uniquely sovereign objectives. Rather, the issue is whether the particular actions that the foreign state performs . . . are the *type* of actions by which a private party engages in "trade and traffic or commerce[.]"

Republic of Arg. v. Weltover, Inc., 504 U.S. 607, 614, 112 S. Ct. 2160, 2166, 119 L. Ed. 2d 394 (1992) (citations omitted). Some have focused on the "private player"

---

1 It may be suggested that whether parishioners donate matters not at all. If so, the result is even more jarring than Doe's proposition.

language, but what is truly significant is the emphasis on the market and on "trade and traffic or commerce." *Id.*

I fail to see how engaging in providing religious counseling is "trade and traffic or commerce." *Id.* Nor, by the way, can a mere private actor give priestly counseling or consolation to a believer. This does not require a focus on purpose; it goes to the very nature of the religious activity itself. Similarly, we have noted that: "[t]he commercial activity exception applies only where the sovereign acts 'in the market in the manner of a private player.'" *Holden v. Canadian Consulate*, 92 F.3d 918, 920 (9th Cir. 1996). Again, Holy See has not acted in the market at all. It has simply supplied religious counseling to a church communicant, a service that this unique sovereign entity is designed for.[2]

I think that the problem this case seems to present lies in the fact that Holy See is an unusual type of foreign sovereign. Most governments do, indeed, exist to afford their citizens a degree of physical protection and guidance, so that they may thrive in this world. Holy See is more focused on the next world, and that makes a universe of difference. Because of that, Holy See's sovereign activities are not simply the passage of mortal laws and the enforcement of those. They, basically, encompass the furnishing of the kinds of services that only Holy See can give: its own kind of religious help, guidance and counseling. It may do more than most sovereigns do, but it is not engaged in the market or in commerce.[3]

In short, Holy See may not be your typical sovereign, but neither is it your typical merchant. Does that lead to some kind of impasse? Of course not. It leads back to the statute itself. Holy See is a foreign state and the commercial activity exception does not strip its immunity from it. Something else may do so, but not that exception.[4] We hierophants of the law are adept at redefining ordinary concepts, but it is no more appropriate to declare that religious services are commercial activities than it would be to declare that ponies are small birds.[5]

Therefore, if we had jurisdiction I would not apply the commercial activity exception to this case.

---

2 Similarly, Father Ronan was not simply supplying commercial advice and services, nor was he a domestic servant. *Cf. Park v. Shin*, 313 F.3d 1138, 1140–41 (9th Cir. 2002) (domestic servant service); *Holden*, 92 F.3d at 919 (commercial officer). Rather, he held his position for the purpose of giving the very kind of ecclesiastical services to the faithful that lie at the heart of this sovereign's reason for being.

3 That is not to say that Holy See could not participate in commercial activities. It is only to say that the activities of the type that are involved here cannot be so dubbed.

4 The Sixth Circuit has reached the same result but for different reasons. *See O'Bryan v. Holy See,* 556 F.3d 361, 377–81, Nos. 07-5078, 07-5163, 2009 U.S. App. LEXIS 2412 at *34–38, 2009 WL 305342, at *9–12 (6th Cir. Feb. 10, 2009). So, too, did the district court in this case. *See Doe v. Holy See*, 434 F. Supp. 2d 925, 946–47 (D. Or. 2006).

5 *See Regina v. Ojibway*, 8 Crim. L.Q. 137 (Oct. 1965).

III. PROCEDURE

8. Exceptions & Limitations

A. Foreign Sovereign Immunities Act

ii. Terrorism Exception*

* Cases are indexed under this subject. The full text of these cases is published in the **volume**-page indicated.

ZACHARY BAUMEL
v.
SYRIAN ARAB REPUBLIC

F. Supp. 2d 39 (D.D.C. 2009)
Decided November 3, 2009

Thomas J. Luz, Karaahmetoglu & Luz Firm, LLP, New York, NY, for Plaintiffs.

Ramsey Clark, Clark & Schilling, New York, NY, for Defendants.

MEMORANDUM OPINION

ROSEMARY M. COLLYER, District Judge.

This is an action brought on behalf of Zachary Baumel against the Syrian Arab Republic and the Popular Front for the Liberation of Palestine and certain of their officials for alleged hostage-taking and torture.[1] Syria moves to dismiss for lack of jurisdiction under Federal Rule of Civil Procedure 12(b)(1) and/or for failure to state a claim upon which relief can be granted under Federal Rule of Civil Procedure 12(b)(6). Plaintiffs oppose. For the reasons explained herein, the motion will be granted under Rule 12(b)(6), and the case dismissed against all Defendants.

I. Facts

The facts are taken from Plaintiffs' Amended Complaint [Dkt. #50] and are assumed to be true. Mr. Baumel, a United States citizen, was a resident of the State of New York who relocated to Israel in 1970 and later joined the Israeli Defense Forces Armored Corps. On June 11, 1982, Mr. Baumel was captured by the Syrian

1 Individual Defendants include Syrian President Bashar Al-Assad; Syrian Foreign Minister Imad Moustapha; former Syrian Foreign Minister Farouq Al-Shaara; former Syrian Defense Minister Moustapha Tlaas; "former high-ranking member of the Syrian Military," Rifaat Assad; John Doe # 1, as Representative of the Estate of Hafez Al-Assad; and Achmed Jibril, leader of the Popular Front for the Liberation of Palestine. Since filing this case on April 14, 2006, Plaintiffs have been attempting to serve the Popular Front for the Liberation of Palestine and the individual Defendants. On June 18, 2009, Plaintiffs filed a mandamus suit against the Secretary of State to compel service of process on the individual Syrian Defendants. *See Baumel v. United States,* Civil Action No. 09-1126 (D.D.C. June 18, 2009).

Army or a Palestinian group loyal to Syria while serving in the Israeli Defense Forces Armored Corps in Southern Lebanon during war between Israel and Syria.[2] Thereafter, Mr. Baumel was taken to Damascus as a hostage of the Syrian Army, where he was displayed as a trophy of war, along with his tank and the other Israeli soldiers captured with him, in a victory parade. Mr. Baumel has not been seen by representatives of Israel, the United States Red Cross, or his family since. Nor has the United States, Israel, news agencies, or the International Committee for the Red Cross been given access to him.

Thereafter, Defendants claimed that Mr. Baumel had died and that they had buried his body with those of other captured Israeli soldiers in the Jewish cemetery in Damascus. With Syria's permission, the International Committee for the Red Cross assisted in the exhumation of four bodies that Syria claimed were bodies of the missing Israeli soldiers. Forensic analysis of the bodies indicated that only one was the body of an Israeli soldier, but not Mr. Baumel. The others were Arabs.

Upon Plaintiffs' "information and belief"

1. Mr. Baumel, his fellow Israeli soldiers, and their tank were taken to Damascus and were stationed in front of Syria's military offices. Thereafter, Mr. Baumel was incarcerated.

2. Mr. Baumel has been "immobilized; blindfolded; held in various and different places for months; transported from location to location; shackled; left in a constant state of disorientation and fear for his life; kept in solitary confinement; confined in cramped, airless rooms, permitted little or no exercise; given only minimal and infrequent access to toilet facilities; fed an unbalanced, monotonous and inadequate diet; physically abused; beaten with fists, guns and sticks; and subjected to verbal abuse, taunts and humiliation." Am. Compl. ¶ 33.

3. Mr. Baumel has been "threatened with death by his captors, denied proper medical attention and medication, denied contact with the outside world, including his family, friends and colleagues, and forced to endure severe physical discomfort, injury, mental anguish, depression, humiliation, anxiety, and pain and suffering." *Id.* ¶ 34.

4. Mr. Baumel has been "deprived of educational and employment opportunities and advancement, and has been unable to provide financially for his family during his captivity." *Id.* ¶ 35.

5. Mr. Baumel has been "deprived of the opportunity to socialize, meet and engage in social contact with people of his age for the purpose [of] social

---

2 The Court notes that at the time of Mr. Baumel's alleged capture by Syria in Lebanon, a state of war existed between Israel and Syria, and Lebanon was at the front of that war. *See, e.g.*, U.S. Department of State, *http://www.state.gov/r/pa/ei/bgn/3580.htm* ("Following the 1982 Israeli invasion of Lebanon, Syrian and Israeli forces clashed in eastern Lebanon.").

interchange and prospects of marriage and concerning the creation and raising of his own family." *Id.* ¶ 36.

Plaintiffs, Mr. Baumel's parents, siblings, and his next friend, sue all Defendants for battery (Count I), assault (Count II), false imprisonment (Count III), economic damages (Count IV), intentional infliction of emotional distress (Count V), loss of solatium (Count VI), and punitive damages (Count VII). The Syrian Arab Republic, the only Defendant served, moves to dismiss.

II. Legal Standards

A motion to dismiss pursuant to Federal Rule of Civil Procedure 12(b)(6) challenges the adequacy of a complaint on its face, testing whether a plaintiff has properly stated a claim. Federal Rule of Civil Procedure 8(a) requires a complaint to contain "a short and plain statement of the claim showing that the pleader is entitled to relief." Fed.R.Civ.P. 8(a). A complaint must be sufficient "to give a defendant fair notice of what the . . . claim is and the grounds upon which it rests." *Bell Atl. Corp. v. Twombly,* 550 U.S. 544, 555, 127 S.Ct. 1955, 167 L.Ed.2d 929 (2007) (internal citations omitted). Although a complaint does not need detailed factual allegations, a plaintiff's obligation to provide the grounds of his entitlement to relief "requires more than labels and conclusions, and a formulaic recitation of the elements of a cause of action will not do." *Id.* The facts alleged "must be enough to raise a right to relief above the speculative level." *Id.* Rule 8(a) requires an actual showing and not just a blanket assertion of a right to relief. *Id.* at 555 n. 3, 127 S.Ct. 1955. "[A] complaint needs *some* information about the circumstances giving rise to the claims." *Aktieselskabet AF 21. Nov. 2001 v. Fame Jeans, Inc.,* 525 F.3d 8, 16 n. 4 (D.C.Cir.2008) (emphasis in original).

In deciding a motion under Rule 12(b)(6), a court may consider the facts alleged in the complaint, documents attached to the complaint as exhibits or incorporated by reference, and matters about which the court may take judicial notice. *Abhe & Svoboda, Inc. v. Chao,* 508 F.3d 1052, 1059 (D.C.Cir.2007). To survive a motion to dismiss, a complaint must contain sufficient factual matter, accepted as true, to state a claim for relief that is "plausible on its face." *Twombly,* 550 U.S. at 570, 127 S.Ct. 1955. When a plaintiff pleads factual content that allows the court to draw the reasonable inference that the defendant is liable for the misconduct alleged, then the claim has facial plausibility. *Ashcroft v. Iqbal,* ___ U.S. ___, 129 S.Ct. 1937, 1949, 173 L.Ed.2d 868 (2009). "The plausibility standard is not akin to a 'probability requirement,' but it asks for more than a sheer possibility that a defendant has acted unlawfully." *Id.*

A court must treat the complaint's factual allegations as true, "even if doubtful in fact." *Twombly,* 550 U.S. at 555, 127 S.Ct. 1955. But a court need not accept as true legal conclusions set forth in a complaint. *Iqbal,* 129 S.Ct. at 1949. "Threadbare recitals of the elements of a cause of action, supported by mere conclusory statements, do not suffice." *Id.* "While legal conclusions can provide the framework of a complaint, they must be supported by factual allegations. When there are well-pleaded factual allegations, a court should assume their veracity and then determine whether they plausibly give rise to an entitlement to relief." *Id.* at 1950.

III. Analysis

Plaintiffs filed this lawsuit on April 14, 2006, under 28 U.S.C. § 1605(a)(7), an exception to the Foreign Sovereign Immunities Act ("FSIA"), 28 U.S.C. § 1602 *et seq.,* that waives the sovereign immunity of a designated foreign state in actions in which money damages are sought for personal injury or death caused by one of the specified acts of terrorism. *Cicippio-Puleo v. Islamic Republic of Iran,* 353 F.3d 1024, 1032 (D.C.Cir.2004). "Section 1605(a)(7) is merely a jurisdiction conferring provision that does not otherwise provide a cause of action against either a foreign state or its agents." *Id.* Under this statutory scheme, a plaintiff could bring suit against a foreign state and a federal court would have jurisdiction under § 1605(a)(7)—but the substance of the claims against the foreign state would be derived from the law of the relevant U.S. state under § 1606. Section 1606 provides: "[T]he foreign state shall be liable in the same manner and to the same extent as a private individual under like circumstances; but a foreign state except for an agency or instrumentality thereof shall not be liable for punitive damages." 28 U.S.C. § 1606. Section 1606 functioned as a "pass through," and in this way foreign states could be liable via § 1606 under another specific source of law, such as state law. *See, e.g., Oveissi v. Islamic Republic of Iran,* 573 F.3d 835, 840 (D.C.Cir.2009) (citing *Acree v. Republic of Iraq,* 370 F.3d 41, 59 (D.C.Cir.2004), *abrogated on other grounds by Republic of Iraq v. Beaty,* ___ U.S. ___, 129 S.Ct. 2183, 173 L.Ed.2d 1193 (2009)); *Heiser v. Islamic Republic of Iran,* 466 F.Supp.2d 229, 265–66 (D.D.C.2006); *Dammarell v. Islamic Republic of Iran,* Civ. No. 01-2224, 2005 WL 756090, at *1 (D.D.C. Mar. 29, 2005). Despite the applicability of other sources of law, § 1606 provided that foreign states were expressly exempt from liability for punitive damages. *Fisher v. Great Socialist People's Libyan Arab Jamahiriya,* 541 F.Supp.2d 46, 53 (D.D.C. 2008).

The Flatow Amendment, 28 U.S.C. § 1605 note, provides a cause of action against "an official, employee, or agent of a foreign state designated as a state sponsor of terrorism" "for personal injury or death caused by acts of that official, employee, or agent for which the courts of the United States may maintain jurisdiction under section 1605(a)(7)." 28 U.S.C. § 1605 note. Thus, "Section 1605(a)(7) merely waives the immunity of a foreign state without creating a cause of action against it," and the Flatow Amendment provides a federal private right of action against officials, employees, and agents of a foreign state, but not against the foreign state itself. *Cicippio-Puleo,* 353 F.3d at 1033.

On January 28, 2008, Congress enacted the National Defense Authorization Act for Fiscal Year 2008 ("NDAA"), Pub.L. No. 110-181, 122 Stat. 3 (2008). Section 1083 of the NDAA revised the state-sponsored terrorism exception to sovereign immunity by repealing § 1605(a)(7) and adding a new exception codified at

§ 1605A. *See* NDAA § 1083. Section 1605A is more advantageous to plaintiffs in several respects—most notably, it creates a federal cause of action against foreign states for which solatium and punitive damages may be awarded. *See* 28 U.S.C. § 1605A ("A foreign state that is or was a state sponsor of terrorism. . . shall be liable . . . for money damages. . . . [D]amages may include economic damages, solatium, pain and suffering, and punitive damages.").

"[A] plaintiff in a case pending under § 1605(a)(7) may not maintain that action based upon the jurisdiction conferred by § 1605A; in order to claim the benefits of § 1605A, the plaintiff must file a new action under that new provision." *Simon v. Republic of Iraq,* 529 F.3d 1187, 1192 (D.C.Cir.2008), *reversed on other grounds sub nom. Republic of Iraq v. Beaty,* ___ U.S. ___, 129 S.Ct. 2183, 173 L.Ed.2d 1193 (2009). However, notwithstanding NDAA § 1083, "courts retain jurisdiction pursuant to § 1605(a)(7) over cases that were pending under that section when the Congress enacted the NDAA." *Id.*

A. Plaintiffs' Cause of Action Against Syria Under § 1605A is Time-Barred

On July 14, 2009, Plaintiffs filed a motion for leave to amend their Complaint under Federal Rule of Civil Procedure 15 to bring a cause of action against Syria under § 1605A. Because Rule 15 "guarantee[s] a plaintiff an absolute right to amend its complaint once at any time before the defendant has filed a responsive pleading," *James V. Hurson Assocs., Inc. v. Glickman,* 229 F.3d 277, 282–83 (D.C.Cir.2000), and because Syria had not filed a responsive pleading, the Court granted Plaintiffs' motion on July 22, 2009.[3]

Syria moves to dismiss the cause of action against it under § 1605A, arguing that it is time-barred. "Plaintiffs with 'pending cases' may invoke new § 1605A in certain circumstances." *Simon,* 529 F.3d at 1192. "Pursuant to § 1083(c)(2) ('Prior Actions'), a plaintiff who detrimentally 'relied upon' former § 1605(a)(7) of the FSIA 'as creating a cause of action' and whose action was 'pending before the courts in any form' when the NDAA became law was given 60 days within which to 'refile' his suit based upon the new cause of action created by § 1605A(c)." *Id.* Section 1083(c)(2) provides that "[a] motion may be made or an action may be refiled under subparagraph (A) *only* within the 60-day period beginning on the date of the enactment of this Act [Jan. 28, 2008]." NDAA § 1083(c)(2)(C)(ii) (emphasis added). Therefore, Plaintiffs had only 60 days from January 28, 2008—that is, until March 28, 2008—to either refile under § 1605A or file a motion requesting that their pending action under § 1605(a)(7) be given effect as if the action had originally been filed under § 1605A. *See In re Islamic Republic of Iran Terrorism Litig.,* Civil Action No. 01-2094, 2009 WL 3112136, at *26 (D.D.C.

---

3 Plaintiffs did not need leave of Court to amend their Complaint because "[a] party may amend its pleading once as a matter of course before being served with a responsive pleading." Fed.R.Civ.P. 15(a)(1)(A).

Sept. 30, 2009) ("Plaintiffs [with cases pending under § 1605(a)(7) at the time the NDAA was enacted] who hope to gain the benefits of the new law by filing a motion or by refiling pursuant to § 1083(c)(2), must file their motions [or refile] 'within the 60-day period beginning on the date of the enactment of the [NDAA],' or no later than March 28, 2008."). Because Plaintiffs did not seek leave to amend their Complaint to bring a cause of action against Syria under § 1605A until July 14, 2009, more than a year too late, that cause of action is time-barred. *See Doe v. U.S. Dep't of Justice,* 753 F.2d 1092, 1115 (D.C.Cir.1985) ("a motion to dismiss [for failure to state a claim] may be granted on the basis that the action is time-barred only when it appears from the face of the complaint that the relevant statute of limitations bars the action").

Plaintiffs argue that they "were permitted to amend their complaint as a matter of course under Rule 15 of the Federal Rules of Civil Procedure" and that they "merely amended their complaint to add a new cause of action under 28 U.S.C. § 1605A, not to retroactively invoke its benefits." Pls.' Mem. in Opp'n to Syria's Mot. to Dismiss ("Pls.' Opp'n") [Dkt. # 54] at 9. Plaintiffs' arguments miss the mark. Under Rule 15, "an amendment adding a new ground for relief to the complaint must contend with the applicable statute of limitations." *Jones v. Bernanke,* 557 F.3d 670, 674 (D.C.Cir.2009).[4] The issue is not whether Plaintiffs had a right under Rule 15 to amend their Complaint to add a new cause of action against Syria under § 1605A, but whether the cause of action under § 1605A must be dismissed for failure to state a claim under Rule 12(b)(6) because it is time-barred. "The 60-day time limit in § 1083(c)(2) is what Congress directed, and counsel has not provided this Court with any case precedent or other authority to suggest that this Court may override or waive the time limit for filing imposed by Congress under the circumstances here." *In re Islamic Republic of Iran Terrorism Litig.,* 2009 WL 3112136, at *52. Nor is the Court persuaded by Plaintiffs' argument that the amendment was timely because it does not seek retroactive application of § 1605A. The 60-day time limit in § 1083(c)(2) applies to all plaintiffs who had cases pending under § 1605(a)(7) at the time the NDAA was enacted and who seek prospective application of § 1605A, as is made clear by § 1083(c)(2)'s use of the future tense "be given effect." *See* NDAA § 1083(c)(2)(A) (upon timely motion or refiling, actions pending under § 1605(a)(7) shall "*be given effect* as if the action had originally

4 "In limited circumstances, Rule 15(c) saves an otherwise untimely amendment by deeming it to 'relate back' to the timely-filed claims the plaintiff alleged in the original complaint." *Jones,* 557 F.3d at 674. Plaintiffs do not argue that the amendment was timely because it relates back to their original Complaint under Rule 15(c). Nor would that argument, had Plaintiffs made it, save the amendment in these circumstances where Congress specifically provided a 60-day time limit within which amendments to add a cause of action under § 1605A must have been made. Were it otherwise, the 60-day time limit in NDAA § 1083(c)(2) would be rendered meaningless.

been filed under section 1605A(c) of title 28, United States Code") (emphasis added).[5]

Finally, Plaintiffs argue that "[i]t is indisputable that, if Plaintiffs had no pending cause of action and filed a new lawsuit alleging violations of § 1605A, they would have standing and the claim would proceed." Pls.' Opp'n at 10–11. This assertion seems doubtful.[6] But, assuming it to be correct, Plaintiffs *did* have a pending cause of action against Syria under § 1605(a)(7) at the time § 1605A was enacted, and NDAA § 1083(c)(2) provided plaintiffs with such a pending action "only a limited window of opportunity to elect the benefits of the new statute." *In re Islamic Republic of Iran Terrorism Litig.,* 2009 WL 3112136, at *26. Plaintiffs failed to take advantage of the new statute within the allotted time frame.

B. Plaintiffs' Cause of Action Under § 1605(a)(7) and the Flatow Amendment Fails Against All Defendants

"Congress had two clear goals behind the state-sponsored terrorism exception to the Foreign Sovereign Immunities Act: (1) deterring terrorism, and (2) accomplishing such deterrence by stripping the states that sponsor terrorism of their foreign sovereign immunity and forcing them to compensate the victims of the terrorist acts they sponsor." *Peterson v. Islamic Republic of Iran,* Civil Action No. 01-2094, slip op. at 5 (D.D.C. Dec.18, 2002). "As the goal of Congress was to deter international terrorism by compensating its victims, it is necessary to determine whether the act that caused the injury to a plaintiff was, in fact, an act of terrorism." *Id.* "Congress has defined terrorism as follows: 'premeditated, politically motivated violence perpetrated against noncombatant targets by subnational groups or clandestine agents.'" *Id.* (quoting 22 U.S.C. § 2656f(d)(2)). "Congress's definition of 'terrorism' makes it clear that a violent act that caused injury to a service member in a combat situation would not qualify as terrorism, and such injury, therefore, would not constitute grounds for recovery under the state-sponsored terrorism exception to the FSIA." *Id.; see also Estate of Heiser v. Islamic Republic of Iran,* 466 F.Supp.2d 229, 258 (D.D.C.2006) ("In *Peterson,* this Court held that a service

---

5 Plaintiffs' reliance on *Clay v. Socialist People's Libyan Arab Jamahirya,* Civil Action No. 06-707, 2008 WL 591008 (D.D.C. Mar. 3, 2008), and *Harris v. Socialist People's Libyan Arab Jamahirya,* Civil Action No. 06-732, 2008 WL 591009 (D.D.C. Mar. 3, 2008), is misplaced. Both of those cases concerned a plaintiff's motion for leave to amend its complaint under Rule 15, not a defendant's motion to dismiss the complaint under Rule 12, like here. Further, the orders in those cases are dated March 3, 2008, prior to the March 28, 2008 expiration of the 60-day period referenced in NDAA § 1083(c)(2).

6 A plaintiff who did not commence a related action under § 1605(a)(7) may bring a new action under § 1605A "if the action is commenced. . . not later than the latter of (1) 10 years after April 24, 1996; or (2) 10 years after the date on which the cause of action arose." 28 U.S.C. § 1605A(b). Insofar as Plaintiffs' cause of action arose on June 11, 1982, when Mr. Baumel is alleged to have been captured, Plaintiffs' cause of action under § 1605A would still be time-barred even if they had not previously commenced an action under § 1605(a)(7).

member and his or her family may recover under the state-sponsored terrorism exception to the FSIA only if the service member was a non-combatant not engaged in military hostilities.").

"On June 11, 1982, while serving in the Israeli Defense Forces Armored Corps in Southern Lebanon," Mr. Baumel "was captured by a unit of the Syrian Army or a Palestinian Group loyal to Syria" and "was taken to Damascus as a hostage by the Syrian Army, where he was displayed as a trophy of war, along with his tank and other persons captured with him, in a Victory parade." Am. Compl. ¶¶ 20 & 21. Assuming these factual assertions to be true, as it must, the Court finds that Mr. Baumel was captured as an Israeli combatant while engaged in military hostilities against Syria. Accordingly, the Court concludes that Mr. Baumel's capture was not an act of "terrorism" within the meaning of the state-sponsored terrorism exception to the FSIA, and, for that reason, Plaintiffs' cause of action under § 1605(a)(7) and the Flatow Amendment fails to state a claim against all Defendants.

Plaintiffs resist this conclusion. They argue that "Mr. Baumel's status as a 'combatant' in the Israeli Defense Forces necessarily changed to that of a 'non-combatant' when hostilities ended and Syria failed to release him." Pls.' Opp'n at 12. "At that point," Plaintiffs argue, "Mr. Baumel's status as a U.S. citizen permitted him to bring this action regardless of his past military service." *Id.* They note that "[t]he United Nations Secretary-General concluded that as of June 16, 2000, Israel had withdrawn its forces from Southern Lebanon in accordance with United Nations Security Council Resolution 425 of 1978, thereby bringing an official conclusion to the war" and that "the United States Department of State also considers Israel's occupation of Southern Lebanon to have ended in May 2000." *Id.* at 12–13. Because "[i]t is a clearly established principle of the law of war that detention may last no longer than active hostilities," *Hamdi v. Rumsfeld,* 542 U.S. 507, 521, 124 S.Ct. 2633, 159 L.Ed.2d 578 (2004), they argue that "once Syria failed in its obligation to return Mr. Baumel [in 2000], he became a hostage and Syria became liable for hostage-taking under the FSIA." *Id.* at 13–14. In support of their conversion theory, Plaintiffs note that "[i]n addition to creating a private right of action against foreign states, [in the NDAA] Congress also amended the terrorist exception of the FSIA to explicitly allow members of the U.S. armed forces to file suit against foreign states for acts of torture and hostage taking." *Id.* at 12. They extrapolate that "[i]n light of this recent amendment, there is no doubt that Congress intended that the FSIA apply to all members of the U.S. armed forces, including soldiers on the front lines who were injured by acts of terror perpetrated by a foreign state or that state's officals." *Id.*

While it is true that § 1605A expands the scope of the state-sponsored terrorism exception to the FSIA to include terrorist acts perpetrated against "a member of the armed forces," it does not change the definition of "terrorism" as being a "premeditated, politically motivated violence perpetrated against noncombatant targets by subnational groups or clandestine agents." 22 U.S.C. § 2656f(d)(2). The Court is not convinced that it is an act of "terrorism" for a designated foreign state to fail to release a combatant captured on the battlefield upon cessation of military hostilities. It may be a violation of the law of war to fail to release, at the war's end, combatants captured as prisoners of war, but Plaintiffs have not persuaded the Court that such a failure also is a terrorist act for which a designated foreign state may be held liable under the state-sponsored terrorism exception to the FSIA. In any event, the expansion does not appear to benefit Plaintiffs inasmuch as their cause of action under § 1605A is time-barred, Mr. Baumel was not a member of the U.S. armed forces, to whom the expansion applies,[7] and the need for the amendment suggests that Congress was concerned that § 1605(a)(7), which does apply here, could be interpreted to exclude members of the U.S. armed forces even when not engaged in military hostilities.

Ultimately, however, the Court need not decide that issue because Plaintiffs have alleged no facts that, as of June 16, 2000, when the war between Israel and Syria ended and Mr. Baumel ceased to be a combatant under Plaintiffs' conversion theory, Mr. Baumel was alive, kept hostage by Syria, and tortured. "Factual allegations must be enough to raise a right to relief above the speculative level." *Twombly,* 550 U.S. at 555, 127 S.Ct. 1955. "[O]nly a complaint that states a plausible claim for relief survives a motion to dismiss." *Iqbal,* 129 S.Ct. at 1950. "[W]here the well-pleaded facts do not permit the court to infer more than the mere possibility of misconduct, the complaint has alleged—but it has not shown—that the pleader is entitled to relief." *Id.* (quotation marks and citation omitted).

According to Plaintiffs' own averments, Mr. Baumel "has not been seen by representatives of Israel, the United States Red Cross or his family since" June 11, 1982. Am. Compl. ¶ 22. Each of Plaintiffs' allegations concerning Syria's treatment of Mr. Baumel since that date is based upon only Plaintiffs' "information and belief," *see id.* ¶¶ 33–36, and is rank speculation. Plaintiffs conjecture that "Mr. Baumel continues to be held in squalid conditions, beaten, abused and denied rudimentary necessities, such as clean air to breathe, access to toilet facilities, a balanced diet or access to medical care," Pls.' Opp'n at 14, but they provide no basis to believe that is fact. Indeed, their only basis for believing that Mr. Baumel is still alive is that none of the bodies Syria thought were the bodies of the missing Israeli soldiers was Mr. Baumel's. Under these circumstances, "the well-pleaded facts," *i.e.,* that Mr. Baumel disappeared on June 11, 1982 in Lebanon while serving in the Israeli army and that his body was never found, "do not permit the court to infer more than the mere possibility of misconduct." *Iqbal,* 129 S.Ct. at 1950. "Because the plaintiffs have not nudged their claims across the line from conceivable to plausible, their complaint must be dismissed." *Twombly,* 550 U.S. at 570, 127 S.Ct. 1955.

---

7 "The term 'armed forces' means the Army, Navy, Air Force, Marine Corps, and Coast Guard." 10 U.S.C. § 101(a)(4). *See* 28 U.S.C. § 1605A(h)(4) ("the term 'armed forces' has the meaning given that term in section 101 of title 10").

IV. Conclusion

For the foregoing reasons, Syria's Motion to Dismiss the Amended Complaint for failure to state a claim against it [Dkt. # 53] will be granted, and this case will be dismissed against all Defendants. A memorializing Order accompanies this Memorandum Opinion.

IN RE ISLAMIC REPUBLIC OF IRAN TERRORISM LITIGATION

659 F. Supp. 2d 31 (D.D.C. 2009)
Decided September 30, 2009

Allen Louis Rothenberg, Philadelphia, PA, Anthony J. Laspada, Tampa, FL, David J. Cook, Cook Collection Attorneys, P.L.C., San Francisco, CA, Ferris Ridgely Bond, Bond & Norman, Robert Peter Feeney, Robert P. Feeney, Esquire, Gaithersburg, MD, Jane Carol Norman, Bond & Norman, PLLC, Kay M. Clarke, Clower & Clarke, Thomas Fortune Fay, Fay Law, PA, Washington, DC, Joseph Peter Drennan, Joseph Peter Drennan, Attorney-at-Law, Alexandria, VA, for Plaintiff.

Rupa Bhattacharyya, Eric R. Womack, Heather R. Phillips, Jacqueline E. Coleman Snead, Varudhini Chilakamarri, U.S. Department of Justice, Francis A. Vasquez, Jr., White & Case LLP, James H. Hulme, Arent Fox LLP, Griffith L. Green, Sidley Austin, LLP, Paul Joseph Lambert, Bingham McCutchen, LLP, Hwan Kim, Alan I. Raylesberg, Jay R. Henneberry, Alex Young K. Oh, Sidley Austin LLP, Bradford A. Berenson, Washington, DC, Jared R. Clark, Joshua Dorchak, Bingham McCutchen LLP, Karl H. Buch, Robert W. Littleton, New York, NY, for Interested Party.

ROYCE C. LAMBERTH, Chief Judge.

INTRODUCTION

For more than a decade now, this Court has presided over what has been a twisting and turning course of litigation against the Islamic Republic of Iran under the state sponsor of terrorism exception of the Foreign Sovereign Immunities Act (FSIA). Despite the best intentions of Congress and moral statements of support from the Executive Branch, the stark reality is that the plaintiffs in these actions face continuous road blocks and setbacks in what has been an increasingly futile exercise to hold Iran accountable for unspeakable acts of terrorist violence.[1]

---

1 The Islamic Republic of Iran was designated by the Secretary of State as a state sponsor of terrorism on January 19, 1984. The State Department maintains a list of countries that have been designated as state sponsors of terrorism on the Department's website. *See* U.S. Dep't of

The cases against Iran that will be addressed by the Court today involve more than one thousand individual plaintiffs. Like countless others before them, the plaintiffs in these actions have demonstrated through competent evidence—including the testimony of several prominent experts in the field of national security—that Iran has provided material support to terrorist organizations, like Hezbollah and Hamas, that have orchestrated unconscionable acts of violence that have killed or injured hundreds of Americans. As a result of these civil actions, Iran faces more than nine billion dollars in liability in the form of court judgments for money damages. Despite plaintiffs' best efforts to execute these court judgments, virtually all have gone unsatisfied.

This consolidated opinion focuses on recent legislative changes in this extraordinary area of the law, as implemented by Congress last term in § 1083 of the 2008 National Defense Appropriations Act for Fiscal Year 2008 (2008 NDAA). *See* Pub. L. No. 110-181, § 1083, 122 Stat. 3, 338–44. Section 1083 completely repeals the original state sponsor of terrorism exception—28 U.S.C. § 1605(a)(7)—which was originally enacted in 1996, and enacts in its place a new exception—28 U.S.C. § 1605A—that is in many ways more favorable to plaintiffs. This new statute provides, among other reforms, a new federal cause of action against state sponsors of terrorism and allows for awards of punitive damages in these cases. Even more significantly, however, the reforms implemented through § 1083 last year add a number of measures that are intended to help plaintiffs succeed in enforcing court judgments against state sponsors of terrorism, such as Iran.

The primary purpose of this opinion is to consider whether and to what extent these recent changes in the law should apply retroactively to a number of civil actions against Iran that were filed, and, in many instances, litigated to a final judgment prior to the enactment of the 2008 NDAA. In this particular instance, Congress has provided express guidance in § 1083(c) with respect to how § 1605A may be applied retroactively to reach a host of cases that were filed under the original terrorism exception, § 1605(a)(7). In considering this retroactivity question, the

---

STATE, STATE SPONSORS OF TERRORISM, www.state.gov/s/ct/c14151.htm (last visited Sept. 29, 2009). As noted at the website, countries designated as state sponsors of terrorism are those countries that the Secretary of State has determined "have repeatedly provided support for acts of international terrorism." *Id.* The Secretary of State makes that determination and designates state sponsors of terrorism pursuant to three statutory authorities: § 6(j) of the Export Administration Act of 1979, 50 U.S.C. app. § 2405(j); § 620A of the Foreign Assistance Act, 22 U.S.C. § 2371; and § 40(d) of the Arms Export Control Act, 22 U.S.C. § 2780(d). Three other countries are designated as State Sponsors of Terrorism: Cuba, Sudan, and Syria. U.S. Dep't of State, *supra* note 1. In April 2009, the State Department published its annual Country Reports on Terrorism, reporting that "Iran remained the most active state sponsor of terrorism" in 2008. U.S. Dep't of State, Country Reports on Terrorism 2008, at 182, available at http://www.state.gov/documents/ organization/122599.pdf. "Iran's involvement in the planning of financial support of terrorist attacks throughout the Middle East, Europe, and Central Asia has had a direct impact on international efforts to promote peace, threatened economic stability in the Gulf, and undermined the growth of democracy." *Id.*

Court will address a variety of other legal and procedural issues relating to what may be another lengthy course of litigation against Iran.

As is often the case in this area of the law that the Supreme Court has called sui generis, *see Austria v. Altmann*, 541 U.S. 677, 698, 124 S. Ct. 2240, 159 L.Ed.2d 1 (2004), this Court must sometimes confront novel legal questions, including constitutional issues of first impression. Today's decision is no different. This Court must address whether § 1083(c) impermissibly directs the reopening of final judgments in violation of Article III of the Constitution. *See Plaut v. Spendthrift Farm, Inc.*, 514 U.S. 211, 241, 115 S. Ct. 1447, 131 L.Ed.2d 328 (1995). The Court's attentiveness to this potentially unconstitutional application of § 1083(c) was heightened significantly by provisions of § 1083(c) that direct courts to essentially disregard the firmly established judicial doctrines of res judicata and collateral estoppel with respect to any matters litigated in a prior FSIA terrorism case.

To the extent that § 1083(c) might be construed as directing the reopening of final judgments entered under the former version of the terrorism exception, § 1605(a)(7), it would usurp the prerogative of the judiciary to decide cases under Article III and thereby offend the principle of separation of powers enshrined within our Constitution. In light of this issue's significance with respect to ongoing litigation against Iran, this Court addresses the Article III question in Part E of this opinion. After careful analysis as set forth below, this Court holds that the statute withstands constitutional scrutiny.

Today, the Court also reaches an even more fundamental conclusion: Civil litigation against Iran under the FSIA state sponsor of terrorism exception represents a failed policy. After more than a decade spent presiding over these difficult cases, this Court now sees that these cases do not achieve justice for victims, are not sustainable, and threaten to undermine the President's foreign policy initiatives during a particularly critical time in our Nation's history. The truth is that the prospects for recovery upon judgments entered in these cases are extremely remote. The amount of Iranian assets currently known to exist with the United States is approximately 45 million dollars, which is infinitesimal in comparison to the 10 billion dollars in currently outstanding court judgments.[2] Beyond the lack of assets available for execution of judgments, however, these civil actions inevitably must confront deeply entrenched and fundamental understandings of foreign state sovereignty, conflicting multinational treaties and executive agreements, and the exercise of presidential executive power in an ever-changing and increasingly complex world of international affairs.

Unfortunately, the enactment of § 1083 of the 2008 NDAA continues and expands the terrorism exception and its failed policy of civil litigation as the means of

---

2 *See* Office of Foreign Assets Control, U.S. Dept of the Treasury, Terrorists Assets Report 14–15, tbls. 1, 3 (2007) [hereinafter Terrorist Assets Report], available at http://www.treas.gov/offices/enforcement/ofac/reports/tar2007.pdf.

redress in these horrific cases. The availability of new federal claims under § 1605A with punitive damages, when combined with the broad retroactive reach accorded to this new statute, means that liability in the form of billions of dollars more in court judgments will continue to mount and mount quickly.

As a result of these latest reforms, the victims in these cases will now continue in their long struggle in pursuit of justice through costly and time-consuming civil litigation against Iran. They will do this at a time in our Nation's history when the President has taken bold and unprecedented steps in an attempt to improve relations with that foreign power while pressing forward on crucial issues, such as the grave threat of nuclear proliferation posed by Iran. Regrettably, the continuation in § 1083 of the same flawed policy that has failed plaintiffs in these actions for over a decade may only stoke the flames of unrealistic and unmanageable expectations in these terrorism victims who so rightly deserve justice, which may in turn serve only to expose the Administration to an unprecedented burden in its management of United States foreign policy towards Iran.

In view of these considerations, the Court will respectfully urge the President and Congress to seek meaningful reforms in this area of law in the form of a viable alternative to private litigation as the means of redress for the countless deaths and injuries caused by acts of terrorism. In Part K of the opinion and in the Conclusion, this Court will speak candidly about the challenges, complexities, and frustrations borne out by these civil actions over the past decade in an effort to urge our political leaders to act. If the decade-long history of these FSIA terrorism actions has revealed anything, it is that the Judiciary cannot resolve the intractable political dilemmas that frustrate these lawsuits; only Congress and the President can. Today, at the start of a new presidential administration—one that has sought engagement with Iran on a host of critical issues—it may be time for our political leaders here in Washington to seek a fresh approach.[3]

To assist this Court in these matters going forward, the Court will invite the United States to participate in these actions by filing a brief in response to the many issues addressed in this opinion. The Court encourages the United States to express its views regarding this litigation, but, more importantly, the Court hopes the Government might take this opportunity to give due consideration to whether there might be a more viable system of redress for these tragic and difficult cases. With the daunting national security challenges that confront the President with respect to Iran, our political leaders should candidly acknowledge the challenges and pitfalls of these terrorism lawsuits. The Court fears that if reforms are not achieved

---

3 Reaching out to the people of Iran and their leaders, President Obama recently stated: "I would like to speak clearly to Iran's leaders: We have serious differences that have grown over time. My administration is now committed to diplomacy that addresses the full range of issues before us and to pursuing constructive ties among the United States, Iran, and the international community." Videotaped Remarks on the Observance of Nowruz, DAILY COMP. PRES. DOC., Mar. 20, 2009.

in the near future, these civil suits against Iran may undermine the President's ability to act at a time when it matters most.

Today's omnibus opinion consists of twelve parts and is intended to serve a case management function in light of the significant changes in the law relating to these civil suits against Iran. Thus, today's ruling is consistent with this Court's inherent authority to manage the docket. *See, e.g.*, *In re Fannie Mae Sec. Litig.*, 552 F.3d 814, 822 (D.C.Cir.2009) ("District judges must have authority to manage their dockets, especially during massive litigation. . . ."). A separate order consistent with this opinion will issue this date.

DISCUSSION

The Foreign Sovereign Immunities Act of 1976 (FSIA), 28 U.S.C. §§ 1330, 1602–1611, is the sole basis of jurisdiction over foreign states in our courts. *E.g.*, *Argentine Republic v. Amerada Hess Shipping Corp.*, 488 U.S. 428, 434, 109 S. Ct. 683, 102 L.Ed.2d 818 (1989); *Prevatt v. Islamic Republic of Iran*, 421 F. Supp. 2d 152, 157–58 (D.D.C.2006) (Lamberth, J.). Enacted in 1976, the FSIA codifies a restrictive theory of foreign state sovereign immunity by which states are generally immune from the jurisdiction of courts of the United States, subject to a few carefully delineated exceptions. *See, e.g.*, *Verlinden B.V. v. Cent. Bank of Nigeria*, 461 U.S. 480, 488–89, 103 S. Ct. 1962, 76 L.Ed.2d 81 (1983); *Price v. Socialist People's Libyan Arab Jamahiriya*, 294 F.3d 82, 87 (D.C.Cir.2002). In the original FSIA enactment, exceptions to foreign sovereign immunity included cases in which a foreign state had either expressly or implicitly waived its immunity and cases relating to the commercial activities of a foreign sovereign within the United States. *See* Act of Oct. 21, 1976, Pub. L. No. 94-583, 90 Stat. 2891; *see also* §§ 1605(a), 1605A (codification of current FSIA exceptions); *Verlinden*, 461 U.S. at 488, 103 S. Ct. 1962 (discussing key exceptions under the FSIA).

The state sponsor of terrorism exception of the FSIA was first enacted in 1996 as part of Mandatory Victims Restitution Act of 1996, which was itself part of the larger Antiterrorism and Effective Death Penalty Act of 1996. Pub. L. No. 104-132, § 221(a)(1)(C), 110 Stat. 1214, 1241 (formerly codified at § 1605(a)(7)). As noted, however, the original exception at § 1605(a)(7) was repealed last year by the 2008 NDAA, § 1083(b)(1)(A)(iii), and replaced with a new exception at § 1605A. It is unclear why Congress chose to repeal rather than simply amend the prior statute. *See* H.R.Rep. No. 110-477, at 1001 (2007) (Conf. Rep.) (discussing § 1605A but omitting discussion of why Congress repealed, instead of amended, § 1605(a)(7)). Perhaps members of Congress wanted to reinforce the significance of their overhaul of the terrorism exception. Whatever the case may be, it is important at the outset for this Court to offer some notes of clarification and historical background information in an effort to avoid any confusion in the ensuing discussion.

The Court's analysis today must simultaneously consider two separate and distinct versions of the terrorism exception of the FSIA—the now-repealed version of the terrorism exception, § 1605(a)(7), and the new version, § 1605A. While the prior version of the exception, § 1605(a)(7), and the new version, § 1605A, differ in many fundamental respects, it is important to keep in mind that the basic grant of subject matter jurisdiction for actions against state sponsors of terrorism remains unchanged. Thus, it makes little difference whether one refers to § 1605(a)(7) or § 1605A when addressing the degree to which foreign sovereign immunity has been removed, subjecting designated state sponsors of terrorism to lawsuits in our courts. Indeed, the language eliminating sovereign immunity in the new exception, § 1605A, is virtually identical to the operative language in § 1605(a)(7). Compare § 1605(a)(7) with § 1605A(a)(1). Accordingly, in those instances in which the Court is merely referring to the grant of subject matter jurisdiction afforded by the virtue of the FSIA's terrorism exception, it will do so broadly, without any additional effort to underscore the two different statutes, as the two provisions are in fact indistinguishable in terms of the basic jurisdiction conferring language.

While the grant of subject matter jurisdiction for suits against state sponsors of terrorism is virtually unchanged, the latest version of the terrorism exception, § 1605A, adds substantive rights and remedies that were not available previously. As noted above, § 1605A is a much more expansive provision, one which provides a federal cause of action, as well as many other statutory entitlements. These new rights and remedies are the central focus of today's decision. The issue is whether the plaintiffs in actions that were filed, at least initially, under the now-repealed § 1605(a)(7), can now avail themselves of the additional entitlements associated with the new exception, § 1605A. Thus, to extent that some of these plaintiffs are unable to claim the benefits of the new terrorism law retroactively, then the prior exception, § 1605(a)(7)—even though now repealed—remains viable and indeed is the controlling source of law in their cases. This is consistent with both the guidance provided by Congress in § 1083(c) of the 2008 NDAA and the general presumption against the retroactive application of laws. *See Landgraf v. USI Film Prods.*, 511 U.S. 244, 286, 114 S. Ct. 1483, 128 L.Ed.2d 229 (1994) ("The presumption against statutory retroactivity is founded upon sound considerations of general policy and practice, and accords with long held and widely shared expectations about the usual operation of legislation."). Thus, when dealing with the nuts and bolts of the retroactivity analysis, especially in Part D below where the Court looks individually at each of the 20 cases in this opinion, it is important to keep the two versions of the exception separate and distinct. As underscored recently by the Court of Appeals for this Circuit, terrorism cases that were filed prior the enactment of the 2008 NDAA, and which do not qualify for retroactive treatment under the new exception, are governed by the prior statute, § 1605(a)(7). *See Simon v. Republic of Iraq*, 529 F.3d 1187, 1192 (D.C.Cir.2008), rev'd on other grounds sub nom. *Republic of Iraq v. Beaty*, ___ U.S. ___, 129 S. Ct. 2183, 173 L.Ed.2d 1193 (2009); accord *Oveissi v. Islamic Republic of Iran*, 573 F.3d 835 (D.C.Cir.2009); *La Reunion Aerienne v. Socialist People's Libyan Arab Jamahiriya*, 533 F.3d 837, 845 (D.C.Cir.2008); *Owens v. Republic of Sudan*, 531 F.3d 884, 887 (D.C.Cir.2008).

A. Historical Overview of the FSIA State Sponsor of Terrorism Exception as it Relates to Actions Against the Islamic Republic of Iran

The new terrorism exception— § 1605A—clears away a number of legal obstacles, including adverse court rulings, that have stifled plaintiffs' efforts to obtain relief in civil actions against designated state sponsors of terrorism. In fact, these reforms are in part a legislative fix to certain adverse precedent from the D.C. Circuit because "§ 1605A(c) abrogates *Cicippio-Puleo v. Islamic Republic of Iran*, 353 F.3d 1024 (D.C.Cir.2004), by creating a federal right of action against foreign states, for which punitive damages may be awarded." *Simon*, 529 F.3d at 1190. Thus, to fully grasp the significance these latest reforms, it is important to have some understanding regarding the manner in which the state sponsor of terrorism exception was shaped over time through the jurisprudence of this Circuit. More fundamentally, however, this historical backdrop is essential to the Court's analysis of the Article III separation-of-powers issue below in Part E, as well as for the Court's conclusion in Part K that even greater reforms in the law are necessary.

Accordingly, the Court will now briefly provide a historical overview of the state sponsor of terrorism exception, as it was originally constituted under § 1605(a)(7) (repealed), and the so-called Flatow Amendment to that exception. This part of the discussion will examine some of the early litigation against Iran before this Court in cases arising out of Iran's provision of material support and resources to terrorist organizations, such as Hamas and Hezbollah. The important historical background that follows breaks down roughly into three parts. The Court will begin with a discussion of *Flatow v. Islamic Republic of Iran*, 999 F. Supp. 1 (D.D.C. 1998) [hereinafter Flatow I] (Lamberth, J.), which was the first case in the country to be decided against Iran under the state sponsor of terrorism exception. After discussing this Court's ruling in Flatow, this Court will then review the decision of the D.C. Circuit Court of Appeals in *Cicippio-Puleo*, 353 F.3d 1024, in which the Court found that neither § 1605(a)(7) nor the Flatow Amendment furnish a cause of action against a foreign state. This Court examines the negative consequences and practical implications of that ruling for plaintiffs in these terrorism cases. After examining the fallout from Cicippio-Puleo, this Court proceeds to address what has been the greatest problem for these plaintiffs, and that is the fact that there are simply not sufficient Iranian assets that are amenable to attachment or execution in satisfaction of judgments entered against Iran under the FSIA terrorism exception.[4]

---

4 For an excellent summary of the litigation and evolution of the law pertaining to the state sponsor of terrorism exception of the FSIA, *see* JENNIFER K. ELSEA, CONGRESSIONAL RESEARCH SERV., SUITES AGAINST TERRORIST STATES BY VICTIMS OF TERRORISM (2008) [hereinafter SUITS AGAINST TERRORIST STATES], available at http://www.fas.org/sgp/crs/terror/RL31258.pdf. This Congressional Research Service report on terrorism lawsuits is the logical starting point for anyone who is hoping to gain a solid grasp of the development of this area of the

1. The Original State Sponsor of Terrorism Exception to Foreign Sovereign Immunity, Section 1605(a)(7) and the Flatow Amendment, Section 1605 Note, and Litigation Against Iran for its Provision of Material Support to Terrorist Organizations

The state sponsor of terrorism exception to foreign sovereign immunity applies only to foreign sovereigns officially designated as state sponsors of terrorism by the State Department. *See* § 1605A(a)(2)(A)(i)(I); § 1605(a)(7)(a) (repealed). This exception to foreign sovereign immunity is commonly known as the "terrorism exception." *See, e.g.*, *Kilburn v. Socialist People's Libyan Arab Jamahiriya*, 376 F.3d 1123, 1126 (D.C.Cir.2004). Under the exception, foreign sovereign immunity is eliminated in two different categories of terrorism cases: (1) those in which the designated foreign state is alleged to have committed certain acts of terrorism, i.e., torture, extrajudicial killing, aircraft sabotage, or hostage taking; and (2) those in which the designated state is alleged to have provided "material support or resources" for such terrorist acts. *See* § 1605A(a)(1); § 1605(a)(7) (repealed). Thus, a designated state sponsor of terrorism might be held to account for its specific acts of terrorism, as well as, more broadly speaking, its "provision of material support or resources" in furtherance of acts of terrorism. *See* § 1605A(a)(1); § 1605(a)(7) (repealed).

The statute is intended to protect American victims of state-sponsored terrorism, and therefore only United States citizens and nationals may rely on its grant of subject matter jurisdiction. *See* § 1605A(a)(1); § 1605(a)(7) (repealed); *see also Acosta v. Islamic Republic of Iran*, 574 F. Supp. 2d. 15, 25–26 (D.D.C.2008) (Lamberth, C.J.) (denying claims of victim, Rabbi Meir Kahane, who had voluntarily renounced his U.S. citizenship years prior to his assassination by Islamic terrorists). Thus, the victim or claimant in an action against a state sponsor of terrorism must have been a United States citizen or national at the time of the incident that gave rise to his claim(s). *See Acosta*, 574 F. Supp. 2d at 26.

Most of the actions in this Court against Iran have proceeded under that portion of the terrorism exception relating to "the provision of material support or resources" for terrorist acts. *See, e.g.*, *Flatow I*, 999 F. Supp. 1; *Eisenfeld v. Islamic Republic of Iran*, 172 F. Supp. 2d 1 (D.D.C.2000) (Lamberth, J.); *Heiser v. Islamic Republic of Iran*, 466 F. Supp. 2d 229 (D.D.C. 2006) (Lamberth, J.). The terrorism exception

law and its many complexities. In addition to chronicling important legislative developments, the report captures and summarizes the civil litigation that has occurred in this Court against Iran under the state sponsor of terrorism exception to the FSIA. This Court is grateful to the Congressional Research Service, and to Ms. Elsea in particular, for their thorough work on this unique and important topic. This Court has examined and relied on many of the original source materials identified in the report for additional insight on these matters beyond the Court's own experience in presiding over dozens of civil actions against Iran.

adopts the definition of "material support or resources" set forth in the criminal code at 18 U.S.C § 2339A(b)(1):

> [T]he term "material support or resources" means any property, tangible or intangible, or service, including currency or monetary instruments or financial securities, financial services, lodging, training, expert advice or assistance, safehouses, false documentation or identification, communications equipment, facilities, weapons, lethal substances, explosives, personnel (1 or more individuals who may be or include oneself), and transportation, except medicine or religious materials[.]

See § 1605A(h)(3) (incorporating § 2339A(b)(1) by reference); *see also* § 1605(a)(7) (repealed).

This Court has determined that "the routine provision of financial assistance to a terrorist group in support of its terrorist activities constitutes 'providing material support and resources' for a terrorist act within the meaning of the [terrorism exception of the FSIA]." *Flatow I*, 999 F. Supp. 1 at 19. Additionally, this Court has found that "a plaintiff need not establish that the material support or resources provided by a foreign state for a terrorist act contributed directly to the act from which his claim arises in order to satisfy 28 U.S.C. § 1605(a)(7)'s statutory requirements for subject matter jurisdiction." *Id.* In other words, there is no "but-for" causation requirement with respect to cases that rely on the material support component of the terrorism exception to foreign sovereign immunity; "[s]ponsorship of a terrorist group which causes personal injury or death of United States national alone is sufficient to invoke jurisdiction." *Id.*; *see also Kilburn*, 376 F.3d at 1129 (holding that Libya's actions need not be the "but for" causation of an act of terrorism for the purpose of establishing subject matter jurisdiction under the terrorism exception). Once the requirements for jurisdiction over a foreign state are satisfied under the FSIA, then that foreign state can be held liable in a civil action "in the same manner and to the same extent as a private individual under like circumstances." § 1606.

When the FSIA state sponsor of terrorism exception was first enacted in April of 1996, it was far from clear whether that statute, § 1605(a)(7), in and of itself, served as a basis for an independent federal cause of action against foreign state sponsors of terrorism. While the waiver of foreign sovereign immunity was clear, and hence the provision authorized courts to serve as a forum to adjudicate certain terrorism cases, questions remained regarding whether any civil claims or money damages were available by virtue of that enactment. To clarify matters, Congress created what is commonly referred to as the Flatow Amendment, which was enacted a mere five months after the state sponsor of terrorism exception as part of the Omnibus Consolidated Appropriations Act, 1997. *See* Pub. L. 104-208, § 589, 110 (1996), 110 Stat. 3009–1, 3009–172 (codified at 28 U.S.C. § 1605 note). The Flatow Amendment provides in pertinent part that:

> An official, employee, or agent of a foreign state designated as a state sponsor of terrorism . . . while acting within the scope of his office, employment, or agency shall

> be liable to a United States national or the national's legal representative for personal injury or death caused by acts of that official, employee, or agent for which courts of the United States may maintain jurisdiction under section 1605(a)(7) of title 28, United States Code [repealed] for money damages which may include economic damages, solatium, pain, and suffering, and punitive damages if the acts were among those described in section 1605(a)(7).

§ 1605 note.

The amendment is named for Alisa Michelle Flatow, a 20-year-old Brandeis University student from New Jersey who was mortally wounded in a suicide bombing attack on the Gaza strip in April of 1995. Alisa Flatow's father, Stephen Flatow, was one of the prime movers behind the state sponsor of terrorism exception, and he successfully lobbied to have the amendment incorporated as part of § 1605. *See, e.g.*, NEELY TUCKER, PAIN AND SUFFERING; RELATIVES OF TERRORIST VICTIMS RACE EACH OTHER TO COURT, BUT JUSTICE AND MONEY ARE BOTH HARD TO FIND, WASH. POST, Apr. 6, 2003, at F1 [hereinafter TUCKER, PAIN AND SUFFERING] (recalling Stephen Flatow's lobbying efforts on behalf of the anti-terrorism legislation); *see also* RUTHANNE M. DEUTSCH, SUING STATE-SPONSORS OF TERRORISM UNDER THE FOREIGN SOVEREIGN IMMUNITIES ACT: GIVING LIFE TO THE JURISDICTIONAL GRANT AFTER CICIPPIO-PULEO, 38 INT'L LAW. 891 (2004) (discussing legislative history of the Flatow Amendment and collecting sources); SUITS AGAINST TERRORIST STATES, *supra* note 4, at 5–7 (discussing legislative history of § 1605(a)(7) and Flatow Amendment).

Stephen Flatow filed suit in this Court shortly after the enactment of the Flatow Amendment. As administrator of Alisa Flatow's estate, plaintiff asserted a wrongful death claim and a claim for Alisa's conscious pain and suffering prior to her death. *See Flatow I*, 999 F. Supp. at 27–29. Plaintiff also asserted solatium claims for the mental anguish and grief suffered by the decedent's parents and siblings as a result of her murder by terrorists. *See id.* at 29–32. Plaintiff also sought punitive damages. *See id.* at 32–35. Iran did not enter an appearance in the action and has never appeared in any FSIA terrorism action to date. *See id.* at 6.[5]

---

5 Iran has never appeared in these actions even though it is "an experienced litigant in the United States Federal Court System generally and in this Circuit. *See, e.g.*, *Cicippio v. Islamic Republic of Iran*, 30 F.3d 164 (D.C.Cir.1994), cert. denied 513 U.S. 1078, 115 S. Ct. 726, 130 L.Ed.2d 631 (1995); *Foremost-McKesson v. Islamic Republic of Iran*, 905 F.2d 438 (D.C.Cir. 1990); *Persinger v. Islamic Republic of Iran*, 729 F.2d 835 (D.C.Cir. 1984); *Berkovitz v. Islamic Republic of Iran*, 735 F.2d 329 (9th Cir.1984); *McKeel v. Islamic Republic of Iran*, 722 F.2d 582 (9th Cir. 1983)." *Flatow I*, 999 F. Supp. 1 at 6 n. 1. Nevertheless, this Court cannot enter a default judgment against a foreign sovereign unless the plaintiff "establishes his claim or right to relief by evidence satisfactory to the Court." 28 U.S.C. § 1608(e). Thus, this Court must carefully review the plaintiff's evidence with respect to both liability and damages.

While Iran has not defended itself in any of the lawsuits under the terrorism exception, Iran has on occasion come to court to prevent plaintiffs from collecting on default judgments entered under that provision. For example, Iran recently prevailed in an action to prevent the

The Flatow case was the first in the country to be decided against Iran under the terrorism exception to the FSIA. *See* 999 F. Supp. at 6 n. 2. In that decision, this Court examined the statutory language of the terrorism exception, § 1605(a)(7), and the Flatow Amendment, § 1605 note, in pari materia and found that those provisions collectively established both subject matter jurisdiction and federal causes of actions for civil lawsuits against state sponsors of terrorism. *See id.* at 12–13. This Court also ruled that the Flatow Amendment was intended to ensure large punitive damage awards against state sponsors of terrorism. *See id.* In this Court's view, the express provision of punitive damages in the Flatow Amendment, in conjunction with the provisions's legislative history, including statements by the Amendment's co-sponsors, Representative Jim Saxton and Senator Frank Lautenberg of New Jersey, demonstrated that Congress believed punitive damage awards were absolutely necessary to ensure that civil actions against state sponsors of terrorism would effectively deter those nations from perpetuating international terrorism. *See id.* Thus, the Flatow Amendment served as an exception to the general rule, as expressed in § 1606 of the FSIA, that foreign sovereigns are not to be held liable for punitive damages.

During a two-day hearing in March of 1998, plaintiff proceeded in the manner of a non-jury trial. *Id.* at 6. The evidence presented to the Court at that time demonstrated by clear and convincing evidence that Iran was the sole source of funding for the Shaqaqi faction of Palestine Islamic Jihad, a small terrorist cell that claimed responsibility for and in fact perpetuated the suicide bombing that gravely wounded Alisa Flatow on April 9, 1995. *Id.* at 8–9. The suicide bomber rammed a van full of explosives into the number 36 Egged bus that Alisa and others were traveling in on their way to a Mediterranean resort in the Gush Katif community in Gaza. *Id.* at 7. The resulting explosion destroyed the bus and sent shrapnel flying in all directions. *Id.* A piece of that shrapnel pierced Alisa's Flatow's skull and lodged in her brain. *Id.* Once Stephen Flatow learned that his daughter had been injured in the attack, he immediately flew to Israel, and he rushed to the Soroka Medial Center, where Alisa was being treated. Upon his arrival there, however, the attending physician informed Mr. Flatow that his daughter Alisa "showed no signs of brain activity, that all physical functions relied on life support, and that there was no hope for her recovery." *Id.* at 8. In emotionally powerful testimony before this Court, Stephen Flatow described the heart-wrenching decision he made to have his daughter's life support terminated and her organs harvested for transplant. *See id.*

This Court ultimately awarded a total of 22.5 million dollars in compensatory damages. More significantly, however, the Court also awarded 225 million dollars in punitive damages, approximately three times Iran's annual expenditures on terrorist activities at that time. *See id.* at 34. In providing for such a large award of

---

attachment of one of its assets here in the United States. *See, e.g.*, *Ministry of Defense and Support for the Armed Forces of the Islamic Republic of Iran v. Elahi*, ___ U.S. ___, 129 S. Ct. 1732, 173 L.Ed.2d 511 (2009).

punitive damages against Iran, this Court stressed the importance of such awards as a means to deter states like Iran from supporting terrorist organizations. The Court stated as follows:

> By creating these rights of action, Congress intended that the Courts impose a substantial financial cost on states which sponsor terrorist groups whose activities kill American citizens. *This Cost functions both as a direct deterrent, and also as a disabling mechanism: if several large punitive damage awards issue against a foreign state sponsor of terrorism, the state's financial capacity to provide funding will be curtailed.*

Id. at 33 (emphasis added). The Court also recognized that any punitive damage award would have to be substantial enough to have an appreciable impact in light of Iran's significant annual revenues from oil exports. *See id.* at 33–34.

At the time the Flatow decision was announced, there was a certain degree of energy and optimism surrounding the action. Senator Frank Lautenberg held a press conference outside this courthouse with Alisa Flatow's parents and their attorneys. They underscored the importance of the Court's decision as a measure of justice for victims of terrorism, and they stressed the importance of holding state sponsors of terrorism accountable for their support of terrorist groups. *See* BILL MILLER & BARTON GELLMAN, JUDGE TELLS IRAN TO PAY TERRORISM DAMAGES; $247 MILLION AWARD FOR FAMILY OF U.S. VICTIM IN GAZA, WASH. POST, Mar. 12, 1998, at A1. Steven Perles, one of the attorneys for the Flatows, spoke of Iran's wealth and expressed his belief that the Flatows would "collect the entirety of the judgment." *See id.* At the time, the popular sentiment was that terrorism victims were going to "sue the terrorists out of business." *See* TUCKER, PAIN AND SUFFERING, *supra*. In the years immediately following the Flatow decision, many more plaintiffs relied on the original terrorism exception, § 1605(a)(7), in combination with the Flatow Amendment, to successfully litigate cases against Iran. *See, e.g., Stern v. Islamic Republic of Iran*, 271 F. Supp. 2d 286 (D.D.C.2003) (Lamberth, J.); *Hutira v. Islamic Republic of Iran*, 211 F. Supp. 2d 115 (D.D.C.2002) (Lamberth, J.); *Eisenfeld*, 172 F. Supp. 2d 1.[6] Large judgments against the state

---

6 Although this Judge ruled in Flatow that the Flatow Amendment, 1605 note, did furnish a cause of action against a state sponsor of terrorism, this Judge elected to revisit the issue even more thoroughly in *Cronin v. Islamic Republic of Iran*, a case concerning an American Professor who was taken hostage and tortured by Hizbollah in Beirut, Lebanon in 1984. *See* 238 F. Supp. 2d 222 (D.D.C. 2002) (Lamberth, J.). The Court did so in part because the Court of Appeals had flagged the issue in Price by observing that "'the amendment does not list 'foreign states' among the parties against whom an action may be brought.'" *Cronin*, 238 F. Supp. 2d at 231 (quoting *Price*, 294 F.3d at 87). As this Court revisited what was then a crucial question, this Court observed that a majority of the judges of this Court by that time had ruled that the Flatow Amendment did provide for a cause of action against a foreign state in cases in which that state is not entitled to immunity by virtue of the terrorism exception, § 1605(a)(7). *See id.* at 233 (collecting cases). Nonetheless, § 1605 note is not a model of clarity, and as Judge Sullivan pointed out in *Roeder v. Islamic Republic of Iran*, there are a number of valid reasons why § 1605 note should not be construed as furnishing substantive claims against

sponsor of terrorism amassed quickly. Unfortunately, in most cases, the victories obtained by plaintiffs in this courthouse merely signaled the beginning of what would become a long, bitter, and often futile quest for justice.

2. Setbacks for Plaintiffs: The D.C. Circuit's Decision in *Cicippio-Puleo*

Nearly six years following the *Flatow* decision, and contrary to what this Court and others had determined, the D.C. Circuit Court of Appeals held that "[p]lainly neither section § 1605(a)(7) nor the Flatow Amendment, separately or together, establishes a cause of action against foreign state sponsors of terrorism." *Cicippio-Puleo*, 353 F.3d at 1027. According to the Court of Appeals, the original terrorism exception to the FSIA, § 1605(a)(7), was "merely a jurisdiction conferring provision," and therefore it did not create an independent federal cause of action against a foreign state or its agents. *Id.* at 1032. In other words, the prior version of the terrorism exception, § 1605(a)(7), merely waived foreign sovereign immunity for designated terrorist states with respect to actions taken by those states in furtherance of international terrorism, but it did not furnish a legal claim for money damages that a terrorism victim might then assert in a lawsuit against Iran or any other designated state sponsor of terrorism. Instead, plaintiffs in terrorism cases were required to find a cause of action based on some other source of law. *Id.* at 1037.

With respect to the Flatow Amendment, § 1605 note, the Court held that the provision "provides a private right of action only against individual officials, employees, and agents of a foreign state, but not against the foreign state itself." *Id.* at 1027. Thus, the cause of action furnished by the Flatow Amendment is severely restricted because it applies only to claims against foreign state officials, employees, and agents, "in their individual capacities, as opposed to their official capacities." *Id.* at 1034 (emphasis in original). In reaching its holding, the Court of Appeals emphasized that a claim against a foreign state official for actions taken within his official capacity on behalf of a foreign government "'is in substance a claim against the government itself'" *Id.* (citations omitted). As the Court found that neither the plain language nor the legislative history of the Flatow Amendment suggested that Congress intended to impose liability on foreign governments, plaintiffs were precluded from relying on that provision for either claims against Iran or claims based on acts taken by Iranian officials within the scope of their official duties. *Id.* at 1034–1036. After rendering its ruling the Cicippio-Puleo, the Court of Appeals remanded the action back to this Court in order to enable plaintiffs in that case to amend their complaint to state a cause of action against Iran "under some other source of law, including state law." *Id.* at 1036.D

---

foreign states. *See* 195 F. Supp. 2d 140, 171–175 (holding that Flatow Amendment did not furnish a cause of action).

As a result of the Cicippio-Puleo decision, plaintiffs in FSIA terrorism cases under § 1605(a)(7) began to use that provision as a "'pass-through'" to causes of actions found in state tort law. *Bodoff v. Islamic Republic of Iran*, 424 F. Supp. 2d 74, 83 (D.D.C.2006) (Lamberth, J.); *see also Pescatore v. Pan Am. World Airways, Inc.*, 97 F.3d 1, 12 (2d Cir.1996) (describing how FSIA acts as pass-through to state law by virtue of § 1606) (quoting *Zicherman v. Korean Air Lines Co.*, 516 U.S. 217, 229, 116 S. Ct. 629, 133 L.Ed.2d 596 (1996)). By using the pass-through approach under the earlier version of the terrorism exception, § 1605(a)(7), most terrorism victims who pursued FSIA cases against Iran were in fact able to litigate claims based on the tort law of the state jurisdiction where they were domiciled at the time of the terrorist incident giving rise to the lawsuit.

In the large consolidated case of *Peterson v. Islamic Republic of Iran*, for example, this Court found that Iran furnished money, weapons, training, and guidance to Hezbollah in direct support of a terrorist plot that culminated in large-scale suicide bombing attack on the United States Marine barracks in Beirut, Lebanon on October 23, 1983. *See* 264 F. Supp. 2d at 47–59 (D.D.C.2003) [hereinafter Peterson I] (Lamberth, J.).[7] More than 200 American servicemen lost their lives and countless others were injured in the bombing. Prior to September 11, 2001, the attack on the Marines in Beirut was the most deadly terrorist attack ever carried out against American citizens. By examining the claims in that case under a number of sources of state law, this Court awarded to the family members of the deceased servicemen and the injured survivors of the Beirut attack exceeds 2.6 billion dollars and remains one of the largest judgments ever awarded in a FSIA action pursuant to the state sponsor of terrorism exception. *See Peterson v. Islamic Republic of Iran*, 515 F. Supp. 2d 25, 44–45 (D.D.C.2007) [hereinafter Peterson II] (Lamberth, J.). Like Peterson, the majority cases addressed in today's opinion stem from the 1983 bombing of the Marine barracks facility in Beirut, Lebanon.

In another action considered today, *Bennett v. Islamic Republic of Iran*, plaintiffs demonstrated how Iran's financial support of Hamas helped to perpetrate terrorist attacks, including a 2002 suicide bombing incident at Hebrew University in Jerusalem that claimed the life of their 24-year-old daughter. *See* 507 F. Supp. 2d 117 (D.D.C.2007) (Lamberth, J.). In Bennett, the plaintiffs relied on California law. Similarly, in *Beer v. Islamic Republic of Iran*, family members of an American killed in a suicide bombing of a bus in Jerusalem showed how Iran's material support to Hamas in the form of funding, safe haven, training, and weapons, helped to spur on violent suicide attacks in Israel and elsewhere. 574 F. Supp. 2d 1 (D.D.C. 2008) (Lamberth, J.).[8] The plaintiffs in Beer relied on New York common law.

---

7 Peterson is consolidated with *Boulos v. Islamic Republic of Iran*, No. 01-CV-2684-RCL (D.D.C.).

8 This Court has also decided FSIA cases arising from Iran-sponsored terrorist attacks that have occurred here in the United States. Acosta, for example, arose out of the assassination of Rabbi Meir Kahane, an Israeli political figure and a founder of the Jewish Defense League, who

But while larger majority of plaintiffs in actions post-Cicippio-Puleo were able to use the pass-through approach to find relief, hundreds of others equally dissevering plaintiffs had their claims denied because they were domiciled in jurisdictions that did not afford them a substantive claim. In the Peterson case, for example, some family members of the Marines and other servicemen who were killed in the 1983 terrorist bombing were barred from asserting intentional infliction of emotional distress claims (IIED) because they lacked standing under the applicable state tort law. Consequently, this Court had to dismiss the IIED claims of family members who were domiciled in either Pennsylvania or Louisiana at the time of the terrorist attack because those jurisdictions would not permit IIED claims by family members who were not physically present at the site of the incident that gave rise to the emotional distress. *See Peterson II*, 515 F. Supp. 2d at 44–45. Thus, the Pennsylvania and Louisiana plaintiffs in the Peterson action were effectively denied their day in court, and yet they watched as many other similarly situated plaintiffs (including some of their own family members) from different state jurisdictions advanced and ultimately prevailed with their claims for IIED. For those Pennsylvania and Louisiana plaintiffs who were denied relief as so many others succeeded based on precisely the same kinds of claims, based on the same horrific and unquestionably traumatic incident, the result must have seemed both arbitrary and unfair.

In addition to the unfairness caused by a lack of uniformity in the underlying state sources of law, the pass-through approach proved cumbersome and tedious in practical application. In a given case based on a single terrorist incident, this Court would usually have to resolve choice of law problems and then proceed through a lengthy analysis of tort claims under the laws of numerous different state jurisdictions. For example, in the Heiser case, a large consolidated action involving the Khobar towers bombing, this Court issued a 209-page opinion in which it ultimately applied the laws of 11 different state jurisdictions. *See* 466 F. Supp. 2d 229. In Peterson, this Court had to apply the laws of nearly 40 different jurisdictions in order to resolve the victims' claims. *See Peterson II*, 515 F. Supp. 2d 25. To efficiently manage these terrorism cases under the pass-through regime imposed by Cicippio-Puleo, this Court would frequently refer the action to special masters after the Court determined under § 1605(a)(7) that Iran provided material support for a terrorist incident that killed or injured Americans.[9]

---

was gunned down by Islamic Jihadists as he was concluding a lecture in New York City on November 5, 1990. *See* 574 F. Supp. 2d 15.

9 The application of diverse sources of substantive law to claims in accordance with the pass-through approach under § 1605(a)(7) may sometimes requires courts to look to foreign sources of law. *See Oveissi*, 573 F.3d 835. In Oveissi, the Court of Appeals ruled that this Court must apply French law to resolve emotional distress and wrongful death claims brought by an American grandson of General Gholam Oveissi, who was the head of the Iranian armed forces under the Shah's regime. General Oveissi was assassinated in France by Hezbollah operatives in February of 1984.

Another consequence of the Cicippio-Puleo decision was that the Flatow Amendment could not serve as independent basis for punitive damages awards against Iran. As the Court of Appeals found that the amendment was not intended to provide for claims against foreign states, the bar on punitive damages in § 1606 of the FSIA remained in tact, even with respect to state sponsors of terrorism. Accordingly, large awards of punitive damages, like that which this Court granted in Flatow to deter Iran from sponsorship of terrorist groups, were no longer available in actions against the state of Iran under § 1605(a)(7).[10]

---

10 In all of the civil actions against the Islamic Republic of Iran considered here today, Iran's Ministry of Information and Security (MOIS) is also named as a defendant. One of the actions also includes the Iranian Islamic Revolutionary Guard Corps (IRGC) as a defendant. *See Rimkus v. Islamic Republic of Iran*, No. 06-CV-1116-RCL (D.D.C.).

As noted, § 1606 of the FSIA provides that foreign states may not be held liable for punitive damages, and, as a result of Cicippio-Puleo, that exemption from punitive damages applies to state sponsors of terrorism in actions under § 1605(a)(7), notwithstanding the Flatow Amendment. Section 1606 also provides, however, that an "agency or instrumentality" of a foreign state, as opposed to the state itself, may be liable for punitive damages. Thus, certain entities of a foreign government may be liable for punitive damages. In terrorism cases against Iran in this Court under § 1605(a)(7), plaintiffs have never identified an appropriate Iranian agency that would qualify as an "agency or instrumentality" of Iran for the purpose of a punitive damages award.

In *Roeder v. Islamic Republic of Iran*, a case that was decided only a few months prior to Cicippio-Puleo, the Court of Appeals emphasized that it follows a categorical approach when determining whether a foreign governmental entity should be considered "'a foreign state or political subdivision' rather than an 'agency or instrumentality of the nation'" for purposes of the FSIA. 333 F.3d 228, 234 (D.C.Cir.2003) (quoting *Transaero, Inc. v. La Fuerza Aerea Boliviana*, 30 F.3d 148, 149–50 (D.C.Cir. 1994)). Under the categorical approach, "if the core functions of the entity are governmental, it is considered the foreign state itself; if commercial, the entity is an agency or instrumentality of the foreign state." *Id.* In Roeder, the Court determined that Iran's Ministry of Foreign Affairs is part of the foreign state itself, rather than an "agency of instrumentality" because the Ministry of Foreign Affairs, like a nation's armed forces, is governmental in nature. *Id.* Following the *Roeder* decision, this Court found that MOIS must be considered part of the state of Iran itself and is therefore exempt from liability for punitive damages. *See, e.g., Haim v. Islamic Republic of Iran*, 425 F. Supp. 2d 56, 71 n. 2 (D.D.C.2006) (Lamberth, J.).

In *Rimkus v. Islamic Republic of Iran*, a case that is addressed in today's consolidated opinion, the plaintiffs asserted claims against IRGC as well as MOIS. In rendering the decision in *Rimkus*, this Court again followed the categorical approach from Roeder and determined that IRGC, like MOIS, is part of the state itself and is therefore exempt from punitive damage under the FSIA. *See* 575 F. Supp. 2d 181, 198–200 (D.D.C.2008) (Lamberth, C.J.); *see also Blais v. Islamic Republic of Iran*, 459 F. Supp. 2d 40, 60–61 (D.D.C. 2006) (Lamberth, J.) (concluding that both MOIS and IRGC must be treated as the state of Iran itself for purposes of liability); *Salazar v. Islamic Republic of Iran*, 370 F. Supp. 2d 105, 115–16 (D.D.C.2005) (Bates, J.) (same). Consequently, in the years following Cicippio-Puleo, plaintiffs in actions under the original terrorism exception, § 1605(a)(7), lacked a basis for claiming punitive damages in actions arising out of Iran-sponsored terrorism.

Because claims against MOIS or IRGC are not legally distinguishable from claims against Iran itself, this opinion refers to Iran as the only defendant.

3. The Never-Ending Struggle to Enforce Judgments Against Iran

In the years since the *Flatow* decision, a number of practical, legal, and political obstacles have made it all but impossible for plaintiffs in these FSIA terrorism cases to enforce their default judgments against Iran. This Court has examined this fundamental and longstanding problem time and again as plaintiffs before this Court have sought, with very little success, to locate and attach Iranian Government assets in aid of execution of their civil judgments. *See, e.g.*, *Bennett v. Islamic Republic of Iran*, 604 F. Supp. 2d 152 (D.D.C.2009) (Lamberth, C.J.); *Peterson v. Islamic Republic of Iran*, 563 F. Supp. 2d 268 (D.D.C.2008) [hereinafter Peterson III] (Lamberth, C.J.); *Weinstein v. Islamic Republic of Iran*, 274 F. Supp. 2d 53 (D.D.C.2003) (Lamberth, J.); *Flatow v. Islamic Republic of Iran*, 76 F. Supp. 2d 16 (D.D.C.1999) [hereinafter Flatow III] (Lamberth, J.); *Flatow v. Islamic Republic of Iran*, 74 F. Supp. 2d 18 (D.D.C.1999) [hereinafter Flatow II] (Lamberth, J.). To even begin to appreciate the difficulties plaintiffs face with respect to locating Iranian property in the United States, it is important to first understand the significance of the Iran-Hostage Crisis and its aftermath and, more specifically, the Algiers Accords, the bilateral executive agreement between Iran and the United States that brought about the settlement of the hostage crisis in 1981.

On November 14, 1979, ten days after the start of the Iran hostage crisis in which Iranian revolutionaries seized the United States embassy in Tehran and took most embassy personnel as hostages, President Carter exercised his powers under the International Emergency Economic Powers Act (IEEPA), 50 U.S.C. §§ 1701–1706, and "blocked all property and interests in property of the Government of Iran . . . subject to the jurisdiction of the United States." Exec. Order No. 12,170, 44 Fed. Reg. 65,729 (Nov. 14, 1979); *see* Transactions Involving Property in Which Iran or Iranian Entities Have an Interest, 31 C.F.R. § 535.201; *see also Dames & Moore v. Regan*, 453 U.S. 654, 662–664, 101 S. Ct. 2972, 69 L.Ed.2d 918 (1981) (discussing the Iran Hostage Crisis and President Carter's actions in response to the Iran hostage crisis pursuant to his authority under the IEEPA).

Approximately five months later, as the hostage crisis continued to wane on, President Carter severed diplomatic relations with Iran, and the State Department assumed custody of all Iran's diplomatic and consular property here in the United States. *See, e.g.*, *Bennett*, 604 F. Supp. 2d at 162–66 (discussing the termination of diplomatic relations with Iran and the State Department's assumption of custody over Iran's diplomatic and consular properties within the United States). The hostage crisis was finally resolved when Iran and the United States executed the Algiers Accords on January 19, 1981, and all hostages were released the following day, just moments after President Regan took office. *See* Iran-United States: Settlement of the Hostage Crisis, Jan. 18–20, 1981, 20 I.L.M. 223 [hereinafter Algiers Accords]; *Dames & Moore*, 453 U.S. at 664–65, 101 S. Ct. 2972 (discussing the release of the hostages and terms of the Algiers Accords).

As part of the Algiers Accords, the United States agreed in principle to restore the financial position of Iran, in so far as possible, to that which existed prior to November 14, 1979." Algiers Accords, 20 I.L.M. at 223, 224. Additionally, the United States "commit[ted] itself to ensure the mobility and free transfer of all Iranian assets within its jurisdiction." *Id.* at 223–224. Iran and the United States further agreed to settle all litigation between the two governments, to include any outstanding litigation between the nationals of the two countries as of January, 19 1981. *Id.* at 223–224, 230–232. To this end, the Algiers Accords established an Iran-U.S. Claims Tribunal in the Hague to arbitrate any claims not settled within six moths. *Id.* at 226, 230–34. Consistent with these commitments to restore Iran's financial position, to facilitate the transfer of Iranian assets, and to have unresolved claims presented to the Iran-Claims Tribunal, the United States agreed to "bring about the transfer" of all Iranian assets held in this country by American banks, with one billion dollars in those assets set aside on account of the Central Bank of Algeria for the payment of any awards entered against Iran by the Claims Tribunal. *Id.* at 225–27. The Claims-Tribunal would also have jurisdiction to revolve disputes between Iran and the United States concerning each other's compliance with the Algiers Accords. *Id.* at 231.

To comply with the terms of the Algiers Accords, President Carter issued, and President Regan subsequently ratified, a series of Executive Orders in which the President unblocked the majority of Iran assets within the jurisdiction of the United States and directed United States banks to transfer all Iranian assets to the Federal Reserve Bank of New York, where they would be held or transferred to Iran as directed by the Secretary of the Treasury. *See Dames & Moore*, 453 U.S. at 665–66, 101 S. Ct. 2972. Subsequent Executive Orders and treasury regulations have controlled the transfer of Iranian Assets consistent with the Algiers Accords. *See, e.g.*, Iranian Assets Control Regulations, 31 C.F.R. pt. 535. Thus, practically speaking, there are simply few assets within the United States that are available for plaintiffs to seize in satisfaction of their judgments under the FSIA terrorism exception.

In Dames & Moore, the Supreme Court upheld the validity of actions taken by both President Regan and Carter to settle the Iran Hostage Crisis through the implementation of the Algiers Accords. 453 U.S. 654, 101 S. Ct. 2972. Specifically, the Court examined two issues. First, the Court addressed the validity of Executive Orders that nullified all attachments and similar encumbrances on Iranian property in the United States and directed the transfer of Iranian assets to the Federal Reserve Bank of New York for ultimate transfer back to Iran under the terms of the Algiers Accords. Second, the Court addressed Executive Orders that suspended claims pending against Iran in American courts and provided for those claims to be presented to Iran-United States Claims Tribunal for resolution through binding arbitration.

With respect to the termination of attachments on Iran's property and the transfer of Iran's assets, the Court found that Congress had provided in the IEEPA, 50 U.S.C. §§ 1701-1706, specific authorization for the President to take those actions. Dames & Moore, 453 U.S. at 674–75, 101 S. Ct. 2972. Accordingly, the Court relied on the strong presumption of validity traditionally accorded to such Executive action pursuant to a federal statute, as described in Justice Jackson's famous concurrence in *Youngstown Sheet & Tube Co. v. Sawyer*, 343 U.S. 579, 72 S. Ct. 863, 96 L.Ed. 1153 (1952), and held that, in light of this "specific congressional authorization," it could not find that the power exercised by the President had exceeded the bounds of any powers afforded under the Constitution. *Dames & Moore*, 453 U.S. at 675, 101 S. Ct. 2972. The Court observed: "A contrary ruling would mean that the Federal Government as a whole lacked the power exercised by the President, and that we are not prepared to say." *Id.* at 674, 101 S. Ct. 2972 (citation omitted).

With respect to the suspension of claims, the Court ultimately upheld that action as well, but the Court's rationale was a bit more nuanced. While the Court could not identity a specific authorization from Congress, the Court did find that, over more than two centuries, Congress had either acquiesced in or implicitly approved of the settlement of claims of United States nationals through executive agreement. *See id.* at 675–687, 101 S. Ct. 2972. Thus, in light of what the Court deemed as Congress' consent to the President's actions, the Court held that it could not say that the President's actions in suspending claims against Iran exceeded the President's powers. *Id.* at 686, 101 S. Ct. 2972.[11]

What few assets of Iran that might be found within jurisdiction of the United States courts since the Algiers Accords are a subject to a dizzying array of statutory and regulatory authorities due in large part to the federal government's obligations

---

11 As a leading case on the scope of Federal Power, particularly Executive Power, as exercised in the realm of foreign affairs and national security, and as a case concerning the Algiers Accords and Iran specifically, Dames & Moore remains particularly relevant with respect to many of the issues presented in the terrorism cases considered by this Court today. For example, by reaffirming the strong presumption of validity that should attach to actions expressly authorized by both political branches in the area of foreign affairs, Dames & Moore lends supports to this Court's ruling in Part E that § 1083(c) does not offend separation-of-powers principles relating to the independence of the judiciary. Additionally, Dames & Moore provides a historical perspective that helps to illustrate some of the unique challenges that plaintiffs in FSIA terrorism cases against Iran face as a consequence of executive actions implementing and honoring the terms of Algiers Accords.

More generally, then-Justice Rehnquist's discussion in Dames & Moore concerning our nation's rich history and tradition of the use of Executive authority to settle claims between United States nationals and foreign sovereigns, *see* 453 U.S. at 678–687, 101 S. Ct. 2972, provides an even broader historical perspective that this Court finds highly instructive for the purposes of today's opinion. Indeed, as Justice Rehnquist illustrated in his opinion for the Court, the exercise of Federal Power by the President to settle claims of U.S. nationals against foreign sovereigns—a long-standing practice to which the Congress has acquiesced and occasionally supported by legislation—has often proven to be the most effective way to ensure relief to United States Nationals aggrieved by foreign sovereigns. In Part K of this opinion, this Court relies on the time-honored practice of claims settlement by the Executive, as expressed in Dames & Moore, in support of this Court's call for reforms to help victims of Iran-sponsored terrorism find the relief they deserve.

under that bilateral executive agreement, but also in part because of the increasing hostility in the relationship between Iran and the United States in the wake of the hostage crisis and the continuous designation of Iran as a state sponsor of terrorism since 1984. In fact, much like the assets of other state sponsors of terrorism, most of Iran's known property or interests in property are blocked, i.e., frozen, or otherwise regulated under any number of United States sanctions programs.[12]

Beyond the imposition of economic sanctions and other regulatory controls, however, the inviolable doctrines of both foreign sovereign immunity and federal sovereign immunity have often precluded the attachment or execution of property that plaintiffs have identified as belonging to Iran. With respect to foreign sovereign immunity specifically, the FSIA itself has long forestalled plaintiffs' efforts to enforce judgments entered under § 1605(a)(7). This is largely because, much like foreign sovereigns are generally immune from civil suit under the FSIA, *see* § 1604, any property belonging to a foreign nation is similarly immune from attachment and execution by judgment creditors. *See* § 1609. The relevant exceptions to the general rule of immunity from the attachment or execution are listed in § 1610. Prior to the enactment of last year's reforms in the 2008 NDAA, however, these exceptions to the general rule of immunity for foreign government property were limited almost exclusively to property relating to the commercial activities of the foreign sovereign within the United States. *See* § 1610(a) and (b). Given the lack of formal relations between the United States and Iran, these provisions have been of little utility to the judgment creditors of Iran in FSIA terrorism cases. Thus, the FSIA facilitated a somewhat ironic and perverse outcome because on the one

---

12 *See* Terrorist Assets Report, *supra* note 2, at 2, 10. The Office of Foreign Assets Control (OFAC) of the Treasury Department administers economic sanction programs relating to terrorists, terrorist organizations, and officially designated state sponsors of terrorism. Each year, OFAC publishes a report to Congress regarding assets in the United States that belong to terrorist nations and other terrorist actors. This annual report discusses both blocked and non-blocked assets of Iran, as well assets attributable to other state sponsors of terrorism. As such, the Terrorist Assets Report is a good reference point for individuals interested in understanding some of the tremendous difficulties terrorism victims face in their efforts to enforce judgments entered against Iran under the FSIA terrorism exception.

According to the CRS, the blocked assets of Iran in the United States "includes property that is blocked under the Iranian Assets Control Regulations, 31 C.F.R. pt. 535, since the hostage crisis was resolved in 1981. The property blocked in 1981 remains blocked in part because of pending claims before the Iran-U.S. Claims Tribunal." *Id.* at 10. Other blocked assets include Iran's diplomatic and consular properties here in the United States, as well as any proceeds from the leasing of those properties, which are now managed and maintained by the State Department's Office of Foreign Missions. *Id.* "Additionally, other sanction authorities designed to address national emergencies distinct from terrorism have also resulted in the blocking of assets in which the Government of Iran has an interest." *Id.* The report adds that Iran claims "miscellaneous blocked and non-blocked military property that it asserts was in the possession of private entities in the United States when the hostage crisis was resolved in 1981. *Id.* at 12. The United States disputes Iran's claims and the matters are pending before the Claims-Tribunal. *Id.* at 13.

hand, in § 1605(a)(7), it created an opportunity for terrorism victims to sue Iran for money damages, while on the other hand, in §§ 1609 and 1610, it denied these victims the legal means to enforce their court judgments.[13]

In addition to the immunity from attachment or execution that the FSIA has long provided to foreign property, assets held within United States Treasury accounts that might otherwise be attributed to Iran are the property of the United States and are therefore exempt from attachment or execution by virtue of the federal government's sovereign immunity. *See Dep't of the Army v. Blue Fox, Inc.*, 525 U.S. 255, 119 S. Ct. 687, 142 L.Ed.2d 718 (1999); *State of Arizona v. Bowsher*, 935 F.2d 332 (D.C.Cir.1991). As the Supreme Court held in the seminal case of *Buchanan v. Alexander*, United States sovereign immunity is an extremely broad bar to jurisdiction that prevents creditors from attaching funds held by the United States treasury or its agents. 45 U.S. 20, 4 How. 20, 11 L.Ed. 857 (1846).

Because the federal government has assumed control over significant portions of what limited Iranian assets remain in the United States, plaintiffs' efforts to enforce judgments under the FSIA have often pitted victims of terrorism against the Executive Branch. Under successive presidential administrations, the Justice Department repeatedly moved to quash writs of attachment issued by judgment creditors of Iran. Two frequently discussed and well-documented examples concern the efforts of Stephen Flatow to enforce his civil judgment, which culminated in litigation against the United States in this Court. *See Flatow II*, 74 F. Supp. 2d 18; *Flatow III*, 76 F. Supp. 2d 16. In both cases, this Court had to deny plaintiff relief and thereby granted the federal government's motion to quash.

In the first case, plaintiff issued writs that purported to attach credits held by the United States for the benefit of Iran, including more than 5 million dollars in the United States Treasury Judgment Fund, which had been earmarked to pay an award issued in Iran's favor by the Iran-United States Claims Tribunal. *Flatow II*, 74 F. Supp. 2d at 20. Plaintiff pointed to the Iranian Assets Control Regulations in support of his argument that money in the Treasury Judgment Fund should be considered Iranian property that is potentially subject to attachment and execution under the FSIA, 1610. *See id.* (citing 31 C.F.R. § 535.311 (1999)). In rejecting plaintiff's argument, this Court relied on Buchanan and Blue Fox, and held that funds in the

13 Another challenge for plaintiffs looking to collect on their judgments in this context is that many of the world's leading financial institutions are agencies or instrumentalities of foreign nations and are therefore immune from jurisdiction of the United States Courts under the FSIA. *See* §§ 1603-1604. In Peterson, for example, this Court recently quashed writs of attachment issued upon Japan Bank for International Cooperation, Bank of Japan, and the Export Import Bank of Korea. *See Peterson III*, 563 F. Supp. 2d 268. Plaintiffs alleged that these three foreign banks possess Iranian assets, but this Court found that all three banks are foreign state entities that qualify for immunity from jurisdiction under the FSIA. For the same reasons, this Court quashed numerous subpoenas that plaintiffs had issued to those financial institutions and denied plaintiffs' request for the appointment of a receivership for any and all assets of Iran held by those foreign banks.

United States Treasury—regardless of whether those funds have been set aside to pay a debt to Iran—remain immune from attachment by virtue of United States sovereign immunity. *Id.* at 21. "In other words, funds held in the U.S. Treasury—even though set aside or 'earmarked' for a specific purpose—remain the property of the United States until the government elects to pay them to who they are owed." *Id.* Accordingly, as the United States had not waived its sovereign immunity with respect to those funds that had been earmarked to pay a Tribunal Award or other debts to Iran, that money remained exempt from attachment or execution by virtue of federal sovereign immunity. *Id.* at 23; *see also Weinstein*, 274 F. Supp. 2d at 58 (holding that funds allegedly owed to Iran in the Treasury's Foreign Military Sales (FMS) Program are immune from attachment by virtue of federal sovereign immunity).

In the second case, plaintiff issued writs of attachment upon three parcels of real estate owned by Iran that once served as the Iranian Embassy and as residences and offices for Iran's diplomatic personnel. *Flatow III*, 76 F. Supp. 2d at 18. Additionally, plaintiff issued writs of attachment upon two bank accounts that contained funds generated by the State Department's lease of Iran's diplomatic properties. *Id.* The first of the two accounts was used to pay for the maintenance and repair of Iran's properties. *Id.* at 19. The second account contained all the profits generated as a result of the lease of Iran's foreign mission properties. *Id.*

The United States promptly intervened and moved to quash the writs, arguing that real property and the related banks accounts were immune from attachment under the Foreign Missions Act, the FSIA, the IEEPA, the Vienna Convention on Diplomatic Relations, and Article II of the U.S. Constitution. *Id.* at 19. The plaintiffs countered that because Iran's former embassy properties were being managed and leased out to tenets by the Department of the State under the auspices of the Foreign Missions Act, 22 U.S.C. §§ 4301-4313, the property was being used for a "commercial activity" and therefore satisfied the requirements for attachment under § 1610(a)(7) of the FSIA. *See Flatow III*, 76 F. Supp. 2d at 21.

Without reaching any of the more fundamental arguments raised by the government's motion to quash, this Court held that the leasing of Iran's real property by the United States did not qualify as a commercial activity in part because the United States' action in taking custody of Iran's property under the authority of the Foreign Missions Act "was decidedly sovereign in nature." *Id.* at 23; *see also Bennett*, 604 F. Supp. 2d at 169 (relying on Flatow to grant United States' motion to quash writs of attachment recently issued on Iran's foreign mission properties). For similar reasons, the Court found that the bank account that was used by the State Department's Office of Foreign Missions (OFM) for the maintenance and repair of Iran's real property was also immune from attachment because the funds within that account were expended by OFM in exercise of its statutory prerogative to provide for the upkeep properties that once housed Iran's foreign mission. *Flatow III*, at 24. This Court also found that the other account at issue, which simply contained the profits earned on the lease of Iran's property, was immune from attachment as a result of federal sovereign immunity. *Id.*

In some frustration, this Court observed in Flatow that President Clinton's Administration, including President Clinton himself, had both publicly and privately expressed support for the victims of terrorism and for the plaintiffs in these terrorism cases specifically, and yet the Clinton Justice Department repeatedly fought efforts by these victims to enforce court judgments under the FSIA. *See Flatow II*, 74 F. Supp. 2d at 26; *Flatow III*, 76 F. Supp. 2d at 19–20. Moreover, as will be discussed below, President Clinton twice blocked reforms to the FSIA that would have subjected Iran's blocked assets to attachment and execution. *See infra* pp. 56–57; Suits Against Terrorist States, *supra* note 4, at 10–12 (discussing President's exercise of waiver authority with respect to provisions that would have permitted attachment and execution upon frozen assets of state sponsors of terrorism); *see also Flatow III*, 76 F. Supp. 2d 16 (noting President's first exercise of waiver in the interest of national security of provision that would have permitted attachment of blocked assets). In a letter to the Washington Post cited by this Court in two of its published decisions, Stephen Flatow documented his meetings with President Clinton, including private meetings and phone calls, as well as his meetings with other high ranking members of the Clinton Administration. *See* Stephen Flatow, In This Case, I Can't Be Diplomatic; I Lost a Child to Terrorism; Now I'm Losing U.S. Support, Wash. Post, Nov. 7, 1999, at B2. Mr. Flatow explained how he grew tremendously frustrated in his long pursuit of justice in which he received statements of support from the Executive Branch, as well as personal assurances of assistance, only to later find that the administration proved to be the most formidable adversary in his efforts to execute judgment upon the blocked assets of Iran. In reflecting on his experiences some years later, Stephen Flatow referred to his litigation against the United States "as a real cat fight." Tucker, Pain and Suffering, *supra*.

As this Court observed how many plaintiffs struggled to enforce their court judgments in FSIA terrorism cases against Iran, this Court began to refer these judgments as "Pyrrhic Victories." *Eisenfeld*, 172 F. Supp. 2d at 9; *Flatow III*, 76 F. Supp. 2d at 27. Moreover, this Court expressed dismay over the fact that the rule of law was being frustrated in these actions. *Eisenfeld*, 172 F. Supp. 2d at 9. Allowing plaintiffs to go forward with suits under § 1605(a)(7) while not freeing up Iran's assets to satisfy those judgments under § 1610, or through the release of blocked assets under United States' control, was a quintessential example of the federal government promising with one hand what it takes away with the other. In fact, it is not uncommon for plaintiffs to receive mixed signals from Congress and the President in this highly-charged political context. *See, e.g.*, *Roeder*, 195 F. Supp. 2d at 145 (observing that the political branches of the Government "should not with one hand express support for the plaintiffs and with the other leave it to this Court to play the role of the messenger of bad news").

In view of the challenges that plaintiffs encountered in their efforts to execute judgments against the assets of state sponsors of terrorism here in the United States, Congress did make a number of efforts on behalf of the victims of terrorism to free up blocked assets for judgments under § 1605(a)(7). The first law enacted as part of this effort to free up assets of state sponsors of terrorism was included in the Omnibus Consolidated and Emergency Supplemental Appropriations Act, 1999. Pub. L. No. 105-277, div. A, tit. I, § 117(a), 112 Stat. 2681–0, 2681–491 (codified at § 1610(f)(1)(A)). That measure created a new exception— § 1610(f)— which allowed for the first time attachment and execution against blocked assets of state sponsors of terrorism.[14] When Congress passed this measure, however, it also provided that the President could waive the provision "in the interest of national security." § 1610(f)(3). Upon signing the bill into law, President Clinton exercised that waiver authority. *See* Pres. Determ. No. 99-1, 63 Fed.Reg. 59,201 (Oct. 21, 1998). In doing so, the President stated:

> Absent my authority to waive section 117's attachment provision, it would effectively eliminate the use of blocked assets of terrorist States in the national security interests of the United States, including denying an important source of leverage. In addition, section 117 could seriously impair our ability to enter into global claims settlements that are fair to all U.S. claimants, and could result in U.S. taxpayer liability in the event of a contrary claims tribunal judgment. To the extent possible, I shall construe section 117 in a manner consistent with my constitutional authority and with U.S. international legal obligations, and for the above reasons, I have exercised the waiver authority in the in the national security interest of the United States.

Statement on Signing the Omnibus Consolidated and Emergency Supplemental Appropriations Act, 1999, 2 Pub. Papers 1843, 1847 (Oct. 23, 1998). Thus, § 1610(f)(1)(A)—which would have broadly subjected Iranian assets to attachment and execution—was rendered a nullity.[15]

---

14 Section 1610(f)(1)(A) of the FSIA has not changed in substance since its enactment in 1998. It was amended slightly by § 1083 of the 2008 NDAA in order to account for the repeal of § 1605(a)(7) and enactment of § 1605A. The exception now reads as follows:

> Notwithstanding any other provision of law, including but not limited to section 208(f) of the Foreign Missions Act (22 U.S.C. 4308(f)), and except as provided in subparagraph (B), any property with respect to which financial transactions are prohibited or regulated pursuant to section 5(b) of the Trading with the Enemy Act (50 U.S.C.App. 5(b)), section 620(a) of the Foreign Assistance Act of 1961 (22 U.S.C. 2370(a)), sections 202 and 203 of the International Emergency Economic Powers Act (50 U.S.C. 1701-1702), or any other proclamation, order, regulation, or license issued pursuant thereto, shall be subject to execution or attachment in aid of execution of any judgment relating to a claim for which a foreign state (including any agency or instrumentality or such state) claiming such property is not immune under section 1605(a)(7) (as in effect before the enactment of section 1605A) or section 1605A.

15 The Supreme Court has long recognized the important role that blocked assets can play in a President's efforts to manage a foreign policy crisis. *See Dames & Moore v. Regan*, 453 U.S. at 673, 101 S. Ct. 2972 (1981) (relying on *Propper v. Clark*, 337 U.S. 472, 493, 69 S. Ct. 1333, 93 L.Ed. 1480 (1949)). In Dames & Moore, the Court emphasized that blocked assets "serve as a 'bargaining chip' to be used when dealing with a hostile country." 453 U.S. at 673, 101 S. Ct. 2972.

The following term, Congress passed the Victims of Trafficking and Violence Protection Act of 2000 (VTVPA), in which Congress again tried to subject blocked assets of state sponsors of terrorism to attachment of execution. Pub. L. No. 106-386, § 2002, 114 Stat. 1464, 1541. Specifically, Congress aimed in the VTVPA to resurect § 1610(f)(1)(A) of the FSIA and thus repealed the waiver authority that was exercised by President Clinton under § 117(d) of the Omnibus Consolidated and Emergency Supplemental Appropriations Act, 1999. *See* § 2002(f)(2). Oddly enough, however, Congress replaced that earlier waiver provision with a new, and nearly identical provision, that again granted the President the authority to waive § 1610(f)(1)(A) "in the interest of national security." § 2002(f)(1)(B). Upon singing the VTVPA into law, the President again exercised the waiver authority, as granted by Congress, which again rendered § 1610 a nullity. Thus, § 1610(f) remains inapplicable in cases under the FSIA terrorism exception.

More significantly, the VTVPA also directed the Secretary of Treasury to pay the compensatory damages awarded in court judgments to plaintiffs in a limited number of FSIA terrorism cases against Iran or Cuba. § 2002(a). With respect to the payment of judgments against Iran specifically, the VTVPA directed the Secretary of Treasury to make those payments out of the rental proceeds that had been accrued as a result of the federal government's lease of Iranian diplomatic and consular property and from appropriated funds "not to exceed the total of the amount in the Iran Foreign Military Sales Program account within the Foreign Military Sales Fund." § 2002(b).[16] Once an eligible plaintiff accepts a payment of compensatory damages from the United States Treasury on a judgment against Iran, the plaintiff's right to pursue that claim is "fully subrogated" to the United States. *Id.* As a result of the VTVPA, precisely ten cases against Iran qualified for payments from the United States Treasury. *See* Terrorist Assets Report, *supra* note 2, at 12–15, app. A (discussing VTVPA program for payment of compensatory damage in judgments entered against Iran and Cuba and listing cases). Flatow was among the cases that qualified, and Stephen Flatow, along with plaintiffs in all

---

Notably, the Court also observed how subjecting frozen assets "to attachments, garnishments, and similar encumbrances" would enable "individual claimants throughout the country to minimize or wholly eliminate this 'bargaining chip.'" *Id.* at 673, 101 S. Ct. 2972. The efforts by Congress to subject the blocked assets of terrorists states to attachment and execution has been one of the most controversial issues pertaining to the FSIA terrorism exception. The tug of war between Congress and the President over this thorny issue serves as a great example of the ways in which the FSIA terrorism exception and its related enactments constitute a "delicate legislative compromise." *Price*, 294 F.3d at 86.

16 The Foreign Military Sales (FMS) Program account for Iran is a United States Treasury account, subject to federal sovereign immunity, which contains funds relating to military transactions with Iran that pre-date the Iran-hostage crisis and which are currently the subject of ongoing litigation before the Iran-U.S. Claims Tribunal. *See Weinstein*, 274 F. Supp. 2d at 58 (discussing the FMS Program account and holding that federal sovereign immunity bars attachment); Terrorist Assets Report, *supra* note 2, at 16–17 (discussing both the VTVPA and the FMS Program account).

of the nine other qualifying cases, opted to have their compensatory damages paid by United States. *See id.*; *see also* TUCKER, PAIN AND SUFFERING, *supra* (discussing Stephen Flatow's acceptance of payment of compensatory damages from the United States Treasury and his ongoing efforts to enforce the punitive damages portion of his judgment against Iran). Subsequent legal enactments have expanded the number of cases with judgments against Iran that are eligible for payments from the United States Treasury. *See* Foreign Relations Authorization Act, Fiscal Year 2003, Pub. L. No. 107-228, § 686, 116 Stat. 1350, 1411 (2002); Terrorism Risk Insurance Act of 2002 (TIRA), Pub. L. No. 107-297, § 201, 116 Stat. 2322, 2337–39.

In the TRIA, Congress not only expanded the class of plaintiffs eligible for payment from the United States Department of Treasury under the VTVPA, but, even more fundamentally, Congress finally succeeded in subjecting the assets of state sponsors of terrorism to attachment and execution in satisfaction of judgments under § 1605(a)(7). *See* § 201. The TRIA provides that "[n]otwithstanding any other provision of law," the blocked assets of a terrorist state are subject to attachment or execution to the extent of any compensatory damages awarded against that state under the FSIA terrorism exception. *Id.* The TRIA does, however, continue to exempt diplomatic and consular property from attachment and execution under § 1610. *See* § 201(d)(2)(B)(ii). Nonetheless, the TRIA has opened a wide range of blocked assets to attachment and execution by the judgment creditors of state sponsors of terrorism. Thus, the TRIA appears to represent something of a victory for these terrorism victims—whose interests have been most vigorously advanced by members of Congress—over the longstanding objections of the Executive Branch.

In the case of Iran, however, the simple fact remains that very few blocked assets exist. In fact, according to OFAC's latest report, there are only 16.8 million dollars in blocked assets relating to Iran. TERRORIST ASSETS REPORT, *supra* note 2, at 14, tbl. 1. This amount is inconsequential—a mere drop in the bucket—when compared to the staggering 9.6 billion dollars in outstanding judgments entered against Iran in terrorism cases as of August 2008, which is the last time the Congressional Research Service compiled data on this issue. *Id.* at 75, app. B, tbl. B-1. The amount of Iranian non-blocked assets within the United States, as reported to OFAC, is similarly inconsequential in comparison to Iran's liability under the FSIA terrorism exception. According to OFAC, the amount of non-blocked Iranian assets is merely 28 million dollars. *Id.* at 15, tbl. 3.[17]

The billions of dollars in liability that Iran now faces is likely to increase tremendously as a result of the new federal cause of action under § 1605A, which now

---

17 In fairness, it is important to emphasize here that "there is no requirement for U.S. persons to report non-blocked assets to OFAC." TERRORIST ASSETS REPORT, *supra* note 2, at 10. Thus, arguably, there could be any number of undisclosed, non-blocked Iranian assets within the jurisdiction of the United States courts. In light of the lack of formal relations between Iran and the United States, however, the prospect of large sums of Iranian assets being located within the jurisdiction of the federal courts seems remote.

includes punitive damages. Thus, Congress has continued to fuel expectations in these actions by broadly subjecting Iran to suit for sponsorship of terrorism while simultaneously ignoring the fact that the prospects for recovery are virtually non-existent. This fundamental problem is an issue that the Court will explore later in this opinion in Part K below.

B. Section 1083 of the 2008 NDAA and the Creation of a New Terrorism Exception, Section 1605a

In light of the significant setbacks that plaintiffs experienced in actions under § 1605(a)(7), Congress implemented a number of major reforms last year. Section 1083 of National Defense Appropriations Act (NDAA) completely repeals § 1605(a)(7) and replaces that provision with a new statute, § 1605A. As noted above, it is important to keep in mind that the exception to foreign sovereign immunity under the new provision, § 1605A, is identical to that which is contained in § 1605(a)(7), but this new law is more comprehensive and more favorable to plaintiffs because it adds a broad array of substantive rights and remedies that simply were not available in actions under § 1605(a)(7).

As noted above, § 1605A accomplishes four basic objectives. This new terrorism statute (1) furnishes a cause of action against state sponsors of terrorism; (2) makes punitive damages available in those actions; (3) authorizes compensation for special masters; and (4) implements new measures designed to facilitate the enforcement of judgments. Each of these four key aspects of § 1605A will now be discussed in turn.

1. New Federal Cause of Action

With respect to the first objective, the new law now expressly provides that designated state sponsors of terrorism may be subject to a federal cause of action for money damages if those terrorist states cause or otherwise provide material support for an act of terrorism that results in the death or injury of a United States citizen or national. *See* § 1605A(c). This new federal right of action for money damages abrogates Cicippio-Puleo, 353 F.3d 1024, and is a crucial change in the law for hundreds of FSIA terrorism plaintiffs who were not able to rely on state tort law to create a cause of action against Iran previously.

Thanks to the enactment of § 1605A, the inconsistent and varied result that was reached in Peterson and in similar cases under § 1605(a)(7) will be avoided in actions going forward under the new law. Courts can now work from a single federal cause of action that will ensure a greater degrees of fairness to FSIA terrorism plaintiffs while furnishing a level of consistency and uniformity that is critical in matters of foreign relations.[18]

---

18 Unlike § 1605(a)(7), the Flatow Amendment, § 1605 note, was not repealed by § 1083 of the 2008 NDAA. Thus, technically speaking, the Flatow Amendment remains on the books

The new cause of action included with the new terrorism exception § 1605A has a new and expanded statute of limitations. Specifically, § 1605A(b) provides:

> An action may be brought or maintained under this section if the action is commenced, or a related action was commenced under section 1605(a)(7) (before the date of the enactment of this section) or [the Flatow Amendment] not later than the later of—
>
> (1) 10 years after April 24, 1996; or
>
> (2) 10 years after the date on which the cause of action arose.

§ 1605A(b) (emphasis added). The prior statute of limitations applicable to actions under § 1605(a)(7) was simply 10 years from the date the cause of action arose (leading to a cut-off date in April 2006), subject, in some instances, to equitable tolling. *See* § 1605(f) (repealed by § 1083(b)). Accordingly, many new actions that might have been barred by the statute of limitations for § 1605(a)(7) may now move forward under § 1605A.

As § 1605A establishes a new federal cause of action against state sponsors of terrorism, this Court will have to determine what basic principles of law should be applied to resolve claims sounding in tort pursuant to this new private right of action under the FSIA. This is an important issue that many judges of this Court grappled with through the application of the Flatow Amendment in FSIA terrorism cases that reached final judgments prior to the Circuit's ruling in Cicippio-Puleo.[19] At that time, judges of this Court frequently referred to "federal common law" as providing the rule of decision for claims under the FSIA. *See, e.g., Stethem v. Islamic Republic of Iran*, 201 F. Supp. 2d 78, 89 (D.D.C.2002) (Jackson, J.); *Wagner v. Islamic Republic of Iran*, 172 F. Supp. 2d 128, 134 (D.D.C.2001) (Jackson, J.); *Flatow I*, 999 F. Supp. 1 at 15.

In *Bettis v. Islamic Republic of Iran*, however, which one of the last FSIA terrorism cases decided by the Circuit prior to Cicippio-Puleo, the Court of Appeals cautioned trial judges against the use of the term "federal common law." 315 F.3d 325, 333 (D.C.Cir.2003). The appeal in Bettis involved claims for intentional infliction of emotional distress. In examining those claims, the Court warned that the Flatow Amendment did not "'authorize federal courts to fashion a complete body of

---

even though it was rendered a virtual nullity by the Cicippio-Puleo decision. Moreover, to the extent that the Flatow Amendment might have any operative effect, the provision is now largely superfluous in light of the private right of action contained in the new terrorism exception, § 1605A.

19 *See, e.g., Jenco v. Islamic Republic of Iran*, 154 F. Supp. 2d 27 (D.D.C.2001) (Lambeth, J.) (relying on tort law treatises, including the Restatement (Second) of Torts, as well as leading state court decisions to resolve claims of battery, assault, false imprisonment, and intentional infliction of emotional distress); *Sutherland v. Islamic Republic of Iran*, 151 F. Supp. 2d 27 (D.D.C.2001) (Lamberth, J.) (applying the Restatement (Second) of Torts to resolve claims of battery, assault, false imprisonment, and intentional infliction of emotional distress); *Flatow I*, 999 F. Supp. 1 (applying common law standards for wrongful death, survival pain and suffering, and solatium).

federal law'" to address the claims of plaintiffs under that statute. *Id.* (quoting *Burks v. Lasker*, 441 U.S. 471, 476, 99 S. Ct. 1831, 60 L.Ed.2d 404 (1979)). Instead of relying on "federal common law," the Court looked to § 46 of the Restatement (Second) of Torts, as well as a number of secondary source compilations, such as legal encyclopedias, law reviews, and survey of leading state tort law cases. *See id.* at 333–338.

Admittedly, Bettis was decided under the Flatow Amendment, but this Court finds nonetheless that Bettis should still control now that Congress has clearly established a private right of action against a foreign state sponsor of terrorism for "personal injury or death" in those cases in which terrorism exception to foreign sovereign immunity applies. § 1605A(c). The questions confronted relating to sources of common law for claims sounding in tort under the Flatow Amendment, are, in substance, the same as those that will now confront this Court as result of the new private right of action in § 1605A(c). Thus, the question of what substantive tort law norms should control in these actions is an issue this Court will have to continue to explore in actions under § 1605A, as it once did in actions under the Flatow Amendment prior to Cicippio-Puleo.[20]

---

20 In cautioning against the use of federal common law, the Court of Appeals in Bettis relied heavily on § 1606 of the FSIA. That provision provides in relevant part: "As to any claim for relief with respect to which a foreign state is not entitled to immunity under section 1605 or section 1607 of this chapter, the foreign state shall be liable in the same manner and to the same extent as a private individual under like circumstances." The Court reasoned that § 1606 "in effect instructs federal judges to find relevant law, not to make it." 315 F.3d at 333. At this juncture, however, it is unclear whether § 1606 should even apply in cases that rely on the new federal cause of action in § 1605A. For starters, § 1606 by its plain terms applies only to sections § 1605 and § 1607 of the FSIA. Moreover, § 1606 conflicts with § 1605A because it provides that punitive damages are not available in actions against foreign states, whereas § 1605A expressly authorizes punitive damages in cases against state sponsors of terrorism. Notably, Congress did not make any changes or updates to § 1606 when it repealed § 1605(a)(7) in the 2008 NDAA, and yet Congress did include a lengthy list of "Conforming Amendments" in § 1083(b) to ensure that both § 1605A and other reforms relating to terrorism actions, such as § 1610(g), were properly integrated into the larger statutory scheme of the FSIA. Thus, this Court can reasonably infer that Congress' failure to update § 1606 to include a reference to § 1605A evinces Congress intent that those standards pertaining to the scope of foreign state liability in § 1606 do not apply in actions against state sponsors of terrorism under § 1605A.

Consistent with the approach this Court initially took in Flatow, some commentators have urged courts to fashion federal common law standards as the substantive rules of decision in cases under the FSIA terrorism exception. *See* DEUTSCH, *supra*, at 891 (criticizing Bettis and urging the adoption of federal common law standards to resolve terrorism claims under the FSIA terrorism exception). Ms. Deutsch argues that federal common law standards are needed in this area largely because of the unique nature of claims involving acts of international terrorism, the primacy of the federal interest in terrorism cases, and the potential inconsistencies that may result from reliance on state law standards. In the absence of additional guidance from the Court of Appeals on this issue, this Court is bound to follow the admonishment in Bettis and will therefore eschew any reliance on "federal common law."

As this Court views Bettis as the as the controlling precedent with respect to application of tort law principles to in cases under the FSIA terrorism exception, this Court will therefore look to that decision as the starting point for the analysis of substantive claims under § 1605A. Consistent with Bettis, this Court will rely on well-established principles of law, such as those found in Restatement (Second) of Torts and other leading treatises, as well as those principles that have been adopted by the majority of state jurisdictions. Today, this Court will issue a separate opinion in the consolidated action of *Heiser v. Islamic Republic of Iran*, 466 F. Supp. 2d 229 (D.D.C.), a case concerning the Khobar Towers bombing, in which this Court analyzes new claims for compensatory damages under § 1605A. Plaintiffs looking for more guidance regarding the standards that this Court will apply to claims under § 1605A should review that decision in conjunction with this omnibus opinion.

2. Punitive Damages

The second key reform found in § 1605A is the availability of punitive damages. *See* § 1605A(c). Consequently, the majority of the of the plaintiffs in prior actions under § 1605(a)(7) who were unable to claim punitive damages following the Cicippio-Puleo decision will now have an opportunity to do so. The prospect of large punitive damage awards may help to deter Iran and other states sponsors of terrorism from their support of international terrorist organizations.

Through the separate opinion and judgment entered in Heiser, this Court awards plaintiffs in that action punitive damages under § 1605A(c). In doing so, the Court reaffirms the principles first articulated in Flatow with respect to awards of punitive damages against Iran. Other plaintiffs who now seek punitive damages under § 1605A should review this Court's discussion of punitive damages in Flatow and look to the opinion issued today in Heiser.

3. Compensation for Special Masters

Over the years, a number of attorneys have been appointed by this Court to serve as special masters to assist the Court in determining money damage awards for the many individual plaintiffs and estates represented on this Court's sizable docket of civil actions against Iran. The work completed by these officers of the Court is extraordinarily tedious and time-consuming, and, until recently, the special masters were not entitled to any compensation for their efforts. In last year's NDAA, however, Congress directed that special masters in cases against designated states sponsors of terrorism should receive compensation for their work, and thus the new terrorism exception now provides that special masters should be reimbursed for their work from the Attorney General's Victims of Crime Fund. *See* § 1605A(e).

4. More Robust Provisions for the Execution of Civil Judgments

Like many prior legislative enactments relating to civil suits against designated state sponsors of terrorism, the new terrorism exception in combination with certain other reforms achieved through § 1083 takes aim at what is perhaps the most fundamental problem confronting these actions: the inability of plaintiffs to execute their civil judgments against Iran. As noted above, *supra*, most plaintiffs in FSIA terrorism cases have been thwarted in their efforts to execute civil judgments in part because there are few Iranian Government assets within the jurisdiction of the United States Courts. What little that does exist is generally immune from attachment or execution under § 1609. Additionally, in the past plaintiffs have encountered the problem of United States sovereign immunity because most property or interests in property within the United States that might be attributed to state sponsors of terrorism are subject to federal regulatory control, or are, in a number of instances, within the possession of the federal government. *See, e.g.*, *Weinstein*, 274 F. Supp. 2d 53.

In an apparent effort to overcome some of the challenges relating to the execution of judgments, § 1605A entitles plaintiffs to what are in effect automatic prejudgment liens on property belonging to a designated state sponsor of terrorism.[21] In addition to these new prejudgment attachment procedures, any actions filed or otherwise maintained under § 1605A may benefit from certain reforms to § 1610, which is the section of the FSIA that prescribes the limited circumstances in which the property of a foreign state may be subject to attachment or execution upon a civil judgment. Specifically, § 1083 of the 2008 NDAA adds to § 1610 new provisions that are plainly intended to limit the application of foreign sovereign immunity or United States sovereign immunity as defenses to attachment or execution with respect to property belonging to designated states sponsors of terrorism. *See* § 1083(b) ("Conforming Amendments") (codified at § 1610(g)). The full implications of § 1610(g) are far from clear. Only time will tell whether § 1610(g) will enable plaintiffs going forward with actions under § 1605A to experience greater success in executing civil judgments against Iranian assets. Given the scarcity of assets and the difficulty of locating what assets might be available—it seems unlikely that this provision will be of great utility to plaintiffs. Suffice it to note, however, these latest additions to the FSIA demonstrate that Congress remains

---

21 The procedure in § 1605A(g) entitles plaintiffs to file notices of lis pendens. Generally speaking, a notice of lis pendens concerns specific property belonging to a party involved in civil litigation. *See generally*, 51 Am.Jur.2d Lis Pendens § 2. The lis pendens notice serves to alert third parties that any rights concerning the noticed property are subject to the outcome of the civil litigation. *See generally id.* While it is not technically a lien, the legal effect of a properly filed notice of lis pendens is that any third-party purchaser who receives title to the noticed property is bound by the outcome of the civil case, without any additional rights to that property. *See generally id.* Lis pendens is a creature of state law that has never before been available through the federal courts. Consistent with the new statutory entitlement contained in § 1605A(g), this Court recently approved a form and procedures for plaintiffs to file notices of lis pendens in the consolidated action of *Heiser v. the Islamic Republic of Iran*, No. 00-CV-2329-RCL (D.D.C.) and *Campbell v. Islamic Republic of Iran*, 01-CV-2104-RCL (D.D.C.). *See Heiser*, No. 00-CV-2329-RCL (D.D.C.), Dk. ## 144–145; *Campbell*, 01-CV-2104-RCL (D.D.C.), Dk. ## 132, 135.

focused on eliminating those barriers that have made it nearly impossible for plaintiffs in these actions to execute civil judgments against Iran or other state sponsors of terrorism.

C. Retroactive Application of Section 1605a to Cases Previously Filed Under Section 1605(a)(7)

Today the Court must determine whether the new terrorism exception should be applied retroactively to reach cases that were originally filed under § 1605(a)(7) prior to enactment of the new statute, § 1605A. In this instance, Congress has in § 1083(c) of the 2008 NDAA provided guidance with respect to the retroactive reach of this new provision of law, and so the Court's analysis begins with that statutory guidance. *See, e.g.*, *Hamdan v. Rumsfeld*, 548 U.S. 557, 575–584, 126 S. Ct. 2749, 165 L.Ed.2d 723 (2006) (applying "ordinary principles of statutory construction" to determine whether the Detainee Treatment Act should operate retroactively); *Landgraf*, 511 U.S. at 271, 114 S. Ct. 1483 (noting that when "Congress has expressly prescribed the statute's proper reach[,] there is no need to resort to judicial default rules"). Section § 1083 contains a number of subsections, but two are especially critical for purposes of this Court's analysis. These are subsections (c)(2) and (c)(3), which set forth the qualifying conditions and procedures that must be fulfilled before a prior action under § 1605(a)(7) may be eligible to proceed under the new terrorism law, § 1605A.

Subsection (c)(2) refers to "Prior Actions," but this subsection actually concerns a relatively narrow category of prior cases, all of which are probably best characterized as pending cases. Pending in this instance means cases that were awaiting a disposition by a court at the time of the 2008 NDAA's enactment. This includes actions that were on direct appeal and those with unresolved postjudgment motions.

The next subsection, (c)(3), referring to "Related Actions," reaches a far broader category of cases, including many that simply were not pending with the courts in any form at the time the 2008 NDAA became law. This is because the plain terms of the related-actions provisions in subsection (c)(3) specify that if an action was timely commenced under § 1605(a)(7), then "any other action arising out of the same act or incident may be brought under section 1605A" § 1083(c)(3) (emphasis added). Thus, the heading of § 1083(c)—"Application to Pending Cases"—is something of a misnomer because, in reality, § 1083(c) may encompass cases that are not pending at all—meaning prior actions that have since reached final judgment and are no longer before the courts in any form.

Additionally, there are two other aspects of § 1083(c) that are critical to today's analysis. First, the statute sets up limitaton periods or filing deadlines for plaintiffs desiring to take advantage of the newly enacted terrorism statute. *See* § 1083(c)(2)(C), (c)(3). Second, in a section of the statute referred to as "Defense Waived," the enactment provides that the defenses of res judicata and collateral estoppel are waived to the extent that such defenses are based on a claim that was presented in a prior FSIA terrorism case under § 1605(a)(7). *See* § 1083(c)(2)(B).

As each of these provisions within § 1083(c) are central to today's decision, the Court will now review the specifics of each of these statutory mandates in turn.

1. Section 1083(c)(2)— "Prior Actions"

In accordance with the procedures in § 1083(c)(2), a "prior action" that was timely commenced under either § 1605(a)(7) or the Flatow Amendment is eligible to proceed under the new statute, § 1605A, if three straightforward criteria are satisfied. Specifically, the plaintiff must demonstrate the prior action: (1) relied on § 1605(a)(7) or the Flatow Amendment as creating a cause of action, (2) has "been adversely affected on the grounds that either or both of those provisions failed to create a cause of action against the state," and (3) as of the date of the enactment of the 2008 NDAA, the case was "before the court[] in any form, including on appeal or motion under Rule 60(b) of the Federal Rules of Civil Procedure." § 1083(c)(2)(A)(ii)-(iv). If these requirements are met, then "the action shall, on motion made by plaintiffs to the United States district court where the action was initially brought, or judgment in the action was originally entered, be given effect as if the action had originally been filed under section 1605A(c) of title 28, United States Code." § 1083(c)(2)(A)(iv). This subsection also contemplates that the plaintiff may chose to "refile" his action, rather than make a motion. *See* § 1083(c)(2)(C).

In another action before this Court, Syria argued recently that plaintiffs who filed actions under § 1605(a)(7) following the Court of Appeals' decision in Cicippio-Puleo, or after June 16, 2004, are precluded from taking advantage of § 1083(c)(2) because, as Syria reads the statute, such plaintiffs could not have reasonably relied on § 1605(a)(7) or the Flatow Amendment, as Cicippio-Puleo made plain that those provisions do not furnish a cause of action against a foreign state. *See Gates v. Syrian Arab Republic*, 646 F. Supp. 2d 79 (D.D.C. 2009) (Collyer, J.). In this Court's view, however, such an interpretation of § 1083(c)(2)(A) is a crabbed reading of the statute, which, if accepted, would frustrate the broad remedial purposes Congress sought to achieve through the enactment of § 1083. In fact, the House Conference Report that accompanied § 1083 strongly suggests that Congress envisioned an expansive retroactive reach for § 1605A as a means to overcome the many setbacks plaintiffs encountered under § 1605(a)(7) and the Flatow Amendment. That report states: "The provision would allow any case previously brought under the state sponsor of terrorism exception to the FSIA under the section 1605(a)(7), or under section 101(c) of Public Law 101-208 [the Flatow Amendment], and which is still before a court, to be refiled as if the original claim has been filed under the provisions of this section." H.R.REP. No. 110-477, at 1001 (2007) (Conf. Rep.). Accordingly, this Court construes § 1083(c)(2)(A) broadly, consistent with the remedial purposes of the new anti-terrorism enactment, to include actions adversely impacted by Cicippio-Puleo, regardless of when those actions were filed. For similar reasons, this Court reads the requirement that the prior actions must be adversely impacted on the grounds that § 1605(a)(7) and the Flatow Amendment failed to establish a cause of action against a foreign state to include those instances in which plaintiffs failed to recover punitive damages, a critical component of these terrorism actions.

2. Section 1083(c)(3)— "Related Actions"

Section 1083(c)(3), the provision concerning "related actions" offers another method by which certain prior actions may be filed with the Court as new actions under § 1605A. Specifically, § 1083(c)(3) provides that "[i]f an action arising out of an act or incident has been timely commenced under section 1605(a)(7) . . . , any other action arising out of the same act or incident may be brought under section 1605A." As this Court has recognized in prior decisions, § 1083(c)(3) enables plaintiffs who achieved final judgments under the former terrorism exception, § 1605(a)(7), to pursue new federal causes of action under § 1605A based on the same prior act or incident. In *Bodoff v. Islamic Republic of Iran*, for example, this Court determined that plaintiff was not entitled to relief under § 1083(c)(2) because the case was not before the court in any form, but in reaching that conclusion, this Court emphasized that plaintiff had the right to file a new action, pursuant to § 1083(c)(3). *See* 567 F. Supp. 2d 141, 142–43 (D.D.C. 2008) (Lamberth, C.J.). Thus, § 1083(c)(3) offers an avenue of relief in those cases that reached final judgment some years prior to the enactment of the 2008 NDAA and therefore are less likely to be "before the court[] in any form," as required for treatment on motion under § 1083(c)(2).

Additionally, § 1083(c) allows plaintiffs in a prior action under § 1605(a)(7) to file an action under the new law, § 1605A, as a related case to any other pending action that was timely commenced under § 1605(a)(7) and based on the same terrorist act or incident. In other words, plaintiffs' right to proceed under the new section is not tied exclusively to their prior action; plaintiffs may identify other cases that are pending under § 1605(a)(7) that are based on the same act or incident.

3. The 60-Day Rule—Filing Deadline for Cases Based on Prior Actions Under Section 1605(a)(7)

No matter how plaintiffs wish to qualify their prior actions under the new terrorism exception, § 1605A—that is, regardless of whether they seek to do so pursuant to § 1083(c)(2) or whether they opt to file a new action pursuant § 1083(c)(3)—plaintiffs have only a limited window of opportunity to elect the benefits of the new statute. Plaintiffs who hope to gain the benefits of the new law by filing a motion or by refiling pursuant to § 1083(c)(2), must file their motions "within the 60-day period beginning on the date of the enactment of the [2008 NDAA]," or no later than March 28, 2008. § 1083(c)(2)(c). Plaintiffs who wish to file a new action as a related case"—as related to either their own prior action under § 1605(a)(7) or some other case based on the same act or incident—pursuant to § 1083(c)(3), must do so no later than 60 days after the entry of judgment in the original action or within 60 days after the date of the enactment of the 2008 NDAA, whichever is later. § 1083(c)(3).

4. Section 1083(c)(2)(B)— "Defenses Waived": Res Judicata, Collateral Estoppel, and Statute of Limitations Are Deemed Waived to the Extent that those Defenses Relate to Claims Litigated in a Prior Action Under Section 1605(a)(7)

Subsection § 1083(c)(2)(B), referred to as "Defenses Waived," purports to limit "[t]he defenses of res judicata, collateral estoppel, and limitation period" in any new action under § 1605A. Specifically, the statute provides that any defense based on either the doctrines of res judicata or collateral estoppel or the limitation period shall be deemed waived to the extent that the new action under § 1605A relies, either in whole or in part, on an earlier terrorism case brought under the prior version of the terrorism exception, § 1605(a)(7). *See* § 1083(c)(2)(B). This waiver applies to cases that are converted to § 1605A on motion, consistent with § 1083(c)(2)(A), as well as to any other prior cases that are "refiled under [§] 1605A(c)." In other words, prior judgments under the state sponsor terrorism exception to the FSIA, § 1605(a)(7) are not to be given any preclusive effect in new actions brought under the current version of the terrorism exception, § 1605A.

D. Efforts to Obtain Retroactive Treatment Under the New Terrorism Exception, Section 1605A

In view of the language that Congress has included within § 1083(c)—both with respect to the criteria defining whether a claim is eligible for treatment under the new terrorism section, § 1605A, as well as the time limits for electing treatment under the new statute—this Court is not persuaded by any reading of § 1083 that would have § 1605A apply automatically to prior terrorism cases under § 1605(a)(7). While some counsel before this Court may have glossed over the requirements within § 1083(c), it is the duty of this Court "to give effect, if possible, to every clause and word of a statute." *United States v. Menasche*, 348 U.S. 528, 538–39, 75 S. Ct. 513, 99 L.Ed. 615 (1955) (quotation and citation omitted). This Court presumes that Congress "says in a statute what it means and means in a statute what it says there." *Conn. Nat'l Bank v. Germain*, 503 U.S. 249, 252–54, 112 S. Ct. 1146, 117 L.Ed.2d 391 (1992). These time-honored cannons of statutory construction are particularly critical in this context because the FSIA terrorism exception is a "delicate legislative compromise" that balances a host of competing foreign policy considerations. *See Price*, 294 F.3d at 89. More fundamentally, however, this Court never presumes that a law applies retroactively; instead, Congress must clearly instruct courts as to whether and to what extent a new law is to apply to cases that preceded its enactment. *See Plaut*, 514 U.S. at 237, 115 S. Ct. 1447. In this case, Congress has done just that by setting forth specific parameters in § 1083(c).

Thus, the framework established by § 1083(c) is the template that this Court must apply when determining whether prior actions under the old exception for state sponsors of terrorism, § 1605(a)(7), are entitled to go forward as new actions under the recently enacted § 1605A with all the benefits that new section entails. Consistent with § 1083, this Court has held on prior occasions that the latest revision of the state sponsor of terrorism exception to sovereign immunity, § 1605A does not have automatic, retroactive application to cases filed under the now-repealed § 1605(a)(7). *See Kirschenbaum v. Islamic Republic of Iran*, 572 F. Supp. 2d 200, 204 n. 1 (D.D.C.2008) (Lamberth, C.J.); *Beer*, 574 F. Supp. 2d at 5 n. 1. Similarly our Court of Appeals observed recently that failure to adhere to those procedures means that the prior action remains under § 1605(a)(7), rather than § 1605A, and thus plaintiffs are not entitled to any of the benefits of the new enactment under those circumstances. *See Simon*, 529 F.3d at 1192; *see also Oveissi*, 573 F.3d 835 (holding that § 1605A provides a federal cause of action for those plaintiffs who meet the statutory criteria).

Notwithstanding the guidance offered in § 1083(c), as well as recent decisions that have applied those provisions to prior terrorism cases, it appears to this Court that there is some degree of confusion among counsel regarding the scope and application of § 1083(c) to FSIA cases that were previously filed against Iran under the former version of the terrorism exception, § 1605(a)(7). In their efforts to avail themselves of the new provision, § 1605A, counsel for plaintiffs in many of these prior actions have taken a variety of different approaches, as § 1083(c) contemplates, but some attorneys have pursued seemingly conflicting tactics. For instance, some attorneys have invoked (c)(2) as well as (c)(3) in their efforts to qualify a single earlier action under § 1605A. Perhaps this sort of move should be viewed by the Court as something of a "belt and suspenders" approach that has been taken out an abundance of caution. Other attorneys have relied on § 1083(c)(3) exclusively, by filing new complaints that assert the right to now pursue a federal cause of action under § 1605A. Many of the new complaints, however, do little more than regurgitate the very same state tort law claims that plaintiffs litigated in prior FSIA terrorism actions in accordance with the Cicippio-Puleo precedent under § 1605(a)(7).

Numerous other attorneys have missed the filing deadlines imposed by the 2008 NDAA, and thus it appears that these individuals were laboring under the false assumption that § 1083 of the 2008 NDAA made the new terrorism exception applied automatically to their terrorism cases. As will be discussed in the analysis that follows, at least one attorney claims that his reading of § 1083 led him to conclude that § 1605A applied retroactively to his cases. Other attorneys have not claimed as much, but they have filed motions that appear to rest on the erroneous assumption that § 1083 somehow makes § 1605A retroactive to any cases under § 1605(a)(7) that were pending as of the date § 1605A was enacted. For instance, this Court recently denied several motions requesting that this Court provide for payment to the special masters who assisted this Court with the determination of damages in the large consolidated action of *Peterson v. Islamic Republic of Iran*. *See* No. 01-CV-2094-RCL (D.D.C.), Dk. # 430. While § 1605A now includes a provision enabling special masters in FSIA terrorism cases to receive payment for their services in certain instances, *see* § 1605A(e), no similar entitlement exists for actions like Peterson, which remain under § 1605(a)(7). Counsel in Peterson never addressed the retroactivity issues; it appears that they simply presupposed that any relief included in the new law, § 1605A, applied automatically to their case. As counsel failed to follow the procedures in § 1083(c), this Court had to deny those motions seeking payment of the special masters.

In sum, there is in this Court's view, a good deal of confusion regarding how parties should avail themselves of the benefits of the new statute. Having to deny relief to so many plaintiffs is particularly regrettable in light of the fact that the recent reforms to the FSIA, as enacted through § 1083, are plainly intended to help these victims of terrorism. It is therefore the hope of this Court that today's decision and the articulation of the statutory framework of § 1083(c) may lend greater clarity to this area for counsel prosecuting these important actions.[22] It should be noted at the outset that there are both winners and losers in today's omnibus opinion. While a number of cases have not obtained retroactive treatment under the new terrorism statute, many in fact have. At this juncture, however, guidance from this Court across this range of cases should lend the greatest degree of clarity to these matters for the benefit of all plaintiffs, and that in turn should help facilitate litigation going forward. The bottom line is that there should no more confusion, guesswork, or misguided notions regarding the retroactive application of § 1605A. If counsel for plaintiffs in these action have in good faith misunderstood or misapplied § 1083(c) to their respective actions—and are time-barred from taking advantage of the new state sponsor of terrorism exception—then they may consider filing a motion for relief under Rule 60 and consistent with the guidance provided by the Court in Part G of this opinion.

E. Examination of Section 1083(c) of the 2008 NDAA Under Article III of the United States Constitution

Before proceeding any further, however, there is a critical threshold matter that this Court must address and that is the question of whether § 1083(c) directs the

22 This is not to say that all counsel with cases pending against Iran in this Court have failed to adhere to procedures set forth in § 1083(c). That is certainly not the case. Some attorneys have managed to get it right, and this Court has recently granted a number of motions permitting prior actions under § 1605(a)(7) to go forward under § 1605A. *See, e.g., Spencer v. Islamic Republic of Iran*, 06-CV-750-RCL (D.D.C.), Dk. # 20; *Heiser v. Islamic Republic of Iran*, 00-CV-2329-RCL (D.D.C.), Dk. # 143. As noted *supra*, p. 60, this Court issues a separate opinion today in Heiser in which this Court analyzes new claims for both compensatory and punitive damages under § 1605A. As the Court has determined that plaintiffs are entitled to relief under the new statute, the Court will also enter a judgment for plaintiffs in Heiser pursuant to § 1605A.

reopening of final judgments in violation of Article III of the United States Constitution. *See Plaut*, 514 U.S. at 241, 115 S. Ct. 1447; *see also Miller v. French*, 530 U.S. 327, 344, 120 S. Ct. 2246, 147 L.Ed.2d 326 (2000). In this instance, the Court is troubled by the related-case provisions of § 1083(c)(3), to the extent that those measures enable individuals who litigated FSIA actions against Iran previously to now file new cases against Iran under § 1605A. For similar reasons, the Court is troubled by § 1083(c)(2)(B) ("Defenses Waived") which directs that in any new action under § 1605 courts must deem as waived "[t]he defenses of res judicata and collateral estoppel" with respect to any claims that were brought previously under § 1605(a)(7). The question presented is whether these particular legislative enactments abrogate final judgments in a manner that the Supreme Court has determined is "repugnant to the text, structure, and traditions of Article III." Plaut, 514 U.S. at 217–18, 115 S. Ct. 1447. As no court has had the opportunity to address this issue, it now confronts this Court as a substantial question of first impression, and one of great and immediate consequence to hundreds of plaintiffs who have filed new actions against Iran consistent with the related-case procedures of § 1083(c).

Examining the constitutionality of an act of Congress requires a journey into treacherous waters, to say the least. It is at these times that a mere district judge would prefer to take refuge in the doctrine of "constitutional avoidance" or "constitutional doubt" rather than engage in a confrontation on such fundamental matters. *See, e.g., Boumediene v. Bush*, ___ U.S. ___, 128 S. Ct. 2229, 2271, 171 L.Ed.2d 41 (2008); *French*, 530 U.S. at 341, 120 S. Ct. 2246; *Nat'l Mining Ass'n v. Kempthorne*, 512 F.3d 702, 711 (D.C.Cir.2008); *Citizens for Responsibility and Ethics in Washington v. U.S. Dep't of Homeland Sec.*, 592 F. Supp. 2d 127 (D.D.C.2009) (Lamberth, C.J.). Consistent with this cardinal rule of statutory construction, courts are obligated to construe legislative enactments in a manner that avoids constitutional questions whenever there is a saving construction that is "not plainly contrary to the intent of Congress." French, 530 U.S. at 341, 120 S. Ct. 2246 (quoting *Edward J. DeBartolo Corp. v. Fla. Gulf Coast Bldg. & Constr. Trades Council*, 485 U.S. 568, 575, 108 S. Ct. 1392, 99 L.Ed.2d 645 (1988)).

Regrettably, the constitutional question is presented squarely and unavoidably in this case. The import of § 1083(c)(3) and § 1083(c)(2)(B) could not be clearer: An individual who received a final judgment in a prior case against Iran, under an earlier version of the FSIA state sponsor of terror exception, § 1605(a)(7), is now permitted to file a new action against Iran under the current version of the terrorism exception, § 1605A. Moreover, this Court is instructed that it may not give any preclusive effect to its prior judgment, even though the prior action was based on the very same act or incident. Thus, there is a legitimate question of whether this enactment offends deeply entrenched constitutional principles relating to the separation of powers and the ability of the judiciary to function independently without interference from the political process. *See, e.g., United States v. Klein*, 80 U.S. 128, 147, 13 Wall. 128, 20 L.Ed. 519 (1871) (emphasizing that the powers afforded to the Congress and the Courts under the Constitution must be kept separate and distinct). This Court must not shirk from its duty, where, as here, the question of the constitutional validity of an act of Congress is starkly presented. French, 530 U.S. at 341, 120 S. Ct. 2246 (quoting *Commodity Futures Trading Comm'n v. Schor*, 478 U.S. 833, 841, 106 S. Ct. 3245, 92 L.Ed.2d 675 (1986)); *see also Boumediene*, 128 S. Ct. at 2271 ("We cannot ignore the text and purpose of a statute in order to save it."); *Citizens for Responsibility and Ethics in Washington*, 592 F. Supp. 2d at 131 ("[I]n the absence of statutory ambiguity the constitutional avoidance doctrine has no place.").

There are other important considerations that militate in favor of this Court addressing the constitutional question in this case. More than a decade ago when this Court first considered the "novel enactments" of the FSIA terrorism exception, § 1605(a)(7) and the Flatow Amendment, § 1605 note, this Court underscored its "special role in the development of foreign sovereign immunity jurisprudence." *Flatow I*, 999 F. Supp. at 6 (citing 28 U.S.C. 1391(f)(4)) ("providing that this Court is a designated venue for actions brought against a foreign state or political subdivision thereof"). Consistent with this role, this Court undertook in Flatow "a systemic review of the dispositive legal issues," including a number of constitutional issues, in an effort to ensure that the plaintiff was fully entitled to relief under the law. *Id.* The plaintiffs before the Court today certainly deserve no less. In light of the substantial personal, financial, and emotional investments that these victims have made in these cases over the years, this Court simply cannot afford to overlook potential legal infirmities that could prove fatal to their cause. Thus, similar to Flatow, and consistent with this Court's historical role in the development of jurisprudence under the FSIA, this Court should examine carefully whether the latest terrorism exception, § 1605A, can be applied retroactively to cases that were litigated to a final judgment under § 1605(a)(7) in a manner that comports with Article III of the Constitution.

More fundamentally, however, the Court is mindful that these FSIA actions under the state sponsor of terror exception involve a handful of rogue nations, who, like Iran, have had an extremely rocky relationship with the United States. On the other side of this difficult problem, are hundreds of victims of international terrorism who have long suffered, and who desperately hope to see Iran held accountable for its role in perpetuating terrorist acts that have destroyed countless lives. In this highly charged and inevitably political context—and especially where the offending nation is in default—this Court needs to be extremely leery of overreaching by Congress. It is also out of respect for the principle of comity between nations that this Court must assure itself that any lawsuit against a foreign power, no matter how unpopular that foreign sovereign may be, is an action that comports with our Constitution.[23] It is precisely at these challenging moments that our Courts must be

23 By working from the general proposition that foreign sovereigns should be immune from suit in our courts, *see* § 1604, the FSIA builds from the principle of comity among nations.

ever vigilant to uphold the rule of law and take full stock of our Article III responsibility "to say what the law is." *Marbury v. Madison*, 5 U.S. 137, 177, 1 Cranch 137, 2 L.Ed. 60 (1803).

In candor, this Court is not the first to observe that certain parts of § 1083(c) might suffer from constitutional infirmities in violation of the principles expounded by the Supreme Court in its jurisprudence concerning the independent authority of Article III courts to decide civil cases. The potential infirmities analyzed here were first noted by Jennifer Elsea in the report she authored for the Congressional Research Service. *See* SUITS AGAINST TERRORIST STATES, *supra* note 4, at 61.[24]

Moreover, this time-honored principle is reinforced throughout the FSIA. Even in cases in which a foreign state is in default, the Court may not enter judgment unless the plaintiff "establishes his claim or right to relief by evidence satisfactory to the court." 28 U.S.C. § 1608(e).

24 The Court's analysis of the Article III question is limited to the procedures for related actions in § 1083(c)(3). Specifically not considered are the procedures for prior actions in § 1083(c)(2). For the sake of argument, this Court assumes that § 1083(c)(2) does not raise any constitutional issues under Article III because that subsection reaches only those cases that were "before the court[] in any form" at the time of the enactment of the 2008 NDAA. As will be discussed in further detail in this part of the opinion, the Supreme Court has made clear that Article III is not offended when courts are directed to apply changes in the law to pending cases, including those on direct appeal. *See Plaut*, 514 U.S. at 227, 115 S. Ct. 1447. Thus, to the extent that § 1083(c)(2) reaches cases that were in fact "pending" under § 1605(a)(7) at the time the new terrorism exception was enacted, the constitutional issue regarding the finality of Article III court judgments is not implicated. The problem, however, is that it is not entirely clear what constitutes the range of cases that might qualify as "pending cases" for Article III purposes, as it was not necessary for the Supreme Court to fully explore this issue in Plaut.

The Court's opinion in Plaut strongly suggests that a "pending case" under Article III is one that is simply awaiting either the entry of a final judgment in district court or the outcome of a direct appeal. *See id.* If this common sense definition is applied here, then § 1083(c)(2), much like § 1083(c)(3), might also present some constitutional concerns. Section 1083(c)(2) provides that cases that were "before the courts in any form, including on appeal or motion under rule 60(b) of the Federal Rules of Civil Procedure" may be eligible for treatment under the new law. *See* § 1083(c)(2)(A)(iv) (emphasis added). While the broad categorization of "in any form" undoubtedly includes cases that are actually "pending" consistent with Plaut, it may also reach back to closed cases that just happen to be before the court in some form because of ongoing litigation relating to efforts to enforce the judgment. In this default context involving Iran, it is not uncommon for the Court to preside over extensive postjudgment litigation with respect to efforts to enforce judgments. The Peterson action is a prime example. *See* No. 01-CV-2094, Dk. # 434 (Memorandum Opinion and Order denying motions to appoint receivers for various Iranian assets); *Bennett*, 604 F. Supp. 2d 152 (granting motion to quash five writs of attachment issued against the property that once comprised the Iranian embassy here in Washington, DC).

This Court is satisfied, however, that it need not subject § 1083(c)(2) to scrutiny under Article III because the Court finds today that even § 1083(c)(3)—which has far greater retroactive reach than § 1083(c)(2)—does not offend the principle of the finality of court judgments. Consequently, if there is no Article III problem with the related-actions procedures of § 1083(c)(3), which enable a plaintiff to file as a new action under § 1605A a case that was previously closed under § 1605(a)(7), and which was not "pending" before this court in any

The issue presented here today is troubling, but, this Court is of the view that § 1083(c)(3) and § 1083(c)(2)(B) withstand constitutional scrutiny.

1. Principles of Law—The Independence of the Federal Judiciary Under Article III and the Finality of Judgments

More than two centuries of Supreme Court jurisprudence has reinforced the basic understanding that the Federal Judiciary has sole responsibility for deciding cases and controversies arising under the federal law. *See, e.g.*, Hayburn's Case, 2 U.S. 408, 2 Dall. 409, 1 L.Ed. 436 (1792); Klein, 80 U.S. 128; Plaut, 514 U.S. 211, 115 S. Ct. 1447. As Justice Scalia observed in Plaut:

> The record of history shows that the Framers crafted this charter of the judicial department with an expressed understanding that it gives the Federal Judiciary the power, not merely to rule on cases, but to decide them, subject to review only by superior courts in the Article III hierarchy—with an understanding, in short, that "a judgment conclusively resolves the case" because "'a judicial power'" is one to render dispositive judgments.

Plaut, 514 U.S. at 218–19, 115 S. Ct. 1447 (quoting Frank J. Easterbrook, Presidential Review, 40 Case W. Res. L. Rev. 905, 926 (1990)) (emphasis in original). Thus, a case submitted to the federal judiciary and resolved in a final judgment is settled conclusively and may not be reversed, undone, or otherwise revisited as a result of subsequent actions taken by the political branches.

In Hayburn's Case, five out the six Supreme Court justices, while sitting in their capacities as circuit judges, considered a federal statute that gave the Secretary of War complete discretion to either accept or reject Circuit Court findings regarding the appropriate amounts of pensions owed to Revolutionary War Veterans. The Justices explained in a recorded opinion how they each found that the statute violated the separation of powers established by the Constitution. The Justices noted that the statute allowed for court judgments to be "revised and controlled by the legislature, and by an office in the executive department," a practice "deemed radically inconsistent with the independence of that judicial power which is vested in the courts." 2 U.S. at 410.

Following the Civil War, the Supreme Court decided the Klein case in which the Court rejected an effort by the Congress to "prescribe rules of decision to the Judicial Department of the Government in cases pending before it." 80 U.S. at 146. At issue in Klein was a measure by Congress intended to direct the outcome in certain cases brought by former confederates who sought compensation for property that was either captured by the United States Government or abandoned during the course of the War. Congress had originally provided, by statute, that such cases would be decided by the Court of Claims. The right to recovery depended on proof

---

sense when the 2008 NDAA was enacted, then, a fortiori, the procedures in § 1083(c)(2) concerning prior actions that are still before the court in some form must also withstand scrutiny.

to the satisfaction of the court demonstrating that the claimant both owned the property at issue and had not supported the rebellion in any way. *Id.* at 131. In deciding such cases, the Court of Claims determined that a presidential pardon was sufficient to cure claimants of their participation in the rebellion. *Id.* at 132–33. The Supreme Court expressly affirmed that principle, holding that the pardon showed the claimant "was innocent in law as though he had never participated [in the rebellion], and that his property was purged of whatever offence he had committed and relieved of any penalty that he might have occurred." *Id.* at 133 (citing *United States v. Padelford*, 76 U.S. 531, 9 Wall. 531, 19 L.Ed. 788 (1870)).

Shortly thereafter, Congress sought to abrogate the Supreme Court's ruling. Congress passed a new statute providing that the courts were no longer permitted to consider a pardon as evidence curing a claimant of his participation in the rebellion. *Id.* at 133–34. Instead, courts were instructed to deem the pardon as conclusive proof that the claimant had supported the rebellion, and, moreover, once proof of a claimant's pardon was furnished by either party, the Court would cease to have jurisdiction over the case and was therefore required to dismiss the action accordingly. *Id.* at 134.

In holding that Congress had exceeded its authority under the Constitution, the Supreme Court stated:

> We must think that Congress has inadvertently passed the limit which separates the legislature from the judicial power.
>
> It is of vital importance that these powers be kept distinct. The Constitution provides that the judicial power of the United States shall be vested in one Supreme Court and such inferior courts as the Congress shall from time to time ordain and establish.
>
> . . .
>
> Congress has already provided that the Supreme Court shall have jurisdiction of the judgments of the Court of Claims on appeal. Can it prescribe a rule in conformity with which the court must deny to itself the jurisdiction thus conferred, because and only because its decision, in accordance with settled law, must be adverse to the Government and favorable to the suitor. The question seems to answer itself.
>
> The rule prescribed is also liable to just exception as impairing the effect of a pardon, and thus infringing on the constitutional power of the Executive.

Id. at 147.

The precise meaning of Klein is subject to much debate in part because the Court's decision appears to rest as much on the principle that Congress cannot nullify the President's authority under Article II as much as it is based on any sense that the Congress had interfered with the Judicial Department's authority to independently decide cases under Article III. *See generally* ERWIN CHEMERINSKY, FEDERAL JURISDICTION 183–88 (3d ed.1999); *see also Nat'l Coalition to Save Our Mall v. Norton*, 269 F.3d 1092, 1096–1098 (D.C.Cir.2001) (noting that "Klein's exact meaning is far from clear" and discussing differing interpretations). While the full implications of Klein will likely be subject to debate for years to come, the Supreme Court has recognized that, at a minimum, Klein stands for the proposition that Congress cannot dictate a rule of decision to courts in pending cases without amending the underlying substantive law. Plaut, 514 U.S. at 218, 115 S. Ct. 1447 ("Whatever the precise scope of Klein, however, later decisions have made clear that its prohibition does not take hold when Congress 'amend[s] applicable law.'") (quoting *Robertson v. Seattle Audubon Soc'y*, 503 U.S. 429, 441, 112 S. Ct. 1407, 118 L.Ed.2d 73 (1992)); accord *French*, 530 U.S. at 349, 120 S. Ct. 2246.

The Supreme Court has decided two cases in which it has considered federal statutes that waived res judicata and collateral estoppel in civil actions. *See United States v. Sioux Nation*, 448 U.S. 371, 100 S. Ct. 2716, 65 L.Ed.2d 844 (1980); *Cherokee Nation v. United States*, 270 U.S. 476, 46 S. Ct. 428, 70 L.Ed. 694 (1926). Both cases, however, concerned a waiver of those preclusion defenses by the United States Government in ongoing litigation with Indian tribes. Neither of those decisions required the Court to examine whether or to what extent Congress may pass a statute waiving res judicata or collateral estoppel as defenses by parties other than the Federal Government, such as private litigants or foreign governments, and the Court did not express any views on the matter.

In Cherokee Nation, the Court reviewed the passage of a special act by Congress that permitted the Court of Claims to adjudicate Cherokee claims against the United States Government that were previously considered in a prior action that the Court had decided several years earlier. 270 U.S. at 485–86, 46 S. Ct. 428. In declining to give res judicata effect to the prior adjudication, the Court stressed that Congress has the authority to deem the prior judgment as waived in actions against the Federal Government. *Id.* at 486, 46 S. Ct. 428.

More than half a century later, the Court considered a similar issue in the case of Sioux Nation. The Sioux alleged that their ouster from the Black Hills of South Dakota by the United States during the late 1800s amounted to a taking under the Fifth Amendment for which just compensation was due. *See* 448 U.S. at 384, 100 S. Ct. 2716. The question was subject to considerable litigation over a period of several decade, and Congress consistently passed legislation in an effort to help the Indians press their claim against the federal government. At each step of the way, the Sioux Indians were opposed in litigation by the Executive Branch.

At the end of the first wave of litigation in 1942, the Court of Claims first ruled against the Indians on the merits, holding that the Sioux had merely presented "a moral claim not protected by the Just Compensation Clause." *Id.* at 384, 100 S. Ct. 2716. Subsequent to that decision, Congress established the Indian Claims Commission, which again considered the Sioux Indians' Takings Clause claim regarding the Black Hills and ultimately decided the question in favor of the Indians. *Id.* at 384–85, 100 S. Ct. 2716. The Federal Government then appealed the Commission's ruling to the Court of Claims. *Id.* Without reaching the merits, the Court of Claims ruled that the Sioux Indians' claim against the Federal

Government was barred by the res judicata effect of the Court's 1942 decision. Shortly after the Court's ruling, Congress passed special legislation directing the Court of Claims to reconsider the Takings Clause question de novo and without regard to the defenses of res judicata and collateral estoppel. *See id.* at 390, 100 S. Ct. 2716. Following that special enactment by Congress, the Court of Claims promptly reconsidered the Sioux Indian case on the merits and found in favor the Indians. *Id.* at 380–390, 100 S. Ct. 2716. The Supreme Court granted the Federal Government's petition for certiorari.

In a lengthy opinion, the Supreme Court considered carefully whether Congress has "inadvertently passed the limit which separates the legislative from the judicial power" by directing the Court of Claims to reconsider the Sioux Indians' taking case. *Id.* at 392, 100 S. Ct. 2716 (quoting *Klein*, 80 U.S. at 147). In holding that Congress had not encroached on the independent powers of the Judiciary under Article III, the Court relied heavily—if not exclusively—on its prior decision in Cherokee Nation. The Court stated:

> The Holding in Cherokee Nation that Congress has the power to waive the res judicata effect of a prior judgment entered in the Government's favor on a claim against the United States is dispositive of the question here. Moreover, that holding is consistent with a substantial body of precedent affirming the broad Constitutional power of Congress to define and "to pay the Debts . . . of the United States." U.S. Const. art. I., § 8, cl. 1. That precedent speaks directly to the separation-of-powers objections discussed above.

Sioux Nation, 448 U.S. at 397, 100 S. Ct. 2716. The Court emphasized, that consistent with Cherokee Nation, numerous cases throughout history "have recognized or acted upon Congress' power to waive the defense of res judicata to claims against the United States." *Id.* at 398 n. 24, 100 S. Ct. 2716 (collecting cases).

Despite the Court's conclusion that the issue was resolved by the waiver principles announced in Cherokee Nation, the majority did examine the Klein precedent in some detail. The Court explained that unlike the statute that was found unconstitutional in Klein, the waiver of res judicata with respect to actions brought by the Cherokee and Sioux Nations did not amount to an effort by Congress to control the outcome of those cases on the merits. *Id.* at 404–407, 100 S. Ct. 2716. According to the Court, Congress was merely providing a "forum so that a new judicial review of the Black Hills claim could take place." *Id.* at 407, 100 S. Ct. 2716.

Justice Rehnquist vigorously dissented. Among other points, he argued that the legislature had impermissibly taken on a judicial function by directing the rehearing of a case that had reached a final judgment. *See id.* at 428–32, 100 S. Ct. 2716 (Rehnquist, J., dissenting). The Justice noted that Congress' broad powers to pay public debts under Article I had nothing to do with the question of whether Congress could direct the federal courts to rehear cases that courts had already heard and decided pursuant to the judiciary's own independent authority under Article III. *See id.* at 429, 100 S. Ct. 2716. The Justice suggested that if Congress truly wanted to pay debts owed to Indians, then it could simply do so consistent with its authority to make such appropriations under Article I. *See id.* at 429–32, 100 S. Ct. 2716. It was offensive to the Constitution, however, for Congress to insist that Courts keep hearing cases until Congress received the outcome it desired. *Id.* at 430–32, 100 S. Ct. 2716. Moreover, Justice Rehnquist emphasized that res judicata is a long-standing judicial doctrine that may be exercised sua sponte by Courts consistent with the obligation to efficiently manage the business that comes before the them. *Id.* at 432–33, 100 S. Ct. 2716.

The very next term, the Supreme Court emphasized that res judicata is "a rule of fundamental and substantial justice, 'of public policy and of private peace,' which should be cordially regarded and enforced by the courts." *Federated Dep't Stores, Inc. v. Moitie*, 452 U.S. 394, 401, 101 S. Ct. 2424, 69 L.Ed.2d 103 (1981) (quoting *Hart Steel Co. v. R.R. Supply Co.*, 244 U.S. 294, 299, 37 S. Ct. 506, 61 L.Ed. 1148 (1917)). The Supreme Court has since stated that the Cherokee Nation and Sioux Nation decisions are narrow rulings that merely stand for the proposition that the doctrine of separation of powers is not offended when Congress waives res judicata effect with respect to a "judgment entered in the Government's favor on a claim against the United States." Plaut, 514 U.S. at 230, 115 S. Ct. 1447 (quoting *Sioux Nation*, 448 U.S. at 397, 100 S. Ct. 2716).[25]

In the watershed case of *Plaut v. Spendthrift Farm*, the Supreme Court reviewed its Article III separation-of-powers jurisprudence spanning more than three centuries—from Hayburn's case to Sioux Nation—and held that Congress may not direct the reopening of final judgments in civil actions for money damages. 514 U.S. at 218–219, 115 S. Ct. 1447. At issue in Plaut was an act of Congress that allowed plaintiffs to reinstate stock fraud cases that had been dismissed previously as time-barred. The dismissals were required by a set of companion Supreme Court decisions in which the Court construed the limitation period for such stock fraud actions and then determined that its ruling on the matter would be applied retroactively to pending cases. *Id.* at 214, 115 S. Ct. 1447 (citing *Lampf, Pleva, Lipkind, Prupis & Petigrow v. Gilbertson*, 501 U.S. 350, 111 S. Ct. 2773, 115 L.Ed.2d 321 (1991); *James B. Beam Distilling Co. v. Georgia*, 501 U.S. 529, 111 S. Ct. 2439, 115 L.Ed.2d 481 (1991)). A few months after those decisions were issued on June 20, 1991, Congress passed a law directing that plaintiffs who had their claims dismissed as time-barred were allowed to reinstate their actions under the limitation period that would have been applicable to their claims on June 19, 1991. *Id.* Thus, the statute purported to save all those cases that were dismissed as a result of the Supreme Court's rulings.

25 Even though the Supreme Court acknowledged in Sioux Nation that Congress has the power to waive the defense of res judicata to claims against the United States, this Court is not aware of any decision in which the Supreme Court has upheld the waiver of res judicata with respect to claims against a third party, which is the case presented here.

The Court found that the statute clearly presented a separations-of-power issue because the enactment provided in plain terms that an individual who had received a final judgment of dismissal could nonetheless "reinstate" his previously dismissed case. *Id.* at 215–217, 115 S. Ct. 1447. Writing for the Court, Justice Scalia stressed that the finality of judgments issued by Article III Courts and the separation of powers under the Constitution were the fundamental principles implicated by the case. In light of those fundamental principles, neither the motive of Congress nor the manner in which it sought to have Article III courts revisit the final judgments were relevant to the Court's determination. *Id.* at 227–28, 115 S. Ct. 1447. "The issue here is not the validity of the source of the legal rule that produced the Article III judgments, but rather the immunity from legislative abrogation of the judgments themselves." *Id.* at 230, 115 S. Ct. 1447. Justice Scalia elaborated on this point for the Court:

> To be sure, [the statute] reopens (or directs the reopening of final judgments in a whole class of cases rather than in a particular suit. We do not see how that makes any difference. The separation-of-powers violation here, if there is any, consists of depriving judicial judgments of the conclusive effect that they had when they were announced, not of acting in a manner—viz., with particular rather than general effect—that is unusual (though, we must note, not impossible) for a legislature. To be sure, a general statute such as this one may reduce the perception that legislative interference with judicial judgments was prompted by individual favoritism; but it is legislative interference with judicial judgments nonetheless. Not favoritism, nor even corruption, but power is the object of the separation-of-powers prohibition. The prohibition is violated when an individual final judgment is legislatively rescinded for even the very best of reasons, such as the legislature's genuine conviction (supported by all the law professors in the land) that the judgment was wrong; and it is violated 40 times over when 40 final judgments are legislatively dissolved.

Id. at 227–228, 115 S. Ct. 1447 (emphasis in original). Thus, the fundamental question, and perhaps the only question, that was critical to the Court's holding in Plaut was whether the statute had directed the reopening of final judgments entered prior to the statute's enactment.

In defining final judgment for the purpose of its analysis under Article III, the Court was careful to explain that a final judgment is one in which the time for appeal has expired. *Id.* at 226–227, 115 S. Ct. 1447. Thus, the Court emphasized that courts must apply new law retroactively to any pending cases, including those on appeal, when Congress clearly instructs the Courts to do so. *Id.* at 226, 115 S. Ct. 1447 (citing *United States v. Schooner Peggy*, 5 U.S. 103, 1 Cranch 103, 2 L.Ed. 49 (1801); *Landgraf*, 511 U.S. at 273–280, 114 S. Ct. 1483). As the Court explained, Article III creates a single judicial department, and thus no judgment in a case is truly the final judgment of the Article III Judiciary until all potential appeals have either been foregone or exhausted. *Id.* at 227, 115 S. Ct. 1447. Accordingly, separation of powers concerns are generally not implicated when Congress directs that a new law should be applied to cases still pending anywhere within the federal judiciary, including on appeal.

The Court concluded its opinion by underscoring the very remarkable and unique nature of the statute Congress had enacted in its effort to "reinstate" certain stock fraud actions that the Court had previously dismissed. The Court stated:

> We know of no previous instance in which Congress has enacted retroactive legislation requiring an Article III court to set aside a final judgment, and for good reason. The Constitution's separation of legislative and judicial powers denies it the Authority to do so. [The statute] is unconstitutional to the extent that it requires federal courts to reopen final judgments entered before its enactment.

Id. at 241, 115 S. Ct. 1447.[26]

Thus, the Court's holding in Plaut appears based at least in part on the truly extraordinary nature of Congress' action in directing the Article III Courts to set aside final judgments entered in certain stock fraud actions prior the legislation's enactment.

2. Analysis of the Constitutional Question in Light of the Supreme Court's Jurisprudence

In view of the Supreme Court's jurisprudence in this area, the fundamental question remains whether § 1083(c) violates Article III to the extent that it applies to FSIA terrorism cases that were terminated in final judgments under § 1605(a)(7). This Court is the view that the Article III question presented in this case, requires the consideration of two distinct but related issues, each of which, when considered either individually or in concert with one another, may lead to the conclusion that § 1083(c) is unconstitutional as applied to prior FSIA actions. The first question is whether § 1083(c)(3) calls for the reopening of final judgments entered before its enactment and therefore contravenes Article III as construed by the Supreme Court in Plaut. The second question is assuming that § 1083(c)(3) does not direct the reopening of final judgments, does § 1083(c)(2)—the waiver of res judicata and collateral estoppel effect of any prior terrorism FSIA action—nonetheless offend Article III because Congress has directed the Courts to ignore fundamental and longstanding judicial doctrine. Both issues are constitutional questions of first impression.

---

26 In *Miller v. French* the Court revisited Plaut in a case involving an act of Congress that in effect required a district court to revisit a remedial injunction issued against a state correctional facility. 530 U.S. 327, 120 S. Ct. 2246. The Court held that the statute did not offend any separations of powers principles. *Id.* at 350, 120 S. Ct. 2246. In reaching that conclusion, the Court emphasized that the Article III principle emphasized in Plaut regarding the finality of civil judgments for money damages does not apply to the same degree with respect to a court order issuing an equitable remedy like an injunction or other kinds of prospective relief. *Id.* at 347–48, 120 S. Ct. 2246. The Court also stressed, that, unlike judgments for money damages, court orders providing for prospective relief are "subject to the continuing supervisory jurisdiction of the court, and therefore may be altered according to subsequent changes in the law." *Id.* at 347, 120 S. Ct. 2246 (citation omitted).

a. Does Section 1083(c)(3) Direct the Reopening of Final Judgments Entered Before its Enactment and Therefore Contravene Article III as Construed by the Supreme Court in Plaut?

Applying the principles articulated by the Supreme Court in Plaut, this Court is of the view that § 1083(c) does not violate Article III of the United States Constitution. Critical to this decision today is this Court's understanding that by enacting § 1083—thereby repealing § 1605(a)(7) and replacing it with § 1605A—Congress and the President have accomplished a fundamental change in substantive federal law with respect to civil actions against state sponsors of terrorism. The former terrorism exception to the FSIA, § 1605(a)(7), which still controls in certain actions, *see Simon*, 529 F.3d at 1192, is "merely a jurisdiction conferring provision" devoid of any substantive law claims against foreign states. Cicippio-Puleo, 353 F.3d at 1032. The new terrorism exception, § 1605A, is a fundamentally different law, however, because it creates a federal cause of action against foreign states, *see* § 1605A(c), thereby allowing for new actions that simply were not available to terrorism victims prior to the enactment of § 1083 last year. Accordingly, this case is distinguishable from Plaut, in which the statute the Supreme Court found unconstitutional made no changes in substantive law and, in fact, was nothing more than a directive instructing courts to reopen stock fraud actions that had been previously dismissed as time-barred.

The change in federal substantive law that has occurred in this case should not be understated. As our Circuit first observed in the case of Cicippio-Puleo: "Plainly, neither section 1605(a)(7) nor the Flatow Amendment, separately or together, establishes a cause of action against foreign state sponsors of terrorism." 353 F.3d at 1027. As a mere jurisdiction conferring statute, § 1605(a)(7) does little more than offer a pass-through to causes of actions that may exist under state law or other sources of law. *Bodoff*, 424 F. Supp. 2d at 83. In practical application before this Court, plaintiffs in actions under § 1605(a)(7) have relied on state tort law as the source of law for substantive causes of actions. *See, e.g.*, *Rimkus*, 575 F. Supp. 2d at 196–99 (applying Missouri law); *Peterson II*, 515 F. Supp. 2d at 41–60 (applying laws from 34 different state jurisdictions, the District of Columbia, and the Philippines); *Greenbaum v. Islamic Republic of Iran*, 451 F. Supp. 2d 90, 101–108 (D.D.C.2006) (Lamberth, J.) (applying California and New Jersey law); *Prevatt*, 421 F. Supp. 2d at 159–162 (D.D.C.2006) (Lamberth, J.) (applying Georgia law).

The reliance on state tort law in the "pass-through" mechanism of § 1605(a)(7) has resulted in a total lack of uniformity in civil cases under that provision. Moreover, the lack of uniformity in turn has caused a certain degree of unfairness to plaintiffs, as the differences in tort law among the many state and territorial jurisdictions has naturally resulted in significant disparities with respect to the availability of relief for similarity situated plaintiffs. Given the unbending supremacy of the federal government in matters of foreign relations, combined with the basic aim of the anti-terrorism provision—which is to hold state sponsors of terror accountable for their role in perpetuating terrorist acts that have injured or killed Americans—this Court has long thought it odd that Congress chose to, in effect, rely on state tort law to achieve its national objectives. Ordinarily, individual state laws must "yield to the National Government's policy, given the 'concern for uniformity in this country's dealings with foreign nations' that animated the Constitution's allocation of foreign relations power to the National Government in the first place." *Am. Ins. Ass'n v. Garamendi*, 539 U.S. 396, 413, 123 S. Ct. 2374, 156 L.Ed.2d 376 (2003) (quoting *Banco Nacional de Cuba v. Sabbatino*, 376 U.S. 398, 427 n. 25, 84 S. Ct. 923, 11 L.Ed.2d 804 (1964)). Why then, for purposes of liability under the state sponsor of terror exception, should it matter at all which particular State in the Union the American plaintiff happens to hail from? But that is precisely the kind of perverse result that § 1605(a)(7) mandates. In Peterson, for example, hundreds of plaintiffs, all victims of the Marine barracks bombing in Lebanon, and all Americans, sought relief for a variety of claims. *Peterson II*, 515 F. Supp. 2d 25. Many family members hoped to receive compensation for their emotional distress, and many were successful, but many others with precisely the same kinds of emotional distress cases, had no recovery whatsoever because they happened to be domiciled in a state that denied them standing to assert such claims. *See id.* at 44–45. With § 1605(a)(7), Congress sent something of a mixed message: The United States is serious about deterring states sponsors of terrorism and compensating victims, but only to the extent that our individual state jurisdictions allow. If you happen to live in a state that will not permit you a substantive claim for relief, so be it.

Rather than leave the substantive law for actions under the FSIA terrorism exception at the disposal of the 50 individual states and numerous other territories, this Court expressed the view in Flatow that the preferable approach would have been to have a federal cause of action consistent with the traditional principle of uniformity in this Country's dealings with foreign nations. *See* 999 F. Supp. 1 at 15. In the Cicippio-Puleo decision, the Court of Appeals even noted how a federal cause of action might better achieve the goals of § 1605(a)(7). The Court stated:

> Clearly, Congress's authorization of a cause of action against officials, employees, and agents of a foreign state was a significant step toward providing a judicial forum for the compensation of terrorism victims. Recognizing a federal cause of action against foreign states undoubtedly would be an even greater step toward that end, but it is a step Congress has yet to take. And it is for Congress, not the courts, to decide when a cause of action should lie against foreign states.

353 F.3d at 1036 (emphasis added). Thus, this Court and our Circuit both stressed how a federal cause of action against foreign states could help to further the purposes of the state sponsor of terrorism exception to foreign sovereign immunity.[27]

---

27 As noted above in Part A, *supra*, in Flatow I, this Court actually read § 1605(a)(7) as providing for a federal cause of action against foreign state sponsors of terror, and "in the

Congress was listening, and it of course responded by implementing a cause of action within the new version of the terrorism exception, § 1605A, through the passage of the § 1083 of the 2008 NDAA. By doing so, Congress completely changed the landscape with respect to actions against state sponsors of terror. This latest version of the terrorism exception is not a mere jurisdiction conferring or "pass-through" statute, but rather it is a source of substantive federal law—a uniform federal standard designed to hold rogue nations accountable for their promotion of terrorists acts.

But as fundamental as this shift to federal law surely is, § 1605A also contains a broad array of substantive rights and remedies that simply were not available under § 1605(a)(7). As emphasized in the introduction to this opinion, the changes implemented through § 1083 are in effect a new statutory regime designed to accomplish a variety of objectives in addition to the creation of a new federal cause of action. Unlike its predecessor exception, § 1605A includes, among other new entitlements, the availability of punitive damages against foreign states, *see* § 1605A(c), the ability to assert pretrial liens on property, *see* § 1605A(g), and plaintiffs in actions under this new exception may take advantage of new restrictions on the types of immunities that have historically protected the properties of foreign states from attachment and execution, *see* § 1610(g). Thus, § 1605A not only creates a new substantive federal claim, but it includes greater remedies, more robust judgment enforcement provisions, and other mechanisms intended to better promote and execute the federal interest in deterring terrorist attacks and compensating victims. Consequently, § 1605A is qualitatively distinct, and, frankly, many times removed from the mere "pass-through" mechanism of § 1605(a)(7).

Ultimately, § 1083—in both its design and practical application—does not portend to achieve an overruling or abrogation of final judgments under § 1605(a)(7), and thus Congress in this case has not sought to impose a legislative veto of court rulings of the kind that the Supreme Court rejected in both Plaut and Klein. Nothing in § 1083 directs this Court to revisit or reopen any judgments entered under § 1605(a)(7). Indeed, that sort of action is not even contemplated by the statute. Section 1083(a) simply repeals § 1605(a)(7) entirely and replaces it with the new provision § 1605A. Noticeably absent from § 1083 are any procedures or directives that might instruct this Court to re-look, reopen, or otherwise abrogate any judgments entered on the basis of state tort law in accordance with the "pass-through" regime of § 1605(a)(7); those prior judgments remain intact as final judgments. Rather than revisiting prior cases under the old "pass-through" system of § 1605(a)(7), § 1083 is geared instead toward bringing into existence a whole new

---

interest of promoting uniformity with respect to liability determinations" this Court chose to "employ interstitial federal common law" to determine liability and damages. 999 F. Supp. at 15. Regardless of our different views on the issue at the time, both this Court's decision in Flatow I and the Circuit's decision in Cicippio-Puleo nonetheless highlighted the potential advantages of a federal cause of action in this area.

statutory regime—one that has as its cornerstone a new federal cause of action against foreign states, for which punitive damages may be awarded.

Some may argue that this Court is merely embracing form over substance here, and, thus they might suggest that this Court has limited Plaut or otherwise given that decision much too narrow of an application with respect to § 1083(c). They might argue that, regardless of whatever differences might exist between causes of actions based in state tort law under § 1605(a)(7) and the new federal cause of actions authorized under § 1605A(c), the fundamental problem is that § 1083(c) offers a mechanism by which a previously determined tort case against Iran may be resurrected from the dead and brought back into court disguised as a new federal claim under federal law. Thus, some may believe today's ruling rests on an overly narrow or technical view of the definition of cause of action, and, consequently, attaches too much significance to the change from state law to federal law with respect to the determination of liability in these actions. *See Apotex v. FDA*, 393 F.3d 210 (D.C.Cir.2004) (holding that, for claims preclusion purposes, "[w]hether two cases implicate the same cause of action turns on whether they share the same 'nucleus of facts'") (citations omitted).

Absent further guidance from the Supreme Court or from this Circuit, however, it is not up to this Court to expand upon the basic holding in Plaut—that a statute is unconstitutional as a violation of the separations of power to the extent that it requires the reopening of a final judgment for money damages. 514 U.S. at 240, 115 S. Ct. 1447. As no reopening of a final judgment under § 1605(a)(7) occurs by virtue of our courts honoring the terms of § 1083(c), that statute withstands scrutiny under the controlling precedent. To rule otherwise, would require this Court to reach well beyond existing precedent, and that is something this trial judge is loathe to do.

Even if the fundamental shift away from the jurisdiction-conferring approach of § 1605(a)(7) is viewed as little more than a than a change in the rule of decision for liability in federal terrorism actions, Congress in this instance has amended all the underlying law by virtue of its complete repeal of § 1605(a)(7) and substitution of § 1605A. Accordingly, this case does not run afoul of Klein in the way the Supreme Court has construed that foundational decision. *See Plaut*, 514 U.S. at 218, 115 S. Ct. 1447; *see also Klein*, 80 U.S. at 146. Moreover, the kind of across-the-board change in the terrorism exception that Congress undertook and ultimately accomplished with the passage of § 1083 is not the kind that embodies or otherwise enhances the risk that certain politically connected groups might twist the lawmaking process into a tool for the unraveling of disfavored civil judgments. *See Plaut*, 514 U.S. at 219–226, 115 S. Ct. 1447 (noting how the Nation's founders viewed finality of court judgments as a safeguard against the risk that politically connected groups might use the legislative process to unravel civil court judgments); *see also id.* at 240–247, 115 S. Ct. 1447 (stressing that the Article III principle of finality in civil judgments is generally intended to prevent the legislative process from being used to direct the reopening of specific civil judgments) (Breyer, J., concurring).

Moreover, while the question of whether the statute impacts the outcome of a civil case on the merits is not a central consideration, *see id.* at 228–29, 115 S. Ct. 1447, it is worth noting that § 1083(c), much like the enactments that were upheld in Cherokee Nation and Sioux Nation, and in sharp contrast to the enactment struck down in Klein, does not dictate the outcome of a case on the merits. *See Sioux Nation*, 448 U.S. at 405, 100 S. Ct. 2716; *Cherokee Nation*, 270 U.S. at 486, 46 S. Ct. 428; *Klein*, 80 U.S. at 146. Plaintiffs still must prove that they are entitled to relief under the new terrorism enactment, § 1605A(c). There is no guarantee that federal law will provide relief to plaintiffs any more or less than state tort law might have in an action under § 1605(a)(7).

Finally, this Court is not convinced that the principles announced in Plaut apply with the same degree of force in actions under the FSIA. As the Supreme Court observed in *Austria v. Altmann*, FSIA questions are sui generis. 541 U.S. at 697, 124 S. Ct. 2240. To begin with, the FSIA is a far-reaching, retrospective law—the statute reaches conduct by foreign powers that long predates its enactment and it directly addresses sensitive matters of foreign relations, which, as the Court emphasized, are inherently subject to "current political realities and relationships." *Id.* at 696, 124 S. Ct. 2240. It is beyond question that foreign relations matters are soundly committed to the political branches. *Oetjen v. Cent. Leather Co.*, 246 U.S. 297, 302–04, 38 S. Ct. 309, 311, 62 L.Ed. 726 (1918); *see also United States v. Curtiss-Wright Export Corp.*, 299 U.S. 304, 319, 57 S. Ct. 216, 81 L.Ed. 255 (1936) (holding that the Federal Government's powers over foreign affairs differ "in origin and essential character" from its powers over domestic law matters). And while neither the retrospective nature of the FSIA, nor the fact that it directly concerns our relationships with foreign nations, is enough to justify a usurpation of the federal courts' powers and responsibilities under Article III, there must be at least be some recognition—as there was in Altmann—that the political branches have greater authority and leeway with respect to decisions apportioning the liability of foreign nations.

In the realm of foreign affairs, our Courts must attach a strong presumption of validity to actions in which both the Congress and President are in agreement. *See Dames & Moore v. Regan*, 453 U.S. 654, 669, 101 S. Ct. 2972, 69 L.Ed.2d 918 (1981); *see also Youngstown Sheet & Tube*, 343 U.S. at 637, 72 S. Ct. 863 (Jackson, J., concurring). As our Circuit has emphasized time and again, the FSIA terrorism exception represents a "delicate legislative compromise." *See Price*, 294 F.3d at 89; accord Cicippio-Puleo, 353 F.3d at 1035. Here, § 1083 represents precisely the kind of "delicate legislative compromise" involving foreign affairs that is best left to the political branches of our Federal Government. Indeed, President Bush vetoed the first attempt by Congress to enact § 1605A. *See* Memorandum to the House of Representatives Returning Without Approval the "National Defense Authorization Act for Fiscal Year 2008," 43 Weekly Comp. Pres. Doc. 1641 (Dec. 28, 2007). At that time, the President expressed concerns about how these reforms to the FSIA terrorism exception would negatively impact Iraq's economy and reconstruction efforts as the United States worked to help that nation rebuild. *See id.* Shortly thereafter, Congress redrafted its proposed legislation to accommodate the President's concerns by adding a provision that authorized the President to waive any part of § 1083 with respect to Iraq. *See* § 1083(d). As a result, the President signed § 1083 into law on January 28, 2008, *see* Pub. L. No. 110-181, thereby enacting the sweeping reforms to the FSIA contained in § 1605A.[28] When, as here, both the President and Congress— the two branches vested with responsibility for our conduct of foreign affairs—are working together toward a common foreign policy objective, the Judicial Branch should be extremely hesitant about intervening in a way that would unravel those efforts.

Under the former version of the terrorism exception, § 1605(a)(7), Congress and the President had in a sense left an important federal policy relating to state sponsors of terrorism to the many diverse substantive bodies of law within state and territorial jurisdictions. The new law, § 1605A, however, demonstrates that both Congress and the President have come to an agreement that this federal policy aimed at deterring foreign state sponsors of terror should now fall squarely under federal law and control. Moreover, Congress and the President have greatly expanded the range of remedies and legal processes available in these federal actions. It may well be that Iran will not be pleased with the changes implemented by § 1083, but whatever concerns Iran may have are best addressed through diplomatic channels.

Important questions concerning how best to deal with state sponsors of terrorism will most certainly be a topic of ongoing debate and discussion between the Legislative and Executive Branches for many years to come. With the enactment of § 1083, the political branches have ordained a fundamental shift in policy pertaining to state sponsors of terrorism. In recognition of these significant reforms, this Court cannot say that § 1083 offends Article III of the Constitution to extent that this new law offers certain victims of state-sponsored terrorism an opportunity to lay claim to new federal rights and remedies in actions under the FSIA. While it is the Federal Judiciary that decides individual cases and controversies arising under federal law, it is our political branches that ultimately bear full responsibility for our relations with foreign powers.

b. Assuming that Section 1083(c)(3) Does Not Direct the Reopening of Final judgments, Does the Waiver of the Res Judicata or Collateral Estoppel Effect of an Prior Terrorism FSIA Action Nonetheless Offend Article III because Congress has Directed the Courts to Ignore Fundamental and Longstanding Judicial Doctrines?

Having decided that § 1083(c)(3) does not direct the reopening of final judgments in violation of Article III, this Court is of the view that the waiver of res judicata and collateral estoppel in § 1083(c)(2)(B) should also withstand Constitutional

28 The President immediately exercised the waiver in § 1083(d) and waived the entire section with respect to Iraq. *See* Pres. Determ. No. 2008-9, 73 Fed.Reg. 6571 (Jan. 28, 2008); *see also Republic of Iraq v. Beaty*, ___ U.S. ___, 129 S. Ct. 2183, 2191–2193, 173 L.Ed.2d 1193 (2009) (discussing President's waiver of § 1083 concerning Iraq.)

scrutiny under the narrow facts of these cases. In this Court's opinion, the holding that there is not prohibited reopening of final judgments—because any terrorism action brought under § 1605A is fundamentally different from an action under § 1605(a)(7)—largely resolves any question regarding the constitutional validity of Congress' decision to waive the preclusive effect (if there is any) of a prior court adjudication under § 1605(a)(7). In practical terms, this Court recognizes that the issue of whether a statute violates the constitutional prohibition against Congress directing the reopening of final civil judgments for money damages, is really an issue that is separate and apart from the question of when and to what extent the preclusion doctrines—res judicata and collateral estoppel—should apply in a given case. Nonetheless, these two important questions raise overlapping concerns and are in many ways inextricably connected. Thus, this Court finds that some additional scrutiny of the statute is warranted with regard to the waiver of claim and issue preclusion defenses in § 1083(c)(2)(B).

Generally speaking, the doctrine of res judicata precludes the parties from relitigating claims only when the parties previously litigated the claims or could have litigated them in a prior civil action that reached a final judgment on the merits. *See, e.g., Allen v. McCurry*, 449 U.S. 90, 92–94, 101 S. Ct. 411, 414, 66 L.Ed.2d 308 (1980); *Drake v. FAA*, 291 F.3d 59 (D.C.Cir.2002). The related doctrine of collateral estoppel provides that parties may be precluded from litigating any issue of fact or law that was previously resolved by a court in the course of reaching a final judgment in another action between those parties. *See, e.g., McCurry*, 449 U.S. at 94–96, 101 S. Ct. 411, 415; *U.S. Postal Serv. v. Am. Postal Workers Union*, 553 F.3d 686, 696 (D.C.Cir.2009).

A fundamental precept of common-law adjudication, embodied in the related doctrines of collateral estoppel and res judicata, is that a "'right, question or fact distinctly put in issue and directly determined by a court of competent jurisdiction . . . cannot be disputed in a subsequent lawsuit between the same parties or privies.'" *Montana v. United States*, 440 U.S. 147, 153, 99 S. Ct. 970, 59 L.Ed.2d 210 (1979) (quoting *S. Pac. R.R. Co. v. United States*, 168 U.S. 1, 48–49, 18 S. Ct. 18, 42 L. Ed. 355 (1897)). Both doctrines serve to "relieve parties of the cost of and vexation of multiple lawsuits, conserve judicial resources, and, by preventing inconsistent decisions, encourage reliance on adjudication." *Id.* at 153–54, 99 S. Ct. 970 (1979). Thus, the primary purpose served by the doctrines of res judicata and collateral estoppel is the preservation of the finality of judgments. *See, e.g., Crist v. Bretz*, 437 U.S. 28, 33, 98 S. Ct. 2156, 57 L.Ed.2d 24 (1978). More fundamentally, however, the Supreme Court has stated that the "[a]pplication of res judicata and collateral estoppel is central to the purpose for which civil courts have been established, the conclusive resolution of disputes within their jurisdictions." Montana, 440 U.S. at 154, 99 S. Ct. 970 (citing *Southern Pacific Railroad Co.*, 168 U.S. at 49, 18 S. Ct. 18; *Hart Steel v. Railroad Supply Co.*, 244 U.S. 294, 37 S. Ct. 506, 61 L.Ed. 1148 (1917)). Thus, a statutory directive instructing courts to waive res judicata and collateral estoppel may raise separation of powers concerns under Article III.

Indeed, in Plaut, the Supreme Court suggested that a waiver of res judicata that is not subject to "the control of the courts themselves" might raise separations-of-powers issues. 514 U.S. at 232–33, 115 S. Ct. 1447; *see also Sioux Nation*, 448 U.S. at 432–434, 100 S. Ct. 2716 (Rehnquist, J., dissenting). The language waiver res judicata at issue is particularly troublesome because, as noted previously, *supra*, only two Supreme Court decisions have considered a waiver of that doctrine by Congress, and both decisions involved cases brought against the United States by Indian tribes. *See Sioux Nation*, 448 U.S. 371, 100 S. Ct. 2716; Cherokee Nation, 270 U.S. 476, 46 S. Ct. 428. And, as underscored by the Supreme Court more recently in Plaut, those two decisions are narrowly tailored to the specific facts of those cases—meaning the basic proposition established by those rulings is simply that Congress may "waive the res judicata effect of a prior judgment entered in the Government's favor on a claim against the United States." 514 U.S. at 230, 115 S. Ct. 1447. In fact, the Court pointed to Justice Rehnquist's dissent in Sioux Nation, and emphasized that Court had yet to consider whether Congress could prohibit the Federal Judiciary from applying the doctrine of res judicata in specific cases. The Court wrote:

> The statute at issue in *United States v. Sioux Nation* seemingly prohibited courts from raising the res judicata defense sua sponte. The Court did not address that point; as far as it appears it saw no reason to raise the defense on its own. Of course the unexplained silences of our decisions lack precedential weight.

Id. at 232 n. 6, 115 S. Ct. 1447 (citations omitted).

The bottom line is that both Sioux Nation or Cherokee Nation leave open the question of whether Congress may waive res judicata or collateral estoppel with respect to a litigant other than the Federal Government—but this is precisely what Congress has sought to achieve with § 1083(c)(2)(B). By its terms, that statutory provision requires this Court to ignore any defense of res judicata or collateral estoppel that Iran may wish to assert in a new action under § 1605A.

Because res judicata and collateral estoppel are long held judicial doctrines that are central to the judiciary's purpose in rendering final judgments in civil cases, this Court is inclined to agree with the opinion expressed by Justice Rehnquist in Sioux Nation. It seems to this Court that Congress has little business directing whether or when those judicial doctrines should be invoked any more than this Judge should play a role in directing federal appropriations. This Court, however, must, at least in this particular instance, separate out the question of whether there has been some effort by the legislative branch to claim those salutary judicial doctrines in pursuit of their own legislative ends, from the more fundamental question of whether there has in fact been a prohibited reopening of final judgments for money damages in contravention of Plaut, the Supreme Court's last word on this matter. While the two issues may be overlapping at times, they are nonetheless distinct. For Article III purposes, the question is not necessarily whether the preclusion doctrines of res judicata or collateral estoppel have been invoked by the Legislative Branch; it is simply whether Congress has in effect directed the reopening of final judgments for money damages. Here, that sort of Article III violation—albeit in the most technical sense—has not occurred.[29] Accordingly, this judge cannot say that the waiver of res judicata or collateral estoppel are offensive under the circumstances presented in this case.[30]

Moreover, this Court is of the view that—regardless of Congress' wishes on the matter—it simply would not be appropriate for this Court to give res judicata or collateral estoppel effect to a prior action under § 1605(a)(7). With respect to res judicata, that doctrine cannot be applied, where, as here, the claims now being asserted could not have been raised in the prior litigation. *See, e.g., McCurry*, 449 U.S. at 92–94, 101 S. Ct. 411, 414; Montana, 440 U.S. at 154, 99 S. Ct. 970; *Nat'l Res. Def. Council v. EPA*, 513 F.3d 257, 260 (D.C.Cir.2008); *Drake*, 291 F.3d at 67. Prior to the enactment of the 2008 NDAA last year, § 1605A and the new federal cause of action it creates did not exist in any shape or form. As our Circuit has emphasized, res judicata "does not bar a litigant from doing in the present what he had no opportunity to do in the past." Drake, 291 F.3d at 67. Accordingly, res judicata, as a doctrine, does not afford preclusive effect to those cases presented here that were litigated in accordance with state law under § 1605(a)(7) at a time when no federal cause of action existed.[31]

Similarly, with respect to collateral estoppel, our Circuit has recently emphasized that issue preclusion is generally not appropriate when the legal context has

---

29 It might very well be a different case if Congress had directed that res judicata and collateral estoppel are waived in any cases brought under the very same cause of action. The appropriate example here would be if Congress had directed the Courts to reinstate, under § 1605(a)(7), all the claims that this Court and others had previously dismissed under that very same provision. As Congress in this case has seen fit to create an entirely new cause of action under § 1605A, and has repealed § 1605(a)(7) outright, this Court need not reach that more difficult issue.

30 In light of the Court's cautionary remarks regarding Sioux Nation in the Plaut decision, the Supreme Court may one day take the opportunity to consider and decide whether res judicata, and perhaps even collateral estoppel, are so intrinsic or central to the Federal Judiciary's responsibilities under Article III that Congress should not limit the ability of the Courts to independently apply those doctrines. It is not the role of this trial court, however, to reach beyond the essential holdings within the Supreme Court's decisions. Those decisions are binding on this Court until the Supreme Court rules otherwise.

31 It is true that subsequent changes in decisional law or case law is normally not sufficient to overcome res judicata. *E.g., Moitie*, 452 U.S. at 398, 101 S. Ct. 2424 (holding that res judicata effect "of a final unappealed judgment on the merits is not altered by the fact that the judgment may have been wrong or rested on a legal principle that is subsequently overruled in another case"); *Hardison v. Alexander*, 655 F.2d 1281, 1288–89 (D.C.Cir. 1981) (holding that res judicata is not overcome by a subsequent change in the law of the Circuit); accord *Apotex*, 393 F.3d at 218. A change in the applicable case law, however, must be distinguished from a change in statutory law. Many Circuits have recognized that a change in statutory law can be sufficient to overcome res judicata. *See Alvear-Velez v. Mukasey*, 540 F.3d 672, 678–80 (7th Cir.2008) (collecting and discussing cases from the Circuits and holding that res judicata does not necessarily apply when the change in the law "is statutory in nature, as opposed to a change in case law").

changed. *See U.S. Postal Serv.*, 553 F.3d at 696; *Pharm. Care Mgmt. Ass'n v. District of Columbia*, 522 F.3d 443, 447 (D.C.Cir.2008). The decisions of our Circuit build on the Supreme Court's decision in *Montana v. United States*, in which the Court observed that a "a change in the controlling legal principles" may be sufficient to prevent the application of collateral estoppel. 440 U.S. at 161, 99 S. Ct. 970. As emphasized throughout this opinion, the enactment of § 1083 of the 2008 NDAA altered the entire legal context pertaining to litigation against state sponsors of terrorism because the underlying substantive legal basis for the such actions has been shifted from state law to federal law. As the legal analysis in these actions will now be determined by a uniform federal standard—rather than the laws of numerous state and territorial jurisdictions—the collateral estoppel doctrine should not be invoked in any of the new actions proceeding under § 1605A(c).

More fundamentally speaking, many of the purposes served by the preclusion doctrines are not as easily realized in this sui generis context involving civil actions against foreign states. In the domestic law context, private citizens involved in civil litigation may certainly achieve settled expectations that are reinforced and well served by the application of preclusion doctrines, but the same cannot be said of foreign states acting within the vast international arena. As Altmann underscored, foreign states order their affairs primarily on the basis of their understanding of how present political realties within the global sphere might influence their standing vis-à-vis other nations. *See* 541 U.S. at 696, 124 S. Ct. 2240; *see also Price*, 294 F.3d at 97 ("Relations between nations in the international community are seldom governed by the domestic law of one state or the other.") (citing LORI FISLER DAMROSCH, FOREIGN STATES AND THE CONSTITUTION, 73 VA. L. REV. 483, 520 (1987)). Thus, while individual lawsuits by United States citizens and nationals against state sponsors of terrorism may have some bearing on how rogue nations, like Iran, might perceive and manage their relations with the United States, it strains credulity to assert that Iran has any reliance interests or settled expectations with respect to prior civil actions litigated against it under § 1605(a)(7). Indeed, the notion is almost laughable because that nation has never appeared in any of the terrorism actions that have been litigated against it in this Court.

Finally, applying any of the preclusion doctrines with respect to actions that were previously litigated to a final judgment under the former version of the state sponsor of terrorism exception, would completely undermine the purpose behind the most recent enactment § 1605A. As noted, *supra*, Part B, the new statute aims to provide a uniform federal cause of action in lieu of the old "pass-through" regime under § 1605(a)(7) that was viewed as unjust and ineffective largely because it was beholden to the laws of the many state and territorial jurisdictions. Thus, the application by courts of preclusion defenses in new actions under § 1605A would lead to a result entirely at odds with the aim of the new statute because our courts, by granting preclusive effect to prior judicial determinations under state law, would, practically speaking, allow those individual state sources of law to again control outcomes in civil actions against state sponsors of terror. Such a perverse result should be avoided, especially in this foreign affairs context in which both the President and Congress have expressed a clear policy preference in favor of a uniform federal standard. *See Dames & Moore*, 453 U.S. at 668–69, 101 S. Ct. 2972 (1981) (suggesting that Courts should be extremely hesitant about undermining foreign policy initiatives when both Congress and the President are in agreement); *Garamendi*, 539 U.S. at 414–15, 123 S. Ct. 2374 (emphasizing that state law touching on foreign policy matters must give way to federal policy in the light of the strong need for uniformity in this country's dealings with foreign sovereigns); *Alvear-Velez*, 540 F.3d 672 (stating that preclusion doctrines should not be applied when doing so would frustrate Congress' purpose for changes in the statutory law).

In sum, where, as in this case, Congress and the President have provided for a new federal cause of action against a foreign state, application of res judicata or collateral estoppel with respect to prior actions that relied on the "pass-through" regime of § 1605(a)(7) would be inconsistent with the Judiciary's own principles regarding the application of those salutary preclusion doctrines. Thus, under the circumstances presented here, the waiver of res judicata and collateral estoppel expressed in § 1083(c)(2)(B) is perhaps best understood as nothing more than a poor choice of statutory language that is merely intended to reinforce the understanding that Congress and the President have accomplished a fundamental change in public policy with respect to actions against state sponsors of terrorism.

As a caveat to this analysis, this Court wishes to stress that this decision does not consider whether the waiver of basic and long-established common law defenses in § 1083(c)(2)(B) might offend the Due Process Clause, as some commentators have suggested recently. *See* Suits Against Terrorist States, *supra* note 4, at 6, 61 nn. 231–232; Debra M. Strauss, Reaching out to the International Community: Civil Lawsuits as the Common Ground in the Battle Against Terrorism, 19 Duke J. Comp. & Int'l L. 307 (2009). Technically speaking, it is an open question whether a foreign state is even entitled to Due Process under the Fifth Amendment because the Supreme Court expressly declined to consider the question in *Republic of Argentina v. Weltover, Inc.*, and has not revisited the issue since. 504 U.S. 607, 619, 112 S. Ct. 2160, 119 L.Ed.2d 394 (1992). Both the Court of Appeals in Price and this Court in Flatow have emphasized how the Supreme Court has never squarely addressed this matter. *See Price*, 294 F.3d at 97; *Flatow I*, 999 F. Supp. 1 at 19. Nonetheless, this Court finds that—unlike the Article III question—the issue of whether the statutory waiver of preclusion defenses like res judicata offends the Due Process Clause is not ripe for consideration at this time.

In contrast to the Article III question, which speaks to the power of this Court to decide cases independently, free from interference from the political branches, the Due Process issue (if there is any) speaks to the degree of fairness to which Iran may or may not be entitled as a party named in these FSIA terrorism cases. To the extent that there is an argument that the statutory waiver of res judicata or collateral estoppel amounts to a violation of Due Process with respect to the treatment of Iran as a civil defendant, that argument is best articulated in the first instance by Iran itself. As emphasized, *supra*, n. 5, Iran is an experienced litigant in this Court and throughout the federal courts generally, but the Iranian Government has elected not to defend itself during the merits phases of these actions. It should also be stressed again here that Iran has appeared repeatedly before the federal courts during the postjudgment phases of these actions, and has successfully defeated efforts by plaintiffs to execute the default civil judgments entered against the Government of Iran. *See, e.g., Ministry of Defense and Support for the Armed Forces of the Islamic Republic of Iran v. Elahi,* ___ U.S. ___, 129 S. Ct. 1732, 173 L.Ed.2d 511 (2009) (demonstrating how Iran litigated an action from the district court all the way through to the Supreme Court and thereby prevented certain FSIA judgment creditors from attaching one of its assets here in the United States). In view of these facts, this Court sees no reason to sua sponte examine whether the waiver of preclusion doctrines in new actions under § 1605A might somehow compromise purported Due Process rights of that foreign sovereign. This Court is certainly not interested in affording constitutional rights to Iran, especially when Iran has not asserted its right to defend itself in the actions filed here.

Thus, the only constitutional issue considered today has nothing to do with Due Process and everything to do with the separation of powers and the independent authority of the Article III judiciary to conclusively resolve cases and controversies. Accordingly, this Court has scrutinized the statutory waiver of res judicata and collateral estoppel in § 1083(c)(2)(B) only to consider whether that measure— either in isolation or in concert with § 1083(c)(3)—amounts to a prohibited usurpation of judicial power by Congress. This basic question does not implicate a legal defense of Iran so much as it concerns the delicate system of checks and balances envisioned under our Constitution and, ultimately, the authority and integrity of this Court. No other constitutional issues warrant the Court's attention at this time.

Moreover, this Court is rather dubious of any suggestion that Due Process would prevent or otherwise limit the application of § 1083(c) to matters that were previously litigated to final judgments against Iran under § 1605(a)(7). As the D.C. Circuit held in Price, "foreign nations are external to the constitutional compact[,]" and therefore foreign states do not have Due Process rights. 294 F.3d at 97. In its extensive analysis of the issue, the Court of Appeals relied heavily on the Supreme Court's decision in *South Carolina v. Katzenbach*, in which the Court held that the "'the word 'person' in the context of the Due Process Clause of the Fifth Amendment, cannot, by any reasonable measure of interpretation, be expanded to encompass the States of the Union.'" 383 U.S. 301, 323–24, 86 S. Ct. 803, 15 L.Ed.2d 769 (1966), quoted in Price, 294 F.3d at 96. Accordingly, as Court of Appeals explained that "it would be highly incongruous to afford greater Fifth Amendment rights to foreign nations, who are entirely alien to our constitutional system, than are afforded to the states, who help make up the very fabric of that system." Price, 294 F.3d at 97. Four years earlier, in the Flatow decision, this Court reached the precisely the same conclusion for similar reasons. *Flatow I*, 999 F. Supp. 1 at 19–21.

In Price, the D.C. Circuit also underscored several practical problems with respect to the extension of Due Process rights to foreign nations. The Court observed, for example, that the freezing of assets of foreign nations by Congress and the President, or the imposition of sanctions, might be challenged as deprivations of property without due process of law. Price, 294 F.3d at 100. "The courts would be called upon to adjudicate these sensitive questions, which could in turn tie the hands of the other branches as they sought to respond to foreign policy crises. The Constitution does not demand this." *Id.* at 99 (citations omitted). For all the sound reasons expressed by the Court of Appeals in Price, this Court finds it unlikely that the Supreme Court would extend Due Process protections to foreign states like Iran. The clear weight of authority suggests otherwise.

3. Additional Considerations

There are other aspects of § 1083 of the 2008 NDAA that—while not directly at issue here—nonetheless give this Court pause and lead it to question whether today's ruling finding no Constitutional infirmities with respect to § 1083(c) is truly the right decision. For instance, within the new terrorism exception, § 1605A, which is implemented at § 1083(a), Congress suggests that this Court should rehear "Case Number 1:00CV03110(EGS) in the United States District Court for the District of Columbia." *See* § 1605A(a)(2)(B). The case that the statute is referring to in this instance is *Roeder v. Islamic Republic of Iran*, an action that Judge Sullivan dismissed in April 2002 because it was barred by the Algiers Accords. 195 F. Supp. 2d 140 (D.D.C.2002) (Sullivan, J.), aff'd, 333 F.3d 228 (D.C.Cir. 2003).

Roeder concerns the more than 50 U.S. diplomatic and military personnel taken hostage, held captive, and tortured at the U.S. Embassy in Tehran from 1979 through 1981. The victims and their loved ones brought a class action lawsuit under the prior version of the state sponsor of terrorism exception, § 1605(a)(7). As the litigation moved forward, it became clear that the action was barred by the Algiers Accords. Once this became apparent, and as dismissal of the case was imminent, Congress passed legislation instructing Judge Sullivan to go forward with the case, and to do so notwithstanding the unmistakable fact that the action was plainly barred under the terms of the Algiers Accords.[32]

Needless to say, Judge Sullivan found himself facing an Article III problem in the Roeder case. Judge Sullivan was able to avoid the Constitutional question, however, because Congress had not clearly expressed its intent to abrogate the Algiers Accords, as is required before Courts will hold that an international agreement is abrogated by a subsequent act of Congress. *See id.* at 145 ("Ultimately, however,

32 Following the entry of default judgment with respect to liability, and on the eve of the date set for trial on the issue of damages, the United States intervened as a matter of right under Fed. R. Civ. Pro. 24(a) and moved the Court to dismiss the case. *See Roeder*, 195 F. Supp. 2d at 150–52, 154–59.

this Court need not resolve these important Constitutional questions because while Congress' intent to interfere with this litigation was clear, its intent to abrogate the Algiers Accords was not."). Thus, Judge Sullivan was able to dismiss the action on the narrow ground that the Algiers Accords remained intact as binding legal authority and therefore required dismissal of any claims arising out of the Iran hostage taking. *Id.* at 178–183.[33]

Judge Sullivan also went to some length in his opinion to explain that, while our Court cannot ignore or refuse to give effect to the Algiers Accords, both Congress and the President have the authority to abrogate them, if they so desire. *Id.* at 183–84. The opinion could not have been any clearer on this point. To date, however, neither branch has taken such action; the political consequences are likely too great, but that is precisely why it is a decision best left to the political branches, and not the Courts. *See id.* at 145.[34]

Unfortunately, § 1605A(a)(2)(B) suggests that at least some members of Congress still believe that Judge Sullivan should decide the Iran hostage case, notwithstanding the Court's determination that the action is barred by the Algiers Accords. Indeed, consistent with § 1605A(a)(2)(B) plaintiffs in Roeder have filed a new action in this Court. *See Roeder v. Islamic Republic of Iran*, No. 08-CV-487-RCL (D.D.C.), Dk. #1 (Complaint filed Mar. 21, 2008).[35] Despite these realities, however, this Court refuses to believe members of Congress—in a nation of committed to the rule of law—would willingly direct our Courts to turn a blind eye to our longstanding and binding international agreements. That certainly cannot be the case, especially now when our current administration appears committed more than ever to the spirit of international engagement and cooperation.

---

33 While Judge Sullivan was able to avoid the Article III constitutional question, he did so in an exceedingly thoughtful and careful manner. *See id.* at 163–67. This Court is grateful to Judge Sullivan for his excellent opinion and thoughtful discussion of the jurisprudence relevant to the consideration of the difficult issues Courts must inevitably face when confronted with the possibility of overreaching by Congress in violation of Article III.

34 Some members of Congress sharply criticized the administration for its role in urging the dismissal of the Iran hostages' case and have flatly rejected the notion that the Algiers Accord bars the victims' claims. For example, Senator Tom Harkin of Iowa issued a statement in 2001 in which he proclaimed: "The Algiers Accord is not a treaty and was never submitted to the Congress for ratification. It is a kidnapping and ransom agreement that entered into under duress while the Ayatollah was threatening to put the Americans on trial as 'spies' and execute them." *See* PATRICK GOODENOUGH, CARTER ERA AGREEMENT AGAIN CITED IN BID TO BLOCK IRAN HOSTAGE LAWSUIT, CYBERCAST NEWS SERV., Apr. 23, 2009, http://www.cnsnews.com/Public/Content/Article.aspx?rsrcid=47064.

35 As it did in the prior action under § 1605(a)(7), the United States has again intervened under Fed. R. Civ. Pro. 24(a) and has filed a Motion to dismiss the action, arguing that the plaintiffs' claims remains barred by the Algiers Accords. *See* Roeder, No. 08-CV-487-RCL (D.D.C.), Dk. # 23 (Motion to Intervene as Defendant, filed by the United States Apr. 21, 2009), Dk. # 24 (Minute Order, entered May 5, 2009, granting Government's Motion to Intervene), Dk. # 26 (Motion to Dismiss, filed by the United States May 5, 2009).

Nonetheless, the troubling language does suggest that perhaps certain interest groups were able to tuck the offensive language into the voluminous Defense Appropriations Act, realizing that perhaps it might not receive the same level of scrutiny there. The meddlesome draftsmanship might be easy enough to dismiss as an empty political gesture, if it were not for the Article III problem. Our Courts are here to uphold the rule of law and will not serve as ready accomplices in what appears as yet another political maneuver designed to make an end run around important international obligations.

Suffice it to note, what appears to this Court as an effort in § 1083 by Congress to reopen a specific case that was previously dismissed as barred by the Algiers Accords is extremely troubling. As a result, this Judge must now think long and hard about whether the questionable aspects of § 1083(c) considered in this decision should be viewed as nothing more than a vehicle to reopen an array of cases against Iran that were already litigated to final judgment prior to this new enactment. Congress has made some difficult constitutional questions even more difficult.

In the end, however, this Court is of the view that if it can it come to rest in its determination that § 1083(c)—to the extent that it allows cases closed under § 1605(a)(7) to now move forward as new actions under § 1605A—can withstand Constitutional scrutiny on its own terms, and thus any language outside of that particular section should not alter this Court's conclusion. To hold otherwise, would effectively bootstrap one Constitutional issue to another. Moreover, relying on language pertaining to the other litigation not pending before this judge, runs the risk of presenting an advisory opinion and one that might interfere with a case pending before another Article III judge in this courthouse. In this case, that would be a particularly undesirable result. As noted, Judge Sullivan produced an exceptional opinion addressing the fundamental problem with Congress' efforts to create a cause of action for the victims of the Iran Hostage crisis, and there is no doubt that Judge Sullivan can appropriately address that question again in the event that the issue becomes ripe for consideration once more.

This Court is also troubled by the way in which a large defense appropriations bill was used in this instance to effectuate an overhaul of the substantive law governing lawsuits against foreign sovereigns. Like Judge Sullivan observed in Roeder, however, this Judge too recognizes that Congress is free to accomplish changes in substantive law through an appropriations bill. *See Roeder*, 195 F. Supp. 2d at 184 (citing *Robertson*, 503 U.S. at 440, 112 S. Ct. 1407). Nonetheless, as Justice Scalia noted in Plaut, the independence of Article III courts serves a fundamental purpose in our system of limited government guarded by checks and balances. The judiciary's independent authority to decide cases with finality protects against the risk that influential groups might use—indeed exploit— the legislative process to make an end run around civil judgments that they find adverse to their own personal interests or desires. *See Plaut*, 514 U.S. at 219–226, 115 S. Ct. 1447. This Court has a suspicion that is precisely what may have occurred in this case. To be sure, there are many aspects of § 1083 of the 2008 NDAA are remarkable much like the statute that did not withstand Constitutional scrutiny in Plaut. In the end, however, this Court cannot allow its suspicion to shift the analysis of these important issues away from the plain text of the statute before it.

In sum, this Court holds that § 1083(c) withstands constitutional scrutiny because that provision does not require the reopening of final judgments issued under § 1605(a)(7). Critical to today's ruling is the Court's determination that the political branches of our government have in essence wiped the slate clean by creating an entirely new statutory provision that is chock full of rights and remedies that never existed under § 1605(a)(7). In so holding, this Court recognizes that this ruling may rest on a narrow view of the terms cause of action and judgment. Absent some clear authority suggesting a contrary result, however, it is not the province of this Court to expand existing Supreme Court precedent.

F. Analysis of Whether Actions Under Section 1605(a)(7) Have Qualified for Retroactive Treatment Under Section 1605A

With the statutory framework of § 1083(c) of the 2008 NDAA to guide the analysis, this Court now examines those efforts by a variety of counsel in these Iran cases to bring their prior actions under § 1605(a)(7) within the ambit of the new enactment, § 1605A. The cases this Court will examine here break down into roughly three categories, and so the analysis will be framed accordingly. The first category of cases are those in which counsel for plaintiffs have taken a "belt and suspenders" approach by invoking both § 1083(c)(2) and (c)(3). In these instances, plaintiffs' counsel have not only filed motions under subsection (c)(2) seeking to have their prior actions under § 1605(a)(7) given effect as if these actions had been filed under § 1605A originally, but they have also filed new actions entirely, relying on the related case procedures of (c)(3) and citing in their complaint, the new terrorism exception, § 1605A. The second category of cases involves those actions in which plaintiffs' counsel rely only on § 1083(c)(3), and so the attorneys in these actions have simply filed new actions under § 1605A as related actions to their prior cases, or as related to other cases pending under § 1605(a)(7) based on the same act or incident. The third category of cases are those in which plaintiffs' counsel have failed to invoke either § 1083(c)(2) or (c)(3), and yet, strangely, the attorneys in this category of cases have nonetheless filed motions that presume the right to relief under § 1605A. Without saying as much, it appears that counsel in this last category of cases have operated under the flawed assumption that § 1605A is automatically retroactive to their cases.

With few exceptions, each of the cases addressed below represents two separate civil actions on this Court's docket, even though the two docketed actions are based on the same act or incident and involve the same plaintiffs and defendants. This odd posture with respect to these matters did not come about because plaintiffs wished to be duplicative or believed that there is some tactical advantage in maintaining two actions based on the same act or incident. Quite the contrary, what has occurred here in many instances is that plaintiffs' counsel—whether they were required to or not—invoked the procedures of § 1083(c)(3), thereby filing their prior cases as new actions under § 1605A, instead of simply filing a motion, pursuant to § 1083(c)(2), that would have enabled this Court to treat their original action as if it was filed under § 1605A, as Congress intended.

As will be underscored in the Court's analysis of these FSIA terrorism cases, § 1083(c)(3) pertaining to related actions— as it may be invoked for certain cases that were previously filed under § 1605(a)(7)— is really a vehicle best reserved for those cases that had reached a final judgment and were not before the courts at time of the enactment of the 2008 NDAA. In other words, it is best reserved for those civil actions that were never eligible for § 1083(c)(2) and therefore could not have been simply transformed on motion into an action under § 1605A. More liberal use of § 1083(c)(3), invites unnecessary duplication of effort, requiring this Court to maintain two nearly identical actions on the docket—one under § 1605(a)(7) and one under § 1605A—by the very same plaintiffs, at approximately the same time, and will inevitably require this Court to flip back and forth between dozens of related cases involving hundreds upon hundreds of repeat plaintiffs. Suffice it to say, such a result wastes time and resources, and invites great confusion. Thus, as this Court understands the new statute, § 1083(c)(3) is the appropriate avenue for relief in those cases that reached final judgment sometime prior to the enactment of the 2008 NDAA and which were not "before the court[] in any form," as required for treatment on motion pursuant to § 1083(c)(2). With these initial observations in mind, this Court turns its attention toward many of the individual terrorism actions now pending against Iran.

1. The "Belt and Suspenders" Plaintiffs: Those Who Have Invoked Both Section 1083(c)(2) and (c)(3)

Nine of the 20 cases considered today fall within the "belt and suspenders" category. As noted, this category of cases involves prior actions under § 1605(a)(7) in which counsel have sought to obtain retroactive treatment under the new terrorism exception by filing both a motion under § 1083(c)(2) and a new complaint consistent with (c)(3). To the extent the use of these dual approaches leads to duplicative actions on the docket, this Court will exercise its docket management prerogative as appropriate to stay the most recently filed actions, pending resolution of efforts by counsel to move forward on motion in accordance with § 1083(c)(2). These actions are addressed here in chronological order

Kirschenbaum, 03-CV-1708 and 08-CV-1814. These cases arise out a suicide bombing in Jerusalem and were brought under § 1605(a)(7). Plaintiffs are an American citizen injured in that attack and several of his family members. An opinion was published and judgment was entered in favor of all plaintiffs on August 26, 2008. *Kirschenbaum*, 572 F. Supp. 2d 200. In reaching that judgment, this Court found liability against Iran based on the underlying causes of action, which were all based in state tort law, and then awarded compensatory damages but declined to award any punitive damages against Iran. *Id.* at 204 n. 1. In making that determination, this Court stressed that § 1605A does not have automatic, retroactive application to cases that were filed under § 1605(a)(7), and because plaintiffs had failed to follow the procedures in § 1083(c), punitive damages were not available. *Id.*

Kirschenbaum's Motion Pursuant to Section 1083(c)(2). Shortly after the judgment, plaintiffs sought reconsideration under Rule 59(e) of the Federal Rules of Civil Procedure and requested leave to file a motion nunc pro tunc under § 1083(c)(2), thereby enabling plaintiffs to proceed under the new terrorism exception § 1605A. Kirschenbaum, No. 03-CV-170-RCL (D.D.C.), Dk. #32. Counsel for plaintiffs argues that, based on a careful analysis of the entire § 1083, he honestly but mistakenly concluded that § 1605A applied retroactively to his case.

Beginning his analysis with § 1083(c)(2), counsel claims he believed that particular provision did not apply to his clients because, in his view, these plaintiffs were not "adversely affected on the ground that 28 U.S.C. § 1605(a)(7) failed to create a cause of action against a foreign state," as § 1083(c)(2)(iii) expressly requires. Dk. # 32, at 3. Counsel explains that the law recognizes a clear distinction between a "cause of action"—essentially the right to bring a civil suit—and the special remedy of punitive damages that may be awarded in certain kinds of lawsuits. *Id.* at 3–4. Counsel relies on a variety of legal authorities, including treatises and case precedent from many other jurisdictions, all of which support the proposition that a cause of action is necessarily separate and distinct from punitive damages. Indeed, as counsel asserts, punitive damages are dependent entirely on the underlying cause of action and cannot exist independently of an underlying claim. *Id.*; *see, e.g.*, *Burke v. Deere & Co.*, 6 F.3d 497, 511 (8th Cir.1993) ("[T]here is no separate cause of action for punitive damages under Iowa law. . . .").

Additionally, plaintiffs' counsel notes that the language in (c)(2)(iii) regarding the failure "to create a cause of action against a foreign state" appears to specifically address the problems encountered by certain plaintiffs in the Peterson litigation involving the 1983 bombing of the United States Marine barracks in Beirut, Lebanon. *Id.* at 4. In that case, for instance, a large number of plaintiffs with claims under § 1605(a)(7) were in fact barred from even presenting a cause of action by the applicable state tort law of certain jurisdictions. *See, e.g.*, *Peterson II*, 515 F. Supp. 2d at 44–45 (denying certain emotional distress claims of plaintiffs from Pennsylvania on the ground that they did not have standing to bring such claims under Pennsylvanian law). Counsel suggests that some of the legislative history, specifically statements from Senator Arlen Specter, reinforces the view that the (c)(2) provision was intended to apply only to plaintiffs, who, like the Pennsylvania litigants and others in Peterson, were barred from presenting their claims for recovery under the former pass-through regime that existed pursuant to § 1605(a)(7). Dk. # 32, at 4.

Thus, counsel reads § 1083(c)(2) in light of the legal distinction between an underlying cause of action and the special remedy of punitive damages, and thereby argues that he determined, in good faith, that he was not entitled to rely on (c)(2) because all the plaintiffs in his case had succeeded in their underlying causes of action under § 1605(a)(7). Consistent with this argument, counsel stresses that his clients neither need nor desire to pursue new claims under federal law; instead, their only request at this time is the additional remedy of punitive damages against Iran, as the new law, § 1605A, now makes available.

With respect to availability of § 1083(c)(3), plaintiffs again relies on the distinction between an action and damages. Counsel states:

> Plaintiffs did not interpret § 1083(c)(3) to apply to the instant case, especially where the original complaint already included a demand for punitive damages against the Defendant. [Section] 1083(c)(3) states that "any other action arising out of the same act or incident may be brought under section 1605A." Under Plaintiffs' interpretation of the word "action" this provision did not cover a situation such as Plaintiffs' where the only difference was in damages, and there was no separate action to bring.

Dk. # 32, at 5 (citations omitted). Accordingly, plaintiff ultimately concluded that neither § 1083(c)(2) nor (c)(3) governing the applicability of § 1605A to pending cases applied to the Kirschenbaum case.

Having determined that his clients had no recourse under § 1083(c), counsel claims that he finally reached the conclusion that actions like Kirschenbaum must fall under § 1605A automatically because of the language within § 1605A(b) that provides "an action may be . . . maintained under this section if the action is commenced . . . under section 1605(a)(7) (before the date of the enactment of this section)." § 1605A(b) (emphasis added).

While today's decision makes clear that this Court finds counsel's interpretation of § 1083 unpersuasive, counsel's reading of the statute is not unreasonable. To be sure, this new enactment is hardly a model of clarity and is "somewhat disjointed in its organization," as counsel observes. On a matter of first impression, such as was presented by this new statute, reasonable legal minds can, and often do, differ in their interpretations. This Court appreciates counsel's candor, insightful analysis, and prompt action in this matter.

At this time, however, the Court must deny the motion for reconsideration under Rule 59(e). This Court is not inclined to overlook a deadline for filing motions that Congress has imposed by statute. The 60-day time limit in § 1083(c)(2) is what Congress directed, and counsel has not provided this Court with any case precedent or other authority to suggest that this Court may override or waive the time limit for filing imposed by Congress under the circumstances presented here. Absent such authority, this Court is compelled to abide by the time limit Congress imposed. Accordingly, plaintiffs' motion will be denied, as will the motion requesting a hearing on this matter (Kirschenbaum, No. 03-CV-170-RCL (D.D.C.), Dk. # 33). A separate order denying these motions will issue this date. If, however, counsel is able to find some authority that might permit this Court to grant relief, notwithstanding the deadline imposed by statute, then Counsel may wish to file another motion for reconsideration under Rule 59(e) or a motion under Rule 60(b) seeking relief from today's order. Any motion and argument under Rule 60(b) should comply with the guidance expressed in Part G below.

Kirschenbaum's New Action Pursuant to § 1083(c)(3). About a month after filing their motion for reconsideration, plaintiffs also filed an action under § 1605A in accordance with the related case procedures set forth in § 1083(c)(3). *See Kirschenbaum*, No. 08-CV-1814-RCL (D.D.C.), Dk. # 3 (filed Oct. 17, 2008). This new action complies with the procedures in § 1083(c)(3) because it relates to plaintiffs' prior case under § 1605(a)(7), and the complaint in this new action was filed with 60 days of "the date of entry of judgment in the original action." *See* § 1083(c)(3)(A). Accordingly, this new case may proceed under § 1605A as a related action. The Court observes, however, that the complaint in this new action continues to assert New York common law as the source of plaintiffs claims against Iran, but reliance on state law is no longer necessary or appropriate under § 1605A because it expressly provides plaintiffs with a federal cause of action. Moreover, as plaintiffs in this new action previously succeeded with claims under New York law by utilizing the pass-through approach in their prior action under § 1605(a)(7), the doctrine of double recovery would likely bar or severely limit plaintiffs' efforts to claim additional compensatory damages in this new case under § 1605A. *See, e.g., Consol. Edison Co. of N.Y., Inc. v. Bodman*, 445 F.3d 438, 451 (D.C.Cir.2006); *Peterson II*, 515 F. Supp. 2d at 40 n. 7. As counsel stressed in their Rule 59(e) motion, however, plaintiffs are not seeking additional compensatory damages in this action. Instead, plaintiffs are now proceeding under § 1605A in order to claim punitive damages, which were not available under § 1605(a)(7). Accordingly, determining an award of punitive damages in this new action will not require this Court to consider any double recovery problems.

Beer, 06-CV-473 and 08-CV-1807. These cases arise out of the suicide bombing of a bus in Jerusalem on June 11, 2003. Plaintiffs are family members of one of the victims, the late Alan Beer, who was killed in that bombing. Plaintiffs in this action are represented by the same attorney who is handling the Kirschenbaum case, and therefore it should come as no surprise that the issues and arguments presented in this action are identical to those addressed above.

This Court issued an opinion and entered a judgment in favor of the plaintiffs on August 26, 2008. *See Beer*, 574 F. Supp. 2d 1. As in the Kirschenbaum case, this Court denied punitive damages because plaintiffs' action fell under § 1605(a)(7), not § 1605A. On September 10, 2008, plaintiffs filed a motion pursuant to Rule 59(e) for reconsideration and requested leave to file a motion nunc pro tunc under § 1083(c)(2) to enable plaintiffs to proceed under § 1605A. Beer, No. 06-CV-473-RCL (D.D.C.), Dk. # 30. That motion is in all critical respects identical to the motion for reconsideration filed in the Kirschenbaum action. Also like Kirschenbaum, plaintiffs in this case have made an additional effort to move forward under the new law by filing a new action in accordance with the related case procedures set forth in § 1083(c)(3). Incorporating by reference the analysis applied to the Kirschenbaum case above, this Court addresses both the motion and the newly filed action.

Beer's Motion Pursuant to § 1083(c)(2). For the reasons expressed above, this motion for reconsideration (*id.* Dk.# 31) must be denied at this time. If plaintiffs wish for this Court to reconsider the judgment and decide whether to grant leave for plaintiffs to proceed under § 1083(c)(2) on motion, then counsel must direct this Court to some authority suggesting that this Court need not comply with a time limit imposed by Congress under the circumstances presented here. The motion for a hearing on this matter, *id.*, will also be denied in a separate order issued this date.

Beer's New Action Pursuant to Section 1083(c)(3). Plaintiffs also filed a new action under § 1605A on October 17, 2008, *see Beer*, 08-CV-1708-RCL (D.D.C.), in accordance with the procedures for related actions under § 1083(c)(3). Like the plaintiffs in Kirschenbaum, plaintiffs in this case have met the requirement of § 1083(c)(3) and therefore may proceed under § 1605A as a related action. The Court again observes, however, that the complaint in this new action continues to assert New York common law as the source of plaintiffs' claims against Iran. In light of the new federal cause of action in § 1605A reliance on state law is no longer necessary or appropriate. Moreover, much like Kirschenbaum, the plaintiffs in this new action also succeeded previously with claims under New York law by utilizing the pass-through approach in their prior case under § 1605(a)(7). Thus, as noted above, the doctrine of double recovery should bar or severely limit plaintiffs' efforts to claim additional compensatory damages in this new case under § 1605A. As counsel stressed in their Rule 59(e) motion, however, plaintiffs are not seeking additional compensatory damages in this action. Instead, plaintiffs are now proceeding under § 1605A in order to claim punitive damages, which were not available under § 1605(a)(7). Accordingly, determining an award of punitive damages in this new action will not require this Court to consider any double recovery problems.

Haim, 02-CV-1811 and 08-CV-520. These cases arise from the same terrorist attack that claimed the life of Alisa Flatow. As noted in Part A, *supra*, a suicide bomber belonging to and acting on behalf of the Palestine Islamic Jihad drove a van loaded with explosives into the passenger bus traveling on the Gaza Strip on April 9, 1995, and the resulting explosion destroyed the bus and killed eight of the passengers. Many others were injured in the explosion. The plaintiffs in these actions are a United States citizen who was injured in that attack and members of his family. They first brought an action under § 1605(a)(7) on September, 12, 2002. Plaintiffs achieved a final judgment in their favor on March 24, 2006. *See Haim*, 425 F. Supp. 2d 56. As that case was under § 1605(a)(7), no punitive damages were awarded against Iran. *See id.* at 71.

Like plaintiffs in Kirschenbaum and Beer, plaintiffs in this action have taken a belt and suspenders approach in their efforts to take advantage of the new law, § 1605A. Following the enactment of the 2008 NDAA, plaintiffs first filed a new action, Haim, No. 08-CV-520-RCL (D.D.C.), on March 26, 2008, in accordance with the related cases provisions of § 1083(c)(3), thereby seeking punitive damages against Iran under the revised terrorism exception, § 1605A. Plaintiffs also filed a motion in their original action in an effort to obtain treatment under § 1605A by using the procedures in § 1083(c)(2). *See Haim*, 02-CV-1811-RCL (D.D.C.), Dk. # 32. As their prior case was no longer "before the court[] in any form" at the time of the enactment of the 2008 NDAA (January, 28, 2008), this Court denied the motion. *See Haim v. Islamic Republic*, 567 F. Supp. 2d 146 (D.D.C.2008) (Lamberth, C.J.).

Unlike a number of other cases addressed by the Court today, Haim was never eligible for treatment under § 1083(c)(2). Accordingly, the only way plaintiffs in this case can claim the benefits of § 1605A is through the related case provisions in § 1083(c)(3). Plaintiffs filed their new action within 60 days of the enactment of the 2008 NDAA, and therefore plaintiffs have properly applied the related case provisions of § 1083(c)(3) in this instance. As plaintiffs have taken the appropriate steps to avail themselves of § 1605A, no further action is required of the Court at this time.

Bland, 05-CV-2124. This civil action was filed under § 1605(a)(7) and arises out of the bombing of the United States Marine barracks in Beirut, Lebanon on October 23, 1983. *See Bland*, No. 05-CV-2124-RCL (D.D.C.), Dk. # 2 (Complaint). There are nearly 100 plaintiffs in this action, including numerous estates of those service members killed in the terrorist attack and dozens of family members of those who were killed or injured during the terrorist incident. On December 6, 2006, this Court took judicial notice of the findings of fact and conclusions of law in the Peterson action, which also concerns the Marine barracks bombing, *see Peterson I*, 264 F. Supp. 2d at 47, and entered judgment in favor of the Plaintiffs and against Iran with respect to all issues of liability. Bland, No. 05-CV-2124-RCL (D.D.C.), Dk. # 16. This Court then referred this action to a special master for consideration of plaintiffs' claims for damages. *See id.* Dk. ## 15-16.

On March 10, 2008, and while this action was still pending with the special master under § 1605(a)(7), counsel for plaintiff timely filed a motion seeking to proceed in their action under the newly-enacted terrorism exception, § 1605A. *See id.* Dk. # 17. As counsel followed the proper procedures and qualified for retroactive treatment in accordance with § 1083(c)(2), this Court granted the motion, thereby enabling plaintiffs to taken advantage of the new statute in their claims before the special master. *See id.* Dk. # 19. While plaintiffs' motion was still under consideration, however, and apparently out of an abundance of caution, counsel added the plaintiffs from this case to a complaint in a new action, styled *Brown v. Islamic Republic for Iran*, which is discussed below and also arises from the Marine barracks bombing incident. *See Brown*, 08-CV-531-RCL (D.D.C.), Dk. #1 (Complaint, filed Mar. 27, 2008). As will be discussed in more detail below, the Brown action includes plaintiffs from one another action, *Spencer v. Islamic Republic of Iran*, No. 06-CV-750-RCL (D.D.C.), which, like Bland, has qualified for treatment under § 1605A in accordance with the requirements of § 1083(c)(2) and arises out the Marine barracks bombing. Plaintiffs in Bland, Spencer, and now Brown, are all are represented by the same counsel, and thus counsel have taken a belt and suspenders approach by filing a new action in their cases, Bland and Spencer, that were eligible—and in fact qualified for—retroactive treatment under the terms of § 1605A.

To date, Bland is still pending with the special master. At a status conference set by the Court in accordance with this opinion and by separate order issued this date, this Court will see what must be done to sort out the claims and move matters forward on behalf of these Marine barracks bombings plaintiffs that are now spread out among three actions under § 1605A.

Spencer, 06-CV-750. This action also arises out of the Marine barracks bombing and was originally filed on April 24, 2006 under the § 1605(a)(7). *See Spencer*, No. 06-CV-750-RCL (D.D.C.), Dk. # 3 (Complaint). As the plaintiffs in this action are represented by the same counsel as plaintiffs in Bland, the issues and procedural history of this case largely mirror those discussed in Bland above. On October 10, 2007, this Court took judicial notice of the findings of fact and conclusions of law in the Peterson action, which also concerns the Marine barracks bombing, *see Peterson I*, 264 F. Supp. 2d at 47 (D.D.C.2003), and entered judgment in favor of the plaintiffs and against Iran with respect to all issues of liability, Spencer, No. 06-CV-750-RCL (D.D.C.), Dk. # 18. At that time the Court, referred this action to a special master for consideration of plaintiffs' claims for damages. *See id.*

On March 10, 2008, and while this action was still pending with the special master under § 1605(a)(7), counsel for plaintiffs timely filed a motion, pursuant to § 1083(c)(2), seeking to proceed in their action under the newly enacted terrorism exception, § 1605A. *See id.* Dk. # 19. As counsel followed the proper procedures and qualified for retroactive treatment in accordance with § 1083(c)(2), this Court granted the motion, thereby enabling plaintiffs to taken advantage of the new statute in their claims before the special master. *See id.* Dk. # 20. While plaintiffs' motion was still under consideration, however, counsel also added the plaintiffs from this case to a complaint in a new action, styled *Brown v. Islamic Republic for Iran*, which is discussed below and also arises from the Marine barracks bombing incident. *See Brown*, No. 08-CV-531-RCL (D.D.C.), Dk. # 1 (Complaint, filed Mar. 27, 2008). As noted above, the Brown action also includes plaintiffs from Bland, and the plaintiffs in Bland, Spencer, and now Brown, are all are represented by the same counsel. Thus, it appears that counsel have taken a belt and suspenders approach by filing a new action for the plaintiffs in their cases, Bland and Spencer, even those plaintiffs were eligible for—and in fact qualified for—retroactive treatment on motion in accordance with § 1083(c)(2).

Spencer is still pending with the special master. At the status conference set by the Court in accordance with this opinion and by separate order issued this date, this Court will see what must be done to sort out the claims and move matters forward under § 1605A.

Brown, 08-CV-531. As noted, the new case of *Brown v. Islamic Republic of Iran*, No. 08-CV-531-RCL (D.D.C.), includes plaintiffs from both Bland and Spencer, as discussed above. Accordingly, those plaintiffs who are now proceeding under § 1605A in their original cases, either Bland or Spencer, should be dismissed from the Brown action. To the extent that there any new plaintiffs in the Brown action, those plaintiffs may, of course, proceed in this new case.

Currently, service of process in Brown is being carried out through diplomatic channels, as that is the standard procedure in these actions against Iran. *See* § 1608(a). Once that process is completed, counsel for plaintiffs shall provide this Court with the names of all plaintiffs in Brown who appear in either the Bland or Spencer cases. As these plaintiffs now have the right to proceed under § 1605A in their original actions, they must be dismissed from this new action. Along with the list of names identifying the duplicative plaintiffs, counsel shall furnish the Court with a proposed order of dismissal of those plaintiffs. If these plaintiffs have any reason to oppose being dismissed from the Brown case, such opposition shall be filed with the Court at that time. An order consistent with the guidance expressed herein shall issue this date.

2. The "Related Action" Plaintiffs: Those Who Have Filed New Actions Pursuant to Section 1083(c)(3)

The next five civil cases to be addressed by the Court today are those in which counsel have invoked the procedures for related actions in § 1083(c). By doing so, plaintiffs' counsel have filed a new case under § 1605A as a "related action." Consistent with § 1083(c)(3) the new action must be related to either the plaintiffs' own prior action under § 1605(a)(7) or to some other currently pending action that is based on the same underlying terrorist incident. The Court will now examine these actions in chronological order.

Rimkus, 06-CV-1116 and 08-CV-1615. These cases arise from the bombing of the Kobar Towers, a residential military complex operated by the United States Air Force in Dhahran, Saudi Arabia. Plaintiff is the father of one of the 19 servicemen killed in that terrorist attack. On August 26, 2008, this Court issued an opinion and entered judgment in favor of plaintiff in accordance with § 1605(a)(7). *See Rimkus*, 575 F. Supp. 2d 181. Even though his action was pending at the time the 2008 NDAA was enacted, plaintiff never moved the Court, pursuant to § 1083(c)(2), to treat his case as if it were filed under the new law, § 1605A. Instead of following those straightforward procedures, plaintiff opted to file what he has styled as a "Complaint For Punitive Damages Pursuant to Section § 1083(c)(3)." *See Rimkis*, No. 08-CV-1615-RCL (D.D.C.). The only purpose of this new action is affix punitive damages against Iran for the claims that were litigated previously in Rimkis, No. 06-CV-1116-RCL (D.D.C.).

Notwithstanding the questionable validity of a complaint for punitive damages, plaintiff was undoubtedly entitled to relief under § 1083(c)(3) when he filed it. Similarly, plaintiff was also eligible for treatment on motion as the litigation in his prior action, No. 06-CV-1116-RCL, wound to a close. While plaintiff's new complaint for punitive damages under § 1083(c)(3) is not the best or most straightforward way to achieve the relief plaintiff desires, it was filed in a timely manner and with recognition of the applicable procedures in § 1083(c). In view of these considerations, plaintiff's new case, No. 08-CV-1615-RCL, is permitted to proceed under § 1605A.

Bonk, 08-CV-1273. This action, like many considered today, emanates from the terrorist bombing of the United States Marine Barracks in Beirut, Lebanon on October 23, 1983. The plaintiffs in this action were all originally part of the large consolidated action *Peterson v. Islamic Republic of Iran*, No. 01-CV-2094-RCL (D.D.C.). As noted Part A, *supra*, Peterson was brought under § 1605(a)(7), the case proceeded to trial, and this Court ultimately awarded damages to most of the plaintiffs in the case. *See Peterson II*, 515 F. Supp. 2d 25.

Bonk is a new case that was filed several months ago by the plaintiffs who were dismissed from the Peterson action because the applicable state tort law—specifically Louisiana and Pennsylvania law—did not provide them standing to assert their claims for the intentional infliction of emotional distress. *See id.* at 45. Bonk is brought in accordance with § 1083(c)(3) as a related action to several other cases that were timely commenced under § 1605(a)(7). Plaintiffs point to the cases of Valore, No. 03-CV-1959-RCL (D.D.C.); Bland, No. 05-CV-2124-RCL (D.D.C.); and Davis, No. 07-CV-1302-RCL (D.D.C.), all of which are open cases pending against Iran, and all of which arise from the bombing of the Marine barracks in Lebanon. As these plaintiffs seek relief based on that same terrorist incident, § 1083(c)(3) by its plain terms authorizes them to file this new action under § 1605A. Accordingly, Bonk has been filed properly as a related action, and so these plaintiffs who were dismissed from Peterson my now move forward with their claims under § 1605A.

All that said, however, this Court is somewhat baffled by the approach taken by counsel here. As the Peterson action was on appeal at the time of the enactment of the 2008 NDAA, counsel could have simply moved this Court, pursuant to § 1083(c)(2), to treat the Peterson case as if it were filed under § 1605A. Had counsel made such a motion within 60 days of the enactment of the 2008 NDAA, this Court could have easily revisited and reconsidered the claims of the Pennsylvania and Louisiana plaintiffs within their original consolidated case, and that, of course, would have avoided the need to file this new civil action. Converting Peterson to an action under § 1605A would have enabled this Court to give effect to many of the other advantages of the new statute, such as the increased availability of punitive damages, within the confines of the original Peterson case and for the benefit of all of the hundreds of plaintiffs in that action.

Perhaps counsel in Peterson did not believe that the appeal by the Pennsylvania and Louisiana plaintiffs—a small subset of the nearly one thousand plaintiffs in Peterson—was sufficient to satisfy the requirement that the action be "before the court[] in any form, including on appeal" for treatment on motion under § 1605A. § 1083(c)(2)(iv) (emphasis added).[36] Perhaps counsel in Peterson also reached a conclusion, similar to that reached by counsel in Kirschenbaum and Beer, that certain aspects of the statute were automatically retroactive and therefore did not implicate the provisions of § 1083(c). Whatever the reasons for the apparent confusion, counsel would do well to consider whether they have a good faith basis for a motion under Rule 60(b). In considering such a motion, plaintiffs should take heed of the guidance provided in Part E, *infra*, of this opinion.

Valore, 03-CV-1959. This action is one of the many other cases in addition to Peterson that arises from the terrorist bombing of the United States Marine Barracks in Beirut, Lebanon in 1983. The case involves nearly fifty plaintiffs, and it is currently an open case, as the Court is awaiting the recommendations from the special masters with respect to the issue of damages. As this was an open case with the Court at the time the 2008 NDAA was enacted, plaintiffs were eligible to convert their action to § 1605A on motion in accordance with the procedures specified in § 1083(c)(2). Several weeks ago, however, plaintiffs filed an amended complaint. *See Valore*, No. 03-CV-1959-RCL (D.D.C.), Dk. # 27. While the complaint is very similar to the original complaint in the sense that it continues to rely on District Columbia law for wrongful death and survivorship claims, it adds § 1605A as the basis for a variety of tort claims, including battery, intentional infliction of emotional distress, and the derivative claim of loss of solatium. To the extent that the complaint continues to assert District of Columbia law, this Court has in the past recognized that the laws of this District are an appropriate model for the development of a federal standard with respect to liability in actions against state sponsors of terrorism. *Flatow I*, 999 F. Supp. at 15, n. 6. Thus, the Court is of the view that the plaintiffs' amended complaint sufficiently comports with the related case filing procedures of § 1083(c)(3), and thus this action may now proceed under § 1605A. Moreover, as this action is a pending case that was eligible for treatment under § 1083(c)(2), this Court will exercise it prerogative to manage the docket by treating this case as if it were converted on motion.

---

36 Approximately one month after the enactment of the 2008 NDAA, on February 27, 2008, the plaintiffs now included in Bonk had their appeal dismissed without prejudice by the Court of Appeals. In a subsequent filing by counsel in Peterson, counsel for plaintiffs informed this Court that the dismissal without prejudice was on their own motion. *See Peterson*, No. 01-CV-2094, Dk. # 388, at 2 (Plaintiffs' Motion and Memorandum in Support of Extension to File a Supplemental Memorandum in Support of Plaintiffs' Motion Pursuant to Fed. R. Civ. Pro. 59(e), filed July 28, 2008).

Davis, 07-CV-1302. This is the last action the Court will address in this section and it too stems from the terrorist bombing of the Marine barracks in Beirut. This case involves more than 200 plaintiffs. The complaint has been amended several times and it appears that a sizable number of the plaintiffs in this action are those who had their claims dismissed without prejudice from the Peterson case due to lack of evidence. *See Peterson II*, 515 F. Supp. 2d at 46-47. Many of the other plaintiffs in this action, however, appear to be coming before the Court for the first time. To lend some clarity to this matter going forward, counsel for plaintiff shall file a separate document with the Court that identifies all the plaintiffs in this new action who were dismissed from Peterson and list the grounds for each of those dismissals. Additionally, counsel should be certain to identify in a like manner any other plaintiffs who may have appeared in any of the other prior actions arising from the Marine barracks bombing. A separate order consistent with this guidance shall issue this date.

3. The "Do-Nothing" Plaintiffs: Those Who Have Invoked Neither Section 1083(c)(2) Nor (c)(3) in Their Efforts to Retroactively Claim the New Entitlements Under Section 1605A

The last five actions considered today are those in which plaintiffs' counsel have not seen fit to invoke either § 1083(c)(2) or (c)(3) in their efforts to claim the entitlements available in terrorism cases under § 1605A. In most of these actions, however, plaintiffs' counsel have proceeded as if § 1605A is automatically retroactive to prior terrorism actions under § 1605(a)(7). Each of these cases will now be addressed in chronological order.

Peterson, 01-CV-2094 and 01-CV-2684. As noted throughout this opinion, this case arises out the suicide bombing of the United States Marine Barracks facility in Beirut, Lebanon in 1983. This large consolidated case is essentially the lead action of the cases filed based on the Beirut attack, and with nearly 1000 plaintiffs, it is by far the largest of the group. As noted above in the discussion concerning Bonk, No. 08-CV-1273-RCL (D.D.C.), *supra*, and at other points throughout today's decision, counsel for plaintiffs in this large action never filed a motion pursuant to § 1083(c)(2) and they have not filed a new action under § 1083. As will be made clear in both Parts H and I of this opinion, counsel for plaintiffs have, however, filed numerous motions that have presumed the right to relief under § 1605A. For example, they filed several motions for payments to the special masters under § 1605A(e), which this Court ultimately denied. *See Peterson*, 01-CV-2094-RCL (D.D.C.), Dk. # 430 (MEMORANDUM OPINION AND ORDER, issued Jan. 5, 2009). Similarly, plaintiffs' counsel filed numerous motions seeking appointment of receivers to locate and take hold of a variety of Iranian assets. *See, e.g., id.* Dk. ## 251, 259, 404. All of the motions for receivers, however, were premised on the new provisions in § 1610(g) that purport to limit the availability of sovereign immunity defenses in efforts by plaintiffs to satisfy judgments entered under the new law, § 1605A. Accordingly, this Court has denied all motions for the appointment of receivers in Peterson. *See, e.g., id.* Dk. # 434 (Memorandum Opinion and Order, dated Mar. 31, 2009, denying all motions for receivers).

As plaintiffs' counsel have not complied with the requirements set forth in § 1083(c), the action remains under § 1605(a)(7). At this juncture, counsel in Peterson may want to consider filing an amended complaint, consistent with the procedures for related actions in § 1083(c), and similar to that which was filed in Valore, *supra*, as there are several cases still pending with the special masters that relate to the Marine Barracks Bombing and which were timely commenced under § 1605(a)(7). Valore, *supra*; Bland, *supra*; Spencer, *supra*; Arnold, *infra*; and Murphy, *infra* are five good examples of actions arising out of the Beirut Bombing that were commenced under § 1605(a)(7).

When considering whether to file an amended complaint pursuant to § 1083(c)(3), counsel also look to the new action they filed on behalf of the Pennsylvania and Louisiana plaintiffs in Bonk, *supra*. As noted, counsel have properly invoked the related case procedures for those plaintiffs. The complaint filed in Bonk is a good example in that it not only expressly identifies the related case provision of § 1083(c)(3), but it also identifies pending actions on this Court's docket that the Bonk action relates to. Additionally, in the event that counsel file such an amended complaint, counsel should address what impact, if any, the Bonk action will have on Peterson going forward. Absent use of the procedures for related cases, counsel should consider this Court's guidance below in Part G with respect to a motion pursuant to Rule 60(b).

Bennett, 03-CV-1486. This case concerns a suicide bombing at Hebrew University in Jerusalem in July of 2002. The bombing claimed the life of Marla Ann Bennett, an American citizen and a resident of California. Marla's parents filed an action under § 1605(a)(7). Plaintiffs ultimately demonstrated that Iran provided material support to Hamas in furtherance of terrorist objectives, including suicide bombing attacks in Israel, including the one that claimed their daughter's life in July of 2002. *See Bennett*, 507 F. Supp. 2d 117. Plaintiffs were awarded a judgment in excess of 12 million dollars. To date, that judgment remains unsatisfied.

Recently, this Court quashed five writs attachment issued by plaintiffs against properties that once comprised the Iranian Embassy compound here in Washington, DC. *See Bennett*, 604 F. Supp. 2d 152. In one of the arguments in support of that motion, plaintiffs stated that § 1610(g) renders Iran's former diplomatic properties subject to attachment. In one of their arguments in support of the writs of attachment, plaintiffs asserted that § 1610(g) strips away any immunity that might otherwise exempt that former embassy from attachment and execution upon a civil judgment. In quashing the writs of attachment, this Court noted that plaintiffs could not take advantage of the new measures in § 1610(g) because they never elected to proceed under the new terrorism exception, § 1605A. *Id.* at 162. Moreover, this Court observed that a plain reading of § 1610(g) offers no indication that Congress intended to eliminate the immunity that has long been afforded to diplomatic properties, like Iran's former embassy here in the United States, that are maintained in protective custody by the State Department pursuant to the Foreign Missions Act. *Id.* While this Court is not convinced that there any reading of § 1610(g) that would permit plaintiffs to attach any of the properties that once comprise the Iranian Embassy, plaintiffs may certainly hope to avail themselves of § 1610(g) in pursuit of other Iranian assets. For this reason, plaintiffs' counsel should consider the guidance in Part G and weigh options for moving forward in the postjudgment phase of this action.

Murphy, 06-CV-596. This action, like so many others on this Court's docket, arises out of the Marine barracks bombing. It was filed on March 31, 2006 under § 1605(a)(7). *See Murphy*, No. 06-CV-596-RCL (D.D.C.), Dk. #1 (Complaint). Plaintiffs include the estate of a United States Marine killed in that attack and several other Marines who were injured in the explosions. *See id.* On October 10, 2007, this Court took judicial notice of the findings of fact and conclusion of law in the Peterson action, and entered judgment in favor of the plaintiffs and against Iran with respect to all issues of liability. *Id.* Dk. # 27. This Court also referred this case to special masters for consideration of the plaintiffs' claims for damages. *See id.*

To date, this action remains pending with the special masters. Notably, counsel for plaintiffs in this case have not taken any action to qualify their case for treatment under § 1605A. Accordingly, this action remains under § 1605(a)(7). As the 60-day window in which counsel for plaintiffs could have filed a motion to bring this action under § 1605A has long since passed, *see* § 1083(c)(2), counsel may want to consider a motion under Rule 60, as discussed in Part G, or, alternately, the related case procedures in § 1083(c)(3). At any rate, the few claims presented in this case have been pending for nearly two years, and thus this Court will want to determine at a status conference what must be done to enter final judgment in this action in due course.

O'Brien, 06-CV-690. This action also arises out of the Marine barracks bombing. It was filed on April 17, 2006 under § 1605(a)(7). *See O'Brien*, 06-CV-690-RCL (D.D.C.), Dk. # 3, (Complaint). Plaintiffs include several United States Marines who were injured in that attack and several of their family members. For over a year, plaintiffs' counsel sought to effect service of process by mailing the summons and complaint to the Iranian Ministry of Information and Security and Tehran. *See id.* Dk. ## 3–11. Those efforts proved unsuccessful, and thus plaintiffs moved this Court for an order authorizing service though diplomatic channels, consistent with § 1608(a)(4). *Id.* Dk. # 12. This Court granted that motion on October 12, 2007, and service of process is now being carried out through the Department of State. *See Id.* Dk. # 14.

Notably, counsel for plaintiffs in this case have not taken any action to qualify their case for treatment under § 1605A. Accordingly, this action remains under § 1605(a)(7). As the 60-day window in which counsel for plaintiffs could have filed a motion to bring this action under § 1605A has long since passed, *see* § 1083(c)(2), counsel may want to consider a motion under Rule 60, as discussed in Part G, or, alternately, the related case procedures in § 1083(c)(3).

Arnold, 06-CV-516. This case is another one of the many actions arising out of the bombing of the Marine barracks in Beirut, Lebanon. This case, like Valore above, was filed under § 1605(a)(7) and is now pending with the special masters. Like both Peterson and Valore, this action was eligible for the procedures in § 1083(c)(2) that would have permitted this Court, on motion by the plaintiffs, to treat this action as if it was filed under § 1605A. As the 60-day period in which plaintiffs counsel could have filed such a motion has passed, plaintiffs' only remaining option is to invoke the procedures for related actions in § 1083(c)(3).

A few points should be stressed in connection with the issue of whether this action might obtain retroactive treatment under § 1605A. First, plaintiffs' counsel have not filed any motions seeking entitlements under the § 1605A. As this case is still pending with the special masters, however, this observation is not all that surprising because the kinds of postjudgment motions and actions undertaken by counsel in Peterson and Bennett would obviously be premature at this stage in the case. Nonetheless, most of the attorneys in this case are also counsel in Bennett and Peterson, and thus they are the same attorneys who appear have taken the erroneous view that § 1605A is automatically retroactive. Thus, in the interest of judicial economy, and in furtherance of the docket management function of this opinion, this Court has elected to address this case now, as it appears that the same issues that have challenged Peterson and Bennett above are likely to apply here. What is surprising about this case is that the lead counsel in this action is also lead counsel in Valore, as discussed above, in which counsel actually filed a new complaint under § 1605A pursuant to the procedures for related actions in § 1083(c)(3). The inconsistency in the approaches taken by counsel in these two actions is rather curious and seems to this Court to underscore the degree of confusion among counsel with respect to how they might ensure that § 1605A is applied retroactively to actions originally filed under § 1605(a)(7). The Court hopes that this opinion, and the analysis in the part of the discussion in particular, serves to eliminate any further confusion going forward.

4. General Guidance for All Cases

As has become evident during the course of the Court's analysis here, many of these cases are very large actions involving hundreds of plaintiffs each. In view of the recent wave of new actions under § 1605A, the Court encourages counsel in these new matters to identify those plaintiffs who pursued claims in a prior case under § 1605(a)(7). It would be helpful for the Court to know at the outset of a new action which plaintiffs, if any, appeared previously, in what cases, as well as the ultimate disposition of the prior claims. Counsel can provide this information through a separate filing, or, going forward, counsel may simply identify the earlier plaintiffs within the complaint. The Court recognizes and appreciates that counsel for some of the plaintiffs have already taken this proactive approach in the filing of their new complaints under § 1605A. As plaintiffs well know, these cases can go on for quite some time and often require the assistance of special masters to assist the Court in culling through voluminous data with respect to the losses suffered by these hundreds of victims of terrorism. Providing the Court with the appropriate reference points in any new filings, will greatly assist with the management of this massive body of litigation and avoid delay in providing appropriate redress to the plaintiffs.

G. Service of New Claims in Pending Cases

Because § 1605A applies retroactively to Court actions under § 1605(a)(7), this Court must now decide whether and to what extent new claims asserted under § 1605A should be served on Iran pursuant to § 1608 of the FSIA, which is the statutory provision that governs service on foreign states. As there is no question that new civil actions under § 1605A, such as Brown and Bonk, *supra*, must be served on Iran, the Court's analysis here is concerned strictly with cases that were pending under § 1605(a)(7) but which have now been converted to § 1605A, either on motion, consistent with § 1083(c)(2) of the 2008 NDAA, or through the filing of an amended complaint, consistent with the procedures for related actions under § 1083(c)(3). With respect to these actions, this Court holds that service of claims is not required under § 1608 of the FSIA.

The question of whether new federally based claims under § 1605A should be served on Iran under the unique circumstances presented here appears to be a matter of first impression. This Court finds, however, that principles espoused in two prior decisions of this Court, *Dammarell v. Islamic Republic of Iran*, 370 F. Supp. 2d 218 (D.D.C.2005) (Bates, J.), and *Bodoff*, 424 F. Supp. 2d 74, guide the resolution of this matter and strongly suggest that service is not required in actions that were pending under § 1605(a)(7) and which have since been converted to § 1605A through the procedures in § 1083(c) of the 2008 NDAA.

In Dammarell, Iran was found in default for failing to appear and plaintiffs' substantive claims were initially considered by the Court under § 1605(a)(7) and the Flatow Amendment, § 1605 note. 370 F. Supp. 2d 218. As the action was pending, the Court of Appeals ruled in both Cicippio-Puleo, 353 F.3d 1024, and *Acree v. Republic of Iraq*, 370 F.3d 41 (D.C.Cir. 2004), that § 1605(a)(7) and the Flatow Amendment do not furnish a cause of action against foreign states. In so ruling, however, the Court of Appeals suggested that other sources of law, including state common law or statutory law, might furnish viable claims for plaintiffs in actions pursuant § 1605(a)(7). *See Dammarell*, 370 F. Supp. 2d at 220 (quoting *Acree*, 370 F.3d at 59); *see also* Part A, *supra*, (discussing Cicippio-Puleo and Acree and the use of § 1605(a)(7) as a pass-through to causes of actions found in state law). Consequently, Judge Bates instructed plaintiffs to file an amended complaint identifying particular causes of action based on state common law or statutory law. *Dammarell*, 370 F. Supp. 2d at 221. Thereafter, plaintiffs filed a motion in which they sought, among other relief, an order stating that they were not required to serve the amended complaint on Iran pursuant to § 1608. *Id.*

After considering supplemental briefing on the issue, Judge Bates held that service of an amended complaint is not required by § 1608 where "the defendant foreign state has failed to appear, and is therefore in default, and where the amendment does not add any claims but instead clarifies existing claims." *Id.* at 224. In reaching this holding, Judge Bates carefully reviewed both the text and legislative history of § 1608, finding that both supported the conclusion that the statute "is concerned with service of the initial complaint that commences the lawsuit, and not with the ensuing pleadings or papers." *Id.* Moreover, Judge Bate noted that his decision to dispense with service under § 1608 was consistent with Federal Rule of Civil Procedure Rule 5(a), which requires service of "new claims" on a party in default. *Id.* (citing FED. R. CIV. P. 5(a)). Judge Bates reasoned that simply identifying the specific sources of state law that would furnish causes of action in plaintiffs' case under the FSIA terrorism exception should not constitute "new claims" within the meaning of Rule 5. *Id.* In Judge Bates's view, the amended complaint would simply clarify existing claims under § 1605(a)(7). Thus, Dammarell appears to rest, at least in part, on the view that changes in the substantive rules of decision governing these actions against state sponsors of terrorism does not amount to the creation of new claims for purposes of the service requirements under the Federal Rules.

In Bodoff, this Judge reached a decision that is largely consistent with Judge Bates's ruling. *See* 424 F. Supp. 2d 74. As in Dammarell, Iran was in default, and the plaintiffs in Bodoff initially proceeded with federal claims under § 1605(a)(7) and the Flatow Amendment. However, plaintiffs failed to amend their complaint to identify state law causes of action following the D.C. Circuit's decisions in Cicippio-Puleo and Acree. *Id.* at 78. In ruling that the plaintiffs were not required to amend their complaint, this Court stated:

> [P]laintiffs' original complaint is sufficiently detailed to provide fair notice of the claims: it delineates the claims asserted and relief requested. For purposes of the complaint, it is not significant that the source of the law underlying the cause of action may have changed. Courts have not construed the pleading requirements of [Fed. R.Civ.P.] 8 to require a plaintiff to recite specific source(s) of law in a complaint. *See MacIntosh v. [Bldg.] Owners & Managers Ass'n Int'l*, 355 F. Supp. 2d 223, 228 (D.D.C.2005) (Sullivan, J.) (citing FED. R. CIV. P. 8(f) for the proposition that "pleadings shall be construed so as to do substantial justice").

Bodoff, 424 F. Supp. 2d at 78. Thus, similar to Dammarell, this Court found that a defendant foreign state in default need not receive an amended complaint when the amendment would merely reflect a change in the source of substantive law applicable to the Court's adjudication of a case under the FSIA terrorism exception. *Id.*; accord *Prevatt*, 421 F. Supp. 2d at 155.

The situation presented in Dammarell and Bodoff following the Court of Appeals' decisions in Cicippio-Puleo and Acree is analogous to the situation the Court finds itself in today. Instead of shifting from federal law to state law, however, the Court is now shifting away from state law under § 1605(a)(7) to federal law under § 1605A. Now, as emphasized in Parts B and E, *supra*, it is certainly not insignificant for purpose of this Court's adjudication that claims under § 1605A are based on federal law, and are thus subject to a federal analytical framework, whether it is considered federal common law or otherwise. The simple fact remains, however, that these new claims are nonetheless actions for personal injury or death, which sound in tort, and which are based on the same underlying terrorist act or incident as the failed state law claims that were originally advanced under § 1605(a)(7). Additionally, plaintiffs in all the actions considered today sought punitive damages in their complaint under § 1605(a)(7), and plaintiffs have consistently pressed for such relief in their prosecution of these cases.

Thus, consistent with Dammarell and Bodoff, even though actions converted to § 1605A are now presenting what are new claims in the sense that the substantive law is now federal law, they need not be considered as new claims for purposes of the pleading requirements applicable to these actions. This determination is consistent with the requirements of § 1608, which requires little more than "notice of the suit" and concerns the initiation of an action against a foreign state, rather than any intermediate filings in the case. Similarly, this ruling is consistent the notions of fair play and substantial justice embraced by the liberal concept of "notice pleading" under the Federal Rules of Civil Procedure. *See, e.g., Hanson v. Hoffmann*, 628 F.2d 42, 53 (D.C.Cir.1980). In these pending cases under § 1605A, Iran has sufficient notice of the nature of the suit and the type of claims against it. While the source of law applicable to these terrorism actions sounding in tort under the FSIA has changed, nothing else has.[37]

As an important caveat to today's ruling, it must be noted that Judge Collyer recently held in circumstances identical to those presented here that a new claim asserted under § 1605A must be served on the foreign state defendant. *See Gates*, 646 F. Supp. 2d at 90–91. In Gates, plaintiffs made a motion, pursuant to § 1083(c)(2), to convert their pending case under § 1605(a)(7) to an action under § 1605A. Judge Collyer ruled, however, that the new claim had to be served on Syria before plaintiffs could proceed under the terms of the new statute. *Id.* at 90–91.

---

37 Out of concern that some parties may read this part of the decision concerning service of claims too broadly, this Court wishes to stress that this is a sui generis context. Today's ruling is limited to the circumstances of these actions, which are pending suits against a foreign state in default in which the substantive source of law for personal injury and wrongful death claims has been converted, by retroactive application of a new federal statute, from state law sources to federal law. In reaching this determination today, this Court is particularly mindful of the distinct requirements in § 1608 for service of process on a foreign state. It would therefore not be prudent for either this Court or the parties before it to assume that today's holding or the underlying rationale should apply with any force in civil actions involving ordinary civil litigants.

This Judge respectfully disagrees with Judge Collyer for several reasons. As an initial matter, it is not entirely clear whether Rule 5 should even apply in actions against foreign state sponsors of terrorism, as there are specific requirements governing service on a foreign state in § 1608 of the FSIA. Assuming, however, that Rule 5(a)(2) is generally applicable in actions involving foreign states, the plain language of that provision indicates that it should not apply to new claims asserted on motion by way of § 1083(c)(2). Rule 5(a)(2) reads as follows: "No service is required on a party who is in default for failing to appear. But a pleading that asserts a new claim for relief against such a party must be served on that party under Rule 4." FED.R.CIV.P. 5(a)(2) (emphasis added). Thus, by its very terms, Rule 5(a)(2) applies only to new claims presented in a "pleading" and therefore should not apply when plaintiffs are proceeding on motion under § 1083(c)(2).

For those who might suggest that this Court's determination hinges on a technical or overly narrow interpretation of Rule 5, this Court adds that there is a clear distinction between pleadings and motions with respect to civil practice in the federal courts. Rule 7 provides that the following documents are considered pleadings: "(1) a complaint; (2) an answer to a complaint; (3) an answer to a counterclaim designated as a counterclaim; (4) an answer to a crossclaim; (5) a third-party complaint; (6) an answer to a third-party complaint; and (7) if the court considers one, a reply to an answer." FED.R.CIV.P. 7(a). Motions, however, are specifically excluded from the list of "pleadings" in Rule 7(a). In fact, a motion is described separately under Rule 7(b), as "a request for an order." FED.R.CIV.P. 7(b); *see also Structural Concrete Prods. v. Clarendon Am. Ins. Co.*, 244 F.R.D. 317, 321 (E.D.Va.2007) (emphasizing that a motion is not a pleading and citing Rule 7(a)).

Additionally, the text of § 1083(c)(2) warrants consideration. Under the terms of that provision, when the requisite conditions are satisfied in a pending case under § 1605(a)(7), the action "shall[] on motion made by the plaintiffs . . . be given effect as if the action had originally been filed under section 1605A(c)." § 1083(c)(2)(A)(iv) (emphasis added). Thus, by its plain terms, § 1083 indicates that no further action—under Rule 5 or otherwise—should be required of plaintiffs before their case may move forward under § 1605. More fundamentally, however, as emphasized above, this Court does not find that a change in the rule of decision applicable to personal injury or wrongful death claims under the FSIA terrorism exception results in new claims of relief for purposes of the pleading requirements in these cases.

In light of the foregoing, this Court holds that service of new federal claims is not required under § 1608 of the FSIA in actions that were pending under § 1605(a)(7) and have since converted to § 1605A in accordance with § 1083 of the 2008 NDAA. In an abundance of caution, however, counsel might well consider serving Iran with their new claims that now fall under § 1605A. Needless to state, however, reasonable judges can, and apparently do, differ on this issue, which suggests counsel may want to take the cautious approach by serving their § 1605A claims on Iran. Service of process is a jurisdictional requirement, and thus on this issue of first impression, counsel is well advised to take the most cautious approach.

H. Guidance for Plaintiffs who may Wish to Pursue Relief Under Rule 60 of the Federal Rules of Civil Procedure

Today's decision is likely to have negative consequences for many of these FSIA plaintiffs—all of whom are victims of terrorism perpetrated by Iran. For years now, these victims—individually and as representatives of the deceased—have come before this Court in the hopes of holding Iran to account for its sponsorship of terrorist organizations and their relentless attacks on innocents. In short, these victims hope to find justice. That goal, however, has proven very elusive, and today's decision will undoubtedly come as yet another setback for many of these FSIA plaintiffs who have not been able to take advantage of the new terrorism exception, § 1605A. That enactment, which was intended to aid them specifically, with its new language providing for a federal cause of action and punitive damages against Iran, as well as enhanced measures for the enforcement of judgments, simply will not extend to a number of plaintiffs addressed here. This is an undeniable fact that deeply troubles the Court.

This Court is particularly concerned that counsel for at least some of the plaintiffs who have failed to quality for treatment under § 1605A, appear to have been laboring under an erroneous view of the law, as provided by section 1083 of the 2008 NDAA. Some, like counsel for the plaintiffs in Beer and Kirschenbaum, may have erroneously, but in good faith, believed that they were not bound by certain procedures in § 1083(c) because they were not seeking to assert a new cause of action, but were merely looking to take advantage of other entitlements within § 1605A, such as the right to an award of punitive damages against Iran directly. It may well be that counsel in other actions also had their own good faith reasons for failing to adhere to the requisite procedures. Whatever those reasons may be, the indisputable fact is that many different attorneys before this Court, representing plaintiffs in a diverse range of cases against Iran, have failed to take the necessary steps to bring their actions under § 1605A. Whether and to what extent this result stems from strategic choices, misunderstandings of the law, tactical blunders or omissions, or other reasons, is difficult for this Court to say. It does appear, however, that at least some of these apparent failures to qualify actions under § 1605A are due to misunderstanding or misapplication of the statutory language within § 1083.

As this Court has recognized here today, § 1083 is hardly a model of clarity and the requirements and conditions with respect to "Pending Cases" are presented in a disjointed manner. *See* Part C, *supra*. Moreover, counsel for most plaintiffs in these actions had only 60 days from the enactment of § 1083 in which they had to elect to proceed under § 1605A. During those first two critical months of the statute's existence, there was not sufficient opportunity for the courts of this Circuit to examine § 1083 in written opinions that counsel might have looked to in an effort to better understand the statute. Indeed, the leading decision on this matter, *Simon v. Iraq*, was not decided until June 2008, nearly three months after the 60 day window of opportunity had passed for most plaintiffs. 529 F.3d 1187. Thus, the lack of clarity with respect to the statutory language in this instance was compounded by a lack of decisional law that might have otherwise aided counsel in their efforts.

In view of the very real potential for injustice these statutory issues of first impression may work for plaintiffs, this Court hereby emphasizes that the denial of relief under § 1605A is without prejudice. Plaintiffs may want to consider whether this Court has authority under Rule 60(b) to grant relief under the circumstances presented by their respective cases. As this Court has recognized in the past, Rule 60(b) is a powerful tool that grants judges broad authority to accomplish justice in certain limited circumstances. *See Bryson v. Gere*, 268 F. Supp. 2d 46, 53 (D.D.C.2003) (Lamberth, J.). It is well established that a

> district judge, who is in the best position to discern and assess all the facts, is vested with a large measure of discretion in deciding whether to grant a Rule 60(b) motion, and the district court's grant or denial of relief under Rule 60(b), unless rooted in an error of law, may be reversed only for abuse of discretion.

Twelve John Does v. District of Columbia, 841 F.2d 1133, 1138 (D.C.Cir.1988) (citing *Browder v. Director*, 434 U.S. 257, 263 n. 7, 98 S. Ct. 556, 54 L.Ed.2d 521 (1978)).

Plaintiffs should be cautioned, however, that they will have to overcome a significant burden under Rule 60(b). To be clear, this Court expresses no view with respect any potential motion seeking relief under Rule 60(b) for any of the groups of plaintiffs who have suffered adverse consequences as a result of the Court's action today. It is, of course, the responsibility of counsel—not of this Court—to articulate what grounds, if any, exist for Rule 60 relief within the parameters set by that rule, as applied to the specific circumstances in their respective cases. Whether counsel assert reasons of "mistake, inadvertence, surprise, or excusable neglect" under (b)(1) or "any other reason that justifies relief" under (b)(6), empty rhetoric or post hoc justifications will not suffice. This Court's discretion is not unfettered. *See Kramer v. Gates*, 481 F.3d 788, 792 (D.C.Cir.2007) (reversing district judge's decision to grant relief to plaintiffs pursuant to Rule 60(b)(6)). Nothing in today's decision should be read as an invitation to "take a mulligan." *Id.*

Regardless of what part of Rule 60(b) may be relied upon, this Court would certainly have to consider the length of time that has passed since the enactment of the 2008 NDAA over one year ago. Perhaps more importantly, however, this Court would have to factor into its analysis the passage of time since June of last year, when our Court of Appeals issued its decision in Simon, which construed § 1083, the very provision at issue here today. *See* 529 F.3d at 1192. This is to say nothing of the numerous opinions published by this Court last July and August that applied § 1083(c) to a number of prior actions filed under § 1605(a)(7). *See, e.g.*, *Bodoff*,

567 F. Supp. 2d 141 (D.D.C.2008) (Lamberth, C.J.); *Stethem v. Islamic Republic of Iran*, 568 F. Supp. 2d 1 (D.D.C.2008) (Lamberth, C.J.). Counsel who have not moved promptly to see that their actions fall under § 1605A will have to explain to the Court why they have not seen fit to file for relief prior to now.

Additionally, counsel for plaintiffs interested in pursuing relief under Rule 60 must also detail how their prior actions under § 1605(a)(7) would have fit within the framework established by § 1083(c) and therefore qualified for treatment under the new terrorism exception, § 1605A. In so doing, plaintiffs should hone in Parts B and C, *supra*, of the discussion section of this opinion. In particular, plaintiffs who would rely on the § 1083(c)(3) concerning related actions need to carefully and specifically identify the new federal causes of action, presumably based on federal common law as applied in FSIA actions. *See, e.g., Flatow I*, 999 F. Supp. at 15. This type of detailed analysis with respect to the merits of the underlying claims is necessary to ensure that any decision granting relief under Rule 60(b) "will not be an empty exercise of futile gesture." *See Norman v. United States*, 467 F.3d 773, 775 (D.C.Cir.2006) (quoting *Murray v. District of Columbia*, 52 F.3d 353, 355 (D.C.Cir.1995)).

Finally, plaintiffs who believe in good faith that they can assert a basis for relief under Rule 60 should heed these words and act with dispatch. Whether this Court can in fact grant Rule 60 relief to plaintiffs who did not timely comply with § 1083(c)(2) of the 2008 NDAA should also be briefed by the parties and will of course have to be addressed by this Court before rendering any rulings on the matter.

I. Compensation for Special Masters

In the course of addressing the variety of issues presented by these civil actions, this Court considered, and ultimately denied, three motions requesting that certain special masters receive compensation for the work that they completed on behalf of the Court in the large consolidated case of *Peterson v. Islamic Republic of Iran*. *See* No. 01-CV-2094-RCL (D.D.C.), Dk. # 430. The special masters have rendered crucial assistance by helping the Court to determine the appropriate amount of monetary damages for hundreds and hundreds of plaintiffs. As alluded to earlier in this opinion, calculating damages in an action like Peterson is not an easy task. The special masters are required to review hundreds, if not thousands of documents, including economic reports and deposition testimony. Needless to say, the work required of the special masters to achieve justice in these terrorism cases demands great attention to detail and is extraordinarily time-consuming.

In Peterson, the three special masters who were denied payment were but a few of the more than one dozen special masters who have been called upon by this Court to examine hundreds of claims in that large consolidated case and in many other large actions under § 1605(a)(7). These three special masters alone performed more than eight months worth of work in Peterson. *See* No. 01-CV-2094-RCL

(D.D.C.), Dk. ## 242, 243, 245. Had this Court been required to take on the functions preformed by these special masters, the work of this Court with respect to numerous other pending civil and criminal cases would have come screeching to a halt.

But the sheer volume of the endeavor surely pales in comparison to the emotional toll that such work extracts from these individuals who have worked diligently to achieve justice for victims of terrorism. This Court listened first-hand to some of the heart-wrenching stories of the victims during live testimony in the bench trial in Peterson. The testimony in that case, as in others, was extraordinarily powerful. As a human being and a fellow American, it is difficult not to be moved by a sense of sorrow and grief for these victims who have long suffered. This is a basic reality that is true in all of these horrific cases from Flatow to Peterson. While this Court is sometimes spared all the intimate and excruciatingly painful details of the lives that have been shattered, the special masters are not. It is their job to undertake a very thorough, painstaking review of all the relevant testimony, medical evidence, economic reports, and other evidence in order to make clear, accurate recommendations to this Court. In going about their important work in these actions, these special masters learn over and over again of the senseless carnage—the horrific deaths and grievous injuries—and of the real and often very personal ways that the deliberate slaughtering of innocents inflicts deep emotional wounds. During a recent status conference, counsel in Peterson spoke of how some of the special masters experienced a sort of emotional fatigue. A special master in another action also spoke at that time about the emotional toll that his responsibilities have exerted on him personally. Thus, it is important to keep in mind that the special masters are handling emotionally wrenching matters as they revisit acts of carnage over and over again and hear the stories of hundreds of Americans whose lives will never be the same.

It was therefore with some regret that this Court was not able to afford compensation to several of the special masters in Peterson. The specific provision at issue was § 1605A(e), which provides:

> (e) SPECIAL MASTERS.—
>
> (1) IN GENERAL.—The courts of the United States may appoint special masters to hear damage claims brought under this section.
>
> (2) TRANSFER OF FUNDS.—The Attorney General shall transfer, from funds available for the program under section 1404C of the Victims of Crime Act of 1984 (42 U.S.C. 10603c) to the Administrator of the United States district court in which any case is pending which has been brought or maintained under this section such funds as may be required to cover the costs of special masters appointed under paragraph (1). Any amount paid in compensation to any such special master shall constitute an item of court costs.

The three motions for payment, as noted above in Part D, *supra*, were based on the erroneous assumption that this new provision allowing for compensation, which did not exist prior to the enactment of the 2008 NDAA, somehow automatically and retroactively applied to their case. In denying relief, this Court emphasized that the special masters in Peterson are not entitled to the benefits of the new statute because plaintiffs have not taken appropriate action, consistent with § 1083(c), to convert their case to an action under § 1605A. Thus, the new statutory entitlements do not apply to their case, which remains under the former state sponsor of terrorism exception—Section 1605(a)(7).

The Court was very careful to render the most narrow ruling possible; the determination that the special masters have not qualified for payment from the Victims of Crime Fund hinged exclusively on the fact that the plaintiffs had failed to follow the requisite procedures in § 1083(c). That ruling stands. Note, however, that the Court did not address the prospect of retroactivity problems or other arguments that the United States presented in a brief submitted on the issue by invitation of this Court. *See Peterson*, No. 01-CV-2094-RCL (D.D.C.), Dk. # 389. The Court declined to comment on those issues at the time of its ruling because this Court anticipated that a Rule 60(b) motion or other action by plaintiffs in Peterson might otherwise permit these plaintiffs to move forward under § 1605A, and that, in turn, might require this Court to revisit the issue of compensation for the special masters.

Having had an opportunity recently to take a close look at the issue of retroactivity, this Court is not convinced that any sort of retroactively problem would serve as a bar to payment of the special masters in these cases. It is difficult for this Court to conceive of how § 1605A(e) operates retroactively in the disfavored sense by impairing previously established rights of the parties or by imposing new duties with respect to past conduct. *See Altmann*, 541 U.S. at 694, 124 S. Ct. 2240. Moreover, § 1083(c), provides a clear mechanism by which cases that were previously decided or pending under § 1605(a)(7) may be brought within the reach of the revised terrorism exception § 1605A, and so this Court need not resort to speculation or judicial default rules to infer Congress' intent in that regard. *See Simon v. Republic of Iraq*, 529 F.3d 1187, 1191 (D.C.Cir.2008), rev'd on other grounds sub nom. *Beaty*, 129 S. Ct. 2183. More fundamentally, however, to the extent that retroactivity analysis should apply, affording payment to the special masters is, in this Court's view, much more akin to the court ordering payment of attorneys' fees, which are collateral to the litigation and therefore do not trigger retroactivity concerns. *See Landgraf*, 511 U.S. at 277, 114 S. Ct. 1483.

This Court must also keep in mind that Congress has exceedingly broad power to acknowledge and pay debts under Article I, Section 8, Clause 1 of the Constitution. *Sioux Nation*, 448 U.S. at 397, 100 S. Ct. 2716. With § 1083 of the 2008 NDAA, Congress has plainly acknowledged the services rendered by the special masters, and, through the enactment of § 1605A(e) provided a means, consistent with the legislature's Article I powers of the purse, to compensate the special masters for service previously rendered in terrorism cases. Thus, assuming the procedures in

§ 1083(c) are complied with, or assuming that there is some way for plaintiffs to overcome the procedural deficiencies in their cases by way of Rule 60(b) motion, or otherwise, this Court sees no reason why it would not have authority to issue an order directing that the special masters receive payment from the Victims of Crime Fund.

Recently, plaintiffs in Peterson filed a new motion for payments to the special masters. *See* No. 01-CV-2094-RCL (D.D.C.), Dk. # 435. This most recent motion seeks payment for nine of the special masters, to include two of the special masters who were denied payment previously as a result of the Court's denial of the three prior motions for payment under § 1605A(e). *See id.* Dk. # 430. The current motion seeks more than $200,000 in total payments.

In contrast to the prior motions, the current motion does not rely on the new authorization in § 1605A(e) for payments from the Victims of Crime Fund, and it does not request or otherwise require the expenditure of government funds. Instead, plaintiffs have made arrangements to have a private organization known as the Peace Through Law Foundation, Inc. pay the nine special masters directly. Dk. # 436. Under the terms of the arrangement that the plaintiffs have asked this Court to endorse, the Peace Through Law Foundation, Inc. will first remit payments to the special masters directly. *Id.* Following those payments, and only after satisfactory proof of the payments is submitted to this Court, this Court will then enter a money judgment against Iran and in favor of plaintiffs for the total amount paid by the Peace Through Law Foundation, Inc. *Id.* Plaintiffs also ask that this Court include in its initial order directing the payments that the plaintiffs are to repay the Peace Through Law Foundation, Inc. once they collect on the judgment entered under the terms of compensation scheme proposed in their current motion. *Id.*

This Court appreciates the persistency, hard work, and creativity of counsel in their efforts to obtain compensation for the special masters. In this Court's view, the special masters have rendered a great service not only to the plaintiffs and this Court but also to the nation as a whole.[38] In light of today's opinion, however, it is not appropriate for this Court to consider the novel approach proposed by the plaintiffs at this time. It seems to this Court that the most prudent course of action at this juncture is to allow counsel to first determine whether, consistent with the guidance offered in this opinion, they might be able to qualify the Peterson action for retroactive treatment under § 1605A. If that can be achieved, then the special masters may have recourse to the Victims of Crime Fund, consistent with the plain terms of § 1605A(e)(2), rather through the privately subsidized subrogation scheme that plaintiffs have proposed in their most recent motion. For this reason, the

38 One of the Special Masters included in the current motion, Judge Howard P. Rives of Florida, passed away shortly after concluding his work. The Court is grateful for Judge Rives's assistance and expresses it condolences to Judge Rives's family.

current motion for payment of the special masters will denied without prejudice in a separate order issued this date.[39]

J. Motions for Appointment of Receivers

This Court also recently denied three motions for the appointment of receivers in Peterson. *See* No. 01-CV-2094-RCL (D.D.C.), Dk. # 434. Like the motions for payments to the special masters discussed above, these three motions for receivers were based on the erroneous assumption that the Peterson action should automatically fall under § 1605A. Two of the motions for appointment of receivers, *id.* Dk. # 3251, 259, sought what counsel referred to as "broad-based" receiverships that would have operated under a sweeping mandate to seek out and take hold of a wide range of Iranian Government assets. *See* Dk. ## 251, at 7; 259, at 4. The first of these two broad-based receiverships urged by plaintiffs would have sought possession of any assets of Iran held by financial institutions within the United States. *See* Dk. # 251. The second broad-based receivership urged by the plaintiffs would have sought possession of "all oil, natural gas, petroleum, hydro-carbon and similar revenues due to and in favor of the Islamic Republic of Iran." *See* Dk. # 259, at 1.[40]

In each of the two motions, plaintiffs recommended that this Court appoint three members of the Gavel Consulting Group to serve as the receivers. The three individuals proposed by plaintiffs were Eugene R. Sullivan, Retired Chief Judge of the United States Court of Appeals for the Armed Forces; Stanley Sporkin, Retired United States District Court Judge for the District of Columbia and Former General Counsel to the Central Intelligence Agency; and Louis Freeh, Former Director of the Federal Bureau of Investigation and Former United States District Court Judge for the Southern District of New York. *See* Dk. ## 251, at 4; 259, at 4. Plaintiffs noted that "[e]ach one of these individuals are former federal judges, all with backgrounds in national security, military, and intelligence matters, and all of them would be more than capable of performing this assignment, and meeting the expectations of all parties." Dk. ## 251, at 22; 259, at 26. Thus, plaintiffs' two motions would have effectively established one large receivership headed by members of the Gavel Consulting Group and with sweeping powers to identify, take possession

---

39 The Court expresses no opinion at this time regarding the reasonableness of the requested payments.

40 One of the three motions, Peterson, No. 01-CV-2094-RCL (D.D.C.), Dk. #404, concerned specific assets held by a financial institution in New York. That matter remains under seal and subject to a protective order in part because plaintiffs have alleged that Iran is the beneficial owner of approximately two billion dollars in specific debt securities. These securities have been restrained and are subject to ongoing garnishment action initiated by plaintiffs in the United States District Court for the Southern District of New York. This section of today's opinion concerning the prior motions for receivers concerns only the two broad-based requests, Dk. ## 251 and 259, and does not speak to plaintiffs' prior effort to establish a receivership for the interests in securities identified in the action in New York.

of, and liquidate a host of undisclosed Iranian Government assets. Plaintiffs argued that a properly appointed receivership in their case would have the authority to demand possession of any of Iran's assets located within the jurisdiction of the United States Courts.[41]

In support of their motions, plaintiffs relied on § 1610(g), a new FSIA provision that was enacted in conjunction with § 1605A last year. *See* § 1083(b). As noted above, § 1610(g) is intended to limit the application of sovereign immunity defenses that have often protected Iran's property from attachment and execution upon civil judgments entered under the terrorism exception. As enacted through § 1083(b) of the 2008 NDAA, 1610(g) reads as follows:

> (g) PROPERTY IN CERTAIN ACTIONS.—
>
> > (1) IN GENERAL.—Subject to paragraph (3), the property of a foreign state against which a judgment is entered under section 1605A, and the property of an agency or instrumentality of such a state, including property that is a separate juridical entity or is an interest held directly or indirectly in a separate juridical entity, is subject to attachment in aid of execution, and execution, upon that judgment as provided in this section, regardless of—
> >
> > > (A) the level of economic control over the property by the Government of the foreign state;
> > >
> > > (B) whether the profits of the property go to that government;
> > >
> > > (C) the degree to which officials of that government manage the property or otherwise control its daily affairs
> > >
> > > (D) whether the government is the sole beneficiary in interest of the property; or
> > >
> > > (E) whether establishing the property as a separate entity would entitle the foreign state to benefits in United States Courts while avoiding its obligations.

---

41 Plaintiffs rely on a variety of different publicly available sources of information concerning Iranian assets. With respect to the receivership proposed for Iran Assets in United States banks, plaintiffs observe that the TERRORIST ASSETS REPORT, which is published periodically by the United States Treasury Department's Office of Foreign Asset Control, indicates that upwards of 49 million dollars in non-blocked funds belonging to Iran may currently be in the possession of United States financial institutions. *See* Dk. # 251, at 5, Ex. D. Similarly, with respect to oil, gas, and hydrocarbon revenues, plaintiffs observe that various Government reports, including reports prepared by the Energy Information Administration of the United States Department of Energy, confirm that Iran earns billions and billions of dollars each year as a result of its diversified oil and gas industries. *See id.* at 4–9. Similarly, plaintiffs point to a number of cases that have been litigated before the Iran-U.S. Claims Tribunal over payments or other assets owed to Iran's oil and gas industries. *See id.* at 5–9, Exs. E-I. While acknowledging that most of Iran's oil assets are located in other foreign countries and outside the jurisdiction of the United States, plaintiffs nonetheless stress that a receivership for these assets would "not be futile" because certain subsidiaries or other entities connected with Iran's state-run enterprises might "have some type of nexus in and to the United States, and therefore might be subject to United States jurisdiction." *Id.* at 15. In fact, plaintiffs identify eight specific oil companies that they believe can and should be reached by the receivership they propose. *Id.* at 1, 15.

> (2) UNITED STATES SOVEREIGN IMMUNITY INAPPLICABLE.—Any property of a foreign state, or agency or instrumentality of a foreign state, to which paragraph (1) applies shall not be immune from attachment in aid of execution, or execution, upon a judgment entered under [§] 1605A because the property is regulated by the United States Government by reason of action taken against that foreign state under the Trading With the Enemy Act or the International Emergency Powers Act.

Plaintiffs argue that this new provision removes Iran's sovereign immunity with respect to its property, as well as any United States sovereign immunity that might otherwise apply, and that therefore Iran's assets "are now subject to clear levy and execution." *See, e.g.*, Dk. # 259, at 4. Consistent with this Court's prior decision denying the special masters motions under § 1605A(e), this Court denied the motions for receivers on the narrow basis that plaintiffs had failed to follow the necessary steps, pursuant to § 1083(c), to obtain treatment under the new terrorism exception. *See* Dk. # 434, at 3. The Court was careful in its ruling not to express any view with respect to the merits of plaintiffs' argument concerning the utility of § 1610(g), as a means to enforce a judgment under § 1605A, as that question was not ripe for consideration. As the Court explained:

> Whatever might be said of § 1610(g), the simple fact is that provision does not apply here. By its express terms, § 1610(g) applies only to "judgments entered under [§] 1605A." Notably, plaintiffs could have converted their judgment under § 1605(a)(7) into a new action under § 1605A. *See* § 1083(c). Plaintiffs failed to do so.

Dk. # 434, at 3. Thus, plaintiffs' action remains under § 1605(a)(7), they are not entitled to take advantage of any of the new limitations in immunities pertaining to Iran's assets that might otherwise facilitate efforts to satisfy their 2.5 billion dollar judgment against Iran.

In the event that the Peterson action were to qualify for treatment under § 1605A as the result of a motion pursuant to Rule 60, or through some other approach, this Court could of course reconsider the plaintiffs' motions for receivers. The Court is well aware of the outstanding professional reputations of the three individuals that plaintiffs proposed to oversee a receivership in their case. The depth of the experience that these three former judges would bring to the table, especially in light of their backgrounds in national security matters, could certainly prove advantageous to plaintiffs. Thus, there is at least some possibility that the sort of broad-based receivership that plaintiffs envisioned for their case might offer them a better chance to overcome some of the challenges that have thus far prevented these terrorism victims from obtaining the compensation they deserve. This Court will keep an open mind about the potential for a receivership in the event that this issue comes up for consideration again under the new terrorism exception, § 1605A.

In the interest of both candor and fairness to plaintiffs, however, the Court wishes to offer some additional guidance on this unique matter. As this Court has emphasized on several occasions in this very case, "the appointment of a receivership is 'an equitable remedy of rather drastic nature.'" Dk. # 434, at 3 (quoting *Peterson III*, 563 F. Supp. 2d 268) (citations omitted). For this reason, the Court must proceed cautiously and will take a critical view of any renewed motions for the appointment of receivers. Among other issues, this Court will need to consider what the realistic probability is that a broad-based receivership would actually succeed in efforts to take hold of Iranian government assets of sufficient value to compensate plaintiffs. On this critical issue, the Court might solicit the opinions of whatever experts the plaintiffs propose to serve as the receivers in their case. Government reports and generalized assertions about the wealth of Iran simply do not provide an adequate basis for this Court to make an assessment of whether there are sufficient assets of Iran available for turnover to a receivership in the sweeping manner that plaintiffs have envisioned. This Court will also have take a closer look at § 1610(g) and consider in what ways this new provision might apply in legal proceedings to seize Iranian assets in satisfaction of judgments in terrorism cases under § 1605A. It is not at all clear to this Court that § 1610(g) is the panacea that the plaintiffs believe it is.

Second, this Court is mindful that in some cases the costs associated with the receivership can actually exceed the value of the funds that the receivers might make available to satisfy the plaintiffs' money judgment. As a consequence, the Court is dragged into a long, costly, and futile exercise that is entirely inconsistent with the basic purpose of a receivership. In view of this potential problem, this Court would undoubtedly want to get some idea of what costs—whether attorneys' fees, expenses, or others—would be associated with any proposed receivership and how those costs would compare with any success the proposed receivers might anticipate with respect to the obtainment of Iranian assets to compensate the actual plaintiffs.

Third, in reviewing any equitable considerations that may or may not militate in favor of a receivership, this Court would want to gauge the potential impact on similarly situated plaintiffs in the many FSIA terrorism cases that have been litigated against Iran in this Court. While there are nearly one thousand plaintiffs in Peterson, there are also hundreds of other victims of Iran-sponsored terrorism who are equally challenged in their ability to enforce judgments against Iran. What should not be overlooked here is that it is for the most part a small, local, and highly specialized bar that handles the vast majority of these cases. Indeed, the attorneys in Peterson serve as counsel in many of the other Iran actions in this Court and vice versa. Thus, it seems to this Court that if certain members of this specialized bar believe that a receivership offers plaintiffs the best chance of collecting on their judgment, then fairness might dictate that such a receivership should work for the benefit of all the plaintiffs as a class, rather than just a select group in a single action.

Most importantly, this Court must bear in mind that the receivership that plaintiffs have urged with respect to Iran's assets is rather extraordinary and unprecedented.

It is therefore difficult to contemplate all the practical and legal implications of such a drastic measure, but the establishment of any kind of receivership in the Peterson case would likely have a significant and negative impact on the to ability of the President to conduct foreign relations with Iran. More problematically, the sort of receivership that the plaintiffs have proposed in the Peterson case might serve as a precedent that would prove troublesome with respect to our relations with other foreign sovereigns. The very thought of imposing a receivership on another foreign sovereign seems to conflict with the principles of comity and mutual respect that have traditionally governed our relations with foreign powers.

With respect to these larger concerns relating to principles of foreign sovereignty and the conduct of foreign relations, this Court should note that there was another motion for the appointment of receivers in Peterson that this Court found very troubling. Specifically, plaintiffs asked this Court to establish a receivership to take the place of Iran at the Iran-United States Claims Tribunal ("Tribunal") established by the Algiers Accords. *See Peterson*, No. 01-CV-2094-RCL (D.D.C.), Dk. # 260. This remarkable and unprecedented proposal by plaintiffs called for court-appointed receivers vested with, among other powers, the authority to "prosecute all Tribunal claims in the name of Iran." *Id.* at 2. As part of this truly extraordinary request, plaintiffs asked the Court to "specifically authorize" the receivers to go before the Tribunal in The Hague, Netherlands in order to dispose of Iran's claims "in any manner which may include settlement, resolution, dismissal" without any requirement to consult with or report to Iran in that process. *Id.* Accordingly, the receivership envisioned by plaintiffs would have received authorization from this Court to replace Iran's lawyers at the Tribunal with counsel appointed by the receivership. *Id.* at 3, 17. Counsel on behalf of the receivership would then continue to advance Iran's claims at the Tribunal, and they would attempt to engage in settlement negotiations with the United States in an effort to convince the United States Government to pay the plaintiffs' multi-billion dollar judgment against the Islamic Republic Iran. *Id.* at 2, 12, 17, 24–25.[42]

While plaintiffs' motion was pending, the United States filed a Statement of Interest in the matter. Dk. # 432. The United States asserted that the receivership proposed by the plaintiffs' is squarely foreclosed by the sovereign immunity of the United States, as well as the basic understanding under our Constitution that "the operation and implementation of international agreements is a matter left to the exclusive province of the political branches." *Id.* at 3. In response, plaintiffs promptly withdrew their motion. *Peterson*, No. 01-CV-2094-RCL (D.D.C.), Dk. # 433. In their notice of withdrawal to this Court, plaintiffs state:

> The statement of interest filed by the United States raises certain issues which indicate that the court should deny Plaintiffs' motion based upon the court's prior rulings, the impact upon the interest of the United States, the sovereign immunity of the

42 Counsel argued that the substitution of Iran with a receivership "might prompt a faster settlement (albeit at a discount) in which the beneficiaries of the settlement would be the victims of terror, and not the terrorist." Dk. # 260, at 12.

> United States, issues which relate to FSIA, international geopolitical concerns, issues which arise out of the U.S.-Iran Claims Tribunal, public policy, and the like. This list is descriptive and illustrative only.

Id. at 1. While not expressly conceding as much, the notice of withdrawal suggests that counsel for plaintiffs came to the realization that their motion was not likely to succeed.

The authorities and legal arguments presented by the United States in this matter clearly demonstrate why this Court cannot appoint a receivership to oust Iran from the Tribunal. A few of the points raised by the United States are worth reinforcing at this time, however, in the interest of ensuring that these controlling legal principles are fully considered by plaintiffs' counsel in any additional requests for extraordinary relief.[43] First and foremost, a critical legal doctrine that is almost always implicated in this context is the sovereign immunity of the United States. The sovereign immunity of the United States is an exceedingly broad jurisdictional bar that precludes attempts by creditors to obtain government funds or property to collect on a debt. *See, e.g.*, *Blue Fox*, 525 U.S. at 264, 119 S. Ct. 687. More to the point, this Court has previously rejected an effort to attach United States Treasury funds that were earmarked for the payment of a Tribunal award to Iran. As noted in Part A, *supra*, in Flatow this Court ruled that "funds held in the U.S. Treasury—even though set aside or 'earmarked' for a specific purpose—remain the property of the United States until the government elects to pay them to whom they are owed." *Flatow II*, 74 F. Supp. 2d 18 at 21 (D.D.C.1999) (Lamberth, J.) (emphasis added) (citing *Buchanan*, 45 U.S. at 21; Blue Fox, 525 U.S. 255, 119 S. Ct. 687).

Plaintiffs attempted to distinguish Flatow in their submission to this Court. They argued that, in contrast to plaintiff's effort to go directly after United States Treasury Funds through writs of attachment in Flatow, receivers would merely "stand in the shoes of Iran" and would simply receive whatever funds the United States might designate for payment to Iran in satisfaction of Tribunal Awards in Iran's favor or in settlement of Iran's pending claims. Dk. # 260, at p. 12, 24. Accordingly, the plaintiffs claimed that the mere creation of a receivership to oust Iran-U.S. Claims Tribunal would not implicate any issues of United States sovereign immunity unless and until the receivers found it necessary to further action in the Courts to enforce Iran's awards and claims against the United States. *Id.* at 7, 24–25. Plaintiffs' argument wholly lacked merit. As this Court emphasized to these very plaintiffs previously, they may not use receivers "to do indirectly what they cannot do directly." *Peterson III*, 563 F. Supp. 2d at 278 (emphasis in original). As the funds within the United States Treasury are immune from the jurisdiction of this Court, this Court is therefore without jurisdiction to appoint receivers whose express objective would be to take hold of any of those funds that the

43 The Court should also note that plaintiffs and the United States stipulated to a withdrawal of plaintiffs' motion without prejudice. *See* Dk. # 433, at 2. The notice of withdrawal also suggests that plaintiffs are considering filing another motion regarding the Iran-U.S. Claims Tribunal.

United States might, within its discretion, use to resolve Tribunal Claims with Iran. Simply put, to allow court-appointed receivers on behalf of the plaintiffs to inject themselves into a process involving payments from the United States Government to Iran would violate the basic purpose of sovereign immunity, as the powers of this Court would be harnessed in a way that would burden the United States in the exercise of its broad discretion to appropriate and allocate federal dollars as it deems fit.

Even if § 1610(g)(2) were to apply in this case—and it does not—this new measure would not alter the analysis. Section § 1610(g)(2) by it plain terms speaks only to funds that were originally held by a state sponsor of terrorism but which later came under the control of the United States by virtue of Executive Orders blocking those assets pursuant to the Trading With the Enemy Act or the International Emergency Economics Powers Act. There is no indication, however, that Congress intended to waive the sovereign immunity of the United States with respect to the Federal Government's own funds within the United States Treasury. Accordingly, § 1610(g)(2) simply does not reach these federal dollars, which the political branches of our Government may, within their discretion, decide to disperse to Iran consistent with the United States' obligations to settle claims under the terms of the Algiers Accord.

Moving beyond the controlling legal precedent that squarely forecloses the relief requested by plaintiffs, this Court finds utterly disturbing the way in which plaintiffs' counsel described in some detail their strange vision of how receivers might invoke the powers of this Article III court to assert control over Iran's affairs before an international tribunal. *See* Dk. # 260, at 15–21. In a rather bizarre and perverse twist of events, counsel would have the Court oversee receivers as they advanced Iran's claims against the United States. Plaintiffs' counsel candidly acknowledged that the ultimate objective of this proposed scheme was to leverage the powers of this Court through the appointment of a receivership in order to pressure the United States into settling its claims with Iran, at least up to the amounts needed to satisfy plaintiffs' 2.5 Billion dollar judgment. Plaintiffs' counsel actually referred to this perverse result as an "elegant outcome." *Id.* at 21.

Putting aside the enormous practical and political obstacles that a receivership conceived to take Iran's place at the Tribunal would instantly confront, this Court is simply without authority to assert any level of control or supervision over the affairs of an international body established to resolve disputes between two sovereign nations. As the United States correctly observed, this Federal Court may not involve itself in the operation or implementation of a bilateral agreement between the United States and Iran. *See* Dk. # 432, at 12–16 (Statement of Interest by the United States). As bilateral agreements that resolved a crisis between two foreign powers, the Algiers Accords are precisely the sort of international agreements that depend exclusively on the political branches for its implementation and enforcement. *See, e.g.*, *Bancoult v. McNamara*, 370 F. Supp. 2d 1, 14 (D.D.C.2004);

Kucinich v. Bush, 236 F. Supp. 2d, 1, 16 (D.D.C.2002); *Antolok v. United States*, 873 F.2d 369, 380 (D.C.Cir.1989); *see also Dames & Moore*, 453 U.S. at 664, 101 S. Ct. 2972 (describing how the United States and Iran entered into the Algiers Accords and established the Iran-United States Claims Tribunal to bring about an end to the hostage crisis).

Plaintiffs' proposal for the appointment of a receivership to oust Iran from the U.S.-Iran Claims Tribunal illustrates how litigation in these FSIA terrorism cases can run amuck as plaintiffs desperately seek out ways to enforce their court-judgments. The default judgment context of these actions only adds to this problem, as there is a risk that unopposed counsel may at times overreach and float meritless, even preposterous arguments. In the end, however, these postjudgment actions—no matter how creative or vigorously pursued—hardly ever net results for plaintiffs, and yet these actions frequently threaten the foreign policy interests of the United States while consuming significant amounts of court time and other resources.

This Court is grateful for the well-crafted statement of interest that apparently brought counsel to their senses and ultimately saved this Court some valuable time and energy. For this reason, this Court will solicit the views of the United States before considering any further motions for the appointment of receivers in any of these terrorism cases pending against Iran. This Court also appreciates that plaintiffs' counsel ultimately withdrew their motion when confronted with clear legal authority that precluded the relief they sought. This Court wishes to remind plaintiffs' counsel, however, that before they file any motion in this Court, they have a duty to fully consider any controlling legal authority—including adverse precedent—that may be dispositive of the relief they request.

There is one statement, however, in the plaintiffs' notice of withdrawal that this Court finds rather heartening. Plaintiffs note that the executive and legislative branches may be able to offer "alternative remedies" and that the type of relief sought through plaintiffs' proposed receivership "may be pursued through an alternative forum, or pursued after addressing the issues raised by the United States." Perhaps plaintiffs have come to realize—as this Court has—that only the political branches have the authority to grant the kinds of extraordinary relief that the victims in these actions require. This Court hopes that there may indeed be some real opportunities in the near future for the plaintiffs in Peterson and in other cases to work closely with our political leaders, including those in the new administration, to move beyond civil litigation in the Courts as a means to achieve the justice that these victims of terrorism so rightly deserve. Unless these actions are to exist in perpetuity as empty promises—which drain the resources of our courts and undercut the foreign affairs prerogative of the President—then some alternative to the private litigation approach must be found. Frankly, plaintiffs have waited far too long for meaningful reforms, and they have exhausted themselves in a seemingly endless quest for justice. The time for real reform is now, and it is to this critical issue that the Court now turns.

K. A Call for Meaningful Reform

The most difficult issues confronting this unique area of the law relate to how plaintiffs in these FSIA terrorism cases might enforce their court judgments against the Islamic Republic of Iran. While this highly charged topic of debate has been the subject of numerous legislative proposals and enactments over the last decade—and is again the subject of many of the most recent reforms implemented by the 2008 NDAA—very little has been achieved. Today, the overwhelming majority of successful FSIA plaintiffs with judgments against Iran still have not received the relief that our courts have determined they are entitled to under the law.[44]

In speaking to this critical issue today in light of the nineteen civil actions addressed in this opinion—and the more than one thousand American victims of Iran-sponsored terrorism that these actions represent—the Court fully appreciates first and foremost the delicate nature of the political compromise the FSIA terrorism exception embodies. "While such legislation had long been sought by victims' groups, it had been consistently resisted by the executive branch." *See Price*, 294 F.3d at 89 (citations omitted). As our Court of Appeals has emphasized, certain features of the terrorism exception "reveal the delicate legislative compromise out of which it was born." *Id.* Among these is the restriction providing that only "state sponsors of terrorism," as officially designated by the State Department, may be subject to suit under the terms of the statute. *Id.* (citing § 1605(a)(7)(A) (repealed)). Additionally, only United States nationals are entitled to file lawsuits under the statute, and the offending state must be given a reasonable opportunity to arbitrate any claims based on an incident that occurred within its borders. *Id.* (citing § 1605(a)(7)(B) (repealed)).

In this Court's view, however, the compromise is perhaps best evinced by the resistance of the Executive Branch to legislation permitting the execution of court judgments through assets of state sponsors of terrorism. As discussed in Part A,

---

44 This Court's observations and comments in this part of the opinion and throughout relate only to civil actions against the Iran under the FSIA terrorism exception. The Court therefore does not express any views with respect to the viability of actions against other state sponsors of terrorism. While it appears that similar issues as those that impact actions against Iran may also be present in civil actions against other state sponsors of terrorism under either § 1605(a)(7) or § 1605A, cases against Iran face a number of unique challenges, such as the Algiers Accords and the establishment of the Iran-United States Claims Tribunal, which make it particularly difficult for plaintiffs to recover in these actions. Finally, the vast majority of cases that have been filed in this Court under the FSIA terrorism exception, have been filed against Iran. Thus, this Court does not want to assume problems or issues in other FSIA terrorism cases in which it has much more limited experience.

Additionally, it should be noted that the Court's opinion today concerns only the FSIA terrorism exception. This Court does not address the Antiterrorism Act, 18 U.S.C. §§ 2331-38; the Torture Victim Protection Act, 28 U.S.C. § 1350 note; the Alien Tort Claims Act, 28 U.S.C. § 1350; or any other civil statutes that may permit civil actions for personal injury or death caused by terrorist acts.

supra, the enforcement of judgments through the attachment and execution of the assets of terrorist states, whether those assets are blocked or not, has been a particularly controversial issue, and it is one that has been tackled continuously in legislative enactments almost since the inception of the FSIA terrorism exception ten years ago. For instance, the enactment of the VTVPA, the TRIA, and now § 1083 of the 2008 NDAA, which provides the most sweeping judgment enforcement authority to date, illustrates the gradual progress that terrorism victims have achieved though Congress over the Executive Branch in their efforts to obtain more power to enforce judgments under the FSIA terrorism exception. Thus, § 1083 is just the latest chapter in what has been a longstanding political debate over how best to achieve some measure of justice for these victims.[45]

In view of the incremental nature of these reforms as meted out through the political process over the years, perhaps the Court's words here will make little difference. This Court is certainly mindful of its limited authority under Article III, and this Court certainly does not wish to wade into the politics of these matters, but it is precisely because this Court's authority is so very limited in this context that this Court has grown increasingly frustrated by the way the political process has treated the terrorism victims in these cases under the FSIA. The experience of this Court in presiding over these actions for over a decade now has revealed that the political compromise achieved through the FSIA terrorism exception and its related enactments is superficial, filled with contradictions, and utterly in denial of practical and political realities—to say nothing of separation-of-powers problems—that courts can do little to address. Moreover, if this Court's experience in any indicator, the most recent reforms in § 1083 are not only destined to fail, but these new measures may even make matters worse.

To be sure, the changes to the FSIA enacted through § 1083 of the 2008 NDAA appear, on the surface at least, to be extraordinarily advantageous to plaintiffs. The direct cause of action contained in the new terrorism exception § 1605A will make it easier for most plaintiffs to file and litigate cases against Iran, and the availability of punitive damages in these actions creates a tremendous incentive for these lawsuits. With respect to the substantial problems plaintiffs in these actions have encountered in their efforts to execute judgments, the provision allowing for prejudgment liens of lis pendens, *see* § 1605A(g), and the new measures added to § 1610 that purport to limit the applicability of both foreign sovereign immunity and United States sovereign immunity are the most significant legislative initiatives to date that aim to overcome the inability of plaintiffs to execute judgments against Iran.

45 Executive Branch resistance to legislation permitting the enforcement of judgments through the assets of terrorist states is probably best documented in Suits Against Terrorist States, *supra* note 4, at 7–23.

From the bench of this Article III Judge, however, what the Court sees in § 1083 is not so much meaningful reform, but rather the continuation of a failed policy and an expansion of the empty promise that the FSIA terrorism exception has come to represent. Through the enactment of § 1083, the political branches have promoted or otherwise acquiesced in subjecting Iran to sweeping liability while simultaneously overlooking the proverbial elephant in the room—and that is the fact that these judgments are largely unenforceable due to the scarcity of Iranian assets within the jurisdiction of the United States courts. As noted Part A, *supra*, few Iranian assets remain with the jurisdiction of the United States courts since the transfer of those assets out of the United States was accomplished in 1981 in fulfillment of the Federal Government's obligations under the terms of Algiers Accords. OFAC's latest report on blocked assets indicates that the total value of blocked assets relating to Iran in the United States is approximately 16.8 million dollars, an infinitesimal amount in comparison to the more than 9.6 billion dollars in civil judgments against Iran under the FSIA terrorism exception. *See* Terrorist Assets Report, *supra* note 2, at 14, tbl. 1. Similarly, OFAC's records suggest that there are very few non-blocked assets within the United States—perhaps no more than 28 million dollars worth. *See id.* at 15, tbl. 3.

Even if one assumes, however, that there are sufficient Iranian assets within the jurisdiction United States courts to satisfy the billions of dollars in judgments entered in these civil suits, proceedings before this District Court have revealed that whatever non-blocked assets might be found may be held by certain large financial institutions that are in fact agencies of instrumentalities of other foreign nations, which are in and of themselves subject to sovereign immunity under the FSIA. *See* § 1604. Indeed, this is precisely the problem that foiled plaintiffs' efforts to enforce their judgment in Peterson; it is the sovereign immunity from jurisdiction afforded to the financial entities of other foreign states—and not of Iran—that frequently frustrates recovery. *See Peterson III*, 563 F. Supp. 2d 268 (quashing writs of attachment issued against Japan Bank for International Cooperation, the Bank of Japan, and the Export and Import Bank of Korea).

Moreover, plaintiffs still have the burden of proving Iranian ownership—whether beneficial or otherwise—of the assets at issue, which can be extraordinary challenging in this context.[46] In this regard, this Court observes that § 1610(g) expressly protects the rights of third parties in actions to levy or execute upon a judgment entered against Iran. Section 1610(g)(3) states:

> Nothing in this subsection shall be construed to supersede the authority of a court to prevent appropriately the impairment of an interest held by a person who is not liable

46 *See Flatow v. Islamic Republic of Iran*, 67 F. Supp. 2d 535 (D.Md.1999) (quashing writs of attachment issued against the Alavi Foundation and rejecting argument that this separately incorporated entity should be considered an agent or alter ego of the Iranian Government). For more detailed analysis of the difficulties of establishing foreign state ownership in these actions, *see* Suits Against Terrorist States, *supra* note 4, at 54–59.

> in the action giving rise to the judgment in property subject to attachment in aid of execution or execution upon such judgment.

Thus, the tremendous complexities and challenges with respect to proving Iranian ownership of the assets in this thorny context are likely to persist.

Finally, United States sovereign immunity will remain an issue under § 1610(g), as nothing prevents the President from seizing Iranian assets and vesting title to them in the U.S. Treasury, as Presidents have often done in the interest of important foreign policy objectives.[47] Accordingly, the language in § 1610(g)(2) purporting to render United States sovereign immunity "inapplicable" may be of utility because, while it speaks to sovereign immunity that might be inferred by virtue of the Federal Government's regulation of assets under either the Trading with the Enemy Act or the International Emergency Economic Powers Act, it does not abrogate United States sovereign immunity with respect to funds held in the United States treasury.[48]

In terms of real and tangible property that Iran owns in the United States, much of it was once used for diplomatic or consular purposes by Iran and is therefore subject to the Vienna Conventions on Diplomatic and Consular Relations. This property is thus immune from attachment and execution because it is currently

---

47 *See, e.g.*, *Smith v. Fed. Reserve Bank of N.Y.*, 346 F.3d 264 (2d Cir.2003). In Smith, the Court held that certain blocked assets of Iraq were not susceptible to attachment because the President had, in the interest of national security, confiscated those assets and vested title to those assets in the United States Treasury.

48 This Court is not overlooking the possibility of execution of judgments through enforcement proceedings in foreign jurisdictions, as least one scholar has recently suggested as a still-viable means of recovery in these actions. *See Strauss*, *supra*, at 307 (arguing for broader, multilateral approach to suits against sponsors of terrorism with leadership from the United Nations and other international organizations, and involving courts worldwide, that would enable victims of terrorism to more effectively execute civil judgments in foreign jurisdictions). The possibility of widespread enforcement of these terrorism judgments in foreign jurisdictions is a difficult prospect in these actions, as Professor Strauss concedes. *See id.* at 325–327 (discussing reluctance of foreign courts to honor U.S. terrorism judgments); *see also* Michael T. Kotlarczyk, Note, "The Provision of Material Support and Resources" and Lawsuits Against State Sponsors of Terrorism, 96 GEO. L.J.2029 (2008). Mr. Kotlarczyk discusses the difficulties in enforcing judgments against liable states respect and stresses how terrorism cases under the FSIA terrorism exception lack legitimacy under international law. Kotlarczyk, *supra* note 48, at 2044–47. "The United States remains essentially alone in international law in applying the jurisdiction of its civil courts to actions performed overseas by foreign sovereigns." *Id.* at 2047.

More fundamentally, however, the continued focus in Congress on the private litigation model, and ad hoc litigation fixes around the failed concept, may be limiting the opportunity for the types proposals that can result in more meaningful and systemic reforms. In short, the focus on the terrorism exception is a distraction from the long-term, practical, and political dilemmas that challenge this area of the law.

being held in protective custody by the Department of State under the auspices of the Foreign Mission Act. *See, e.g.*, *Bennett*, 604 F. Supp. 2d 152.[49]

In sum, § 1610(g) is unlikely to be the cure-all that some plaintiffs perceive it to be. As with past measures intended to help victims execute judgments, a myriad of legal issues still await to befuddle plaintiffs at every turn. Thus, these victims will continue to struggle in their attempts to execute court judgments, whether those efforts involve the very limited disclosed Iranian assets known to OFAC or other yet-undisclosed Iranian property that may or may not be within the jurisdiction of the courts of the United States.[50]

The lack of available Iranian assets to satisfy court judgments has contributed to a rather harsh and unseemly unfairness in these actions because a few dozen plaintiffs in the earliest cases managed to obtain compensation for their losses, but hundreds of other equally deserving victims of terrorism—including the more than one thousand plaintiffs in the actions considered in today's decision—have gotten nothing. As noted in Part A, *supra*, the VTVPA directed the Secretary of the Treasury to pay the compensatory damages portion of court judgments entered in a select number of cases against Iran. Under the terms of the VTVPA, payments of compensatory damages in qualifying cases were made from either funds that had accrued as a result of the Federal Government lease of Iran's diplomatic and consular properties or from appropriated funds up to the total amount of funds contained in Iran's FMS Program account. Ultimately, plaintiffs in 16 cases against Iran received payments of compensatory damages. *See* SUITS AGAINST TERRORIST STATES, *supra* note 4, at p. 11–23, app. A. By as early as 2004, however, the funds made available for payment to plaintiffs under the VTVPA were totally exhausted and the program has not been continued. *Id.* at app. A.

---

49 Recent OFAC estimates indicate that the total value of Iran's diplomatic property, to include any remaining furnishings for that property, is unlikely to exceed 23.2 million dollars. Again, this figure represents little more than a drop in the bucket when compared to the nearly 10 billion dollars owed judgment creditors of Iran under the FSIA terrorism exception.

50 The Court recognizes that plaintiffs are optimistic that § 1610(g) is a tool that will finally enable them to execute judgments, and it appears that some victims have invested a great deal of emotional stock in this provision. *See Strauss*, *supra*, at 331–336, 354–355 (discussing § 1083 of the 2008 NDAA, and in particular the measures now codified at § 1610(g), and observing positive reactions expressed by the victims upon the signing of the law). As Professors Strauss observes: "Victims of terrorism and their families have praised the new law and voiced their intention to put it quickly to action." *Id.* at 335. Professor Strauss quotes Lynn Derbyshire, who serves as national spokesperson for the victims of the Beirut Marine Corps Barracks Bombing, as stating: "'Our focus now turns back to the court system, where we intend to move vigorously and rapidly to identify and attach the $2.6 billion in Iranian assets' awarded by the U.S. Court to the victims and their families.'" *Id.* It is precisely because these victims appear to have placed so much emotional stock in this provision, however, that this Judge finds that it is important to speak candidly about the continuing problems that await these victims in their efforts to execute judgments in these cases. This Court believes it is especially important to engage in an honest dialog with these victims who have waited so long for justice; it hopes our political leaders will do the same.

Thus, there has not only been a race to this federal courthouse in these civil actions, but there also appears to have been something of a race across the street to Capitol Hill. In the end, the terrorism victims who had access to a Congressman or a Senator—or who could otherwise afford to spend the time or money to lobby Congress—obtained millions of dollars in compensation under the VTVPA program, but those victims who were not able to get in early and gain access to Congress have been left to fend for themselves. This inequitable result is not only unseemly, it is just plain wrong.[51]

The harsh reality is that the promise of relief in these actions—if there ever was one—is more distant and seemingly illusory today than it was when this exercise started more than a decade ago, when judgment creditors in these terrorism cases first encountered resistance in their efforts to execute judgments against Iran. The reforms enacted through § 1083 of the 2008 NDAA to the FSIA terrorism exception and related provisions in § 1610 are in all likelihood destined to fail because these changes remain premised on the same flawed private litigation concept that has proven unworkable since the original terrorism exception was first enacted in 1996. In fact, the availability of punitive damages under § 1605A, when combined with the authorization in § 1083(c) for claims that were compromised or failed on state law grounds under § 1605(a)(7) to now be reinstated as federal causes of action under § 1605A, means that both the total amount of liability and the overall quantity of civil judgments against Iran is likely to increase exponentially, and in short order. Indeed, in the immediate aftermath of the enactment of § 1083, dozens of new cases against Iran were filed in this Court. With virtually no Iranian assets within the jurisdiction of our courts to satisfy judgments in these many additional cases, the great travesty in all this is that our political branches have essentially told victims of terrorism to continue their long march to justice down a path that leads to nowhere.

Beyond the scarcity of Iranian assets, however, there are a number of other fundamental problems that confront these actions against Iran under the FSIA

---

51 Washington Post Staff Writer Neely Tucker has reported extensively on terrorism lawsuits in this Courthouse and on suits against Iran in particular. *See, e.g.*, NEELY TUCKER, IRAN HOSTAGES SEEK SUIT'S REINSTATEMENT; CASE REFLECTS HILL-WHITE HOUSE DIVIDE, WASH. POST, May 13, 2003, at A10; NEELY TUCKER, IRAN STANDS ON TRIAL IN 1983 SUICIDE BOMBING IN BEIRUT, Wash. Post, Apr. 8, 2003, at A9. Mr. Tucker's work Pain and Suffering; Relatives of Terrorist Victims Race Each Other to the Court, but Justice and Money are Both Hard to Find, *supra*, is particularly insightful. In it, Mr. Tucker chronicles the plight of terrorism victims, to include Stephen Flatow and many others, in their struggles to achieve justice though civil lawsuits under the FSIA terrorism exception. Mr. Tucker reports on interviews with these victims, which adds a human touch that is often missing in the discussion of these terrorism lawsuits. More significantly, Mr. Tucker's article highlights the perils, contradictions, and unintended consequences that victims face in these actions. His reporting on the race to the courthouse and Congress, in which victims compete against each other for what limited assets might be available, that helped this Court to see the inherent and unseemly unfairness that these actions create among the victims.

terrorism exception. In terms of United States foreign policy and national security objectives, one of the perverse outcomes of Congress' legislative victories over the Executive Branch is that what limited resources might have served as a bargaining chip that the President could have used in dealings with Iran are now subject to depletion as a result of the TRIA. These frozen assets, once at the disposal of the President in his management of foreign policy crises under the IEEPA and other authorities, are now largely subject to the jurisdiction of the Article III courts to be divided up among what few plaintiffs first lay claim to them in satisfaction of judgments under § 1605(a)(7) or § 1605A.[52]

Finally, because of the potential for these lawsuits to interfere with the foreign policy prerogatives of the President, another fundamental problem is that these actions have often pitted victims of terrorism against the Executive Branch, engendering a tremendous amount of acrimony in these victims toward the Federal Government, and, at times, the President. Beyond the wrangling back and forth over legislative initiatives intended to aid victims in these lawsuits—which is best ex-emplified by the blocked assets issue, discussed Part A, *supra*,—the victims in these cases often face stiff resistance in court from Department of Justice lawyers. In fact, in the absence of Iran, which never shows to defend itself in these actions, the Federal Government has turned out to be the number one adversary of these victims in litigation before this Court.

As noted in Part E, *supra*, the victims of the Iran hostage crisis—and their backers in Congress—have been opposed repeatedly by the Federal Government in their efforts to sue Iran in this Court. The administration has consistently maintained that such a lawsuit is barred by the Algiers Accords. Similarly, as noted in Part A, *supra*, successive presidential administrations have intervened to quash writs of attachment issued by judgment creditors of Iran against Iranian diplomatic properties here in Washington, DC and against other assets under the control of either the Department of State or the Department of Treasury. Thus, victims of Iran-sponsored terrorism have grown increasingly frustrated as the Department of Justice has repeatedly opposed them in this context and defeated them in litigation. This frustration has been exacerbated by the fact that many high-level Executive officials, to include the President at times, have expressed sympathy for these victims and have even made public pronouncements of support for their cause, thereby sending mixed, and even outright contradictory signals.

The Executive Branch, in its dealings with Congress and in litigation before this Court, often takes the position that these actions threaten to undermine United States foreign policy and national security interests, both with respect to Iran

---

52 Another troubling aspect of litigation under the FSIA terrorism exception is that it appears to have spurred on reciprocal lawsuits in the courts of Iran against the United States for actions allegedly committed against Iran and its citizens by United States agencies and officials. *See* TUCKER, PAIN AND SUFFERING, *supra* (discussing antiterrorism lawsuits in the Iranian courts against the United States).

specifically, as well as with respect to our relations with other nations more broadly. The victims in these cases counter with what are often extremely emotional retorts to the Executive Branch's opposition. In frustration and anger, the victims, their lawyers, and even some members of Congress, have unfairly accused the Administration of defending Iran and siding with terrorists. While such extreme rhetoric undoubtedly reveals the depth of the frustration experienced by the victims in these civil actions against Iran, it inaccurately characterizes the position of the Executive Branch and the true nature of the interests at stake in these important actions. What the victims, their attorneys, and backers in Congress apparently fail to see, or perhaps conveniently overlook, is that these actions frequently run into direct conflict with other sources of law, including bilateral Executive agreements, multilateral treaty obligations, and numerous other statutory and regulatory authorities relating to foreign policy and the President's powers to manage national security crises.

Nonetheless, the victims in these lawsuits are right to feel abandoned and frustrated to a certain extent. After all, these Americans are merely pursuing justice under the terms of a federal statute that, twice now, the Congress has passed and two Presidents have signed. Yet, in taking action in accordance with that federal law, these victims are all too frequently stopped in their tracks by their own Government, which quickly and poignantly reveals in open Court, that the promise of justice that they thought they had achieved in the FSIA terrorism exception is nothing more than an illusion.

In the end, both the victims of terrorism and the Federal Government each have valid concerns—and both sides are ultimately seeking to achieve the same broad objectives of holding terrorists accountable and eliminating terrorism against United States nationals—but the private litigation model for resolving these terrorism claims has had the very unfortunate consequence of casting the United States Government and American victims of terrorism as constant and bitter adversaries. This cold reality will undoubtedly continue under § 1605A.

As Congress usually backs the victims in their desire to press forward with lawsuits against Iran in the courts, the FSIA terrorism exception has had another unfortunate consequence of turning these already extraordinary lawsuits against a foreign power into high stakes contests between the two political branches. As this inter-branch feud over terrorism suits has heated up over the years, the Executive Branch and Congress have in essence waged a war by proxy against one another through these FSIA terrorism lawsuits. As difficult separation-of-powers problems and other challenging legal questions loom large in these supercharged actions, the victims are often relegated to the role of bystanders, stuck in the middle, caught up, and emotionally torn up in the cross-fire of an inter-branch political feud turned-litigation event.

But it is not only the victims who are caught up in the middle of this volatile political mix; this Court itself is also stuck in the middle and forced to referee these highly charged and highly political disputes. Like the victims, this Court finds itself relegated to the role of a powerless and frustrated bystander at times because under Article III this Court has neither foreign affairs powers nor any of the plenary authorities that are rightly vested in the political branches under our Constitution. It is these powers of governance, and not the powers of the courts, that must be used to help these victims overcome the significant challenges they face. Thus, this Court is caught in something of a political quagmire in which it is called upon to consume judicial resources chewing on novel legal issues and jurisprudential problems while carefully dodging delicate political questions. All the while the victims in these actions are no closer to justice. More fundamentally, respect for this Court and for the rule of law are undermined as judges in these actions are cast as the perennial bearers of bad news and as the designated apologists for the meaningless charade that our the political branches have created.

All these problems might be easy enough to ignore, if it were not for the real people involved. As this Court and others continue to wrestle with and mete out judicial solutions to the variety of legal issues that stem from this delicate political compromise that is the terrorism exception to foreign sovereign immunity, it can be all too easy to lose sight of the human beings whose lives have been torn apart. These victims have poured much of their emotional energy and time, to say nothing of their financial resources, into these civil cases in the hope of finding justice for themselves and for the loved ones they have lost due to terrorist violence. Over the last decade, this Court has listened to live testimony of these victims in dozens of tragic cases, and this Court will not forget—and no one familiar with the harsh and intimate details of these cases could ever forget—the stories these victims have to tell of lives destroyed by unjustifiable violence committed against them or their family members and against the laws of all civilized nations.

These Americans pour their hearts out in these actions, and yet with more than ten years gone by now, the notion of suing the terrorists out of business has not been realized, and the vast majority of victims have not collected so much as a dime on their court judgments against Iran. In fact, as discussed Part A, *supra*, it was almost ten years ago to this date that this Court regrettably had to deny some of Stephen Flatow's first efforts to execute his civil judgment. This Court held that Mr. Flatow could not attach certain Iranian diplomatic property and related bank accounts. *See Flatow III*, 76 F. Supp. 2d 16. Following that tough decision, the Washington Post published an editorial in which it called for the repeal of the FSIA terrorism exception. The Post stated in part:

> Judge Lamberth quashed an effort by a man whose daughter was killed in a suicide bombing in the Gaza Strip to satisfy a judgment he had obtained against Iran by tapping such frozen assets as that country's old embassy. The opinion is not just, but it is correct. The executive branch's ability to conduct foreign policy simply must trump the right of any individual plaintiff to collect money damages against a sovereign state.
>
> . . .

> The administration and Congress both deserve blame for a law that is, in large measure, a lie. Because frozen assets— whether consular or otherwise—are tools of foreign policy, the executive branch has to resist their being turned over to private plaintiffs. Congress never should have passed, nor President Clinton signed, a law that could only offer Mr. Flatow justice by depriving the administration of control over important instruments of foreign policy. This law should be repealed.

Editorial, WASH. POST, Dec. 26, 1999, at B6.

While this Court will not go so far as to call for an outright repeal of the terrorism exception, this Judge has come to the conclusion, after careful deliberation and reflection, that substantial reforms in the law are needed with respect to civil actions against Iran. This judge has taken a special interest in these cases since their inception, and after presiding over these actions for over ten years now, this Court has grown increasingly troubled by the fact that no matter how hard they struggle—and struggle they must—it is virtually impossible for the victims in these terrorism cases to collect on the civil judgments entered against Iran in this Court.

Thus, as a measure devised to achieve justice for victims, the FSIA terrorism exception has failed, and judged by the plaintiffs before the Court today, it has failed one thousand times over and seems all but certain to fail again, unless a real— rather than a superficial and politically convenient solution—is found, and found soon. Our political branches should not continue to tell victims of terrorism to come into this Court in search of justice for unspeakable harms that they have suffered at the hands of terrorists when our political leaders know, or should know, that these lawsuits will not offer redress of any kind for the vast majority of victims in these actions against Iran. In fact, to the extent any of the judgments have been paid in these cases, those payments have come from U.S. Treasury funds under the VTVPA, and these costs may ultimately be borne by U.S. taxpayer. Thus, Iran has not been held accountable and the vast majority of victims have not received compensation of any kind. In the final analysis, the terrorism exception is at best an empty promise, and at worst, it is a provision that has demoralized—and in some ways exploited—these victims of horrific acts of violence.

By other important measures, the private litigation model as a means to resolve terrorism cases against Iran has not achieved success. It has not deterred Iran. Today, Iran is still the world's foremost sponsor of terrorism, and the same oppressive regime is in power and appears committed to staying in power at all costs. United States relations with Iran remain openly hostile, and it appears that this is likely to continue into the foreseeable future. Thus, if the goals of the FSIA terrorism exception are justice in terms of compensation for victim and accountability for Iran, as well as deterrence of Iran from its material support for terrorists, civil litigation against Iran has not brought our nation any closer to these goals today than we were when the terrorism exception was first enacted in 1996. Yet, in addition to imposing tremendous costs on the victims who have invested their hopes, time, money, and emotions into these lawsuits, civil litigation against Iran in this context has undermined the President's ability to handle some of our most sensitive foreign relations matters, exposed the United States to reciprocal lawsuits in Iran, and wastefully consumed the resources of our Courts here at home.

Now today, in 2009, and ten years after this Court first found itself in the disquieting predicament of having to quash the first efforts of victims to enforce judgments achieved in this Court under the original version of the FSIA terrorism exception, this Court finds itself committed to a new round of litigation under the terms of § 1083 of the 2008 NDAA and a new, and supposedly improved, FSIA terrorism exception, § 1605A. Candidly, this Court has grown increasingly frustrated as the political branches have now enabled new lawsuits and new claims against Iran to populate this Court's docket without first addressing the more fundamental problems that will again condemn these actions, if successful before this Court, to the status of "Pyrrhic victories." Quite simply, this is déjà vu all over again.

The new terrorism exception § 1605A— much like § 1605(a)(7) before it—is in many respects a lie. The truth is, as long as civil litigation is the means by which our political branches choose to redress the harms suffered as a result of terrorism sponsored by Iran, the victims in these cases will continue to be unwitting participants in a meaningless charade. And let no one forget that both political branches are responsible for this problem, as Congress drafted both the original and the most recent version of the state sponsor of terrorism exception, and now two different Presidents, one Democrat, and one Republican, signed these provisions into law. Accordingly, the frustrations and anger of the victims in these actions, which are often manifested in emotional outbursts and extreme rhetoric directed toward the Executive, are in many ways a direct result of the overblown expectations that the political branches have themselves created.

What this Court hopes our political branches will realize and appreciate today is that it is extraordinarily difficult to tell these victims that the rights and remedies they believe they are entitled to under the FSIA terrorism exception either do not exist or cannot be enforced. These victims have been waiting for years, and, in many cases, decades, for justice. How much longer should this meaningless kabuki dance continue?

This is not the first time that this Court has been critical of the FSIA terrorism exception and nothing said here is all that original. Numerous commentators in the legal community, among others, have called for the repeal of the terrorism exception or have otherwise proposed significant reforms intended to improve this provision of law that virtually all recognize has not achieved redress for victims of terrorism.[53] More significantly, there have been some efforts at systemic reforms

---

53 *See, e.g.*, Kotlarczyk, *supra* note 48, at 2030 (arguing that the "provision of material support and resources" clause of the FSIA terrorism exception should be eliminated thereby limiting suits to those case in which the state or its officials have directly participated in a specified act of terrorism); Keith Sealing, "State Sponsors of Terrorism" Is a Question,

introduced in Congress in recent years in the form of proposals for alternative compensations scheme that shift away from the private litigation paradigm. Most of these proposals would have established what would in essence function as a government insurance program in which qualifying victims of terrorism and their loved ones could file claims with the government for compensation. To date, none of these proposals has gotten any traction on Capitol Hill.[54]

Perhaps nothing said here can add to what has already been stated by legal commentators, critics, and those that have explored alternative proposals on the Hill and in other policy-making circles, but unlike political leaders, academic pundits, and media commentators, this Court has the benefit of years of experience—difficult experience—with these cases. By just looking at these actions on the Court's docket, this Court sees today all too clearly just how unsustainable these actions have become. Our political branches have opened the floodgates to even greater numbers of actions against Iran and have added the lure of punitive damage awards. Reforms are needed now before things get out of hand. This Court senses the enactment of § 1083, which greatly expands the failed private litigation concept and all its pitfalls, while combined with the start of a new Administration—one which has promoted a policy of engagement with Iran and with the Middle East more broadly— may offer something of a perfect storm, which may perhaps serve as the perfect opportunity to accomplish something meaningful for the victims in these tragic cases.

Looking back on these matters now, the Court cannot help but see the wisdom in two of Justice Rehnquist's opinions, both of which formed part of this Court's analysis of issues addressed earlier in today's decision, *see* Parts A & E, *supra*, and appear particularly relevant now to the Court's request of our political leaders to find meaningful reform. The first is Justice Rehnquist's opinion for the Court in

---

NOT AN ANSWER: THE TERRORISM AMENDMENT TO THE FSIA MAKES LESS SENSE NOW THAN IT DID BEFORE 9/11, 38 TEX. INT'L L.J. 119, 122 (2003) (arguing for the outright repeal of the FSIA terrorism exception); JONATHAN FISCHBACH, Note, THE EMPTY POT AT THE END OF THE RAINBOW: CONFRONTING "HALLOW-RIGHTS LEGISLATION" AFTER FLATOW, 87 CORNELL L.REV. 1001 (arguing that, in addition to the existing jurisdictional requirements for an action under the FSIA terrorism exception, jurisdiction should also be predicated on a court determination that there are sufficient assets available to satisfy any money judgment awarded in such an action). But *see* Strauss, *supra*, at 307 (arguing that a multilateral strategy focused on both the freezing of assets and civil litigation against terrorist groups and states would serve as the most effective deterrent of international terrorism and would best ensure justice for terrorism victims).

54 The proposals introduced in Congress recently, including a comprehensive alternative compensation scheme proposed by Bush Administration, are well documented in SUITS AGAINST TERRORIST STATES, *supra* note 4, at 20, 23, 47. *See also* KOTLARCZYK, *supra* note 48, at 2044 (suggesting a terrorism victim compensation fund similar to the September 11th Victim Compensation Fund as an alternative to civil actions under the FSIA state sponsor of terrorism exception).

Dames & Moore, 453 U.S. 654, 101 S. Ct. 2972, and the second is the Justice's dissenting opinion in Sioux Nation, 448 U.S. 371, 100 S. Ct. 2716.

Dames & Moore is most relevant for a number of reasons. Historically speaking, the decision documents the Iran Hostage Crisis and upholds the Algiers Accords and related Executive actions taken to bring about the end of that crisis, including, most importantly, the transfer of Iranian assets outside the jurisdiction of the United States courts and the settlement of claims of United States nationals. Thus, Dames & Moore reveals the inviolability of the Algiers Accords and related Executive actions as large stumbling blocks standing in the way of meaningful redress of terrorism claims against Iran. More significantly, Justice Rehnquist's opinion for the Court underscores the very limited powers of Article III Courts to resolve issues relating to a foreign policy crisis and places emphasis on the role of Executive power and discretion in the resolution of sensitive matters with hostile nations like Iran. Indeed, since the implementation of the Algiers Accords, the ability of the political branches—particularly the Executive—to manage our hostile relations with Iran has been in a constant state of tension with the desire of United States nationals to assert claims against Iran for acts of terrorism. This is an inherent tension under our Constitution that this Court is not at liberty to resolve.

Finally, what this Court sees as an essential take-away from Dames & Moore is the discussion of the history of the longstanding practice of Executive claims settlement as a means to redress claims of United States nationals against foreign sovereigns. As Justice Rehnquist's discussion points out, Executive settlement of claims is a practice that reaches far back to the time of President George Washington, and numerous other American Presidents have exercised this authority consistently throughout our history. *See* 453 U.S. at 679–688, 101 S. Ct. 2972. Moreover, as the Court's opinion observes, Executive claims settlement is a practice that has been reinforced by Congress though statutes establishing claims settlement commissions, such as the Foreign Claims Settlement Commission under the International Claims Settlement Act of 1949, 22 U.S.C. §§ 1621-1645o. *See Dames & Moore*, 453 U.S. at 680–81, 101 S. Ct. 2972. Historically speaking, claims settlement by the Executive has often proven to be the only effective means of redress of those claims that originate during a period of strained relations with another nation.

Thus, while private litigation is now authorized under the FSIA against state sponsors of terrorism, Executive action is historically an important and necessary practice to ensure relief for United States nationals who have suffered at the hands of an unfriendly foreign government. Courts can only function at the margins on these matters, if at all. Indeed, in comparison to the long-standing tradition of Executive settlement of claims, these private terrorism suits represent a novel and unprecedented experiment, and one that has failed.

This brings the Court to Justice Rehnquist's dissent in Sioux Nation, which he penned in the term immediately prior to that in which he wrote the opinion for the Court in *Dames & Moore v. Regan*. As discussed Part E, *supra*, Sioux Nation, involved a no less challenging and difficult context—the mistreatment of the Sioux

Indians and their divestment from their lands in the Black Hills of South Dakota. The Court's opinion in the case recounts this American tragedy in painstaking detail. *See* 448 U.S. at 374–384, 100 S. Ct. 2716. Like many difficult political issues, the failure to address that injustice apparently had much to do with money, as the Sioux Indians were claiming upwards of a billion dollars in compensation for the land and mineral rights they lost, as compounded over time. *See id.* at 390, 100 S. Ct. 2716.

As noted in Part E, *supra*, Sioux Nation involved a claim under the Taking Clause of the Fifth Amendment. The Sioux Indians claimed that their ouster from their lands in the Blacks Hills by the Federal Government in 1877 violated the terms of the Fort Laramie Treaty of 1868 and therefore amounted to a taking for which just compensation was owed. *See* 448 U.S. at 384, 100 S. Ct. 2716. Over a series of decades, Congress intervened on no less than three occasions in order to allow the Sioux to press their case against the Federal Government. *See id.* at 384–90, 100 S. Ct. 2716. These efforts were consistently opposed by the Executive Branch.

At the culmination of the first action brought by the Sioux Nation in 1942, the Court of Claims ruled squarely against the Indians, holding that the Sioux had merely presented "a moral claim not protected by the Just Compensation Clause." *See id.* at 384, 100 S. Ct. 2716. Thereafter, Congress established the Indian Claims Commission, and the Sioux Indians then resubmitted their Black Hills takings clause claim to that body. *Id.* at 384–85, 100 S. Ct. 2716. After the Commission ruled in favor of the Sioux, the Federal Government appealed to the Court of Claims. *Id.* at 386–87, 100 S. Ct. 2716. Without reaching the merits of the issue, the Court of Claims held that the Sioux Indian's takings claim was barred by the res judicata effect of its 1942 decision. *Id.* at 387, 100 S. Ct. 2716. In the meantime, however, Congress again passed special legislation in favor of the Sioux Indians in which Congress directed the Court of Claims to hear the Sioux Indians claim "[n]otwithstanding any other provisions of law . . . [and] without regard to the defense of res judicata or collateral estoppel." *Id.* at 389, 391, 100 S. Ct. 2716. Pursuant to that special enactment, the Court of Claims promptly reheard the Sioux Indians' case on the merits and ultimately decided in their favor. *Id.* at 389–390, 100 S. Ct. 2716. The Supreme Court granted the Federal Government's petition for a writ of certiorari to in order to review constitutional "questions not only of long-standing concern to the Sioux, but also of significant economic import to the Government." *Id.* at 390, 100 S. Ct. 2716.

In a narrowly crafted decision, the Supreme Court ruled that the doctrine of separation of powers did not prevent the reinstatement of the Sioux Indians claim on the grounds that Congress was free, if it wished to do so, to waive the res judicata effect of the prior judicial decision in the Government's favor. *Id.* at 407, 100 S. Ct. 2716. The Court found that the Federal Government had effectively waived those defenses though the special legislation allowing the Sioux Nation case to be reinstated. *See id.* at 406–407, 100 S. Ct. 2716. In so doing, the Court emphasized Congress' broad powers to acknowledge and pay debts under the Constitution.

See id. at 397, 100 S. Ct. 2716 (citing U.S. CONST., ART. I, § 8, cl. 1). On the merits, the Court upheld the Court of Claims' determination that the Government actions amounted to a taking in violation of the Fifth Amendment and the Court's award of compensation, plus interest, in favor of the Sioux. *Id.* at 432–424, 100 S. Ct. 2716.

As stressed in Part E, *supra*, Justice Rehnquist mounted a vigorous dissent. *See* 448 U.S. at 424–437, 100 S. Ct. 2716. At the heart of Justice Rehnquist's dissent in Sioux Nation was the basic sense that Congress should not be permitted to co-opt the judicial powers of the Article III Courts to resolve a claim decided previously in a manner not to its liking. *See id.* at 427–32, 100 S. Ct. 2716. The Justice stated, "Congress may not attempt to shift its legislative responsibilities and satisfy its constituents by discarding final judgments and ordering new trials." *Id.* at 431–432, 100 S. Ct. 2716. According to Justice Rehnquist, if Congress really wanted to achieve justice for the Indians, it could have simply passed legislation providing the sizable compensation owed. Unlike the majority of the Court at that time, Justice Rehnquist would hold that Congress had impermissibly attempted to usurp judicial power by reopening a case that was previously resolved in a final judgment—albeit unfavorably to the Indians—long ago. *Id.* at 424–25, 100 S. Ct. 2716.

The parallels between the factual circumstances surrounding the claim of the Sioux Indians against the Federal Government and those that now afflict the claims of victims of state-sponsored terrorism in actions under the FSIA terrorism actions are remarkably striking. Similar to the Sioux Nation case, the difficult problems confronting these FSIA terrorism cases have been foisted upon the Article III Courts in part because of a lack of real consensus between our co-equal political branches of Government on how to deal with this controversial topic. Much like the takings claim of the Sioux, Congress persistently pushes for the litigation of claims of terrorism victims in the Federal Courts, where these victims are opposed by the Federal Government and encounter adverse court rulings.

In the dicey political context of these terrorism cases, that message of Justice Rehnquist's dissent in Sioux Nation reads clarion clear: If Congress and the President are serious about finding redress of the injustices suffered by these terrorism victims, then they should pull together to find meaningful, workable solutions, rather than finding new and creative ways to push these tragic claims back onto the Courts. The private litigation has not worked, and simply is not workable, in this highly sensitive context involving affairs with a hostile nation. It is the plenary powers of governance, and not the powers of the courts, that must be used to help these victims overcome the significant challenges they face.

Even though the President has lost much of his "bargaining chip" with respect to Iran because of the depletion of blocked assets under the VTVPA and the TRIA, there is still room for the President to reassert his prerogative in foreign affairs in this sensitive context. In light of the scarcity of Iranian assets and the tension in

United States relations with Iran, the President might consider renewing efforts to move forward with the establishment of a terrorism claims settlement commission, like those that have been introduced in Congress in recent years. This would be consistent with longstanding historical practice as described in *Dames & Moore v. Regan*.

To succeed, however, any proposal in this area will have to do more than simply provide compensation to victims. Experience in these actions has demonstrated convincingly to this Court that what these victims truly want is justice. This point was underscored poignantly in live testimony in this Court during the trial in Peterson case involving the bombing of the Marine Barrack in Beirut. In finding Iran liable for that terrorist attack, this Court recounted some of the testimony. When Lt. Col Howard Gerlach of the United States Marine Corps, who was paralyzed in the attack, was asked about what he hoped to achieve by participating in these actions, he answered:

> Well, I guess there's three words: accountability, deterrence and justice. And they are interrelated. The accountability, and I swear it was on Sunday, I was listening to a rerun of one of the TV—I don't know, Meet the Press or whatever, but Vice President Cheney was talking and he was saying that they, the terrorists feel that they can do things with impunity, and he said ever since the Marines in '83. Yes, there hasn't been any accountability.
>
> Deterrence effect is, in some way, and this is also what he was talking about, was one thing we have to go after—and I think I'm stating this correctly; this is what I heard, is the funding. It's the funding. Even on the radio coming over here, we heard some talk about funding for terrorist organizations.
>
> Then the third thing is the justice, and this refers to the people, a good portion of [whom] are in this room. . . . They lost a large chunk of their lives, young Marines, sons, husbands, fathers, brothers. They were attempting to do a noble thing. They went as peacekeepers in the tradition of this country. . . . [W]e weren't trying to conquer land, we weren't trying to get anything for ourselves; we were really trying in a humanitarian way to help those people in Lebanon. I think this is . . . the day in court, literally and figuratively speaking, for recognition of just how great these guys were.

Peterson I, 264 F. Supp. 2d at 63–64.

On this salient point, this Court recognizes again today, as it did in Peterson in 2003, that "there is little that the Court can do to add to the eloquent words" of witnesses who came to this Court in an effort to "achieve some small measure of justice." *Id.* at 64. It would indeed be naive and insulting to the victims to suggest that these difficult cases can be resolved through cash pay outs from our Federal Government. Nothing could be further from the truth. Justice requires accountably for Iran, and a claims authority that simply doles out compensation to victims will not achieve that end any more than actions before this Court will.[55]

---

55 But *see* KOTLARCZYK, *supra* note 48, at 2044 (suggesting that a compensation fund similar to the September 11th Fund might be the most appropriate way to redress terrorism claims.)

The accountability aspect of the justice these victims seek certainly does not admit of any easy answers, and this is precisely the sort of challenging question that is best left to the capable minds in the Administration and in Congress. It seems to this Court, however, that such a commission might include administrative law judges within the Executive Branch who could adjudicate claims under the terrorism exception and the body of law around it, as modified for such administrative proceedings. Through that process, the Executive Branch could obtain a thorough record of these horrific cases with the active participation of the victims, and thus these matters could then be more easily presented to the policy makers within the Executive Branch who are in the best position to hold Iran accountable. To enhance the prospect of accountability in these matters, the record from hearings on these case could then be published in an annual report to both Congress and the President and made available publicly to the citizens at large in an effort to keep these matters in focus.

Another advantage of a claims commission process within the Executive Branch is that Executive departments, and particularly the Department of State, have superior access to data and information that can help verify these terrorist incidents, and determine more reliably to what extent Iran may have played a role in supporting a particular act of terrorism. With the benefit of such data, the findings of a terrorism claims commission might carry more weight with the State Department and the President during periods of negotiations with Iran and thus further advance the prospect of settlement with Iran down the road. Similarly, the Executive Branch through the Treasury Department, particularly OFAC, is in the best position to locate assets of Iran in the United States, including unblocked assets. Accordingly, if it is empowered to do so, such a commission would be most capable of tracking down these assets and could more effectively liquidate them in satisfaction of claims, which would provide real accountability and might also defray the costs of the commission.

Finally, the commission might work on an ongoing basis to make recommendations on how best to structure a large settlement with Iran, and perhaps other state sponsors of terrorism as well, in the event of normalization. Whatever the case may be, the commission will have to conduct itself in an open and transparent manner, use all available renounces to verify and document terrorist incidents, speak candidly with the victims, and work aggressively on their behalf. Such a terrorism commission, if well resourced and able to report independently on its findings to both political branches of Government, should provide victims of terrorism with a better opportunity for meaningful redress of their claims.

The need for substantial reforms with respect to terrorism lawsuits has become even more apparent over the last several months. As the events in Iran since that country's presidential election in June have revealed, the affairs of that nation are tremendously complex. There are forces for both good and evil in that society, and there are those who want reform and a new day for Iran, and for its relations with the larger international community. While that day is still undoubtedly a long ways off, we cannot ignore its promise. And while we must decry and condemn the current regime and its use of terror in furtherance of its political objectives—we cannot forget the courage of the people, including women and young people, who took to the streets of Tehran and elsewhere in the hope of a better day.

What we have seen from the citizens of Iran is inspiring and brings a brief flicker of hope for a lasting peace and a chance to settle grievances—real or perceived—whatever they may be. It is in that process of normalization, whenever and however it might occur, that there is the best chance for achieving justice for all those who have suffered over the last thirty years. Regrettably, the same cannot be said of the FSIA terrorism exception—whether § 1605(a)(7) or § 1605A. Frankly, these measures are politically superficial and overly simplistic solutions to much deeper problems. These measures are empty political gestures that offer no justice for so many victims who—whether intentionally or not—have been exploited by the politics of these terrorism lawsuits.

There is an important dialogue occurring in our nation over how best to deal with terrorism, including state sponsors of terrorism like Iran, but neither tough rhetoric nor large, unenforceable court judgments will help to resolve these extraordinarily sensitive and complex matters. By fanning flames and fueling unrealistic exceptions, these court actions do not contribute to a productive dialogue. These actions may even add to the atmosphere of tension and hostility between Iran and the United States that moves that rogue country further down the path of isolation and paranoia, thereby contributing to the conditions that strengthen and further the ends of a regime that seems determined to do us in. Certainly, these actions under the FSIA terrorism exception do nothing to enhance the President's ability to carefully and intelligently respond to a host of sensitive matters pertaining to our relations with Iran, and there are indeed many substantial competing considerations in this context. The most paramount of these is the grave risk of nuclear proliferation.

Make no mistake about it, terrorism is a grave threat to our society. Our citizens will continue to be targeted precisely because they are Americans.[56] The White House may have declared the war on terrorism over,[57] but the threat of terrorism

56 Terrorists attack American targets more often than those of any other country. America's preeminent role in the world guarantees that this will continue to be the case, and the threat of attacks creating massive casualties is growing. If the United States is to protect itself, if it is to remain a world leader, this nation must develop and continuously refine sound counterterrorism policies appropriate to the rapidly changing world around us."

Nat'l Comm'n on Terrorism, Countering the Changing Threat of International Terrorism, at iii (2008), available at http://www.gpo.gov/nct/nct1.pdf.

57 The Administration has apparently decided to stop using the phrase "war on terrorism." *See* John Brennan, Assistant to the President for Homeland Sec. and Counterterrorism, A New Approach for Safeguarding Americans, Address at the Center for Strategic and International Studies (Aug. 6, 2009) ("[T]he president does not describe this as a 'war on terrorism.'") (transcript available at http:// csis.org/files/attachments/090806—brennan—transcript.pdf); *see also* John Ward, U.S. No Longer at War with "Terrorism"; Administration Deems Terms from Bush Era Unacceptable, Wash. Times, Aug. 7, 2009, at A1.

remains very real, and Americans will continue to suffer casualties as a result of this insidious and murderous evil. These victims certainly deserve justice, but the private litigation approach to redress is unsustainable and works at cross purposes of the President's foreign policy initiatives other developments that may lead to lasting change and peace. Nothing that occurs in this Court can achieve those ends.

Thus, today's decision is merely a roadmap for the long road ahead that awaits these victims in renewed litigation before this Court under the FSIA terrorism exception, a provision of law that so far has gotten the victims of terrorism no closer to the justice they seek.[58] What this Court really hopes for, however, is that some of our political leaders may read this opinion and consider the experiences of this Court in a broader effort to obtain meaningful reform. Our political leaders must find a way to muster the commitment and courage it will take to address the fundamental problems—the roadblocks—that will continue to undermine the efforts of these victims to find justice in new lawsuits under § 1605A. This meaningless charade under the FSIA has gone on far too long. It is high time for our political leaders to consider the flaws of this private litigation experience and address the deeper political problems that this Court has no authority to resolve.

This Court's experience with these terrorism lawsuits might not offer any immediate answers, but it may lend some valuable insights, and thus this Court hopes these insights—these lessons learned—will assist in a larger dialogue about reform. Is there a better way to address these important terrorism cases and achieve justice for the victims? It is in this spirit that today's decision is offered. This opinion is in no way intended as a criticism of the victims and their noble efforts, but as a call to action for their cause. If the President and Congress are able to candidly acknowledge the both the legitimate grievances of the terrorism victims and the fundamental problems that undercut the private litigation model long embraced by FSIA terrorism exception, they can undoubtedly develop a workable system of redress for these tragic cases. Key Executive Branch officials, including the Secretary of State, the Attorney General, and the Secretary of the Treasury, among others will likely prove crucial to the success of such an undertaking.

Whatever measures might be advanced to aid terrorism victims in this context should neither limit the President's ability to extend his hand nor encourage Iran to continue to clench its fist. Now more than ever, it is important for our President to be able to speak with one voice and to marshal the full measure of American power and diplomacy in search of better relations with Iran in the interest of all Americans. This Court is concerned, however, that if these unsustainable civil actions continue to fan flames and exhaust terrorism victims who have already suffered enough,

---

58 This opinion speaks only to 20 pending cases, which is only a fraction of the number now pending against Iran in this Court. This judge has several more not included in this opinion, and there dozens of others representing billions in potential liability for Iran that are now pending with other judges of this Court.

judgments entered by this Court will continue to undermine the President's ability to address sensitive matters of national security and will do so at crucial times when the President's ability to act is likely to matter most.

L. An Invitation for the United States to Participate in these Actions

This Court has found on past occasions that the appearance of the United States in actions against Iran has greatly assisted the Court. The United States often brings to light additional, relevant legal authorities and arguments bearing on the questions presented and generally provides the kind of broader perspective that this Court must have when addressing cases against foreign sovereigns. For these reasons, the United States will be invited to file a brief within 60 days in which the United States may express its views regarding any of the issues raised by this consolidated opinion and the accompanying order. Filing a brief by invitation of this Court will not prejudice the United States with respect to any submissions it may wish to make in response to specific filings by plaintiffs in any of the civil actions addressed today.

Additionally, in an effort to further the case-management function of this opinion, this Court will hold a series of status conferences for all the civil cases addressed in this decision. The United States will be invited to attend the status conferences along with the parties. The Court anticipates holding similar status conferences in these cases approximately every 60 days thereafter to ensure that these matters remain on track. Many of these cases have been languishing on the Court's docket for quite some time, and thus the Court is eager to bring these matters to conclusion as expeditiously as possible. The clerk will contact counsel for plaintiffs and the United States to schedule a time on the Court's docket that is convenient for all parties.

CONCLUSION

Nearly thirty years ago, the Hostage Crisis began as Islamic students seized the United States Embassy in Tehran and took more than 50 Americans as hostages. For over four hundred long and painful days, Americans looked on with shock and horror as they followed the nightly news coverage of the events in Tehran. It seemed as if our whole nation was being held hostage. On the eve of Ronald Reagan's Inauguration, the hostage standoff was finally settled peacefully through the conclusion of the Algiers Accords on January 19, 1981. All American hostages were released the following day, only moments after President Reagan took the oath of office. Little did we know at that time that the Hostage Crisis merely signaled the beginning of what would become an increasingly hostile era of relations between the Islamic Republic of Iran and the United States.

Less than three years later, in Beirut, Lebanon, more than two hundred United States Marines and numerous other uniformed service members, most of whom were asleep in their barracks, would die in a tremendously powerful explosion—the result of a highly sophisticated and carefully executed suicide bombing orchestrated by Hezbollah operatives acting with training, guidance, and other material support from Iran's Ministry of Information and Security. By January 1984, Iran was designated as a state sponsor of terrorism by the State Department. In the years that followed, Iran's material support for terrorism would lead to unprecedented suicide bombing attacks throughout the Gaza Strip and Israel. Schools and buses were frequent targets of the terrorist perpetrators of these attacks—unjustified killings of innocents in contravention of all the laws of humanity—which have claimed the lives of many bright young American men and women.

Since 1996, the civil cases brought under the FSIA state sponsor of terrorism exception have chronicled the senseless violence and carnage that have dotted the last three decades of hostile relations between the Islamic Republic of Iran and the United States. These terrorism cases are the tragic stories of the many victims—like the more than one thousand victims represented here today—who have suffered dearly as a result of a campaign of terror that has included hostage takings, torture, suicide bombings, and assassinations.

Regrettably, the tragedies represented by these cases under the FSIA terrorism exception have been compounded by what has turned into a long and often futile quest for justice under this novel provision of law. The reality is that the FSIA terrorism exception, as applied by our Article III Courts of limited jurisdiction and powers, has not provided the victims the relief they deserve. Instead of finding justice, most of these plaintiffs have found themselves holding unenforceable judgments. They have faced years of costly, emotionally draining, and time-consuming postjudgment litigation. They have often been opposed by the Executive Branch, and their struggles have rarely produced positive results. Similarly, these victims have fought in the halls of Congress for ad hoc and often ineffectual legislative fixes in an effort to give some real teeth to this failed provision of law.

This Court commends Stephen Flatow, Deborah Peterson, and the many others who have bravely pursued justice under the terrorism exception. They have brought to light to an important issue, and their cases in the courts provide an important historical record concerning all those who have been injured or killed as a result of state-sponsored terrorism. Our Nation has been served by their efforts. It is out of respect and appreciation for these victims—and out of observance of the frustrations that experience with this terrorism law has borne out over time in proceedings before this Court—that this Court expresses the view that these FSIA terrorism actions cannot achieve justice as intended. In the long and difficult process that this Court has witnessed over the last decade, these cases have consumed substantial judicial resources while achieving few tangible results for the victims. The problems encountered by the Flatows a decade ago are the same problems experienced by Deborah Peterson today. More fundamentally, the rule of law is being frustrated in what now seems to be an increasingly counterproductive and largely academic exercise.

For the sake of these terrorism victims, however, and for the sake of our Nation as a whole, these actions should not continue on as academic exercises. The stakes are far too high, both in terms of the losses sustained, and in terms of the larger foreign policy interests of the United States.

To be sure, the current regime in Iran is apparently not going away any time soon and the problem of state-sponsored terrorism will be with us for years to come, and long after the judges of this Court who have presided over this grand experiment have passed from the bench. But these are complicated matters. If anything, the events of the last few months and weeks have underscored the depth of that complexity. There are forces for evil in that country, as there are in any nation, but there are also forces for good, and with that there is a glimmer of hope for a better future.

Meanwhile, here at home, the reforms implemented as part of § 1083 of the 2008 NDAA last year—which are just now being implemented in individual cases here today—will not, in this Court's humble opinion, lend much support to the cause of these victims or their long march toward justice. These most recent reforms, like others before them, are premised on the same failed private-litigation model that has, in effect, doomed these actions from the start. These terrorism cases—whether under § 1605(a)(7) or § 1605A—are likely to face the same obstacles discussed in this opinion, such as the Algiers Accords, limited assets to satisfy judgments, conflicting laws and regulations, and the President's foreign policy prerogative, among others. These are intractable problems that are more often political, rather than jurisprudential, and so it seems that the new § 1605A, although well intentioned, is destined to prolong and perhaps aggravate the ways in which the same intractable issues have continuously foiled plaintiffs in these cases time and again. Today, more than a decade after these suits began—and with the majority of Iran's blocked assets depleted to pay for earlier judgments—the hope for justice under the terrorism exception is growing increasingly distant and unobtainable.

But these difficult realities should not give license to those who would rather ignore the plight of American victims of terrorism. Instead, this Court sincerely hopes that today, on the dawn of a new presidential administration—one that remains committed to a policy of engagement with Iran and the Middle East as whole—that the President, the Secretary of State, the Attorney General, the Secretary of the Treasury, and leaders in Congress will look at these matters and look for ways to make real change. The President should be commended for his work to foster a dialogue with the Middle East generally and the Muslim world specifically. In light of this fresh and inspiring approach, perhaps today more than ever there is hope for real reform.

The challenges that confront the President with respect to our relations with Iran are as daunting as ever, and thus this Court must leave it to the experts in the political branches to consider whether a balanced and meaningful political compromise can be reached with respect to these difficult terrorism cases. It seems to this judge that it is time for a new approach, and perhaps it is time to think more systematically about how these cases can work in concert, rather than in conflict, with a broader strategy towards the goals of better relations with the Muslim world, peace in the Middle East, and the eradication of terrorism.

To all the plaintiffs, this Court wishes to stress that it, as always, will endeavor to see to it that plaintiffs in these actions get all the relief to which they are entitled under the law. This Court continues to hope that one day soon justice might be achieved.

MINISTRY OF DEFENSE AND SUPPORT FOR THE ARMED FORCES OF THE ISLAMIC REPUBLIC OF IRAN v. DARIUSH ELAHI

129 S. Ct. 1732 (2009)
Decided April 21, 2009

David J. Bederman argued the cause for petitioner.

Douglas Hallward-Driemeier argued the cause for the United States, as amicus curiae, by special leave of court.

Carter G. Phillips argued the cause for respondent.

Breyer, J., delivered the opinion of the Court, in which Roberts, C. J., and Stevens, Scalia, Thomas, and Alito, JJ., joined, and in which Kennedy, Souter, and Ginsburg, JJ., joined as to Parts I and II. Kennedy, J., filed an opinion concurring in part and dissenting in part, in which Souter and Ginsburg, JJ., joined.

Justice Breyer delivered the opinion of the Court.

Dariush Elahi, the respondent, sued Iran, claiming that Iran unlawfully participated in the assassination of his brother, and he obtained a default judgment of about $312 million. Seeking to collect some of the money, he has tried to attach an asset belonging to Iran, namely a $2.8 million judgment that Iran obtained against a California company called Cubic Defense Systems, Inc. (Cubic Judgment). Iran has asserted a defense of sovereign immunity in order to prevent the attachment. See Foreign Sovereign Immunities Act of 1976, 28 U.S.C. § 1610.

Since Iran is a sovereign nation, Elahi cannot attach the Cubic Judgment unless he finds an exception to the principle of sovereign immunity that would allow him to do so. *See Ministry of Defense and Support for Armed Forces of Islamic Republic of Iran v. Elahi*, 546 U.S. 450, 126 S. Ct. 1193, 163 L. Ed. 2d 1047 (2006) *(per curiam)*. As the case reaches us, the Terrorism Risk Insurance Act of 2002 (TRIA), § 201(a), 116 Stat. 2337, note following 28 U.S.C. § 1610, provides the sole possible exception. That Act authorizes holders of terrorism-related judgments against Iran, such as Elahi, to attach Iranian assets that the United States has "*blocked.*"

Ibid. (emphasis added). And we initially decide whether Iran's Cubic Judgment is a "blocked asset" within the terms of that Act.

Even if the Cubic Judgment is a blocked asset, however, Elahi still cannot attach it if he waived his right to do so. And we next decide whether Elahi waived that right when, in return for partial compensation from the Government, he agreed not to attach "*property that is at issue in claims against the United States before an international tribunal.*" Victims of Trafficking and Violence Protection Act of 2000 (VPA), § 2002(d)(5)(B), as added by TRIA § 201(c)(4), 116 Stat. 2339, note following 28 U.S.C. § 1610 (emphasis added).

We ultimately hold that the Cubic Judgment was not a "blocked asset" at the time the Court of Appeals handed down its decision in this case. We recognize that since that time new Executive Branch action may have "blocked" that asset; but, in light of the posture of the case, we do not decide whether it has done so. Rather, we determine that Elahi cannot attach the Cubic Judgment regardless, for the Judgment is "at issue" in a claim against the United States before the Iran-U. S. Claims Tribunal. The Judgment consequently falls within the terms of Elahi's waiver.

I.

We initially set forth key background elements, including in this section the events necessary to understand the "blocked asset" question, while leaving for Part III, *infra,* additional background matters related to Elahi's waiver.

A.

The Cubic Judgment arose out of a 1977 contract between Cubic Defense Systems, a California company and Iran's Ministry of Defense. (We shall refer to the Ministry, for present purposes an inseparable part of the Iranian State, as "Iran." *See Ministry of Defense and Support for Armed Forces of Islamic Republic of Iran v. Cubic Defense Systems, Inc.,* 495 F.3d 1024, 1035–1036 (CA9 2007)). Cubic there promised to supply Iran with certain military goods, namely an air combat training system, for which Iran promised to pay approximately $18 million dollars. In 1979, after Iran had paid some of the money but before Cubic had sent the training system, the Iranian Revolution broke out, militants in Iran seized American hostages, and President Carter "*blocked* all property and interests in property of the Government of Iran . . . subject to the jurisdiction of the United States." Exec. Order No. 12170, 3 CFR 457 (1979 Comp.) (emphasis added), promulgated pursuant to the authority of International Emergency Economic Powers Act (IEEPA), 50 U.S.C. §§ 1701–1702 (2000 ed. and Supp. V); 31 CFR § 535.201 (1980).

About a year later, on January 19, 1981, Iran and the United States settled the crisis, in part with an agreement called the "Algiers Accords." 20 I. L. M. 224. Under the Accords, the United States agreed to "restore the financial position of Iran, in so far as possible, to that which existed prior to November 14, 1979," *ibid.*, and (with some exceptions) to "arrange, subject to the provisions of U. S. law applicable prior to November 14, 1979, for the transfer to Iran of all Iranian properties," *id.*, at 227. The President then lifted the legal prohibitions against transactions involving Iranian property. *See* Exec. Orders Nos. 12277–12282, 3 CFR 105–113 (1981 Comp.); 31 CFR §§ 535.211–535.215 (1981). In doing so, he ordered the transfer to Iran of Iranian financial assets and most other Iranian property "as directed . . . by the Government of Iran," Exec. Order No. 12281, 3 CFR 112 (1981 Comp.). Shortly thereafter, the Treasury Department issued a general license authorizing "[t]ransactions involving property in which Iran . . . has an interest" where "[t]he property comes within the jurisdiction of the United States . . . after January 19, 1981, or . . . [t]he interest in the property . . . arises after January 19, 1981." 31 CFR § 535.579(a).

The Algiers Accords also set up an international arbitration tribunal, the Iran-U. S. Claims Tribunal (or Tribunal), to resolve disputes between the two nations concerning each other's performance under the Algiers Accords. The Tribunal would also resolve disputes concerning contracts and agreements between the two nations that were outstanding on January 19, 1981. 20 I. L. M., at 230–231. The Tribunal's jurisdiction included claims by nationals of one state against the other state, but it did not include claims by one state against nationals of the other state. *Id.*, at 231–232.

B.

In January 1982, Iran filed two Cubic-based claims in the Tribunal. In Case No. B61, Iran claimed that between 1979 and 1981 the United States had wrongly barred the transfer of certain military equipment, including the Cubic air combat training system, to Iran. Iran asked the Tribunal to order the United States either to issue an export license for the equipment or to pay Iran damages. App. to Brief for United States as *Amicus Curiae* 22a, 24a, 31a.

In Case No. B66, Iran claimed that Cubic had breached its contract to deliver the training system partly because the United States had taken actions contrary to the Algiers Accords. Again Iran asked the Tribunal to order either the issuance of an export license for the equipment or the payment of damages. *Id.*, at 1a, 2a, 9a–10a. In April 1987 the Tribunal dismissed this second case (No. B66) on the grounds that the Iran-Cubic contract imposed no obligations on the United States and that the Tribunal lacked jurisdiction to consider a suit by a state (Iran) against a private party (Cubic). *Ministry of Nat. Defense of Islamic Republic of Iran* v. *United States,* 14 Iran-U. S. Cl. Trib. Rep. 276, 277–278.

Iran, believing that Cubic had breached its contract, then went to arbitration before the arbitration tribunal specified in the Cubic contract, namely the International Court of Arbitration of the International Chamber of Commerce. Iran asked that arbitration tribunal to award it restitution and damages.

In May 1997 the arbitrators issued their decision. The arbitrators found that prior to the Iranian Revolution, prior to the hostage crisis, and prior to the blocking of any Iranian assets, (1) Iran and Cubic had themselves agreed that they would temporarily discontinue (but not terminate) the contract; and (2) Cubic had agreed to try to sell the training system to another buyer and to settle accounts with Iran later. The arbitrators further found that after the crisis (in September 1981) (3) Cubic successfully sold a modified version of the system to Canada. *Ministry of Defense and Support for Armed Forces of Islamic Republic of Iran* v. *Cubic Int'l Sales Corp.*, No. 7365/FMC (Int'l Ct. of Arbitration of Int'l Chamber of Commerce), pp. 32–33, 36–40, 50–51, reprinted in 13 Mealey's Int'l Arbitration Report pp. G-4, G-15 to G-18, G-21 (Oct. 1998) (Arbitration Award). The arbitrators concluded that Cubic had not lived up to this modified agreement. And, after taking account of the advance payments that Iran had made to Cubic, the funds that Cubic had spent, the amount that Canada had paid Cubic, and various other items, they awarded Iran $2.8 million plus interest. *Id.*, P C.18.3(a), at G–31.

Cubic refused to pay Iran this money. Iran then sued in the Federal District Court for the Southern District of California to enforce the arbitration award. The District Court confirmed the award and entered a final judgment ordering Cubic to pay $2.8 million plus interest to Iran. That judgment is the Cubic Judgment. *Ministry of Defense and Support for Armed Forces of Islamic Republic of Iran v. Cubic Defense Systems, Inc.,* 29 F.Supp.2d 1168, 1174 (1998) (final judgment entered Aug. 10, 1999).

C.

In February 2000 Elahi brought a tort action against Iran in the Federal District Court for the District of Columbia. Elahi claimed that Iranian agents had murdered his brother. *See* 28 U.S.C. § 1605(a)(7) (2000 ed.) (lifting sovereign immunity of state sponsors of certain kinds of terrorism) (subsequently replaced by National Defense Authorization Act for Fiscal Year 2008, § 1083(a)(1), 122 Stat. 338, 28 U.S.C. A. § 1605A); Foreign Operations, Export Financing, and Related Programs Appropriations Act, 1997, § 589, 110 Stat. 3009-172, note following 28 U.S.C. § 1605 (providing tort cause of action). Iran did not answer the complaint. The District Court found Iran in default, and it awarded Elahi nearly $12 million in compensatory damages and $300 million in punitive damages. *Elahi v. Islamic Republic of Iran*, 124 F.Supp.2d 97 (DC 2000).

In 2001 Elahi filed a notice of lien against Iran's Cubic Judgment. He thereby sought to satisfy from the Cubic Judgment a portion of what Iran owed him under his own default judgment against Iran. Iran opposed the lien. It argued that the Cubic Judgment, as property of the sovereign state of Iran, was immune from attachment or execution. The District Court denied immunity. *Ministry of Defense and Support for Armed Forces of Islamic Republic of Iran v. Cubic Defense Systems, Inc.,* 236 F.Supp.2d 1140, 1152 (SD Cal. 2002).

The Court of Appeals affirmed the denial. *Ministry of Defense and Support for Armed Forces of Islamic Republic of Iran v. Cubic Defense Systems, Inc.*, 385 F.3d 1206 (CA9 2004). The Court of Appeals thought that the Ministry of Defense of

Iran had lost its immunity from attachment because of a special statutory exception that permits a creditor to attach the property of an "agency or instrumentality of a foreign state engaged in commercial activity in the United States"—where the creditor seeks the property to satisfy a terrorism-related judgment. 28 U.S.C. § 1610(b). *See* 385 F.3d at 1219–1222. But, on review here, we pointed out (in a *per curiam* opinion) that the sovereign immunity exception upon which the Ninth Circuit had relied—the exception for the property of an entity that has "engaged in commercial activity," § 1610(b)(2) —applies only to property of an "agency or instrumentality" of a foreign state. It does not apply to property of an entity that itself is an inseparable part of the foreign state. § 1610(a). *Elahi*, 546 U.S., at 452–453, 126 S. Ct. 1193, 163 L. Ed. 2d 1047.

We remanded the case, and on remand, the Ninth Circuit held that the Ministry of Defense fell into the latter category (an inseparable part of the state of Iran), not the former (an "agency or instrumentality" of Iran). 495 F.3d 1024, 1035–1036 (2007). Hence Elahi could not take advantage of the "engaged in commercial activities" exception. The Court of Appeals also found inapplicable a slightly different exception applicable to "property . . . of a foreign state . . . used for a commercial activity in the United States," 28 U.S.C. § 1610(a). 495 F.3d at 1036–1037.

Nonetheless the Court of Appeals found yet another exception that it believed denied Iran its sovereign immunity defense. The court pointed out that in 2002 Congress had enacted the TRIA. That Act permitted a person with a terrorism-related judgment to attach an asset of the responsible "terrorist" state to satisfy the judgment, "[n]otwithstanding any other provision of law," provided that the asset was a "blocked asset." § 201(a), 116 Stat. 2337. The Court of Appeals noted that the Cubic Judgment arose out of a pre-1981 contract with Iran involving an air combat training system for Iran, and that President Carter had blocked virtually all Iranian assets following the Iranian hostage crisis. See Exec. Order No. 12170, 44 Fed. Reg. 65729 ("block[ing] all property and interests in property of the Government of Iran . . . subject to the jurisdiction of the United States"), promulgated pursuant to the authority of International Emergency Economic Powers Act, 50 U.S.C. §§ 1701–1702 (2000 ed. and Supp. V); 31 CFR § 535.201. The Court of Appeals then held that the President had never unblocked the asset in question. 495 F.3d at 1033. In its view, the many unblocking orders that were issued after the 1981 Algiers Accords, *see, e.g.*, Exec. Orders Nos. 12277–12282, 3 CFR 105–113; 31 CFR §§ 535.211–535.215, 535.579(a), did not apply because those unblocking orders omitted "military goods such as the [training system that underlay the Cubic Judgment]." 495 F.3d at 1033.

The Court of Appeals also rejected Iran's argument that Elahi had waived his right to attach the Cubic Judgment regardless (a matter to which we shall turn in Part III). And the court concluded that Elahi was free to attach the Judgment. *Id.*, at 1037.

Iran, with the support of the Department of State, asked us to grant certiorari. We did so, and we shall consider both aspects of the Court of Appeals' determination.

II.

A.

We turn first to the question whether the Cubic Judgment was a "blocked asset." The Ninth Circuit held that the asset in question consisted of Iran's interest in military goods, namely an air combat training system, which it believed the Executive Branch had failed to unblock after the Iranian hostage crisis ended. None of the parties here, however, supports the Ninth Circuit's determination. And neither do we.

The basic reason we cannot accept the Ninth Circuit's rationale is that we do not believe Cubic's air combat training system is the asset here in question. Elahi does not seek to attach that system. Cubic sent the system itself to Canada, where, as far as we know, it remains. Rather, Elahi seeks to attach a judgment enforcing an arbitration award based upon Cubic's failure to account to Iran for Iran's share of the proceeds of that system's sale. And neither the Cubic Judgment nor the sale proceeds that it represents were blocked assets at the time the Court of Appeals issued its decision.

In 1981, the Treasury Department issued an order that authorized "[t]ransactions involving property in which Iran . . . has an interest" where "*[t]he interest in the property . . . arises after January 19, 1981.*" 31 CFR § 535.579(a)(1) (emphasis added). As the Court of Appeals itself pointed out, Iran's interest in the Cubic Judgment arose "on December 7, 1998, when the district court confirmed the [arbitration] award." 385 F.3d at 1224. Since it arose more than 17 years "after January 19, 1981," the Cubic Judgment falls within the terms of Treasury's order. And that fact, in our view, is sufficient to treat the Judgment as unblocked.

Iran's interest in the property that underlies the Cubic Judgment also arose after January 19, 1981. As the International Court of Arbitration held, Cubic and Iran entered into their initial contract before 1981. But they later agreed to discontinue (but not to terminate) the contract. Arbitration Award G-15, G-21. They agreed that Cubic would try to sell the system elsewhere. *Id.*, P C.9.15, at G-14. And they further agreed that they would take "final decisions" about who owed what to whom "only . . . once the result of Cubic's attempt to resell the System" was "known." *Id.*, P B.10.7, at G-17.

Cubic completed its sale of the system (to Canada) in October 1982. *Id.*, P B.12.14, at G-22. And the arbitrators referred to October 1982 as "the date the Parties had in mind when they agreed to await the outcome of Cubic's resale attempts." *Ibid.* Only then was Cubic "in a position to reasonably, comprehensively and precisely account for the reuse of components originally manufactured for Iran and for any modification costs." *Ibid.* For those reasons, and in light of the arbitrators' findings, we must conclude that October 1982 is the time when Iran's claim to proceeds arose.

The upshot is that, whether we consider Iran's "interest in property" as its interest in the Cubic Judgment itself or its underlying interest in the proceeds of the

Canadian sale, the interest falls within the terms of the Treasury Department's general license authorizing "[t]ransactions involving property in which Iran . . . has an interest" where "[t]he interest in the property . . . arises after January 19, 1981." 31 CFR § 535.579(a). And, as we said, that fact is sufficient for present purposes to treat the asset as having been unblocked at the time the Ninth Circuit issued the decision below.

Finally, even if we were to assume (as the Ninth Circuit held) that the relevant asset were Iran's pre-1981 interest in the air combat training system itself, we should still conclude that that asset was not "blocked" at the time of the decision below. As the Government points out, such an interest falls directly within the scope of Executive Order No. 12281, an unblocking order that required property owned by Iran to be transferred "as directed . . . by the Government of Iran." *See also* 31 CFR § 535.215(a). None of the four authorities upon which the Ninth Circuit relied indicates the contrary conclusion. First, the Circuit cited the Arms Export Control Act, 82 Stat. 1321, 22 U.S.C. § 2751 *et seq.*, and its implementing regulations, a statute and regulations which regulate arms shipments. It is true that, notwithstanding Executive Order No. 12281, the export of certain military equipment remained subject to regulation under other statutes, including the Arms Export Control Act. *See* 31 CFR § 535.215(c). But that fact does not show that military equipment remained *blocked* under IEEPA. The Court of Appeals next cited the 1979 Executive Order freezing Iranian assets, Exec. Order No. 12170, 3 CFR 457 (Comp. 1980)—but it failed to consider the effect of the subsequent unblocking order just discussed. The Court of Appeals also relied on a 2005 Presidential notice extending the national emergency with respect to Iran, 70 Fed. Reg. 69039, but that notice did not impose any additional restrictions on Iranian assets. Finally, the Court of Appeals pointed to a Treasury Department guidance document, which states that "[c]ertain assets"—consisting "mainly of military and dual-use property"—"related to . . . claims" by "U. S. nationals . . . against Iran or Iranian entities" still being litigated in the Tribunal "remain blocked in the United States." Office of Foreign Assets Control, Dept. of Treasury, Foreign Assets Control Regulations for Exporters and Importers 23 (2007). But the training system does not fall into the category of assets identified by the guidance document. The system neither "remain[s] . . . in the United States" (having been sent to Canada), nor was it related to claims by "*U. S. nationals . . . against Iran or Iranian entities*" before the Tribunal. In sum, no authority supports the Ninth Circuit's conclusion that an Iranian interest in the training system itself would be a "blocked asset." And none of the parties defend the Ninth Circuit's conclusion here.

B.

Although the Cubic Judgment was not a blocked asset at the time the Court of Appeals reached its decision, the Government believes that it is a blocked asset now. In 2005 the President issued a new Executive Order that blocks assets held by proliferators of weapons of mass destruction. Exec. Order No. 13382, 3 CFR

170 (2005 Comp.). And in 2007, after the Court of Appeals issued its decision, the State Department designated certain component parts of Iran's Ministry of Defense as entities whose property and interests in property are blocked under Executive Order No. 13382. *See* 72 Fed. Reg. 71991–71992. If the Iranian entity to which the Cubic Judgment belongs falls within the terms of the State Department's designation, then presumably that asset is blocked at this time.

The problem for the Government, however, is that Iran does not agree that the relevant parts of its Ministry of Defense fall within the scope of the State Department's designation. Thus the matter is in dispute. The lower courts have not considered that dispute. The relevant arguments have not been set forth in detail here. And in such circumstances we normally would remand the case, permitting the lower courts to decide the issue in the first instance. *See, e.g., F. Hoffmann-La Roche Ltd v. Empagran S. A.*, 542 U.S. 155, 175, 124 S. Ct. 2359, 159 L. Ed. 2d 226 (2004). Consequently, we shall not decide whether the new Executive Branch actions have blocked the Cubic Judgment. Instead, we turn to the "waiver" question. And our answer (that Elahi has waived his right to attach the Cubic Judgment) makes it unnecessary to remand the blocking question for further consideration.

III.

As we have just said, the second question concerns Elahi's waiver of his right to attach the Cubic Judgment. In 2000, Congress enacted a statute that offers some compensation to certain individuals, including Elahi, who hold terrorism-related judgments against Iran. VPA § 2002, as amended by TRIA § 201(c). The Act requires those who receive that compensation to relinquish "*all rights to execute against or attach property that is at issue in claims against the United States before an international tribunal,* [or] that is the subject of awards rendered by such tribunal." § 2002(a)(2)(D), 114 Stat. 1542; *see also* § 2002(d)(5)(B), as added by TRIA § 201(c)(4) (cross-referencing § 2002(a)(2)(D)). In 2003 the Government paid Elahi $2.3 million under the Act as partial compensation for his judgment against Iran. Brief for Respondent 9. And at that time, Elahi signed a waiver form that mirrors the statutory language. App. to Pet. for Cert. 30 (citing 68 Fed. Reg. 8077, 8081 (2003)).

The question is whether the Cubic Judgment "is at issue in claims" against the United States before an "international tribunal," namely the Iran-U. S. Claims Tribunal. If so, the Cubic Judgment falls within the terms of Elahi's waiver. The Court of Appeals believed the Judgment was not "at issue." 495 F.3d at 1030–1031. But we find to the contrary.

A review of the record in Iran-U. S. Claims Tribunal Case No. B61 leads us to conclude that the Cubic Judgment is "at issue" before that Tribunal. In Case No. B61 Iran argued that, between 1979 and 1981, the United States had wrongly prevented the transfer of Cubic's air combat training system to Iran. Iran asked the Tribunal, among other things, to order the United States to pay damages. Statement of Claim, *Islamic Republic of Iran* v. *United States* (filed Jan. 19, 1982), App. to

Brief for United States as *Amicus Curiae* 22a, 24a, 31a. In its briefing before the Tribunal, Iran acknowledged that any amount it recovered from Cubic would "be recuperated from the remedy sought" against the United States. App. 76, n 2. And Iran sent a letter to the United States in which it said that any amounts it actually received from Cubic would be "recouped from the remedy sought against the United States in Case B61." App. to Brief for United States as *Amicus Curiae* 84a. *But* Iran added that the Cubic Judgment could *not* be used as a setoff *insofar as it had been attached by creditors. Id.*, at 85a.

Meanwhile, in a rebuttal brief before the Tribunal, the United States, while arguing that in fact it owed Iran nothing, added that at the very least Iran must set off the amount "already . . . awarded" by the International Court of Arbitration (namely, the $2.8 million awarded to Iran from Cubic) against any money awarded by the Tribunal. *Id.*, at 52a, 80a–81a, and n 32. And the United States' demand for a setoff applies even if third parties have attached the Cubic Judgment. See Tr. of Tribunal Hearing, in No. B61 (Iran-U. S. Cl. Trib., Dec. 7 and 12, 2006), App. to Brief for Respondent 37, 38–39, 41, 42.

The upshot is a dispute about the Cubic Judgment. The United States argues (and argued before the Tribunal) that the Tribunal should set off the $2.8 million that the Cubic Judgment represents against any award that the Tribunal may make against the United States in Case No. B61. Iran argues (and argued before the Tribunal) that the Tribunal should not set off the $2.8 million insofar as third parties have attached the Judgment.

To put the matter in terms of the language of Elahi's waiver, one can say for certain that the Cubic Judgment is "property." And Case No. B61 itself is a "clai[m] against the United States before an international tribunal." We can also be reasonably certain that how the Tribunal should use that property is also under dispute or in question in that claim. Moreover, since several parties other than Elahi have already attached the Cubic Judgment, see Brief for United States as *Amicus Curiae* 20, the question whether an attached claim can be used as a setoff is potentially significant, irrespective of Elahi's own efforts to attach the judgment.

Are these circumstances sufficient to place the Cubic Judgment "at issue" in Case No. B61? Elahi argues not. He points out that the Cubic Judgment does not appear on a list of property contained in Iran's statement of claim in Case No. B61; nor is it the subject of any other claim before the Tribunal. Indeed, Iran and the United States do not dispute the Cubic Judgment's validity; they do not dispute the Cubic Judgment's ownership; and they do not dispute the fact that the United States' asset freeze had no adverse effect on the Cubic Judgment or on Iran's entitlement to the Cubic Judgment. As the dissent correctly points out, the Judgment is not "at issue" in any of these senses.

The Judgment will neither be suspended nor modified by the Tribunal in Case No. B61, nor is the Judgment property claimed by Iran from the United States in that case, *see post*, at ____ – ____, 173 L. Ed. 2d, at 527–529.

But that does not end the matter. The question is whether, for purposes of the VPA, a judgment can nevertheless be "at issue" before the Tribunal *even* when it will not be suspended or modified by the Tribunal and when it is not claimed by Iran from the United States. Here, a significant dispute about the Cubic Judgment still remains, namely a dispute about whether it can be used by the Tribunal as a setoff. And in our view, that dispute is sufficient to put the Judgment "at issue" in the case.

For one thing, we do not doubt that the setoff matter is "under dispute" or "in question" in Case No. B61, and those words typically define the term "at issue." Black's Law Dictionary 136 (8th ed. 2004). In the event that the Tribunal finds the United States liable in Case No. B61, the total sum awarded to Iran by the Tribunal will depend on whether the Judgment is used as a setoff. And whether the Judgment can be so used depends, in turn, on whether the United States is right that an attached judgment should be set off or whether Iran is right that it should not be—a matter in question before the Tribunal. In that sense, the Judgment is "under dispute." We recognize that the dispute is over the *use* of the Judgment, not the validity of the Judgment. But we do not see how that fact matters.

For another thing, ordinary legal disputes can easily encompass questions of setoff. Suppose Smith sues a carrier for wrongfully harming a shipment of goods. The question of liability, the question of damages, and the question of reducing damages through setoff may all be at issue in the case. Which is the more important issue in a particular case depends not upon the category (liability, damages, or setoff) but upon the circumstances of that particular case.

Further, the language of the statute suggests that Congress meant the words "at issue" to carry the ordinary meaning just described. Elahi essentially distinguishes between property that is the subject of a claim (a claim, for example, that the United States took or harmed particular property belonging to Iran) and property that might otherwise affect a Tribunal judgment (say, through its use as a setoff). And he argues that the statutory phrase "at issue" covers only the first kind of dispute, not the second. But the statute does not limit the property that is "*at issue* in a claim" to property that is the *subject* of a claim. To the contrary, the statute says that judgment creditors such as Elahi must

> "relinquis[h] all rights to execute against or attach property [1] that is *at issue in claims* against the United States before an international tribunal *[or]* [2] that *is the subject of awards* rendered by such tribunal."

VPA § 2002(a)(2)(D), 114 Stat. 1542 (emphasis added); *see also* § 2002(d)(5)(B), as added by TRIA § 201(c)(4) (cross-referencing § 2002(a)(2)(D)).

Had Congress wanted to limit the property to which it first refers (namely, property that is "*at issue*" in a claim) to property that is *the subject* of a claim, it seems likely that Congress straightforwardly would have used the words "subject of"—words that appear later (in respect to awards rendered) in the very same sentence.

Finally, the statute's purpose leans in the direction of a broader interpretation of the words "at issue" than that proposed by Elahi. Pointing to the statute's legislative history, Elahi says that the statute seeks to enable victims of terrorism to collect on judgments they have won against terrorist parties. See Brief of Respondent 6–7, 31 (citing H. R. Conf. Rep. No. 107-779 (2002); 148 Cong. Rec. 23119, 23121–23123 (2002) (statement of Sen. Harkin)). He is such a victim, and, he says, Congress would have intended an interpretation that favors his cause. But Congress had a more complicated set of purposes in mind. The statute authorizes the attachment of blocked assets, and it provides partial compensation to victims to be paid (in part) from general Treasury funds. But it does so in exchange for a right of subrogation, VPA § 2002(c), and for the victim's promise not to pursue the balance of the judgment by attaching property "at issue" in a claim against the United States before the Tribunal. VPA §§ 2002(a)(2)(D), (d)(5)(B), as added by TRIA § 201(c)(4). The statute thereby protects property that the United States might use to satisfy its potential liability to Iran.

The Cubic Judgment falls into this category. It is property that the United States could use to satisfy its potential liability to Iran, but which may be unavailable for that purpose if successfully attached. With respect to the statute's revenue-saving purpose, it is difficult to distinguish between property that is the subject of a claim before a tribunal and property that is in dispute before the tribunal in respect to its use as an offset.

The dissent adds that the "better reading" of the words "at issue" is one that limits them to the "foster[ing] [of] compliance with the Government's international obligations." *Post*, at ____, 173 L. Ed. 2d, at 530. We agree with this statement, but we do not see how it adds anything but new phraseology to the dissent's basic claim, namely that arguments before the Tribunal about "setoffs" do not count as "issues." To repeat our own view of the matter, a dispute about whether one country must pay the other country more money because it cannot use particular property (because of an attachment) to satisfy an obligation raises an issue that the Tribunal must resolve, no less and no more than other issues that might be before the Tribunal in that case or other cases.

Contrary to the dissent's suggestion, *post*, at ____, 173 L. Ed. 2d, at 531, there is no unfairness in our holding. Elahi could have chosen to forgo the Government's compensation scheme, and he then could have attached the Cubic Judgment, as have other terrorist victims with judgments against Iran. See Brief for United States as *Amicus Curiae* 20. But that course carried risks: Iran had challenged Elahi's notice of lien and it was uncertain whether Elahi would prevail. In 2003, while litigation over his notice of lien was pending, Elahi chose to participate in the Government's scheme. He thereby received the benefit of immediate, guaranteed partial compensation from the Government—in exchange for a promise not to interfere with property that the United States might need to satisfy potential liability to Iran. Having received $2.3 million in Government funds, there is nothing unfair about holding Elahi to the terms of his bargain.

Elahi makes several other arguments. He points to language in the TRIA (the statute authorizing attachment of blocked assets) which says: "*[n]otwithstanding any other provision of law*" the "blocked assets" of a state "shall be subject to . . . attachment in aid of execution" of a terrorism-related judgment. § 201(a), 116 Stat. 2337 (emphasis added). He also points to VPA § 2002(d)(4), as added by TRIA § 201(c)(4), 116 Stat. 2339, which reads: "*[N]othing in this subsection* [which contains the relinquishment provision] *shall bar . . . enforcement* of any" terrorism-related "judgment . . . *against assets otherwise available* under this section or *under any other provision of law*" (emphasis added). The first provision, Elahi argues, permits him to attach blocked assets notwithstanding the VPA's requirement that he relinquish his right to attach property "at issue" before an international tribunal; and that conclusion, he says, is reinforced by VPA § 2002(d)(4). Our interpretation, he adds, would "bar . . . enforcement" of a terrorism-related judgment "otherwise available" under TRIA § 201(a) —contrary to the statutory language just quoted.

But VPA § 2002(d)(5) requires Elahi, in exchange for having received partial compensation, to relinquish "*all rights*" to attach property "at issue" in an international tribunal. VPA § 2002(a)(2)(D), 114 Stat. 1542 (cross-referenced by § 2002(d)(5)(B); emphasis added). And, as several courts of appeals have apparently assumed, the relinquishment of "all rights" includes the right given by TRIA § 201(a) to attach blocked assets. *See Hegna v. Islamic Republic of Iran*, 376 F.3d 226, 232 (CA4 2004); *Hegna v. Islamic Republic of Iran*, 380 F.3d 1000, 1009 (CA7 2004); *Hegna v. Islamic Republic of Iran,* 402 F.3d 97, 99 (CA2 2005) *(per curiam).*

Moreover, the relinquishment provision that applies to Elahi was added to the VPA by the very same statute, the TRIA, that permitted the attachment of blocked assets, and which contains the "notwithstanding" clause upon which Elahi relies. § 201(a) (blocked assets); § 201(c) (amending VPA). Congress could not have intended the words to which Elahi refers to narrow so dramatically an important provision that it inserted in the same statute. And for those who, like Elahi, argue that the legislative history supports his reading of the statute, we point out that the history suggests that Congress placed the "notwithstanding" clause in § 201(a) for totally different reasons, namely to eliminate the effect of any Presidential waiver issued under 28 U.S.C. § 1610(f) prior to the date of the TRIA's enactment. H. R. Conf. Rep. No. 107-779, at 27.

Elahi makes three final arguments, first that setoff is not "at issue" because the United States has argued in Case No. B61 that it has no liability at all, second that set-off is not "at issue" because the United States has not formally asserted a setoff before the Tribunal, and third that the Government violated his due process rights by inadequately informing that his waiver would deprive him of his right to attach the Cubic Judgment. We find none of these arguments convincing and shall briefly indicate our reasons in summary form.

As to the first, the United States argued setoff in the alternative, thereby placing it, in the alternative, "at issue" before the Tribunal. As to the second, Elahi at most points to a ground for disputing the propriety, under Tribunal rules, for granting a setoff; he does not deny that the Tribunal sometimes can do so, *see, e.g., Futura Trading Inc.* v. *National Iranian Oil Co.*, 13 Iran-U. S. Cl. Trib. Rep. 99, 115–116, P 62 (1986) (preventing collection on a claim because the claimant had already collected the sum at issue from a different party). Hence whether the Tribunal can provide for a setoff here is a matter for the Tribunal to decide, and until it does decide, one way or the other, the matter is "at issue." As to the third, we can find nothing that shows Elahi was unfairly surprised by the scope of his waiver—certainly not to the point of violating any Due Process rights. *See, e.g.*, 14 Iran-U. S. Cl. Trib. Rep., at 278, P 10 (dismissal of Iran's claim against Cubic was "without prejudice to any findings it may make concerning [the Cubic contract] in Case No. B61").

IV.

We conclude: The Cubic Judgment was not blocked at the time the Court of Appeals reached its decision. We do not decide whether more recent Executive Branch actions would block the Judgment at present. Regardless, Elahi has waived his right to attach the Judgment. We reverse the judgment of the Court of Appeals.

It is so ordered.

DISSENT

Justice Kennedy, with whom Justice Souter and Justice Ginsburg join, concurring in part and dissenting in part.

I join Parts I and II of the Court's opinion but, with all respect, dissent from Parts III and IV. As to Parts I and II, the Court is correct, in my view, to hold that the Cubic Judgment was not a "blocked asset" when the Court of Appeals reached its decision. As to Parts III and IV, however, respondent Dariush Elahi has not relinquished his right to attach the Cubic Judgment. By holding otherwise, the Court departs from the plain meaning and the purpose of the statutes Congress enacted to compensate Elahi and other victims of terrorism.

I.

A.

The statutory phrase to be interpreted is "property that is at issue in claims against the United States before an international tribunal." Victims of Trafficking and Violence Protection Act of 2000 (VTVPA), § 2002(d)(s), as added by Terrorism Risk Insurance Act of 2002 (TRIA), § 201(c)(4), 116 Stat. 2339, note following 28 U.S.C. § 1610. The context, of course, is Case No. B61—a suit by Iran against the United States that is pending before the Iran-U. S. Claims Tribunal. The word "property," as used in the statutory phrase, surely can refer both to tangible property, such as real estate or valuables in a safe-deposit box, and to intangible property interests, such as a claim, a cause of action or, as in this case, a judgment rendered by a United States district court. Still, it must be acknowledged that the term "at issue" is neither precise nor much illuminated by its operation in cases or other statutes. The absence of any clear authority on this point makes it imperative to adopt an interpretation that accords with familiar and well-settled principles of law. In this case those principles are the rules designed to give full and proper respect to final judgments rendered by courts of competent jurisdiction.

To determine whether the Cubic Judgment is "at issue" in Case No. B61, the primary consideration must be whether the Claims Tribunal, in the exercise of its own authority and jurisdiction, can affect the ownership, disposition, or control of the property the judgment comprises. Here the property in question is a judgment rendered by the United States District Court for the Southern District of California. As all acknowledge, that court had jurisdiction over the subject and the persons then before it. And, as is further conceded, that court's judgment is valid and has binding force on Cubic Defense Systems, Inc., the nongovernmental party before that court. *See Ministry of Defense and Support for Armed Forces of Islamic Republic of Iran v. Cubic Defense Systems, Inc.*, 29 F.Supp.2d 1168, 1170 (1998). Neither party to Case No. B61 questions the judgment or requests the Claims Tribunal to interpret it—much less to alter, enforce or invalidate it.

Even if one of the parties were to ask the Claims Tribunal to modify the Cubic Judgment, the Tribunal would simply lack power to do so. The judgment arises out of Iran's contractual dispute with Cubic, an American company, and the Tribunal has no "jurisdiction over claims by Iran against United States nationals." *Ministry of Nat. Defence of Islamic Republic of Iran* v. *United States,* 14 Iran-U. S. Cl. Trib. Rep. 276, 278 (1987) (Case No. B66). Iran tried to sue Cubic in the Claims Tribunal 20 years ago, but the Tribunal dismissed that suit for lack of jurisdiction. *Ibid.* In these circumstances the Cubic Judgment is simply an extrinsic fact beyond the Claims Tribunal's power to affect. True, the Tribunal, when it enters its own orders, might or might not give credit to the United States for a payment, or a right to payment, arising out of the Cubic Judgment; but that does not put the judgment itself at issue.

B.

Even if the Court's broad reading of the phrase "at issue" were correct, the Court's conclusion would still be wrong because the relinquishment provision is limited to property that is at issue "in claims against the United States." And the Cubic Judgment is not part of the claims Iran makes in Case No. B61, as both Iran and the United States have made clear in their submissions to the Claims Tribunal. To put the countries' filings in context, a brief review of both the Cubic Judgment and Case No. B61 is necessary.

The Cubic Judgment is the result of a contract dispute between Iran and Cubic. In the late 1970's, Iran hired Cubic to build an air combat training system, and advanced some $12 million for the project. But Iran failed to make all the payments due. App. 43–44. Thus rebuffed, Cubic sold the system to Canada and refused to refund any of Iran's advance payments. Iran brought an arbitration against Cubic. The panel of arbitrators, after ascertaining Cubic's costs of building the system, and after allowing the company a reasonable profit of $3.5 million, ordered Cubic to return to Iran $2.8 million of the $12 million advance. Iran brought this arbitration award to the U. S. District Court for the Southern District of California, which issued the judgment at issue here. The judgment orders Cubic to pay Iran $2.8 million. *Cubic Defense Systems, supra,* at 1171, 1174.

Case No. B61 is in essence a contract dispute between Iran and the United States. Iran accuses the United States of breaking its promise, made in the Algiers Accords, to "arrange . . . for the transfer to Iran of all Iranian properties" located in the United States on January 19, 1981. 20 I. L. M. 224, 227, P 9 (1981). One of the properties Iran claims is Cubic's air combat training system. See Statement of Claim in No. B61, (Iran-U. S. Cl. Trib.), App. to Brief for United States 22a, 24a, 31a. Both parties have confirmed, in their joint report describing all the "property claimed by Iran," that Cubic's system is "at issue" in Iran's claims. Cover Letter to Final Joint Report (July 14, 1989), App. to Brief for Respondent 14.

But the Cubic Judgment, in contrast to Cubic's training system, is not part of Iran's claims in Case No. B61. Both countries made this clear in their submissions to the Tribunal. Their joint report does not list the Cubic Judgment among the properties "at issue." Final Joint Report (July 14, 1989), App. to Brief for Respondent 15–23.

And, in a statement altogether consistent with that omission, Iran told the Tribunal that "[t]he subject matter of [Case No. B61], at variance with the [arbitration] action [against Cubic], is the losses suffered by Iran as a result of the United States' non-export of Iranian properties." Iran's Statement 16, App. 73, 76. The United States agreed, stating that the "only 'property that' . . . is properly at issue" in Case No. B61 is property that "'has already been made the subject of a claim'" by Iran against the United States. U. S. Rebuttal (Sept. 1, 2003), 1 Lodging p. L419 (emphasis deleted) (Sealed). The United States reaffirmed this position in oral argument before the Tribunal: "Any losses in relation to [the Iran-Cubic] contract are not recoverable against the United States and issues regarding losses under that contract do not belong before this Tribunal." Tribunal Hearing 124 (Dec. 12, 2006), App. to Brief for Respondent 42.

Because the Claims Tribunal lacks jurisdiction over the Cubic Judgment, and because that judgment is not part of Iran's claims against the United States in Case No. B61, the judgment is not "property that is at issue in claims against the United States" under the plain meaning of the TRIA's relinquishment provision. TRIA § 201(c)(4), 116 Stat. 2339 (amending VTVPA § 2002(d)).

II.

Even if the text of the relinquishment provision were somehow ambiguous—and it is not—then the purpose of the VTVPA and TRIA would tip the scales in Elahi's favor. The text and the evident purpose of those statutes demonstrate that Congress' primary purpose was to compensate the victims of terrorism, not to secure from those victims a relinquishment of their claims to property owned by entities found to have sponsored terrorism.

The text of the VTVPA, and of the amendments made to it by the TRIA, shows that Congress' primary purpose was to enable the victims of terrorism to execute on the assets of a state found to have sponsored or assisted in a terrorist act. In the first subsection of the TRIA concerning the attachment of state assets by victims of terrorism, Congress provided that "[n]otwithstanding any other provision of law . . . in every case in which a person has obtained a judgment against a terrorist party on a claim based upon an act of terrorism . . . the blocked assets of that terrorist party . . . shall be subject to execution or attachment in aid of execution in order to satisfy such judgment . . . ." TRIA § 201(a), *id.,* at 2337. The effect of this subsection is to ensure that other laws do not bar victims' efforts to enforce judgments against terrorist states. To like effect is another paragraph of the VTVPA concerning victims of Iranian terrorism. Entitled "Statutory Construction," this paragraph reads: "Nothing in this subsection shall bar, or require delay in, enforcement of any judgment to which this subsection applies under any procedure . . . ." § 2002(d)(4), as added by TRIA § 201(c)(4), *id.*, at 2339. Though neither provision refers in direct terms to the relinquishment provision, both provisions show Congress' intent to broaden, rather than limit, the rights of victims like Elahi to execute on property owned by state sponsors of terrorism. Yet the opinion issued by the Court today does just the opposite.

To contravene the statute's clear design, the Court surmises that Congress also had a "more complicated" purpose, namely, to "protec[t] property that the United States might use to satisfy its potential liability to Iran." *Ante*, at ____, 173 L. Ed. 2d, at 525. This imagined purpose, the Court says, requires us to read the relinquishment provision as broadly as possible so as to prevent victims of terrorism from attaching property. But the Court does not point to evidence of this putative purpose, aside from the text of the relinquishment provision itself—a text which, as submitted above, the Court reads the wrong way.

The better reading of the relinquishment provision—and one much more consistent with Congress' protective purpose—is not as a "revenue-saving" device, *ibid.*, but as a way to foster compliance with the Government's international obligations. If Iran has asked the Claims Tribunal to resolve the status of certain property, then Iran and the Tribunal may well take the position that the United States has a responsibility under the Algiers Accords to prevent U. S. nationals from executing against that property. That concern is not present in this case. The ownership of the Cubic Judgment is not disputed, and allowing Elahi to attach it will not affect Iran's right to obtain full recovery from the United States in Case No. B61. At most, the attachment might affect the right of the United States to use the judgment to offset its liability.

The Court purports to agree with this reading of the statute's purpose. *Ante*, at ____, 173 L. Ed. 2d, at 525. But that agreement is hard to square with the Court's insistence upon fulfilling what it sees as the statute's "revenue-saving purpose." *Ibid.* If the Court did in fact believe that the "'better reading'" of the statute's purpose, *ibid.*, is to foster compliance with the United States' international obligations, then the Court would affirm the judgment of the Court of Appeals. Elahi's attachment of the Cubic Judgment does not hinder the U. S. Government's efforts to comply with its obligations under the Algiers Accords. At Algiers, the United States agreed to "arrange . . . for the transfer to Iran of all Iranian properties" located in the United States. 20 I. L. M., at 227, P 9. That is not an obligation to pay Iran money, as the Court seems to believe. *See ante*, at ____, 173 L. Ed. 2d, at 525. It is instead an obligation to take specific action in regard to specific properties. These specific properties do not include the Cubic Judgment—as the Court concedes. *See ante*, at ____, 173 L. Ed. 2d, at 520 (holding that the Cubic Judgment was not blocked). Therefore, Elahi's attachment of the Cubic Judgment does not impede the United States' efforts to make good on its obligations under the Algiers Accords.

To be sure, a judicial lien on one of the specific properties referenced by the Algiers Accords might make it difficult for the U. S. Government to comply with its obligations, under those Accords, to arrange for that property's transfer to Iran.

By encouraging creditors such as Elahi to give up their liens on these specific properties that are subject to the Algiers Accords, the TRIA makes it easier for the Government to comply with its obligation to "arrange . . . for the transfer" of these properties to Iran. This purpose (fostering compliance with the United States' obligation under the Algiers Accords) is more in keeping with the statute's text than is the Court's "revenue-saving" purpose. And this purpose—that is, the purpose of enabling the United States to meet its obligations under the Algiers Accords—is not in the least frustrated by permitting Elahi to attach the Cubic Judgment, a property that, as the Court concedes, is not subject to the Algiers Accords.

III.

The facts of this case show the injustice of the Court's interpretation. The Court today puts an end to Elahi's decade-long quest to hold Iran to account for murdering his brother Cyrus. In 2000, Elahi won a wrongful-death lawsuit against Iran and was awarded some $6 million in compensatory damages. *See Elahi v. Islamic Republic of Iran*, 124 F.Supp.2d 97 (DC). In April 2003, Elahi took what he must have considered a further step toward his goal when he accepted $2.3 million from the U. S. Government under the VTVPA.

After today's ruling, what once appeared Elahi's gain of $2.3 million now seems to be a loss of $500,000. By taking the VTVPA's $2.3 million, the Court holds, Elahi relinquished his right to the $2.8 million Cubic Judgment he had already attached. The practical effect of the Court's ruling is to turn the purpose of the VTVPA on its head. Rather than further Elahi's effort to obtain compensation for the murder of his brother, the Act has instead set him back half a million dollars. For the reasons given above, this result was not what Congress intended when it passed the VTVPA.

IV.

Congress passed the Victims of Trafficking and Violence Protection Act and the Terrorism Risk Insurance Act to compensate victims of terrorism. Congress expressed this purpose both in the text of the principal provision interpreted here and in accompanying sections of the statute. By stripping Elahi of his right to attach the valid judgment against Cubic rendered by the District Court—a judgment not before the Claims Tribunal in any sense—the Court fails to give the statute its intended effect. These reasons explain my respectful dissent.

AMIR REZA OVEISSI
v.
ISLAMIC REPUBLIC OF IRAN

573 F.3d 835 (D.C. Cir. 2009)
Decided July 28, 2009

Before: ROGERS, GARLAND, and BROWN, Circuit Judges. Opinion for the Court filed by Circuit Judge GARLAND.

OPINION

GARLAND, *Circuit Judge*:

The plaintiff in this case is the grandson of Gholam Oveissi, who was chief of the Iranian armed forces under the Shah's regime. Members of the terrorist organization Hezbollah, operating under the name Islamic Jihad, assassinated Oveissi in Paris in 1984. In 2003, the plaintiff sued the Islamic Republic of Iran and the Iranian Ministry of Information and Security (MOIS) in the United States District Court for the District of Columbia, alleging that the defendants had funded and directed Islamic Jihad. The district court found that Iran and MOIS were not entitled to sovereign immunity and that they were culpable in Oveissi's murder, but the court rejected the plaintiff's claims for intentional infliction of emotional distress and wrongful death. We conclude that the court applied the wrong law to the plaintiff's claims because it conducted an erroneous choice-of-law analysis. Accordingly, we reverse the judgment and remand the case for further proceedings.

I.

Gholam Oveissi, an Iranian citizen, served as a four-star general and chief of Iran's armed forces until early 1979. In that year, revolutionaries deposed the Shah and established an Islamic Republic. Oveissi, a supporter of the Shah's government, fled the country, traveling first to the United States and then to France, where he took up residence in Paris. Oveissi's son and daughter-in-law also fled from Iran to the United States. Their son, plaintiff Amir Oveissi, was born during their stay in California. Several months after the plaintiff's birth, his family moved to Paris, where they shared an apartment with Gholam Oveissi.

"While the family lived together in Paris, Gholam was outspoken in his opposition to Iran's revolutionary government and met with other expatriates in the family's apartment." *Oveissi v. Islamic Republic of Iran*, 498 F. Supp. 2d 268, 274 (D.D.C. 2007). Fearing reprisal for his political views, Oveissi hired a bodyguard. Despite this precaution, on February 17, 1984, Oveissi was shot and killed while he walked on a crowded Paris street. Members of the terrorist group Hezbollah, operating under the name Islamic Jihad, "immediately claimed responsibility," and the district court found "[n]o reason . . . to dispute this claim." *Id.* Oveissi's family left Paris as soon as they learned of the assassination, traveling first to Morocco for eighteen months and then to the United States, where they eventually settled in Virginia.

On June 2, 2003, the plaintiff filed a complaint against Iran and MOIS in the United States District Court for the District of Columbia, invoking the court's jurisdiction under the Foreign Sovereign Immunities Act (FSIA), 28 U.S.C. §§ 1602 *et seq.* The complaint alleged causes of action for, inter alia, intentional infliction of emotional distress (IIED) and wrongful death. The plaintiff filed an amended complaint on December 31, 2005, and effected service of process through diplomatic channels on May 30, 2006, pursuant to 28 U.S.C. § 1608(a)(4).

Iran failed to enter an appearance or respond to the complaint. The FSIA, however, "does not automatically entitle a plaintiff to judgment when a foreign state defaults," and instead requires a court "to satisfy itself that [the plaintiff has] established a right to relief." *Roeder v. Islamic Republic of Iran*, 333 F.3d 228, 232, 357 U.S. App. D.C. 107 (D.C. Cir. 2003) (citing 28 U.S.C. § 1608(e)). The district court therefore conducted a bench trial, receiving evidence from the plaintiff, Gholam Oveissi's bodyguard, and an international terrorism expert. The court summarized the expert's testimony as follows:

> [I]n the early 1980s, members of Hezbollah, under the direction of MOIS, engaged in terrorist activities outside the Middle East using the nom-de-guerre "Islamic Jihad." These activities included assassinations of expatriate Iranian dissidents, mainly in France. In [the expert's] opinion, the killings were intended to silence the Iranian regime's critics and to deter French intervention in Lebanon. . . . As well as guiding Hezbollah's terrorist activities, Iran, through MOIS and other entities, provided logistical support and training that, according to [the expert], were crucial to Hezbollah's ability to carry out the assassinations.

Oveissi, 498 F. Supp. 2d at 273–74 (footnote omitted). Based on this evidence, the court concluded that the then-applicable terrorism exception to the FSIA, 28 U.S.C. § 1605(a)(7), stripped Iran of its immunity from suit, and that Iran and MOIS were culpable in Oveissi's assassination.

The court nonetheless dismissed all of the plaintiff's claims. With respect to the IIED claim, the court began by conducting a choice-of-law analysis. Applying District of Columbia choice-of-law rules, it determined that ordinarily the "the law of the plaintiff's domicile at the time of the acts at issue" would govern the claim.

Oveissi, 498 F. Supp. 2d at 280. Although the court found that the plaintiff was a domiciliary of France at the time of the 1984 assassination, it concluded that domiciliary status was not determinative in the instant case. "[T]he United States," the court said, "has a unique interest in having its domestic law apply when its citizens are injured by state-sponsored terrorist acts." *Id.* at 281 (internal quotation marks omitted). Because the plaintiff was born in California and had briefly resided there, the court determined that it should apply California law to the IIED claim. In light of its reading of California law, however, the court concluded that the plaintiff "lack[ed] standing to bring an IIED claim based on [Gholam Oveissi's] death." *Id.* at 283.

Without applying a choice-of-law analysis, the court found the plaintiff's wrongful-death claim barred by Lord Campbell's Act, a law enacted by the British Parliament in 1846 that became the prototype for wrongful-death statutes in many American states. *Id.* at 277–79; *see Sea-Land Servs., Inc. v. Gaudet*, 414 U.S. 573, 579–80, 94 S. Ct. 806, 39 L. Ed. 2d 9 (1974). Lord Campbell's Act permits certain near relatives to bring a wrongful-death action against a tortfeasor if the deceased would have been "entitled . . . to maintain an Action . . . if Death had not ensued" and the deceased had merely been injured. Lord Campbell's Act, 9 & 10 Vict., ch. 93, An Act for compensating the Families of Persons killed by Accidents (Aug. 26, 1846); *see* RESTATEMENT (SECOND) OF TORTS § 925 cmt. a (1979). Although the plaintiff is a U.S. citizen and is thereby entitled to bring an action under the terrorism exception of the FSIA if the other statutory conditions are met, *see* 28 U.S.C. § 1605(a)(7)(A), (B), Gholam Oveissi was an Iranian citizen and could not himself have sued under the terrorism exception had he survived the attack. "Because no action could have been brought by the deceased if still alive," the court thought it had to dismiss the plaintiff's wrongful-death claim. *Oveissi*, 498 F. Supp. 2d at 279 (internal quotation mark omitted).

The plaintiff now appeals from the district court's dismissal of his amended complaint.

II.

We begin with some necessary background regarding the FSIA. The Act "grants United States courts both subject matter and personal jurisdiction (where service of process has been made) over any claim against a foreign state as to which the state is not entitled to immunity." *World Wide Minerals, Ltd. v. Republic of Kazakhstan*, 296 F.3d 1154, 1159 n.5, 353 U.S. App. D.C. 147 (D.C. Cir. 2002) (citing 28 U.S.C. § 1330(a), (b)). Under the FSIA, foreign states generally are entitled to immunity unless the case falls within one of a list of statutory exceptions. 28 U.S.C. § 1604; *see Kilburn v. Socialist People's Libyan Arab Jamahiriya*, 376 F.3d 1123, 1126, 363 U.S. App. D.C. 87 (D.C. Cir. 2004). In 1996, Congress amended the FSIA, adding an exception—§ 1605(a)(7)—"colloquially known as the 'terrorism exception.'" *Kilburn*, 376 F.3d at 1126. In pertinent part, that exception abrogates the sovereign immunity of foreign states in civil cases "in which money damages are sought against a foreign state for personal injury or death that was caused by . . . extrajudicial killing." 28 U.S.C. § 1605(a)(7). "This exception applies only if three additional criteria are also satisfied: the foreign state was designated a 'state sponsor of terrorism' at the time the act occurred; the foreign state was given a reasonable opportunity to arbitrate a claim regarding an act that occurred within the state's borders; and the claimant or victim was a national of the United States." *Kilburn*, 376 F.3d at 1126–27 (citing 28 U.S.C. § 1605(a)(7)(A), (B)).

In this case, the district court correctly determined that it had jurisdiction over the plaintiff's suit under the terrorism exception of the FSIA. The assassination of Gholam Oveissi clearly qualifies as an extrajudicial killing attributable to the Iranian government; "Iran has been designated a state sponsor of terrorism continuously since January 19, 1984, one month prior to Gholam Ali Oveissi's death," *Oveissi*, 498 F. Supp. 2d at 275; there was no need to give Iran an opportunity to arbitrate the claim because the murder occurred outside Iran's borders; and the claimant, Amir Oveissi, is a U.S. citizen.

Although the FSIA grants jurisdiction over certain claims against foreign countries, at the time the plaintiff filed his suit the terrorism exception did not provide a federal cause of action against a foreign state. *See Cicippio-Puleo v. Islamic Republic of Iran*, 353 F.3d 1024, 1027, 359 U.S. App. D.C. 299 (D.C. Cir. 2004). The plaintiff was therefore required to identify, and to bring his claims pursuant to, some other "cause of action arising out of a specific source of law"—for example, state law. *Acree v. Republic of Iraq,* 370 F.3d 41, 59, 361 U.S. App. D.C. 410 (D.C. Cir. 2004), *abrogated on other grounds by Republic of Iraq v. Beaty*, 129 S. Ct. 2183, 173 L. Ed. 2d 1193 (2009). While he did not have to identify the specific source of law in his complaint, the plaintiff did have to do so at an appropriate time in the litigation.[1] The plaintiff satisfied this obligation by identifying his causes of action as arising under state statutory and common law in his submissions to the district court.

One additional development in the statutory scheme merits notice. After the district court issued its opinion in this case, Congress enacted the National Defense Authorization Act for Fiscal Year 2008 (NDAA), which, among other things, amended the terrorism exception by repealing 28 U.S.C. § 1605(a)(7) and adding a new exception codified at § 1605A. Pub. L. No. 110-181, § 1083, 122 Stat. 3, 338–44 (2008). This new exception, which became effective on January 28, 2008,

---

1 *See Acree*, 370 F.3d at 43 (dismissing a suit because "[n]either appellees' complaint, nor their submissions to this court, nor the District Court's decision in their favor offers any . . . coherent alternative causes of action" besides the FSIA itself); *see also Kilburn*, 376 F.3d at 1125 (allowing a suit to proceed, "[a]lthough the complaint did not specify the legal sources of the . . . causes of action," when later pleadings clarified the sources of law underlying the claims); *cf. Owens v. Republic of Sudan*, 531 F.3d 884, 894, 382 U.S. App. D.C. 155 (D.C. Cir. 2008) (rejecting Sudan's argument that "heightened specificity is required of . . . pleading" regarding causation in an FSIA case, and noting that "Sudan points to no Rule or statute that imposes a heightened pleading requirement in the context of the terrorism exception").

is "more advantageous to plaintiffs in several respects"; for example, it "creat[es] a federal right of action against foreign states, for which punitive damages may be awarded." *Simon v. Republic of Iraq*, 529 F.3d 1187, 1190, 381 U.S. App. D.C. 483 (D.C. Cir. 2008), *rev'd on other grounds sub nom. Republic of Iraq v. Beaty,* 129 S. Ct. 2183, 173 L. Ed. 2d 1193 (2009); *see* 28 U.S.C. § 1605A.

In *Simon*, the circuit held that a "plaintiff in a case pending under § 1605(a)(7) may not maintain that action based upon the jurisdiction conferred by [the new] § 1605A; in order to claim the benefits of § 1605A, the plaintiff must file a new action under that new provision." 529 F.3d at 1192. We also determined, however, that "courts retain jurisdiction pursuant to [former] §1605(a)(7) over cases that were pending under that section when the Congress enacted the NDAA." *Id.* Because the plaintiff has not attempted to refile his case under § 1605A, we have no occasion to consider whether he can allege claims under that section. Instead, doing as *Simon* says, we retain jurisdiction and consider this suit pursuant to § 1605(a)(7), the section under which it was filed. *See La Reunion Aerienne v. Socialist People's Libyan Arab Jamahiriya*, 533 F.3d 837, 845, 382 U.S. App. D.C. 365 (D.C. Cir. 2008); *Owens v. Republic of Sudan*, 531 F.3d 884, 887, 382 U.S. App. D.C. 155 (D.C. Cir. 2008).

III.

As noted in Part I, the district court dismissed the plaintiff's IIED claim on the ground that he lacked standing to assert such a claim under California law, and it dismissed his wrongful-death claim on the ground that it was barred by Lord Campbell's Act. Before we can consider whether the court accurately construed California law or Lord Campbell's Act, we must ask whether the district court was right to apply them. And before we can answer that question, we must first determine which jurisdiction's choice-of-law rules tell us which jurisdiction's substantive law to apply.

1. The FSIA does not contain an express choice-of-law provision. FSIA § 1606 does, however, provide that a foreign state stripped of its immunity "shall be liable in the same manner and to the same extent as a private individual under like circumstances." 28 U.S.C. § 1606. This section ensures that, if an FSIA exception abrogates immunity, plaintiffs may bring state law claims that they could have brought if the defendant were a private individual. *See First Nat'l City Bank v. Banco Para El Comercio Exterior de Cuba*, 462 U.S. 611, 622 n.11, 103 S. Ct. 2591, 77 L. Ed. 2d 46 (1983) ("[W]here state law provides a rule of liability governing private individuals, the FSIA requires the application of that rule to foreign states in like circumstances."). In this way, "the FSIA . . . operates as a 'pass-through' to state law principles." *Pescatore v. Pan Am. World Airways, Inc.,* 97 F.3d 1, 12 (2d Cir. 1996).

Relying on the language of § 1606, the Second Circuit has held that courts considering issues governed by state substantive law in FSIA cases should apply the choice-of-law rules of the forum state. *Barkanic v. Gen. Admin. of Civil Aviation of the People's Republic of China,* 923 F.2d 957, 959–60 (2d Cir. 1991); *see also O'Bryan v. Holy See*, 556 F.3d 361, 381 n.8 (6th Cir. 2009) (using the forum state's choice-of-law rules in an FSIA case). As the Second Circuit persuasively reasoned, "[t]he goal of applying identical substantive laws to foreign states and private individuals . . . cannot be achieved unless a federal court utilizes the same choice of law analysis in FSIA cases as it would apply if all the parties to the action were private." *Barkanic*, 923 F.2d at 959–60. The paradigm case involving choice-of-law issues and solely private parties is one brought under the federal courts' diversity jurisdiction. *See* 28 U.S.C. § 1332. In such a case, the court would apply the forum state's choice-of-law rules. *See Klaxon Co. v. Stentor Elec. Mfg. Co.,* 313 U.S. 487, 496, 61 S. Ct. 1020, 85 L. Ed. 1477 (1941). We thus agree with the Second Circuit that applying the forum state's choice-of-law principles, rather than constructing a set of federal common law principles, better effectuates Congress' intent that foreign states be "liable in the same manner and to the same extent as a private individual" in FSIA actions. 28 U.S.C. § 1606. [2]

In this case, the plaintiff's causes of action for IIED and wrongful death are based solely on state substantive law, and the choice-of-law rules of the forum—the District of Columbia—therefore apply to those claims. The district court did rely on D.C. law when conducting its choice-of-law analysis for the plaintiff's IIED claim, and it concluded that California law should supply the rule of decision. *See Oveissi*, 498 F. Supp. 2d at 280–81. We review this determination *de novo. Williams v. First Gov't Mortgage & Investors Corp.,* 176 F.3d 497, 499, 336 U.S. App. D.C. 71 (D.C. Cir. 1999); *see also Felch v. Air Florida, Inc.,* 866 F.2d 1521, 1523, 275 U.S. App. D.C. 403 (D.C. Cir. 1989) ("This court treats choice of law issues as matters of law over which it exercises *de novo* review.").

2. To determine which jurisdiction's substantive law governs a dispute, District of Columbia courts blend a "governmental interests analysis" with a "most significant relationship" test. *Hercules & Co., Ltd. v. Shama Rest. Corp.,* 566 A.2d 31, 40–41 & n.18 (D.C. 1989); *see also Jaffe v. Pallotta TeamWorks,* 374 F.3d 1223, 1227, 362 U.S. App. D.C. 398 (D.C. Cir. 2004); *Stephen A. Goldberg Co. v. Remsen Partners, Ltd.,* 170 F.3d 191, 193–94, 335 U.S. App. D.C. 154 (D.C. Cir. 1999). "Under the governmental interests analysis[,] . . . [a court] must evaluate the governmental policies underlying the applicable laws and determine which jurisdiction's policy would be most advanced by having its law applied to the facts of the case under review." *Hercules*, 566 A.2d at 41 (internal quotation

---

2 By contrast, the Ninth Circuit has stated that, "[i]n the absence of specific statutory guidance [in the FSIA], [it] prefer[s] to resort to the federal common law for a choice-of-law rule." *Harris v. Polskie Linie Lotnicze*, 820 F.2d 1000, 1003 (9th Cir. 1987). In our view, § 1606 provides sufficient statutory guidance to resolve the issue. In any event, as we discuss in Part III.2, all of the usual choice-of-law factors - including those identified as important by the Restatement (Second) of Conflict of Laws—point in the same direction, so there is no reason to believe that applying a federal common law choice-of-law rule would yield a different result in this case.

marks omitted). To determine which jurisdiction has the most significant relationship to a case, a court must "consider the factors enumerated in the Restatement [(Second) of Conflict of Laws] § 145." *Id.* at 40. The four Restatement factors are: (1) "the place where the injury occurred"; (2) "the place where the conduct causing the injury occurred"; (3) "the domicil[e], residence, nationality, place of incorporation and place of business of the parties"; and (4) "the place where the relationship, if any, between the parties is centered." RESTATEMENT (SECOND) OF CONFLICT OF LAWS § 145(2) (1971).

In any given case, these considerations may point in opposite directions and raise difficult questions concerning how each should be weighted. In this case, however, we face no such difficulty because the factors overwhelmingly point in the direction of France. The assassination occurred in France. The victim, Gholam Oveissi, was an Iranian who was domiciled there. Although the plaintiff is a U.S. citizen, he, too, was domiciled in France at the time his grandfather was murdered. Hence, this is not a case in which we must choose between applying the law of the jurisdiction where the tort occurred versus that where the plaintiff was domiciled, as both are the same. Moreover, in addition to having the most significant relationship to the assassination, France has a strong governmental interest in both deterring attacks within its sovereign borders and ensuring compensation for injuries to its domiciliaries.[3] The interest of California, which arises solely out of the fact that the plaintiff was born and briefly resided there—for less than a year and not at the time of the attack—is slight by comparison. *Cf. Jaffe*, 374 F.3d at 1229 (concluding that District of Columbia choice-of-law rules counsel applying Virginia, rather than D.C., law to a suit brought on behalf of a D.C. resident when "Virginia has a public policy which is directly implicated" and "the interests of the District of Columbia are at best attenuated").

The district court recognized that, under ordinary D.C. choice-of-law analysis, French law would apply to the plaintiff's claims. *Oveissi*, 498 F. Supp. 2d at 280. The court noted, however, that "the United States has a unique interest in having its domestic law apply when its citizens are injured by state-sponsored terrorist acts." *Id.* at 281 (internal quotation marks omitted). This consideration, the court said, "elevates the interests of the United States to nearly [their] highest point" and requires resort to California law. *Id.* (internal quotation marks omitted).

To support this proposition, the district court cited another district court opinion, *Dammarell v. Islamic Republic of Iran*, which applied the law of the American plaintiffs' state of domicile—rather than that of Lebanon—to a suit brought by American victims of the 1983 bombing of the United States Embassy in Beirut.

---

3 There is no contention here that application of French law would "conflict [] with a strong public policy" of the District of Columbia. *Cf. Sami v. United States*, 617 F.2d 755, 763, 199 U.S. App. D.C. 173 (D.C. Cir. 1979) (noting that "prevailing conflicts principles in the District of Columbia and elsewhere . . . permit application of an alternate substantive law when foreign law conflicts with a strong public policy of the forum" (footnote omitted)).

2005 U.S. Dist. LEXIS 5343, 2005 WL 756090 (D.D.C. Mar. 29, 2005). As the *Dammarell* court explained, the injuries in that case were "the result of a state-sponsored terrorist attack on a United States embassy and diplomatic personnel [, and the] United States has a unique interest in its domestic law . . . determining damages in a suit involving such an attack." 2005 U.S. Dist. LEXIS 5343, [WL] at *20. The court cited the Restatement (Third) of Foreign Relations Law § 402(3), which provides that a country has jurisdiction to prescribe law with respect to "'certain conduct outside its territory by persons not its nationals *that is directed against* the security of the state or against a limited class of other state interests.'" *Id.* (quoting RESTATEMENT (THIRD) OF FOREIGN RELATIONS LAW § 402(3) (1987)) (emphasis added). The court also cited a comment to the Restatement for the proposition that this principle is "'increasingly accepted as applied to terrorist and other organized attacks *on a state's nationals by reason of their nationality*, or to assassination of a state's diplomatic representatives or other officials.'" *Id.* at *20 n.16 (quoting RESTATEMENT (THIRD) OF FOREIGN RELATIONS LAW § 402 cmt. g) (emphasis added).

We have no doubt that the United States has a strong interest in applying its domestic law to terrorist attacks on its nationals, especially when, as was the case in *Dammarell*, the attacks are "by reason of their nationality." But Gholam Oveissi was not an American national; nor has the plaintiff suggested that the defendants knew Oveissi had an American grandchild or that the United States or its nationals were in any other way the object of the attack. To the contrary, plaintiff's counsel conceded at oral argument that there is no evidence that Oveissi's assassination was intended to affect the United States. *See* Oral Arg. Recording at 4:52–5:03. Moreover, the plaintiff's international terrorism expert testified that assassinations like this one "were intended to silence the Iranian regime's critics *and to deter French intervention in Lebanon.*" *Oveissi*, 498 F. Supp. 2d at 273 (emphasis added). Hence, if any country was the object of the attack, it was France. Accordingly, all of the relevant choice-of-law factors point to the application of French law to the plaintiff's claims.[4]

We close this discussion by emphasizing that we are not setting forth a general choice-of-law rule for terrorism cases, but merely applying the District of Columbia's rules to the facts of a case filed under former § 1605(a)(7). And we note that, for terrorism cases filed under the new § 1605A, plaintiffs whose cases meet the statutory requirements now have a *federal* cause of action. *See* 28 U.S.C. § 1605A(c); *Simon*, 529 F.3d at 1190.

3. Having concluded that French law governs the assassination of French-domiciliary Gholam Oveissi in France, we do not address the plaintiff's arguments

4 We also note that, although choice-of-law rules can point to different sources of substantive law for different claims, *e.g., Logan v. Providence Hosp., Inc.*, 778 A.2d 275, 280 (D.C. 2001), that is not the case for the closely related IIED and wrongful-death claims at issue here.

that the district court misconstrued California law and Lord Campbell's Act in dismissing his claims. We have no reason to suspect that French and California law are the same with respect to IIED claims. And we have every reason to doubt that France has adopted the equivalent of an 1846 British statute to govern wrongful-death claims in its courts. Accordingly, our opining on California law or Lord Campbell's Act would be beside the point. We leave it to the district court on remand to evaluate the plaintiff's claims under French law.

IV.

For the foregoing reasons, we reverse the judgment dismissing the plaintiff's amended complaint, and we remand the case for further proceedings consistent with this opinion.

Reversed and remanded.

REPUBLIC OF IRAQ
v.
JORDAN BEATY

129 S. Ct. 2183 (2009)
Decided June 8, 2009*

Jonathan S. Franklin, for petitioners.

Douglas Hallward-Driemeier, for the United States as amicus curiae, by special leave of the Court, supporting the petitioners.

Thomas C. Goldstein, for respondents.

Andrew C. Hall, Hall Lamb and Hall, P.A., Miami, FL, Counsel of Record for the Beaty Respondents, Stephen A. Fennell, Steptoe & Johnson, LLP, Washington, DC, Counsel of Record for the Simon Respondents, Thomas C. Goldstein, Counsel of Record, Akin, Gump, Strauss, Hauer & Feld LLP, Washington, DC, for respondents.

Timothy B. Mills, Maggs & McDermott LLC, Washington, D.C., Jonathan S. Franklin, Counsel of Record, Robert A. Burgoyne, Tillman J. Breckenridge, Fulbright & Jaworski L.L.P., Washington, D.C., for Petitioners.

James Cooper-Hill, Rockport, Texas, Nelson M. Jones III, Houston, Texas, Andrew C. Hall, Counsel of Record, Roarke Maxwell, Hall, Lamb and Hall, P.A., Miami, Florida, for Beaty Respondents.

Justice SCALIA delivered the opinion of the Court.

We consider in these cases whether the Republic of Iraq remains subject to suit in American courts pursuant to the terrorism exception to foreign sovereign immunity, now repealed, that had been codified at 28 U.S.C. § 1605(a)(7).

---

* Together with No. 08-539, *Republic of Iraq et al. v. Simon et al.,* also on certiorari to the same court.

I.

A.

Under the venerable principle of foreign sovereign immunity, foreign states are ordinarily "immune from the jurisdiction of the courts of the United States and of the States," § 1604. See generally *Schooner Exchange v. McFaddon,* 7 Cranch 116, 3 L.Ed. 287 (1812). But the statute embodying that principle—the Foreign Sovereign Immunities Act of 1976 (FSIA), 28 U.S.C. § 1602 *et seq.*—recognizes a number of exceptions; if any of these is applicable, the state is subject to suit, and federal district courts have jurisdiction to adjudicate the claim. § 1330(a); *Verlinden B.V. v. Central Bank of Nigeria,* 461 U.S. 480, 489, 103 S. Ct. 1962, 76 L.Ed.2d 81 (1983).

In 1996, Congress added to the list of statutory exceptions one for state sponsors of terrorism, which was codified at 28 U.S.C. § 1605(a)(7). Subject to limitations not relevant here, that exception stripped immunity in any suit for money damages

> "against a foreign state for personal injury or death that was caused by an act of torture, extrajudicial killing, aircraft sabotage, hostage taking, or the provision of material support or resources . . . for such an act . . . except that the court shall decline to hear a claim under this paragraph—
>
> > "(A) if the foreign state was not designated as a state sponsor of terrorism under section 6(j) of the Export Administration Act of 1979 (50 U.S.C.App. 2405(j)) or section 620A of the Foreign Assistance Act of 1961 (22 U.S.C. 2371) at the time the act occurred. . . ."

In brief, § 1605(a)(7) stripped immunity from a foreign state for claims arising from particular acts, if those acts were taken at a time when the state was designated as a sponsor of terrorism.

B.

In September 1990, Acting Secretary of State Lawrence Eagleburger formally designated Iraq, pursuant to § 6(j) of the Export Administration Act of 1979, as redesignated and amended, 99 Stat. 135, 50 U.S.C.App. § 2405(j), as "a country which has repeatedly provided support for acts of international terrorism," 55 Fed.Reg. 37793. Over a decade later, in March 2003, the United States and a coalition of allies initiated military action against that country. In a matter of weeks, the regime of Iraqi dictator Saddam Hussein collapsed and coalition forces occupied Baghdad. American attention soon shifted from combat operations to the longer term project of rebuilding Iraq, with the ultimate goal of creating a stable ally in the region.

Toward that end, Congress enacted in April 2003 the Emergency Wartime Supplemental Appropriations Act (EWSAA), 117 Stat. 559. Section 1503 of that Act authorized the President to "make inapplicable with respect to Iraq section 620A of the Foreign Assistance Act of 1961 or any other provision of law that applies to countries that have supported terrorism." *Id.,* at 579. President George W. Bush exercised that authority to its fullest extent in May 2003, declaring "inapplicable with respect to Iraq section 620A of the Foreign Assistance Act of 1961 . . . and any other provision of law that applies to countries that have supported terrorism." 68 Fed. Reg.26459.

Shortly thereafter, the United States Court of Appeals for the District of Columbia Circuit had occasion to consider whether that Presidential action had the effect of rendering inapplicable to Iraq the terrorism exception to foreign sovereign immunity. The Court concluded in a divided panel decision that the President's EWSAA authority did not permit him to waive § 1605(a)(7), and thereby restore sovereign immunity to Iraq, for claims arising from acts it had taken while designated as a sponsor of terror. *Acree v. Republic of Iraq,* 370 F.3d 41, 48 (2004). Because Iraq succeeded in having the claims against it dismissed on other grounds, *id.,* at 59–60, it could not seek certiorari to challenge the D.C. Circuit's interpretation of the EWSAA.

C.

There is yet another legislative enactment, and yet another corresponding executive waiver, that bear on the question presented. The National Defense Authorization Act for Fiscal Year 2008 (NDAA), 122 Stat. 3, was passed in January 2008. That Act (1) repealed the FSIA's terrorism exception, § 1083(b)(1)(A)(iii); (2) replaced it with a new, roughly similar exception, § 1083(a); (3) declared that nothing in § 1503 of the EWSAA had "ever authorized, directly or indirectly, the making inapplicable of any provision of chapter 97 of title 28, United States Code, or the removal of the jurisdiction of any court of the United States" (thus purporting to ratify the Court of Appeals' *Acree* decision), § 1083(c)(4), 122 Stat. 343; and (4) authorized the President to waive "any provision of this section with respect to Iraq" so long as he made certain findings and so notified Congress within 30 days, § 1083(d), *id.,* at 343–344.

The last provision was added to the NDAA after the President vetoed an earlier version of the bill, which did not include the waiver authority. The President's veto message said that the bill "would imperil billions of dollars of Iraqi assets at a crucial juncture in that nation's reconstruction efforts." Memorandum to the House of Representatives Returning Without Approval the "National Defense Authorization Act for Fiscal Year 2008," 43 Weekly Comp. of Pres. Doc. 1641 (2007). Only when Congress added the waiver authority to the NDAA did the President agree to approve it; and on the same day he signed it into law he also officially waived "all provisions of section 1083 of the Act with respect to Iraq," 73 Fed.Reg. 6571 (2008).

II.

We consider today two cases that have been navigating their way through the lower courts against the backdrop of the above-described congressional, military, Presidential, and judicial actions. Respondents in the *Simon* case are American nationals (and relatives of those nationals) who allege that they were captured and cruelly mistreated by Iraqi officials during the 1991 Gulf War. The *Beaty* respondents are the children of two other Americans, Kenneth Beaty and William Barloon, who are alleged to have been similarly abused by the regime of Saddam Hussein in the aftermath of that war. Each set of respondents filed suit in early 2003 against Iraq in the United States District Court for the District of Columbia, alleging violations of local, federal, and international law.

Respondents invoked the terrorism exception to foreign sovereign immunity, and given *Acree*'s holding that the President had not rendered that statutory provision inapplicable to Iraq, the District Court refused to dismiss either case on jurisdictional grounds. In *Beaty,* after the District Court denied Iraq's motion to dismiss, 480 F. Supp. 2d 60, 70 (2007), Iraq invoked the collateral order doctrine to support an interlocutory appeal. See *Mitchell v. Forsyth,* 472 U.S. 511, 524–529, 105 S. Ct. 2806, 86 L.Ed.2d 411 (1985). In *Simon,* the District Court determined that the claims were time barred and dismissed on that alternative basis, *Vine v. Republic of Iraq,* 459 F. Supp. 2d 10, 25 (2006), after which the *Simon* respondents appealed.

In the *Beaty* appeal, Iraq (supported by the United States as *amicus*) requested that the Court of Appeals for the District of Columbia Circuit reconsider *Acree*'s holding en banc. The Court denied that request over the dissent of Judges Brown and Kavanaugh, and a panel then summarily affirmed in an unpublished order the District Court's denial of Iraq's motion to dismiss. No. 07-7057 (Nov. 21, 2007) *(per curiam),* App. to Pet. for Cert. 1a-2a.

While the *Simon* appeal was still pending, Congress enacted the NDAA, and the Court of Appeals requested supplemental briefing addressing the impact of that legislation on the court's jurisdiction. Iraq contended, as an alternative argument to its position that *Acree* was wrongly decided, that even if 28 U.S.C. § 1605(a)(7)'s application to Iraq survived the President's EWSAA waiver, the provision was repealed by § 1083(b)(1)(A)(iii) of the NDAA, 122 Stat. 341; and that the *new* terrorism exception to sovereign immunity—which was created by the NDAA and codified at 28 U.S.C.A. § 1605A (July 2008 Supp.)—was waived by the President with respect to Iraq pursuant to his NDAA authority.

The Court of Appeals rejected that argument, holding instead, based on a close reading of the statutory text, that "the NDAA leaves intact our jurisdiction over cases . . . that were pending against Iraq when the Congress enacted the NDAA." 529 F.3d 1187, 1194 (2008). The panel then reversed the District Court's determination that the *Simon* respondents' claims were untimely, *id.,* at 1195–1196, and rebuffed Iraq's request for dismissal under the political question doctrine, *id.,* at 1196–1198.

Iraq sought this Court's review of both cases, asking us to determine whether under current law it remains subject to suit in the federal courts. We granted certiorari, 555 U.S. ___, 129 S. Ct. 894, 172 L.Ed.2d 769 (2009), and consolidated the cases.

III.

A.

Section 1503 of the EWSAA consists of a principal clause, followed by eight separate proviso clauses. The dispute in these cases concerns the second of the provisos. The principal clause and that proviso read:

> "The President may suspend the application of any provision of the Iraq Sanctions Act of 1990: . . . *Provided further,* That the President may make inapplicable with respect to Iraq section 620A of the Foreign Assistance Act of 1961 or any other provision of law that applies to countries that have supported terrorism. . . ." 117 Stat. 579.

Iraq and the United States both read the quoted proviso's residual clause as sweeping in the terrorism exception to foreign sovereign immunity. Certainly that reading is, as even the *Acree* Court acknowledged, "straightforward." 370 F.3d, at 52.

Title 28 U.S.C. § 1605(a)(7)'s exception to sovereign immunity for state sponsors of terrorism stripped jurisdictional immunity from a country unless "the foreign state was not designated as a state sponsor of terrorism." This is a "provision of law" (indisputably) that "applies to" (strips immunity from) "countries that have supported terrorism" (as designated pursuant to certain statutory provisions). Of course the word "any" (in the phrase "any other provision of law") has an "expansive meaning," *United States v. Gonzales,* 520 U.S. 1, 5, 117 S. Ct. 1032, 137 L.Ed.2d 132 (1997), giving us no warrant to limit the class of provisions of law that the President may waive. Because the President exercised his authority with respect to "all" provisions of law encompassed by the second proviso, his actions made § 1605(a)(7) "inapplicable" to Iraq.

To a layperson, the notion of the President's suspending the operation of a valid law might seem strange. But the practice is well established, at least in the sphere of foreign affairs. *See United States v. Curtiss-Wright Export Corp.,* 299 U.S. 304, 322–324, 57 S. Ct. 216, 81 L.Ed. 255 (1936) (canvassing precedents from as early as the "inception of the national government"). The granting of Presidential waiver authority is particularly apt with respect to congressional elimination of foreign sovereign immunity, since the granting or denial of that immunity was historically the case-by-case prerogative of the Executive Branch. *See, e.g., Ex parte Peru,* 318 U.S. 578, 586–590, 63 S. Ct. 793, 87 L.Ed. 1014 (1943). It is entirely unremarkable that Congress, having taken upon itself in the FSIA to "free the Government" from the diplomatic pressures engendered by the case-by-case approach, *Verlinden,* 461 U.S., at 488, 103 S. Ct. 1962, would nonetheless think it prudent to afford the President some flexibility in unique circumstances such as these.

B.

The Court of Appeals in *Acree* resisted the above construction, primarily on the ground that the relevant text is found in a proviso. We have said that, at least presumptively, the "grammatical and logical scope [of a proviso] is confined to the subject-matter of the principal clause." *United States v. Morrow,* 266 U.S. 531, 534–535, 45 S. Ct. 173, 69 L.Ed. 425 (1925). Using that proposition as a guide, the *Acree* panel strove mightily to construe the proviso as somehow restricting the principal clause of EWSAA § 1503, which authorized the President to suspend "any provision of the Iraq Sanctions Act of 1990," 117 Stat. 579.

In the Court of Appeals' view, the second proviso related to that subsection of the Iraq Sanctions Act (referred to in the principal provision) which dictated that certain enumerated statutory provisions, including § 620A of the Foreign Assistance Act of 1961 and "all other provisions of law that *impose sanctions* against a country which has repeatedly provided support for acts of international terrorism," shall be fully enforced against Iraq. § 586F(c), 104 Stat. 2051 (emphasis added). The panel understood the second EWSAA proviso as doing nothing more than clarifying that the authority granted by the principal clause (to suspend any part of the Iraq Sanctions Act) included the power to make inapplicable to Iraq the various independent provisions of law that § 586F(c) of the Iraq Sanctions Act instructed to be enforced against Iraq— which might otherwise continue to apply of their own force even without the Iraq Sanctions Act. However, the residual clause of § 586F(c) encompasses only provisions that "impose sanctions"; and, in the Court of Appeals' view, that excludes § 1605(a)(7), which is a rule going instead to the jurisdiction of the federal courts. Thus, the EWSAA proviso swept only as broadly as § 586F(c), and therefore did not permit the President to waive the FSIA terrorism exception.

This is a highly sophisticated effort to construe the proviso as a limitation upon the principal clause. Ultimately, however, we think that effort neither necessary nor successful. It is true that the "general office of a proviso is to except something from the enacting clause, or to qualify and restrain its generality." *Morrow, supra,* at 534, 45 S. Ct. 173. But its general (and perhaps appropriate) office is not, alas, its exclusive use. Use of a proviso "to state a general, independent rule," *Alaska v. United States,* 545 U.S. 75, 106, 125 S. Ct. 2137, 162 L.Ed.2d 57 (2005), may be lazy drafting, but is hardly a novelty. *See, e.g., McDonald v. United States,* 279 U.S. 12, 21, 49 S. Ct. 218, 73 L.Ed. 582 (1929). *Morrow* itself came with the caveat that a proviso is sometimes used "to introduce independent legislation." 266 U.S., at 535, 45 S. Ct. 173. We think that was its office here. The principal clause granted the President a power; the second proviso purported to grant him an *additional* power. It was not, on any fair reading, an exception to, qualification of, or restraint on the principal power.

Contrasting the second EWSAA proviso to some of the other provisos illustrates the point. For example, the first proviso cautioned that "nothing in this section shall affect the applicability of the Iran-Iraq Arms Non-Proliferation Act of 1992," 117 Stat. 579, and the third forbade the export of certain military equipment "under the authority of this section." *Ibid.* Both of these plainly sought to define and limit the authority granted by the principal clause. The fourth proviso, however, mandated that "section 307 of the Foreign Assistance Act of 1961 shall not apply with respect to programs of international organizations for Iraq," *ibid.,* and it is impossible to see how that self-executing suspension of a distinct statute in any way cabined or clarified the principal clause's authorization to suspend the Iraq Sanctions Act.

There are other indications that the second proviso's waiver authority was not limited to the statutory provisions embraced by § 586F(c) of the Iraq Sanctions Act. If that is all it was meant to accomplish, why would Congress not simply have tracked § 586F(c)'s residual clause? Instead of restricting the President's authority to statutes that "impose sanctions" on sponsors of terror, the EWSAA extended it to any statute that "applies" to such states. That is undoubtedly a broader class.

Even if the best reading of the EWSAA proviso were that it encompassed only statutes that impose sanctions or prohibit assistance to state sponsors of terrorism, *see Acree,* 370 F.3d, at 54, we would disagree with the Court of Appeals' conclusion that the FSIA exception is not such a law. Allowing lawsuits to proceed certainly has the extra benefit of facilitating the compensation of injured victims, but the fact that § 1605(a)(7) targeted only foreign states designated as sponsors of terrorism suggests that the law was intended as a sanction, to punish and deter undesirable conduct. Stripping the immunity that foreign sovereigns ordinarily enjoy is as much a sanction as eliminating bilateral assistance or prohibiting export of munitions (both of which are explicitly mandated by § 586F(c) of the Iraq Sanctions Act). The application of this sanction affects the jurisdiction of the federal courts, but that fact alone does not deprive it of its character as a sanction.

It may well be that when Congress enacted the EWSAA it did not have specifically in mind the terrorism exception to sovereign immunity. The Court of Appeals evidently found that to be of some importance. *Id.,* at 56 (noting there is "no reference in the legislative history to the FSIA"). But the whole value of a generally phrased residual clause, like the one used in the second proviso, is that it serves as a catch-all for matters not specifically contemplated—known unknowns, in the happy phrase coined by Secretary of Defense Donald Rumsfeld. Pieces of Intelligence: The Existential Poetry of Donald H. Rumsfeld 2 (H. Seely comp.2003). If Congress wanted to limit the waiver authority to particular statutes that it had in mind, it could have enumerated them individually.

We cannot say with any certainty (for those who think this matters) whether the Congress that passed the EWSAA *would have wanted* the President to be permitted to waive § 1605(a)(7). Certainly the exposure of Iraq to billions of dollars in damages could be thought to jeopardize the statute's goal of speedy reconstruction of that country. At least the President thought so. And in the "vast external realm, with its important, complicated, delicate and manifold problems," *Curtiss-Wright Export Corp.,* 299 U.S., at 319, 57 S. Ct. 216, courts ought to be especially wary of overriding apparent statutory text supported by executive interpretation in favor of speculation about a law's true purpose.[1]

C.

Respondents advance two other objections to the straightforward interpretation of the EWSAA proviso. First, in a less compelling variant of the D.C. Circuit's approach, the *Simon* respondents argue that "section 620A of the Foreign Assistance Act of 1961 or any other provision of law that applies to countries that have supported terrorism" means section 620A of the Foreign Assistance Act or any other provision of law cited therein. The provision would thus allow the President to make inapplicable to Iraq the statutes that § 620A precludes from being used to provide support to terror-sponsoring nations. Not to put too fine a point upon it, that is an absurd reading, not only textually but in the result it produces: It would mean that the effect of the EWSAA was to permit the President to *exclude* Iraq from, rather than *include* it within, such beneficent legislation as the Food for Peace Act of 1966, 7 U.S.C. § 1691 *et seq.*

Both respondents also invoke the canon against implied repeals, *TVA v. Hill,* 437 U.S. 153, 190, 98 S. Ct. 2279, 57 L.Ed.2d 117 (1978), but that canon has no force here. Iraq's construction of the statute neither rests on implication nor effects a repeal. The EWSAA proviso *expressly* allowed the President to render certain statutes inapplicable; the only question is its scope. And it did not repeal anything, but merely granted the President authority to waive the application of particular statutes to a single foreign nation. Cf. *Clinton v. City of New York,* 524 U.S. 417, 443–445, 118 S. Ct. 2091, 141 L.Ed.2d 393 (1998).

D.

We must consider whether anything in the subsequent NDAA legislation changes the above analysis. In particular, § 1083(c)(4) of that statute specifically says that "[n]othing in section 1503 of the [EWSAA] has ever authorized, directly or indirectly, the making inapplicable of any provision of chapter 97 of title 28, United States Code, or the removal of the jurisdiction of any court of the United States." 122 Stat. 343. This looks like a ratification by Congress of the conclusion reached in the *Acree* decision.

Is such a ratification effective? The NDAA is not subsequent legislative history, as Iraq claims, cf. *Sullivan v. Finkelstein,* 496 U.S. 617, 632, 110 S. Ct. 2658, 110 L.Ed.2d 563 (1990) (SCALIA, J., concurring in part); rather, it is binding law,

---

1 The eighth proviso of EWSAA § 1503 says that absent further congressional action, "the authorities contained in this section shall expire on September 30, 2004." 117 Stat. 579. The Court of Appeals expressed doubt that Congress would have wanted federal-court jurisdiction to disappear for a year and then suddenly return. *Acree v. Republic of Iraq,* 370 F.3d 41, 56–57 (C.A.D.C.2004). Our analysis of the sunset provision, *see* Part V, *infra,* disposes of that concern.

approved by the Legislature and signed by the President. Subsequent legislation can of course alter the meaning of an existing law for the future; and it can even alter the past operation of an existing law (constitutional objections aside) if it makes that retroactive operation clear. *Landgraf v. USI Film Products,* 511 U.S. 244, 267–268, 114 S. Ct. 1483, 128 L.Ed.2d 229 (1994). To tell the truth, however, we are unaware of any case dealing with the retroactive amendment of a law that had already expired, as the EWSAA had here. And it is doubtful whether Congress can retroactively claw back power it has given to the Executive, invalidating Presidential action that was valid when it was taken. Thankfully, however, we need not explore these difficulties here.

In § 1083(d)(1) of the NDAA, the President was given authority to "waive any provision of this section with respect to Iraq." 122 Stat. 343. The President proceeded to waive "all" provisions of that section as to Iraq, including (presumably) § 1083(c)(4). 73 Fed.Reg. 6571. The Act can therefore add nothing to our analysis of the EWSAA. Respondent Beaty objects that the President cannot waive a *fact.* But neither can Congress legislate a fact. Section 1083(c)(4) could change our interpretation of the disputed EWSAA language only if it has some *substantive* effect, changing what would otherwise be the law. And if the President's waiver does anything, it eliminates any substantive effect that the NDAA would otherwise have on cases to which Iraq is a party.[2]

IV.

Having concluded that the President did render 28 U.S.C. § 1605(a)(7) "inapplicable with respect to Iraq," and that such action was within his assigned powers, we consider respondents' argument that the inapplicability of the provision does not bar their claims, since they arise from Iraq's conduct *prior* to the President's waiver. Any other interpretation, they say, would cause the law to operate in a disfavored retroactive fashion.

This argument proceeds as follows: The FSIA exception becomes "applicable" to a foreign state when that foreign state is designated as a sponsor of terrorism. In parallel fashion, rendering the exception "inapplicable" should be equivalent to *removing* the state's designation. And under § 1605(a)(7), jurisdiction turned on the foreign state's designation "at the time the act [giving rise to the claim] occurred." On this reading, the President's waiver meant only that Iraq could not

2 Respondents contend that the NDAA waiver is irrelevant because the President's veto of the *initial* version of the bill—which did not include the waiver authority—was defective. We need not inquire into that point, since Congress (evidently thinking the veto effective) enacted a new bill that was identical in all material respects but for the addition of presidential waiver authority. Since that authority would be nugatory, and the rest of the new law utterly redundant, if a law resulting from the former bill remained in effect, that law would have been effectively repealed.

be sued pursuant to § 1605(a)(7) for any *future* conduct, even though it technically remained designated as a state sponsor of terrorism.

Respondents support this interpretation with a policy argument and a canon of construction. First, why would Congress have sought to give Iraq *better* treatment than any other state that saw the error of its ways, reformed its behavior, and was accordingly removed from the list of terror-sponsoring regimes? *See Acree,* 370 F.3d, at 56 (calling such a result "perplexing"). Providing immunity for future acts is one thing, but wiping the slate clean is quite another. Second, this Court has often applied a presumption that, absent clear indication to the contrary, statutory amendments do not apply to pending cases. *Landgraf, supra,* at 280, 114 S. Ct. 1483. A narrow reading of "inapplicable" would better comport with that presumption.

As a textual matter, the proffered definition of "inapplicable" is unpersuasive. If a provision of law is "inapplicable" then it cannot be applied; to "apply" a statute is "[t]o put [it] to use." Webster's New International Dictionary 131 (2d ed.1954). When the District Court exercised jurisdiction over these cases against Iraq, it surely was putting § 1605(a)(7) to use with respect to that country. Without the *application* of that provision, there was no basis for subject-matter jurisdiction. 28 U.S.C. §§ 1604, 1330(a). If Congress had wanted to authorize the President merely to cancel Iraq's designation as a state sponsor of terrorism, then Congress could have done so.

As a policy matter, moreover, we do not find that result particularly "perplexing." As then-Judge Roberts explained in his separate opinion in *Acree,* Congress in 2003 "*for the first time* confronted the prospect that a friendly successor government would, in its infancy, be vulnerable under Section 1605(a)(7) to crushing liability for the actions of its renounced predecessor." 370 F.3d, at 61 (opinion concurring in part and concurring in judgment) (emphasis in original). The Government was at the time spending considerable sums of money to rebuild Iraq, *see* ROGERS, CONGRESS GIVES INITIAL APPROVAL FOR WAR FUNDING, AIRLINE AID, Wall Street Journal, Apr. 4, 2003, p. A10. What would seem perplexing is converting a billion-dollar reconstruction project into a compensation scheme for a few of Saddam's victims.

As for the judicial presumption against retroactivity, that does not induce us to read the EWSAA proviso more narrowly. Laws that merely alter the rules of foreign sovereign immunity, rather than modify substantive rights, are not operating retroactively when applied to pending cases. Foreign sovereign immunity "reflects current political realities and relationships," and its availability (or lack thereof) generally is not something on which parties can rely "in shaping their primary conduct." *Republic of Austria v. Altmann,* 541 U.S. 677, 696, 124 S. Ct. 2240, 159 L.Ed.2d 1 (2004); *see also id.,* at 703, 124 S. Ct. 2240 (SCALIA, J., concurring).

In any event, the primary conduct by Iraq that forms the basis for these suits actually occurred prior to the enactment of the FSIA terrorism exception in 1996. *See Saudi Arabia v. Nelson,* 507 U.S. 349, 351, 113 S. Ct. 1471, 123 L.Ed.2d

47 (1993). That is, Iraq was immune from suit at the time it is alleged to have harmed respondents. The President's elimination of Iraq's *later* subjection to suit could hardly have deprived respondents of any expectation they held at the time of their injury that they would be able to sue Iraq in United States courts.

V.

Accordingly, the District Court lost jurisdiction over both suits in May 2003, when the President exercised his authority to make § 1605(a)(7) inapplicable with respect to Iraq. At that point, immunity kicked back in and the cases ought to have been dismissed, "the only function remaining to the court [being] that of announcing the fact and dismissing the cause." *Ex parte McCardle,* 7 Wall. 506, 514, 19 L.Ed. 264 (1869).

In respondents' view, that is not fatal to their claims. They point to the eighth proviso in § 1503 of the EWSAA:

> "*Provided further,* That the authorities contained in this section shall expire on September 30, 2004, or on the date of enactment of a subsequent Act authorizing assistance for Iraq and that specifically amends, repeals or otherwise makes inapplicable the authorities of this section, whichever occurs first." 117 Stat. 579.

The effect of this provision, they contend, is that the EWSAA waiver expired in 2005,[3] and that when it did so § 1605(a)(7) was revived, immunity was again stripped, and jurisdiction was restored. If that is true, then at the very least they ought to be permitted to refile their suits and claim equitable tolling for the period between 2005 and the present, during which time they understandably relied on *Acree*'s holding.

The premise, however, is flawed. It is true that the "authorities contained in" § 1503 of the EWSAA expired, but expiration of the *authorities* (viz., the President's powers to suspend and make inapplicable certain laws) is not the same as cancellation of the *effect* of the President's prior valid exercise of those authorities (viz., the restoration of sovereign immunity). As Iraq points out, Congress has in other statutes provided explicitly that *both* the authorities granted *and* the effects of their exercise sunset on a particular date. *E.g.,* 19 U.S.C. § 2432(c)(3) ("A waiver with respect to any country shall terminate on the day after the waiver authority granted by this subsection ceases to be effective with respect to such country"). The EWSAA contains no such language.

We think the better reading of the eighth EWSAA proviso (the sunset clause) is that the powers granted by the section could be exercised only for a limited time, but that actions taken by the President pursuant to those powers (*e.g.,* suspension of the Iraq Sanctions Act) would not lapse on the sunset date. If it were otherwise, then the Iraq Sanctions Act—which has never been repealed, and which imposes

3 The sunset date was extended by one year in a later bill. 108-106, § 2204(2), 117 Stat. 1230.

a whole host of restrictions on relations with Iraq—would have returned to force in September 2005. Nobody believes that is so.

* * *

When the President exercised his authority to make inapplicable with respect to Iraq all provisions of law that apply to countries that have supported terrorism, the exception to foreign sovereign immunity for state sponsors of terrorism became inoperative as against Iraq. As a result, the courts below lacked jurisdiction; we therefore need not reach Iraq's alternative argument that the NDAA subsequently stripped jurisdiction over the cases. The judgments of the Court of Appeals are reversed.

It is so ordered.

Printed and bound in the UK by
CPI Antony Rowe, Eastbourne

The manufacturer's authorised representative in the EU for product
safety is Oxford University Press España S.A. of El Parque Empresarial
San Fernando de Henares, Avenida de Castilla, 2 - 28830 Madrid
(www.oup.es/en or product.safety@oup.com). OUP España S.A. also acts
as importer into Spain of products made by the manufacturer.
Printed and bound by CPI Group (UK) Ltd, Croydon, CR0 4YY
14/09/2026
02216290-0014